PLAYING EUROPE 92-93

A WHO'S WHO GUIDE TO THE TEAMS AND PLAYERS IN EUROPE'S THREE MAJOR CLUB COMPETITIONS

Published by SPORTS PROJECTS LTD
General Editor MIKE HAMMOND

ACKNOWLEDGEMENTS

Playing In Europe 92/93
First published in Great Britain in August 1992
by Sports Projects Limited

© 1992 Sports Projects Limited
188 Lightwoods Hill, Smethwick, Warley,
West Midlands B67 5EH, England

ISBN 0-946866-07-4

Printed and bound in Great Britain

General Editor: Mike Hammond

Special thanks to:
Marcus Luik, Stefan Welte, Serge Van Hoof, Lakis Avramides,
Michael Hansen, Mike Ritter, Theodore Mantzouranis,
Peter Hekkema, Tamás Dénes, Skapti Hallgrímsson, Kevin
McNamara, Kazimierz Oleszek, Humberto M. Pereira Silva,
Romeo Ionescu, José del Olmo, Steven Bergström,
Marco von Ah, Luciano Zinelli, Jacob Ziv and Terry O'Neill.

Photographs: Empics

Text design and layout: Trevor Hartley

Cover design: Bernard Gallagher

CONTENTS

KEY

● Where players have appeared outside the First Division during the past five seasons it has not always been possible to record their club or record. This is also the case for players that have competed in a non-European First Division.

● When precise dates of birth are unknown only the year of birth is given.

● All international players are indicated with a ★, followed by the country they represent.

● Caps and goals totals are shown only for European players and are correct as at 24 July 1992.

● Foreign players and clubs are indicated using the Olympic three-letter code (see table, right).

● The codes for the three European competitions are:

CC = Champions' Cup
CWC = Cup-Winners' Cup
UC = UEFA Cup

● Where a player has a winners medal in European cup competition this is shown #, followed by the relevant cup code.

● Where a player has a runners-up medal in European cup competition this is shown +, followed by the relevant cup code.

● Appearance totals (Apps) include substitute appearances.

COUNTRY CODES

European

Alb	Albania
Aut	Austria
Bel	Belgium
Bos	Bosnia-Herzegovina
Bul	Bulgaria
Cis	CIS (ex USSR)
Cro	Croatia
Cyp	Cyprus
Tch	Czechoslovakia
Den	Denmark
Eng	England
Est	Estonia
Far	Faeroe Isles
Fin	Finland
Fra	France
Gdr	East Germany
Geo	Georgia
Ger	Germany
Gre	Greece
Hol	Holland
Hun	Hungary
Isl	Iceland
Isr	Israel
Ita	Italy
Lat	Latvia
Lit	Lithuania
Lux	Luxembourg
Mlt	Malta
Nir	Northern Ireland
Nor	Norway
Pol	Poland
Por	Portugal
Irl	Republic of Ireland
Rom	Romania
Rus	Russia
Smr	San Marino
Sco	Scotland
Slo	Slovenia
Esp	Spain
Swe	Sweden
Sui	Switzerland
Tur	Turkey
Ukr	Ukraine
Urs	USSR
Wal	Wales
Yug	Yugoslavia

South American

Arg	Argentina
Bra	Brazil
Bol	Bolivia
Chi	Chile
Col	Colombia
Uru	Uruguay

African

Ben	Benin
Cmr	Cameroon
Egy	Egypt
Gha	Ghana
Civ	Ivory Coast
Lib	Liberia
Mar	Morocco
Nig	Nigeria
Tun	Tunisia
Zai	Zaire
Zam	Zambia
Zim	Zimbabwe

Others

Aus	Australia
Kor	South Korea
Nzl	New Zealand
Pan	Panama
Usa	United States

INTRODUCTION

PLAYING IN EUROPE is a statistical guide to the players and teams competing in the 92/93 Champions' Cup, Cup-Winners' Cup and UEFA Cup competitions.

Produced as a companion to The European Football Yearbook 92/93 this book, unique in its content and presentation, will serve as an important reference for anyone interested in the European game.

A squad of 18 players is listed for each participating club, showing full name, date of birth, playing position, any full international caps /goals and, in most cases, a unique five-year career record in domestic First Division and European competitions. Also featured is each club's all-time record in Europe.

This is the first edition of an annual publication planned to develop and extend the type of information provided each year.

Mike Hammond and his team of researchers have made strenuous efforts to keep everything up-to-date as possible, even allowing for UEFA's decision to admit several new nations into the first round draw made in July.

However, it is impossible to include all the late summer transfers and there had to be a cut-off point for the end-of-August publishing date.

The information within these pages will, I am sure, add to the immense pleasure we all enjoy following the thrills and spills of European Cup football.

BERNARD GALLAGHER Publisher

A celebration hug for Barcelona's match-winner at Wembley, Ronald Koeman

CHAMPIONS' CUP

THERE was considerable controversy last season when UEFA decided to alter the format of the European Champions' Cup and introduce a round-robin league system to replace the traditional quarter and semi-finals.

But despite lingering criticism that the competition has lost some of its appeal because of this change, the powers that be have declared it a success and will continue with the new format in 1992/93.

This means that the primary objective of the established teams in the tournament will be to reach the last eight and thereby reap the lucrative rewards that await in the latter stages.

Two teams which are heavily fancied to achieve that objective, and more besides, are the Italian champions Milan and the Champions' Cup holders, Barcelona. These two set out as joint favourites to win the trophy and few would bet against at least one of these giants of European football making it all the way to the final in May.

Milan are returning to the European stage after a one-year ban, imposed when they were eliminated by Olympique Marseille in the quarter-finals of the 1990/91 competition. At that time Milan were going for a Champions' Cup hat-trick, having taken the trophy at the expense of Steaua Bucharest and Benfica in the two previous years.

Many of that great team remain - the Italians Baresi, Maldini and Donadoni, plus the Dutch trio of Gullit, Van Basten and Rijkaard - but they enter this year's competition with even greater potential thanks to the summer spending of their multi-millionaire president, Silvio Berlusconi, and to the modified rules of the Italian league in respect of the number of foreign players permitted to be registered with each club.

A host of expensive new signings at the San Siro include ace French goal-getter Jean-Pierre Papin, the brilliant Yugoslav midfielder Dejan Savicevic and, for a reported world record transfer fee of over £10 million, the exciting young Torino forward, Gianluigi Lentini.

Barcelona, on the other hand, have largely stuck by the players that carried them to their historic first-ever Champions' Cup triumph at Wembley last spring. That means another stab at the ultimate prize for world-class stars Ronald Koeman, Christo Stoichkov and Michael Laudrup. Johan Cruyff's team will certainly not relinquish their trophy without a fight.

Other top contenders this year include French champions Marseille, who, with a much-changed team, are competing in the Champions' Cup for a fourth consecutive season, determined as ever to become the first French side to win a European trophy.

Scottish champions Rangers have also become regular Champions' Cup participants over the past few years, but as yet, unlike Marseille, they have failed to launch a serious bid for the trophy. Perhaps this could be their year?

The champions of England and Germany - Leeds United and VfB Stuttgart - have been drawn together in what is the pick of the first-round ties. Whichever team wins through that encounter is unlikely to face such stiff opposition again in the second round.

For many of the participating teams, a place in the second round is the extent of their ambitions. Four teams, however, will not even make it into the first round proper. This is because of the increased number of entries this year as a result of the fragmentation of the Soviet Union and Yugoslavia and the admission of several "smaller" nations such as the Faeroe Isles and Israel.

One of the preliminary round ties in particular is sure to be hotly disputed. For waiting to face the winner of the encounter between Slovenia's Olimpija Ljubljana and Estonia's Norma Tallinn is none other than Italian giants Milan!

★ TEN TO WATCH ★

Gianluigi Lentini (Milan), Dejan Savicevic (Milan), Gheorghe Popescu (PSV), Christo Stoichkov (Barcelona), Dmitry Kharin (CSKA Moscow), Rudi Völler (Marseille), Guido Buchwald (VfB Stuttgart), Gary McAllister (Leeds United), Valdas Ivanauskas (FK Austria), Ally McCoist (Rangers).

CHAMPIONS' CUP

PRELIMINARY ROUND

1st Leg - August 19, 1992; 2nd Leg - September 2, 1992

			1st Leg	2nd Leg	Agg.	Away gls	Pens
Shelbourne (Irl)	v	Tavria Simferopol (Ukr)					
Valletta (Mlt)	v	Maccabbi Tel-Aviv (Isr)					
KÍ (Far)	v	Skonto Riga (Lat)					
Olimpija Ljubljana (Slo)	v	Norma Tallinn (Est)					

FIRST ROUND

1st Leg - September 16, 1992; 2nd Leg - September 30, 1992

			1st Leg	2nd Leg	Agg.	Away gls	Pens
Milan (Ita)	v	Olimpija Ljubljana or Norma Tallinn					
Lech Poznan (Pol)	v	KÍ or Skonto Riga					
PSV (Hol)	v	Zhalgiris Vilnius (Lit)					
FC Barcelona (Esp)	v	Viking FK (Nor)					
FC Kuusysi (Fin)	v	Dinamo Bucuresti (Rom)					
Rangers (Sco)	v	Lyngby BK (Den)					
Slovan Bratislava (Tch)	v	Ferencváros (Hun)					
FK Austria (Aut)	v	CSKA Sofia (Bul)					
FC Sion (Sui)	v	Shelbourne or Tavria Simferopol					
Union Luxembourg (Lux)	v	FC Porto (Por)					
Víkingur (Isl)	v	CSKA Moskva (Rus)	`				
Club Brugge KV (Bel)	v	Valletta or Maccabbi Tel-Aviv					
AEK (Gre)	v	Apoel Nicosia (Cyp)					
IFK Göteborg (Swe)	v	Besiktas (Tur)					
Glentoran (Nir)	v	Olympique Marseille (Fra)					
VfB Stuttgart (Ger)	v	Leeds United (Eng)					

1992-93

SECOND ROUND
1st Leg - October 21, 1992; 2nd Leg - November 4, 1992

	1st Leg	2nd Leg	Agg.	Away gls	Pens
v					
v					
v					
v					
v					
v					
v					
v					

SEMI-FINAL GROUP A
November 25; December 9; March 3; March 17; April 17; April 21

	v Team A	v Team B	v Team C	v Team D
A				
B				
C				
D				

SEMI-FINAL GROUP B
November 25; December 9; March 3; March 17; April 17; April 21

	v Team A	v Team B	v Team C	v Team D
A				
B				
C				
D				

FINAL
May 26, 1993

v	

FK AUSTRIA

| FIVE YEAR RECORD | LEAGUE | | EURO CUPS | |
Birthdate/Playing position	Apps	Gls	Cup	Apps Gls

Franz WOHLFAHRT
01/07/64   Goalkeeper

87/88	FK Austria	36	-	UC 2	-
88/89	FK Austria	32	-	UC 4	-
89/90	FK Austria	36	-	UC 4	-
90/91	FK Austria	36	-	CWC 4	-
91/92	FK Austria	27	-	CC 1	-

★ Austria 10 caps, 0 goals

Martin UNGER
23/12/70   Goalkeeper

90/91	FK Austria	-	-
91/92	FK Austria	2	-

Attila SEKERLIOGLU
27/01/65   Defender

88/89	FK Austria	28	-	UC 4	1
89/90	FK Austria	21	-	UC 3	-
90/91	FK Austria	24	-	CWC 2	-
91/92	FK Austria	34	1	CC 2	-

Walter KÖGLER
12/12/67   Defender

87/88	SK Sturm Graz	19	1		
88/89	SK Sturm Graz	12	1	UC 2	-
89/90	SK Sturm Graz	34	-		
90/91	SK Sturm Graz	30	3		
91/92	SK Sturm Graz	21	1	UC 2	-

★ Austria 4 caps, 1 goal

Anton PFEFFER
17/08/65   Defender

87/88	FK Austria	23	5	UC 1	-
88/89	FK Austria	36	2	UC 4	-
89/90	FK Austria	35	3	UC 3	-
90/91	FK Austria	33	2	CWC 3	-
91/92	FK Austria	32	4	CC 2	-

★ Austria 26 caps, 1 goals

Manfred ZSAK
22/12/64   Defender

87/88	FK Austria	33	7	UC 2	-
88/89	FK Austria	35	6	UC 3	-
89/90	FK Austria	32	10	UC 4	-
90/91	FK Austria	31	7	CWC 4	1
91/92	FK Austria	35	5	CC 2	-

★ Austria 41 caps, 5 goals

Ernst AIGNER
31/10/66   Defender

87/88	FC Admira Wacker	30	5	UC 1	-
88/89	FC Admira Wacker	32	6		
89/90	FK Austria	35	4	UC 4	-
90/91	FK Austria	23	1	CWC 4	-
91/92	FK Austria	2	-		

★ Austria 11 caps, 0 goals

Christian PROSENIK
07/06/68   Midfield

87/88	FK Austria	29	2	UC 1	-
88/89	FK Austria	26	1	UC 1	-
89/90	FK Austria	31	1	UC 4	-
90/91	FK Austria	33	2	CWC 4	-
91/92	FK Austria	35	1	CC 2	-

★ Austria 9 caps, 1 goal

Peter STÖGER
11/04/66   Midfield

87/88	First Vienna FC	36	6		
88/89	FK Austria	35	9	UC 3	-
89/90	FK Austria	13	1		
90/91	FK Austria	35	10	CWC 3	-
91/92	FK Austria	34	12	CC 2	1

★ Austria 20 caps, 0 goals

Manfred SCHMID
20/02/71   Midfield

89/90	FK Austria	1	-
90/91	FK Austria	4	-
91/92	FK Austria	2	-

AUSTRIA

FIVE YEAR RECORD	LEAGUE		EURO CUPS		
Birthdate/Playing position	Apps	Gls	Cup	Apps	Gls

Peter POSPISIL
28/10/66   Midfield

		LEAGUE		EURO CUPS		
87/88	FK Austria	-	-			
88/89	SV Stockerau	Div 2				
89/90	SV Stockerau	Div 2				
90/91	SV Stockerau	Div 2				
91/92	SV Stockerau	Div 2		CWC	2	-

Arminas NARBEKOVAS (Lit)
28/01/65   Midfield

		Apps	Gls	Cup	Apps	Gls
87	Zhalgiris Vilnius (Urs)	30	16			
88	Zhalgiris Vilnius (Urs)	26	9	UC	2	-
89	Zhalgiris Vilnius (Urs)	21	4	UC	4	-
90	Zhalgiris Vilnius (Lit)					
90/91	FK Austria	13	6			
91/92	FK Austria	30	10	CC	2	-

★ Lithuania

Thomas FLÖGEL
07/06/71   Midfield

		Apps	Gls	Cup	Apps	Gls
89/90	FK Austria	16	1			
90/91	FK Austria	28	5	CWC	4	-
91/92	FK Austria	35	6	CC	2	-

★ Austria 4 caps, 0 goals

Peter LETOCHA
24/06/69   Midfield

		Apps	Gls	Cup	Apps	Gls
90/91	FK Austria	2	-			
91/92	FK Austria	4	1			

Robertas FRIDRIKAS (Lit)
08/04/67   Midfield

		Apps	Gls	Cup	Apps	Gls
87	Zhalgiris Vilnius (Urs)	1	-			
88	Zhalgiris Vilnius (Urs)	21	6	UC	2	2
89	Zhalgiris Vilnius (Urs)	28	5	UC	4	2
90	Zhalgiris Vilnius (Lit)					
91	Lokomotiv Moskva (Urs)	16	1			
91/92	FK Austria	9	3			

★ Lithuania

Andreas OGRIS
07/10/64   Forward

FIVE YEAR RECORD		LEAGUE		EURO CUPS		
87/88	FK Austria	31	17	UC	1	-
88/89	FK Austria	30	14	UC	4	-
89/90	FK Austria	32	16	UC	4	-
90/91	FK Austria	7	7			
	RCD Español (Esp)	29	4			
91/92	FK Austria	29	8	CC	2	1

★ Austria 43 caps, 8 goals

Valdas IVANAUSKAS (Lit)
31/02/66   Forward

		Apps	Gls	Cup	Apps	Gls
87	Zhalgiris Vilnius (Urs)	25	7			
88	Zhalgiris Vilnius (Urs)	28	7	UC	2	-
89	Zhalgiris Vilnius (Urs)	26	5	UC	4	1
90	Zhalgiris Vilnius (Lit)					
90/91	FK Austria	14	4			
91/92	FK Austria	32	9	CC	2	-

★ USSR 4 cps, 0 goals; Lithuania

Ralph HASENHÜTTL
09/08/67   Forward

		Apps	Gls	Cup	Apps	Gls
87/88	Grazer AK	34	12			
88/89	Grazer AK	27	7			
89/90	FK Austria	34	8	UC	3	2
90/91	FK Austria	25	11	CWC	4	-
91/92	FK Austria	31	10	CC	1	-

★ Austria 5 caps, 3 goals

EUROPEAN HONOURS
none

EUROPEAN CUPS RECORD

	Entries	Pd	W	D	L	F	A
Champions' Cup	14	51	19	11	21	75	76
Cup-winners' Cup	7	35	9	12	14	36	52
UEFA/Fairs' Cup	5	20	8	5	7	38	34
Total - All 3 Cups	26	106	36	28	42	149	162

CLUB BRUGGE KV

FIVE YEAR RECORD	LEAGUE		EURO CUPS		
Birthdate/Playing position	Apps	Gls	Cup	Apps	Gls

Danny VERLINDEN
15/08/63   Goalkeeper

87/88	K Lierse SK	Div 2				
88/89	Club Brugge KV	5	-			
89/90	Club Brugge KV	29	-	UC	1	-
90/91	Club Brugge KV	33	-	CC	4	-
91/92	Club Brugge KV	30	-	CWC	7	-

Hans GALJE (Hol)
21/02/67   Goalkeeper

87/88	KSV Waregem	34	-			
88/89	KSV Waregem	29	-	CC	2	-
89/90	KSV Waregem	21	-			
90/91	Club Brugge KV	1	-			
91/92	Club Brugge KV	5	-	CWC	1	-

Claude VERSPAILLE
21/07/64   Defender

87/88	KV Kortrijk	33	2			
88/89	KV Kortrijk	30	3			
89/90	KV Kortrijk	27	8			
90/91	Club Brugge KV	19	1	CC	2	-
91/92	Club Brugge KV	30	4	CWC	6	2

László DISZTL (Hun)
04/06/62   Defender

87/88	Budapesti Honvéd SE (Hun)	30	-	UC	6	-
88/89	Budapesti Honvéd SE (Hun)	28	-	CC	2	-
89/90	Club Brugge KV	27	3	UC	2	1
90/91	Club Brugge KV	25	1	CC	3	-
91/92	Club Brugge KV	23	1	CWC	4	-
★ Hungary 24 caps, 1 goal

Rudy COSSEY
02/08/61   Defender

87/88	RWD Molenbeek	32	-			
88/89	RWD Molenbeek	26	1			
89/90	RWD Molenbeek	Div 2				
90/91	Club Brugge KV	24	2	CC	2	-
91/92	Club Brugge KV	24	4	CWC	7	-

Vital BORKELMANS
01/06/63   Defender

87/88	KSV Waregem	34	5			
88/89	KSV Waregem	32	3	UC	4	-
89/90	Club Brugge KV	34	2	UC	4	-
90/91	Club Brugge KV	34	1	CC	4	-
91/92	Club Brugge KV	33	3	CWC	8	-
★ Belgium 7 caps, 0 goals

Pascal PLOVIE
07/05/65   Defender

87/88	Royal Antwerp FC	33	1			
88/89	Club Brugge KV	30	-	CC	4	-
89/90	Club Brugge KV	32	-	UC	4	-
90/91	Club Brugge KV	29	1	CC	4	-
91/92	Club Brugge KV	20	-	CWC	4	-
★ Belgium 5 caps, 0 goals

Marc SCHAESSENS
14/09/68   Defender

87/88	K Beerschot VAV	23	-			
88/89	K Beerschot VAV	29	3			
89/90	R Standard Liège	32	2			
90/91	R Standard Liège	33	3			
91/92	Club Brugge KV	17	2	CWC	1	-

Pascal RENIER
03/08/71   Defender

90/91	RFC Liège	4	-			
91/92	RFC Liège	27	-			

Cedomir JANEVSKI (Yug)
03/07/61   Defender

87/88	Vardar Skoplje (Yug)	17	5			
88/89	Vardar Skoplje (Yug)	15	-			
89/90	Club Brugge KV	12	-	UC	2	-
90/91	Club Brugge KV	11	-	CC	2	-
91/92	RSC Charleroi	22	3			
★ Yugoslavia 2 caps, 0 goals

BELGIUM

FIVE YEAR RECORD *Birthdate/Playing position*	LEAGUE Apps Gls	EURO CUPS Cup Apps Gls

Lorenzo STAELENS
30/04/64   Midfield

87/88	KV Kortrijk	32	4		
88/89	KV Kortrijk	32	7		
89/90	Club Brugge KV	34	4	UC	4	1
90/91	Club Brugge KV	33	4	CC	4	1
91/92	Club Brugge KV	31	5	CWC	8	2

★ Belgium 8 caps, 0 goals

Franky VAN DER ELST
30/04/61   Midfield

87/88	Club Brugge KV	32	-	UC	9	1
88/89	Club Brugge KV	34	1	CC	4	-
89/90	Club Brugge KV	34	1	UC	4	-
90/91	Club Brugge KV	34	3	CC	4	-
91/92	Club Brugge KV	29	3	CWC	7	-

★ Belgium 51 caps, 0 goals

Peter CREVE
17/08/61   Midfield

87/88	Club Brugge KV	28	-	UC	10	-
88/89	Club Brugge KV	26	1	CC	4	-
89/90	Club Brugge KV	25	2	UC	2	-
90/91	Club Brugge KV	29	4	CC	3	-
91/92	Club Brugge KV	31	3	CWC	7	-

★ Belgium 3 caps, 1 goal

Alex QUERTER
18/12/57   Midfield

87/88	Club Brugge KV	18	2	UC	7	-
88/89	Club Brugge KV	30	2	CC	3	-
89/90	Club Brugge KV	30	2	UC	4	-
90/91	Club Brugge KV	10	-	CC	2	-
91/92	Club Brugge KV	31	1	CWC	6	-

Stéphane VAN DER HEYDEN
03/07/69   Midfield

87/88	KSK Beveren	16	1	UC	1	-
88/89	KSK Beveren	27	1		
89/90	KSK Beveren	27	2		
90/91	KSK Beveren	Div 2			
91/92	Club Brugge KV	23	1	CWC	8	1

★ Belgium 1 cap, 0 goals

FIVE YEAR RECORD *Birthdate/Playing position*	LEAGUE Apps Gls	EURO CUPS Cup Apps Gls

Foeke BOOY (Hol)
25/08/62   Forward

87/88	FC Groningen (Hol)	29	10		
88/89	KV Kortrijk	31	9		
89/90	Club Brugge KV	27	14	UC	4	2
90/91	Club Brugge KV	33	12	CC	4	1
91/92	Club Brugge KV	26	20	CWC	6	3

Daniel AMOKACHI (Nig)
20/12/72   Forward

90/91	Club Brugge KV	3	-		
91/92	Club Brugge KV	26	12	CWC	6	1

Tomasz DZIUBINSKI (Pol)
08/08/68   Forward

87/88	Bron Radom (Pol)	Div 2			
88/89	Wisla Kraków (Pol)	11	2		
89/90	Wisla Kraków (Pol)	22	7		
90/91	Wisla Kraków (Pol)	29	21		
91/92	Club Brugge KV	19	5	CWC	5	1

EUROPEAN HONOURS
none

EUROPEAN CUPS RECORD

	Entries	Pd	W	D	L	F	A
Champions' Cup	7	31	14	5	12	51	39
Cup-winners' Cup	4	18	10	1	7	31	25
UEFA/Fairs' Cup	10	48	20	6	22	83	77
Total - All 3 Cups	21	97	44	12	41	165	141

CSKA SOFIA

FIVE YEAR RECORD	LEAGUE		EURO CUPS		
Birthdate/Playing position	Apps	Gls	Cup	Apps	Gls

Georgi VELINOV
05/10/57 Goalkeeper

87/88	SC Braga (Por)	16	-		
88/89	Académica Coimbra (Por) Div 2				
89/90	Académica Coimbra (Por) Div 2				
90/91	Sliven	13	-		
91/92	CSKA Sofia	29	-	UC	4	-

★ Bulgaria 33 caps, 0 goals

Rumen NENOV
29/12/68 Goalkeeper

88/89	Vratsa	27	-
89/90	Botev Vratsa	23	-
90/91	CSKA Sofia	2	-
91/92	CSKA Sofia	1	-

Emil DIMITROV
15/04/60 Defender

87/88	Etar Veliko Tarnovo	29	1			
88/89	Etar Veliko Tarnovo	29	1			
89/90	CSKA Sofia	28	-	CC	6	-
90/91	CSKA Sofia	27	6	CC	4	-
91/92	CSKA Sofia	10	1	UC	3	1

★ Bulgaria 8 caps, 0 goals

Velian PARUSHEV
20/03/68 Defender

87/88	Sliven	5	-			
88/89	Sliven	16	-			
89/90	Sliven	30	1			
90/91	Sliven	30	4	CWC	2	-
91/92	CSKA Sofia	15	1	UC	4	1
	Sliven	15	-			

Radoslav VIDOV
23/04/65 Defender

88/89	Vratsa	17	-			
89/90	Botev Vratsa	27	-			
90/91	CSKA Sofia	10	-			
91/92	CSKA Sofia	28	-	UC	3	-

★ Bulgaria 1 cap, 0 goals

Krasimir BEZINSKI
26/09/61 Defender

87/88	CFKA Sredets Sofia	27	1	CC	2	-
88/89	CFKA Sredets Sofia	25	-	CWC	7	-
89/90	Portimonense SC (Por)	32	-			
90/91	Portimonense SC (Por) Div 2					
91/92	Portimonense SC (Por) Div 2					
	CSKA Sofia	15	1			

★ Bulgaria 11 caps, 0 goals

Marius URUKOV
24/08/67 Defender

87/88	Spartak Pleven	11	1			
88/89	Spartak Pleven Div 2					
89/90	CSKA Sofia	27	1	CC	6	1
90/91	CSKA Sofia	26	1			
91/92	Lokomotiv Sofia	22	-			

Georgi NACHOV
18/06/68 Midfield

89/90	Marek Stanke Dimitrov Div 2					
90/91	CSKA Sofia	13	-			
91/92	CSKA Sofia	4	-	UC	2	-

Stefan KOLEV
12/10/66 Defender

87/88	Vitosha Sofia	6	-			
88/89	Spartak Pleven Div 2					
	Etar Veliko Tarnovo	3	-			
89/90	Lokomotiv Gorna Oriahovitsa	30	-			
90/91	Yantra Gabrovo	21	-			
91/92	CSKA Sofia	17	-	UC	1	-

Kiril METKOV
01/02/65 Midfield

87/88	Lokomotiv Sofia	30	7	UC	2	-
88/89	Lokomotiv Sofia	25	4			
89/90	Lokomotiv Sofia	28	5			
90/91	Lokomotiv Sofia	22	6			
91/92	Lokomotiv Sofia	14	3			
	CSKA Sofia	15	11			

★ Bulgaria 3 caps, 0 goals

BULGARIA

FIVE YEAR RECORD *Birthdate/Playing position*	LEAGUE Apps Gls	EURO CUPS Cup Apps Gls

Victorio PAVLOV
28/05/68   Midfield

		Apps	Gls	Cup	Apps	Gls
89/90	CSKA Sofia	3	1			
90/91	CSKA Sofia	20	4	CC	3	-
91/92	CSKA Sofia	8	-	UC	3	-

Yordan MARINOV
23/06/68   Midfield

88/89	Akademik Sofia	Div 2				
89/90	Lokomotiv Gorna Oriahovitsa	27	4			
90/91	Lokomotiv Gorna Oriahovitsa	25	3			
91/92	CSKA Sofia	15	-	UC	4	-

Ivailo ANDONOV
14/08/67   Midfield

87/88	Pirin Blagoevgrad	6	-			
88/89	Pirin Blagoevgrad	28	2			
89/90	Pirin Blagoevgrad	30	7			
90/91	Pirin Blagoevgrad	29	9			
91/92	CSKA Sofia	30	16	UC	4	-

★ Bulgaria 1 cap, 0 goals

Stoicho STOILOV
15/10/71   Midfield

89/90	Pirin Blagoevgrad	11	2			
90/91	CSKA Sofia	10	1			
91/92	CSKA Sofia	14	1	UC	3	-

Anatoli NANKOV
15/07/69   Midfield

88/89	Dunav Ruse	30	-			
89/90	Slavia Sofia	27	2			
90/91	CSKA Sofia	17	1	CC	1	-
91/92	CSKA Sofia	27	5	UC	4	-

FIVE YEAR RECORD *Birthdate/Playing position*	LEAGUE Apps Gls	EURO CUPS Cup Apps Gls

Todor PRAMATAROV
08/08/68   Forward

		Apps	Gls	Cup	Apps	Gls
89/90	Montana Mikhailovgrad	Div 3				
90/91	Lokomotiv Sofia	29	14			
91/92	CSKA Sofia	14	4	UC	2	-

Boris KHVOINEV
19/08/67   Forward

87/88	Trakia Plovdiv	26	2	UC	2	-
88/89	Trakia Plovdiv	24	4	UC	2	-
89/90	Botev Plovdiv	29	6			
90/91	Botev Plovdiv	26	10			
91/92	Botev Plovdiv	30	9			

Anton DIMITROV
12/08/70   Forward

87/88	CFKA Sredets Sofia	1	-			
88/89	CFKA Sredets Sofia	-	-			
89/90	CSKA Sofia	-	-			
90/91	CSKA Sofia	26	7	CC	3	-
91/92	CSKA Sofia	21	3	UC	3	-

EUROPEAN HONOURS
none

EUROPEAN CUPS RECORD

	Entries	Pd	WW	D	L	F	A
Champions' Cup	21	86	35	15	36	124	125
Cup-winners' Cup	4	18	10	0	8	36	22
UEFA/Fairs' Cup	6	16	3	5	8	15	29
Total - All 3 Cups	31	120	48	20	52	175	176

APOEL NICOSIA

FIVE YEAR RECORD	LEAGUE		EURO CUPS		
Birthdate/Playing position	Apps	Gls	Cup	Apps	Gls

Andros PETRIDES
06/12/66   Goalkeeper

87/88	Apoel Nicosia	29	-		
88/89	Apoel Nicosia	24	-	UC	2	-
89/90	Apoel Nicosia	2	-		
90/91	Apoel Nicosia	2	-		
91/92	Apoel Nicosia	15	-		

★ Cyprus 1 cap, 0 goals

Socratis MARANGOS
14/05/59   Goalkeeper

87/88	Apoel Nicosia	1	-		
88/89	Apoel Nicosia	4	-		
89/90	Apoel Nicosia	25	-		
90/91	Apoel Nicosia	25	-	CC	2	-
91/92	Apoel Nicosia	11	-		

★ Cyprus 2 caps, 0 goals

Costas COSTA
04/01/69   Defender

89/90	Apoel Nicosia	7	-		
90/91	Apoel Nicosia	22	6	CC	2	-
91/92	Apoel Nicosia	22	-		

★ Cyprus 7 caps, 0 goals

Demetris KLEANTHOUS
04/07/64   Defender

87/88	Apoel Nicosia	20	1		
88/89	Apoel Nicosia	17	1	UC	2	-
89/90	Apoel Nicosia	25	-		
90/91	Apoel Nicosia	24	-	CC	2	-
91/92	Apoel Nicosia	22	-		

Lefteris KOUIS
22/11/60   Defender

87/88	Keravnos Strovolos	Div 2			
88/89	Keravnos Strovolos	24	2		
89/90	Apoel Nicosia	25	-		
90/91	Apoel Nicosia	16	-	CC	1	-
91/92	Apoel Nicosia	20	-		

FIVE YEAR RECORD	LEAGUE		EURO CUPS		
Birthdate/Playing position	Apps	Gls	Cup	Apps	Gls

Nicos CHARALAMBOUS
03/11/66   Defender

87/88	Olympiakos Nicosia	24	1		
88/89	Olympiakos Nicosia	19	-		
89/90	Olympiakos Nicosia	16	-		
90/91	Olympiakos Nicosia	16	1		
91/92	Olympiakos Nicosia	21	3		

Costas MIAMILIOTIS
01/08/60   Defender

87/88	Apoel Nicosia	25	2		
88/89	Apoel Nicosia	9	-	UC	2	-
89/90	Pezoporikos Larnaca	26	1		
90/91	Pezoporikos Larnaca	23	-		
91/92	Pezoporikos Larnaca	12	-		

★ Cyprus 43 caps, 0 goals

Christodoulos CHRISTODOULOU
04/10/64   Defender

87/88	AEL Limassol	24	2	CWC	1	-
88/89	AEL Limassol	25	-		
89/90	AEL Limassol	19	1	CWC	2	-
90/91	AEL Limassol	20	-		
91/92	Apoel Nicosia	16	-		

Andreas LUCA
27/04/71   Defender

91/92	Apoel Nicosia	1	-	

Christodoulos POUNNAS
18/05/68   Midfield

88/89	Apoel Nicosia	8	2	
89/90	Apoel Nicosia	12	1	
90/91	Apoel Nicosia	8	-	
91/92	Apoel Nicosia	18	1	

Toza SAPURIC (Yug)
28/08/60   Midfield

87/88	Vojvodina Novi Sad (Yug)	28	3		
88/89	Vojvodina Novi Sad (Yug)	28	1		
89/90	Apoel Nicosia	21	3		
90/91	Apoel Nicosia	25	2	CC	2	-
91/92	Apoel Nicosia	24	1		

CYPRUS

FIVE YEAR RECORD	LEAGUE		EURO CUPS		
Birthdate/Playing position	Apps	Gls	Cup	Apps	Gls

Nicos MAGNITIS
27/11/69   Midfield

87/88	Apoel Nicosia	6	·			
88/89	Apoel Nicosia	12	·	UC	2	·
89/90	Apoel Nicosia	24	·			
90/91	Apoel Nicosia	22	·	CC	2	·
91/92	Apoel Nicosia	12	·			

Costas PHASOULIOTIS
19/08/70   Midfield

90/91	Apoel Nicosia	22	2	CC	1	·
91/92	Apoel Nicosia	24	8			

★ Cyprus 1 cap, 0 goals

Nicos SATSIAS
21/06/71   Midfield

91/92	Apoel Nicosia	7	·

Andros SOTIRIOU
07/06/68   Forward

87/88	Apoel Nicosia	3	4			
88/89	Apoel Nicosia	25	8	UC	1	·
89/90	Apoel Nicosia	19	5			
90/91	Apoel Nicosia	25	12	CC	2	·
91/92	Apoel Nicosia	26	19			

★ Cyprus 9 caps, 1 goals

Sinisa GOGIC (Yug)
20/10/63   Forward

87/88	Rad Beograd (Yug)	29	4			
88/89	Rad Beograd (Yug)	22	1			
89/90	Apoel Nicosia	24	19			
90/91	Apoel Nicosia	25	17	CC	2	1
91/92	Apoel Nicosia	24	19			

FIVE YEAR RECORD	LEAGUE		EURO CUPS		
Birthdate/Playing position	Apps	Gls	Cup	Apps	Gls

Yiannos IOANNOU
25/01/66   Forward

87/88	Apoel Nicosia	20	13			
88/89	Apoel Nicosia	25	15	UC	2	·
89/90	Apoel Nicosia	26	11			
90/91	Apoel Nicosia	·	·			
91/92	Apoel Nicosia	22	18			

★ Cyprus 19 caps, 2 goals

Lucas HADJILUCAS
06/06/67   Forward

87/88	Apoel Nicosia	25	9			
88/89	Apoel Nicosia	27	9	UC	1	·
89/90	Apoel Nicosia	25	4			
90/91	Apoel Nicosia	9	2			
91/92	Apoel Nicosia	24	·			

★ Cyprus 3 caps, 0 goals

EUROPEAN HONOURS
none

EUROPEAN CUPS RECORD

	Entries	Pd	W	D	L	F	A
Champions' Cup	5	10	2	0	8	7	27
Cup-winners' Cup	7	18	2	2	14	13	61
UEFA/Fairs' Cup	4	8	0	3	5	8	21
Total - All 3 Cups	16	36	4	5	27	28	109

SLOVAN BRATISLAVA

FIVE YEAR RECORD Birthdate/Playing position	LEAGUE Apps Gls	EURO CUPS Cup Apps Gls

Alexander VENCEL
02/03/67   Goalkeeper

87/88	Slovan Bratislava	Div 2		
88/89	Slovan Bratislava	12	-	
89/90	RH Cheb	28	-	
90/91	Slovan Bratislava	30	-	
91/92	Slovan Bratislava	30	-	UC 2 -

★ Czechoslovakia 2 caps, 0 goals

Vladimír ZENIS
08/09/68   Goalkeeper

91/92	Slovan Bratislava	1	-

Tomas STÚPALA
05/05/66   Defender

87/88	Slovan Bratislava	Div 2		
88/89	Slovan Bratislava	30	-	
89/90	Slovan Bratislava	30	-	CWC 2 -
90/91	Slovan Bratislava	29	-	
91/92	Slovan Bratislava	30	-	UC 2 -

Milos GLONEK
26/09/68   Defender

89/90	Slovan Bratislava	22	1	
90/91	Slovan Bratislava	29	2	
91/92	Slovan Bratislava	29	-	UC 2 -

★ Czechoslovakia 6 caps, 0 goals

Miroslav CHVILA
28/03/67   Defender

87/88	Dukla Banská Bystrica	6	-	
88/89	Slovan Bratislava	16	1	
89/90	Slovan Bratislava	25	2	CWC 2 -
90/91	Slovan Bratislava	21	2	
91/92	Slovan Bratislava	28	2	UC 2 -

★ Czechoslovakia 1 cap, 0 goals

Stanislav GOREL
1970   Defender

90/91	Slovan Bratislava	9	-
91/92	Slovan Bratislava	4	-

FIVE YEAR RECORD Birthdate/Playing position	LEAGUE Apps Gls	EURO CUPS Cup Apps Gls

Zsold HORNYAK
1971   Defender

91/92	Slovan Bratislava	1	-

Vladimír KINDER
14/03/66   Midfield

89/90	VTJ Karlovy Vary	Div 3		
90/91	Slovan Bratislava	10	2	
91/92	Slovan Bratislava	29	2	UC 2 -

Eugen VARGA
24/09/62   Midfield

87/88	Slovan Bratislava	Div 2		
88/89	Slovan Bratislava	27	1	
89/90	Slovan Bratislava	27	4	CWC 2 -
90/91	Slovan Bratislava	29	-	
91/92	Slovan Bratislava	24	1	UC 2 -

Ludovít LANCZ
02/06/64   Midfield

87/88	Inter Bratislava	27	2	
88/89	Inter Bratislava	24	6	
89/90	Inter Bratislava	28	6	
90/91	Inter Bratislava	2	-	
91/92	Slovan Bratislava	26	4	UC 2 1

★ Czechoslovakia 1 cap, 1 goal

Ondrej KRISTOFIK
10/09/66   Midfield

89/90	Slovan Bratislava	9	-	CWC 2 -
90/91	Slovan Bratislava	29	2	
91/92	Slovan Bratislava	24	1	UC 2 -

★ Czechoslovakia 5 caps, 1 goal

Jozef JURIGA
09/09/68   Midfield

87/88	Slovan Bratislava	Div 2		
88/89	Slovan Bratislava	25	1	
89/90	Slovan Bratislava	26	5	CWC 2 -
90/91	Slovan Bratislava	24	-	
91/92	Slovan Bratislava	22	2	UC 1 -

CZECHOSLOVAKIA

FIVE YEAR RECORD *Birthdate/Playing position*	LEAGUE Apps Gls		EURO CUPS Cup Apps Gls		

Peter DUBOVSKY
07/05/72   Forward

		Apps	Gls		Apps	Gls
89/90	Slovan Bratislava	8	1			
90/91	Slovan Bratislava	26	7			
91/92	Slovan Bratislava	30	27	UC	2	1

★ Czechoslovakia 5 caps, 0 goals

Jaroslav TIMKO
28/09/65   Forward

		Apps	Gls		Apps	Gls
87/88	Slovan Bratislava	Div 2				
88/89	Slovan Bratislava	17	3			
89/90	Slovan Bratislava	27	4	CWC	2	1
90/91	Slovan Bratislava	27	6			
91/92	Slovan Bratislava	30	5	UC	2	-

Ladislav PECKO
27/06/68   Forward

		Apps	Gls		Apps	Gls
87/88	Slovan Bratislava	Div 2				
88/89	Slovan Bratislava	24	3			
89/90	Slovan Bratislava	30	5	CWC	2	-
90/91	Slovan Bratislava	29	7			
91/92	Slovan Bratislava	27	3	UC	1	-

★ Czechoslovakia 11 caps, 1 goal

Pavol GOSTIC
05/11/66   Forward

		Apps	Gls		Apps	Gls
87/88	Dukla Banská Bystrica	15	3			
88/89	Dukla Banská Bystrica	30	6			
89/90	Slovan Bratislava	12	1			
90/91	Slovan Bratislava	20	2			
91/92	Slovan Bratislava	27	8	UC	2	-

FIVE YEAR RECORD *Birthdate/Playing position*	LEAGUE Apps Gls		EURO CUPS Cup Apps Gls		

Erik CHYTIL
24/11/70   Forward

		Apps	Gls		Apps	Gls
90/91	Slovan Bratislava	6	1			
91/92	Slovan Bratislava	9	1			

Ivan ZIGA
21/08/72   Forward

		Apps	Gls		Apps	Gls
91/92	Slovan Bratislava	1	-	UC	1	-

EUROPEAN HONOURS
Cup-winners' Cup - (1) 1969.

EUROPEAN CUPS RECORD

	Entries	Pd	W	D	L	F	A
Champions' Cup	4	12	6	1	5	17	19
Cup-winners' Cup	6	25	14	3	8	41	29
UEFA/Fairs' Cup	3	10	4	3	3	25	15
Total - All 3 Cups	13	47	24	7	16	83	63

LYNGBY BK

FIVE YEAR RECORD *Birthdate/Playing position*	LEAGUE Apps	Gls	EURO CUPS Cup	Apps	Gls

Kim BRODERSEN
03/02/63   Goalkeeper

87	Herfølge BK	15	-		
88	Herfølge BK	25	-		
89	Herfølge BK	22	-		
90	Naestved IF	26	-		
91	Lyngby BK	18	-		
91/92	Lyngby BK	32	-		

Claus FALLENTIN
27/06/70   Goalkeeper

89	Greve IF	Div 3			
90	Greve IF	Div 3			
91	Greve IF	Div 3			
91/92	Lyngby BK	-	-		

Claus CHRISTIANSEN
19/10/67   Defender

87	Lyngby BK	12	-		
88	Lyngby BK	23	2		
89	Lyngby BK	23	-		
90	Lyngby BK	25	-	CWC	2	-
91	Lyngby BK	17	-		
91/92	Lyngby BK	30	1		

★ Denmark 4 caps, 0 goals

Michael GOTHENBORG
28/07/64   Defender

87	B 1903	17	-		
88	B 1903	26	-		
89	B 1903	19	1		
90	Lyngby BK	25	-	CWC	2	-
91	Lyngby BK	15	1		
91/92	Lyngby BK	28	1		

Dennis HANSEN
10/11/70   Defender

89	Lyngby BK	-	-		
90	Lyngby BK	-	-		
91	Lyngby BK	8	1		
91/92	Lyngby BK	1	-		

John LARSEN
25/05/62   Defender

87	Lyngby BK	26	2		
88	Lyngby BK	26	4		
89	Vejle BK	26	4		
90	Vejle BK	22	4		
91	Lyngby BK	-	-		
91/92	Lyngby BK	21	-		

★ Denmark 19 caps, 1 goal

Henrik RISOM
24/07/68   Defender

87	Vejle BK	26	6		
88	Vejle BK	25	4		
89	Vejle BK	26	-		
90	Vejle BK	25	1	UC	2	-
91	Lyngby BK	14	-		
91/92	Lyngby BK	31	3		

★ Denmark 9 caps, 0 goals

Jan SØRENSEN
08/04/68   Defender

89	B 1901	Div 3			
90	BK Frem	23	-		
91	BK Frem	18	1		
91/92	BK Frem	11	-		
	Lyngby BK	2	-		

Emeka EZEUGO (Nig)
16/12/65   Midfield

90	Lyngby BK	3	-		
91	Lyngby BK	16	2		
91/92	Lyngby BK	8	-		

★ Nigeria

Anders NIELSEN
23/11/72   Midfield

91	Lyngby BK	9	1		
91/92	Lyngby BK	17	2		

DENMARK

FIVE YEAR RECORD *Birthdate/Playing position*	LEAGUE Apps Gls	EURO CUPS Cup Apps Gls

Henrik LARSEN
17/05/66   Midfield

87	Lyngby BK	20	3			
88	Lyngby BK	24	1			
89	Lyngby BK	26	3			
90	Lyngby BK	10	1			
90/91	Pisa (Ita)	33	1			
91/92	Lyngby BK	29	5			

★ Denmark 22 caps, 4 goals

Morten WIEGHORST
25/02/71   Midfield

90	Lyngby BK	19	3	CWC	2	-
91	Lyngby BK	17	-			
91/92	Lyngby BK	24	1			

Johnny VILSTRUP
27/02/67   Midfield

89	BK Fremad Valby	Div 3		
90	BK Fremad Amager	Div 2		
91	BK Fremad Amager	Div 2		
91/92	Lyngby BK	30	3	

Jan Chico OLSEN
18/02/71   Forward

90	KB	12	4
91	KB	Div 2	
91/92	Vanløse IF	Div 2	

Kim MICHELSEN
02/10/67   Forward

88	IF Skold Birkerød	Div 3	
89	IF Skold Birkerød	Div 3	
90	IF Skold Birkerød	Div 3	
91	IF Skold Birkerød	Div 2	
91/92	Lyngby BK	11	2

FIVE YEAR RECORD *Birthdate/Playing position*	LEAGUE Apps Gls	EURO CUPS Cup Apps Gls

Allan KUHN
02/03/68   Forward

87	Lyngby BK	13	2			
88	B 1903	1	-			
89	B 1903	23	2			
90	Lyngby BK	25	6	CWC	2	-
91	Lyngby BK	14	-			
91/92	Lyngby BK	6	2			

Per PEDERSEN
30/03/69   Forward

87	OB	8	-			
88	OB	11	7			
89	OB	3	1			
90	OB	22	8	CC	1	1
91	Lyngby BK	18	9			
91/92	Lyngby BK	22	10			

★ Denmark 2 caps, 0 goals

Christian CLEM
06/01/73   Forward

91/92	Lyngby BK	4	1

EUROPEAN HONOURS
none

EUROPEAN CUPS RECORD

	Entries	Pd	W	D	L	F	A
Champions' Cup	1	4	2	1	1	7	2
Cup-winners' Cup	2	6	2	2	2	7	8
UEFA/Fairs' Cup	2	4	0	1	3	4	9
Total - All 3 Cups	5	14	4	4	6	18	19

LEEDS UNITED

FIVE YEAR RECORD	LEAGUE		EURO CUPS		
Birthdate/Playing position	Apps	Gls	Cup	Apps	Gls

John LUKIC
11/12/60 Goalkeeper

87/88	Arsenal	40	-		
88/89	Arsenal	38	-		
89/90	Arsenal	38	-		
90/91	Leeds United	38	-		
91/92	Leeds United	42	-		

Neil EDWARDS
05/12/70 Goalkeeper

89/90	Leeds United	-	-		
90/91	Leeds United	-	-		
91/92	Leeds United	-	-		

Mel STERLAND
01/10/61 Defender

87/88	Sheffield Wednesday	38	8		
88/89	Sheffield Wednesday	22	6		
	Rangers (Sco)	9	3		
89/90	Leeds United	Div 2			
90/91	Leeds United	38	5		
91/92	Leeds United	31	6		

★ England 1 cap, 0 goals

Tony DORIGO
31/12/65 Defender

87/88	Chelsea	40	-		
88/89	Chelsea	Div 2			
89/90	Chelsea	35	3		
90/91	Chelsea	31	2		
91/92	Leeds United	38	3		

★ England 10 caps, 0 goals

Chris FAIRCLOUGH
12/04/64 Defender

87/88	Tottenham Hotspur	40	4		
88/89	Tottenham Hotspur	20	1		
	Leeds United	Div 2			
89/90	Leeds United	Div 2			
90/91	Leeds United	34	4		
91/92	Leeds United	31	2		

Chris WHYTE
02/09/61 Defender

87/88	Los Angeles (Usa)				
88/89	West Bromwich Albion	Div 2			
89/90	Leeds United	Div 2			
90/91	Leeds United	38	3		
91/92	Leeds United	41	1		

Jon NEWSOME
06/09/70 Defender

89/90	Sheffield Wednesday	6	-		
90/91	Sheffield Wednesday	Div 2			
91/92	Leeds United	10	2		

David BATTY
02/12/68 Midfield

87/88	Leeds United	Div 2			
88/89	Leeds United	Div 2			
89/90	Leeds United	Div 2	1		
90/91	Leeds United	37	-		
91/92	Leeds United	40	2		

★ England 10 caps, 0 goals

SCOTT SELLARS
27/11/65 Midfield

87/88	Blackburn Rovers	Div 2			
88/89	Blackburn Rovers	Div 2			
89/90	Blackburn Rovers	Div 2			
90/91	Blackburn Rovers	Div 2			
91/92	Blackburn Rovers	Div 2			

Gordon STRACHAN (Sco)
09/02/57 Midfield

87/88	Manchester United	36	8		
88/89	Manchester United	21	1		
	Leeds United	Div 2			
89/90	Leeds United	Div 2			
90/91	Leeds United	34	7		
91/92	Leeds United	36	4		

★ Scotland 50 caps, 5 goals

ENGLAND

FIVE YEAR RECORD	LEAGUE		EURO CUPS		
Birthdate/Playing position	Apps	Gls	Cup	Apps	Gls

Gary McALLISTER (Sco)
25/12/64   Midfield

87/88	Leicester City	Div 2	
88/89	Leicester City	Div 2	
89/90	Leicester City	Div 2	
90/91	Leeds United	38	2
91/92	Leeds United	42	5

★ Scotland 18 caps, 4 goals

David ROCASTLE
02/05/67   Midfield

87/88	Arsenal	40	6		
88/89	Arsenal	38	6		
89/90	Arsenal	33	2		
90/91	Arsenal	16	2		
91/92	Arsenal	39	4	CC	4	-

★ England 14 caps, 0 goals

Gary SPEED (Wal)
08/09/69   Midfield

88/89	Leeds United	Div 2	
89/90	Leeds United	Div 2	
90/91	Leeds United	38	7
91/92	Leeds United	41	7

★ Wales 13 caps, 0 goals

Steve HODGE
25/10/62   Midfield

88/89	Tottenham Hotspur	26	3
88/89	Nottingham Forest	34	7
89/90	Nottingham Forest	34	10
90/91	Nottingham Forest	14	3
91/92	Leeds United	23	7

★ England 24 caps, 0 goals

Rod WALLACE
02/10/69   Forward

87/88	Southampton	15	1
88/89	Southampton	38	12
89/90	Southampton	38	18
90/91	Southampton	37	14
91/92	Leeds United	34	11

FIVE YEAR RECORD	LEAGUE		EURO CUPS		
Birthdate/Playing position	Apps	Gls	Cup	Apps	Gls

Lee CHAPMAN
05/12/59   Forward

87/88	Sheffield Wednesday	37	19
88/89	Chamois Niortais (Fra)	Div 2	
	Nottingham Forest	30	8
89/90	Nottingham Forest	18	7
	Leeds United	Div 2	
90/91	Leeds United	38	21
91/92	Leeds United	38	16

Carl SHUTT
10/10/61   Forward

87/88	Sheffield Wednesday	1	-
	Bristol City	Div 3	
88/89	Bristol City	Div 3	
	Leeds United	Div 2	
89/90	Leeds United	Div 2	
90/91	Leeds United	28	10
91/92	Leeds United	14	1

Eric CANTONA (Fra)
24/05/66   Forward

87/88	AJ Auxerre (Fra)	32	8	UC	2	1
88/89	Olympique Marseille (Fra)	22	5			
	Girondins de Bordeaux (Fra)	11	6			
89/90	Montpellier HSC (Fra)	33	10			
90/91	Olympique Marseille (Fra)	18	8	+CC	3	1
91/92	Nîmes-Olympique (Fra)	16	2			
	Leeds United	14	3			

★ France 27 caps, 12 goals

EUROPEAN HONOURS
Fairs' Cup - (2) 1968, 1971.

EUROPEAN CUPS RECORD

	Entries	Pd	W	D	L	F	A
Champions' Cup	2	17	12	1	4	42	11
Cup-winners' Cup	1	9	5	3	1	13	3
UEFA/Fairs' Cup	8	65	33	20	12	110	53
Total - All 3 Cups	11	91	50	24	17	165	67

FC KUUSYSI

FIVE YEAR RECORD	LEAGUE		EURO CUPS		
Birthdate/Playing position	Apps	Gls	Cup	Apps	Gls

Ismo KORHONEN
10/02/62   Goalkeeper

87	FC Kuusysi	22	-	CC	2	-
88	FC Kuusysi	26	-	CWC	2	-
89	FC Kuusysi	27	-	UC	2	-
90	FC Kuusysi	28	-	CC	2	-
91	FC Kuusysi	10	-			

★ Finland 7 caps, 0 goals

Jyrki ROVIO
04/03/68   Goalkeeper

89	KuPS	27	1			
90	KuPS	24	-	CWC	2	-
91	FC Kuusysi	23	-	UC	2	-

Keijo KOUSA
27/07/59   Defender

87	FC Kuusysi	20	2	CC	2	1
88	FC Kuusysi	27	1	CWC	2	-
89	FC Kuusysi	25	4	UC	2	-
90	FC Kuusysi	20	1			
91	FC Kuusysi	31	4			

★ Finland 18 caps, 0 goals

Mika MOTTURI
26/06/70   Defender

89	FC Kuusysi	1	-			
90	FC Kuusysi	6	-	CC	1	-
91	FC Kuusysi	5	-			

Ilkka REMES
29/07/63   Defender

87	FC Kuusysi	22	2	CC	2	-
88	FC Kuusysi	27	-	CWC	2	-
89	FC Kuusysi	26	1	UC	2	1
90	FC Kuusysi	27	1	CC	2	-
91	FC Kuusysi	31	-	UC	2	-

★ Finland 31 caps, 1 goals

Jari KINNUNEN
12/09/66   Defender

87	Reipas	21	6			
88	Reipas	27	9			
89	Reipas	27	5			
90	FC Kuusysi	23	3	CC	2	-
91	FC Kuusysi	31	2	UC	2	-

★ Finland 1 cap, 0 goals

Jarmo SAASTAMOINEN
20/09/67   Defender

87	Reipas	22	1			
88	Reipas	27	2			
89	FC Kuusysi	25	3	UC	2	-
90	FC Kuusysi	14	1	CC	2	-
91	FC Kuusysi	33	3	UC	2	-

★ Finland 6 caps, 0 goals

Harri MUNUKKA
28/03/65   Defender

87	Reipas	21	-			
88	Reipas	27	2			
89	Reipas	26	2			
90	Reipas	27	1			
91	Reipas	27	2			

Hannu JÄNTTI
01/03/63   Defender

87	FC Kuusysi	19	1	CC	2	-
88	FC Kuusysi	27	-	CWC	2	-
89	FC Kuusysi	24	3	UC	2	-
90	FC Kuusysi	22	3	CC	2	-
91	FC Kuusysi	25	1	UC	2	-

Mika AALTONEN
12/03/67   Midfield

88	Ilves	27	2			
89	Ilves	22	2			
90	Ilves	17	4			
91	Ilves	21	4			

★ Finland 3 caps, 1 goal

FINLAND

FIVE YEAR RECORD Birthdate/Playing position	LEAGUE Apps Gls	EURO CUPS Cup Apps Gls

Juha ANNUNEN
16/04/60   Midfield

87	FC Kuusysi	21	7	CC	2	-
88	FC Kuusysi	26	5	CWC	2	-
89	FC Kuusysi	27	10	UC	2	-
90	FC Kuusysi	26	6	CC	2	-
91	FC Kuusysi	32	6	UC	2	-

★ Finland 16 caps, 1 goal

Petri JÄRVINEN
09/05/65   Midfield

87	Haka	16	2			
88	Haka	26	8			
89	FC Kuusysi	27	1	UC	2	-
90	FC Kuusysi	28	8	CC	1	-
91	FC Kuusysi	32	8	UC	2	-

★ Finland 13 caps, 2 goals

Jari RINNE
04/05/64   Midfield

87	FC Kuusysi	22	2	CC	2	-
88	FC Kuusysi	27	1	CWC	2	-
89	FC Kuusysi	26	4	UC	2	-
90	FC Kuusysi	28	1	CC	2	-
91	FC Kuusysi	30	2	UC	1	-

★ Finland 22 caps, 0 goals

Sami VEHKAKOSKI
06/12/68   Midfield

87	FC Kuusysi	16	-	CC	2	-
88	FC Kuusysi	25	5	CWC	2	-
89	FC Kuusysi	16	1	UC	1	-
90	FC Kuusysi	28	3	CC	2	1
91	FC Kuusysi	17	-	UC	1	-

Mike BELFIELD (Eng)
10/06/61   Forward

87	Ilves	19	6			
88	Reipas	27	7			
89	Reipas	25	12			
90	Reipas	27	11			
91	FC Kuusysi	31	21	UC	2	1

FIVE YEAR RECORD Birthdate/Playing position	LEAGUE Apps Gls	EURO CUPS Cup Apps Gls

Jari SULANDER
14/08/71   Forward

91	FC Kuusysi	-	-			

Kimmo TARKKIO
15/01/66   Forward

87	HJK	12	4			
88	HJK	26	5	CC	2	-
89	Hammarby IF (Swe)	Div 2				
90	HJK	27	16			
91	Haka	28	23			

★ Finland 31 caps, 3 goals

Kalle LEHTINEN
17/08/72   Forward

91	FC Kuusysi	15	6	UC	2	1

EUROPEAN HONOURS
none

EUROPEAN CUPS RECORD

	Entries	Pd	W	D	L	F	A
Champions' Cup	4	12	4	1	7	11	23
Cup-winners' Cup	3	6	0	2	4	3	11
UEFA/Fairs' Cup	2	4	1	1	2	3	9
Total - All 3 Cups	9	22	5	4	13	17	43

OLYMPIQUE MARSEILLE

FIVE YEAR RECORD	LEAGUE		EURO CUPS		
Birthdate/Playing position	Apps	Gls	Cup	Apps	Gls

Pascal OLMETA
07/04/61   Goalkeeper

87/88	Matra Racing Paris	38	-		
88/89	Matra Racing Paris	36	-		
89/90	Racing Paris 1	36	-		
90/91	Olympique Marseille	38	-	+CC	9	-
91/92	Olympique Marseille	38	-	CC	4	-

Fabien BARTHEZ
28/06/71   Goalkeeper

91/92	Toulouse FC	26	-

Manuel AMOROS
01/02/62   Defender

87/88	AS Monaco	37	6			
88/89	AS Monaco	34	6	CC	6	-
89/90	Olympique Marseille	34	1	CC	8	-
90/91	Olympique Marseille	29	1	+CC	7	-
91/92	Olympique Marseille	33	-	CC	4	-

★ France 82 caps, 1 goal

Basile BOLI
02/01/67   Defender

87/88	AJ Auxerre	34	-	UC	2	-
88/89	AJ Auxerre	37	1			
89/90	AJ Auxerre	36	-	UC	10	1
90/91	Olympique Marseille	38	8	+CC	6	2
91/92	Olympique Marseille	34	5	CC	4	-

★ France 38 caps, 1 goal

Bernard CASONI
04/09/61   Defender

87/88	SC Toulon	31	-			
88/89	Matra Racing Paris	27	1			
89/90	SC Toulon	36	-			
90/91	Olympique Marseille	35	-	+CC	9	-
91/92	Olympique Marseille	31	-	CC	4	-

★ France 27 caps, 0 goals

FIVE YEAR RECORD	LEAGUE		EURO CUPS		
Birthdate/Playing position	Apps	Gls	Cup	Apps	Gls

Marcel DESAILLY
07/09/68   Defender

87/88	FC Nantes	11	-	
88/89	FC Nantes	36	1	
89/90	FC Nantes	36	1	
90/91	FC Nantes	34	1	
91/92	FC Nantes	32	2	

Jean-Jacques EYDELIE
03/02/66   Defender

87/88	FC Tours	Div 2	
88/89	FC Nantes	19	1
89/90	FC Nantes	30	1
90/91	FC Nantes	33	1
91/92	FC Nantes	25	1

Eric DI MECO
07/09/63   Defender

87/88	FC Martigues	Div 2				
88/89	Olympique Marseille	33	-			
89/90	Olympique Marseille	33	-	CC	8	-
90/91	Olympique Marseille	20	-	+CC	7	-
91/92	Olympique Marseille	4	-			

★ France 6 caps, 0 goals

Jocelyn ANGLOMA
07/08/65   Midfield

87/88	Lille OSC	32	3			
88/89	Lille OSC	26	3			
89/90	Lille OSC	34	7			
90/91	Paris-Saint-Germain FC	36	6			
91/92	Olympique Marseille	32	2	CC	4	1

★ France 12 caps, 0 goals

Didier DESCHAMPS
15/10/68   Midfield

87/88	FC Nantes	30	2			
88/89	FC Nantes	36	1			
89/90	FC Nantes	19	1			
	Olympique Marseille	17	1	CC	4	-
90/91	Girondins de Bordeaux	29	3	UC	4	-
91/92	Olympique Marseille	36	4	CC	4	-

★ France 24 caps, 3 goals

FRANCE

FIVE YEAR RECORD *Birthdate/Playing position*	LEAGUE Apps Gls	EURO CUPS Cup Apps Gls

Jean-Philippe DURAND
11/11/60   Midfield

87/88	Toulouse FC	15	1			
88/89	Toulouse FC	24	3			
89/90	Girondins de Bordeaux	30	1			
90/91	Girondins de Bordeaux	32	1	UC	6	-
91/92	Olympique Marseille	27	2	CC	1	-

★ France 22 caps, 0 goals

Jean-Christophe THOMAS
16/10/64   Midfield

87/88	FC Sochaux	Div 2				
88/89	FC Sochaux	38	3			
89/90	FC Sochaux	34	7	UC	4	3
90/91	FC Sochaux	33	2			
91/92	FC Sochaux	37	5			

Franck SAUZEE
28/10/65   Midfield

87/88	FC Sochaux	Div 2				
88/89	Olympique Marseille	32	4			
89/90	Olympique Marseille	36	5	CC	7	3
90/91	AS Monaco	28	7	UC	5	-
91/92	Olympique Marseille	22	2	CC	2	1

★ France 27 caps, 6 goals

Dragan STOJKOVIC (Yug)
03/03/65   Midfield

87/88	Crvena zvezda Beograd (Yug)	28	15	UC	3	1
88/89	Crvena zvezda Beograd (Yug)	27	12	CC	4	3
89/90	Crvena zvezda Beograd (Yug)	30	10	UC	6	-
90/91	Olympique Marseille	11	-	+CC	3	-
91/92	Verona (Ita)	19	2			

★ Yugoslavia 41 caps, 9 goals

Alen BOKSIC (Cro)
21/01/70   Forward

87/88	Hajduk Split (Yug)	13	2			
88/89	Hajduk Split (Yug)	26	7			
89/90	Hajduk Split (Yug)	28	12			
90/91	Hajduk Split (Yug)	29	6			
91/92	AS Cannes	1	-			

FIVE YEAR RECORD *Birthdate/Playing position*	LEAGUE Apps Gls	EURO CUPS Cup Apps Gls

Rudi VÖLLER (Ger)
13/04/60   Forward

87/88	Roma (Ita)	21	3			
88/89	Roma (Ita)	29	10	UC	6	2
89/90	Roma (Ita)	32	14			
90/91	Roma (Ita)	30	11	+UC	12	10
91/92	Roma (Ita)	30	7	CWC	4	-

★ Germany 84 caps, 43 goals

Abedi PELE (Gha)
05/01/62   Forward

87/88	FC Mulhouse	Div 2				
	Olympique Marseille	5	-	CWC	4	-
88/89	Olympique Marseille	4	-			
	Lille OSC	24	7			
89/90	Lille OSC	37	9			
90/91	Olympique Marseille	32	5	+CC	8	2
91/92	Olympique Marseille	36	12	CC	3	1

★ Ghana

François OMAM-BIYIK (Cmr)
21/05/66   Forward

87/88	Stade Lavallois	24	11			
88/89	Stade Lavallois	25	4			
89/90	Stade Lavallois	Div 2				
90/91	Stade Rennais FC	38	14			
91/92	AS Cannes	35	7	UC	4	2

★ Cameroon

EUROPEAN HONOURS
none

EUROPEAN CUPS RECORD

	Entries	Pd	W	D	L	F	A
Champions' Cup	5	27	15	6	6	53	28
Cup-winners' Cup	3	14	8	2	4	18	13
UEFA/Fairs' Cup	5	12	6	0	6	21	19
Total - All 3 Cups	13	53	29	8	16	92	60

VFB STUTTGART

FIVE YEAR RECORD *Birthdate/Playing position*	LEAGUE Apps Gls	EURO CUPS Cup Apps Gls

Eike IMMEL
27/11/60   Goalkeeper

		LEAGUE Apps	Gls	Cup	Apps	Gls
87/88	VfB Stuttgart	29	-			
88/89	VfB Stuttgart	29	-	+UC	12	-
89/90	VfB Stuttgart	27	-	UC	6	-
90/91	VfB Stuttgart	34	-			
91/92	VfB Stuttgart	38	-	UC	4	-

★ Germany 19 caps, 0 goals

Eberhard TRAUTNER
07/02/67   Goalkeeper

		Apps	Gls			
87/88	VfB Stuttgart	6	-			
88/89	VfB Stuttgart	5	-			
89/90	VfB Stuttgart	7	-			
90/91	VfB Stuttgart	-	-			
91/92	VfB Stuttgart	-	-			

Slobodan DUBAJIC (Yug)
19/02/63   Defender

		Apps	Gls			
88/89	Proleter Zrenjanin (Yug)	Div 2				
89/90	Proleter Zrenjanin (Yug)	Div 2				
90/91	Proleter Zrenjanin (Yug)	34	2			
91/92	VfB Stuttgart	38	2	UC	4	-

Günther SCHÄFER
09/06/62   Defender

		Apps	Gls			
87/88	VfB Stuttgart	28	2			
88/89	VfB Stuttgart	19	-	+UC	9	-
89/90	VfB Stuttgart	22	-	UC	5	-
90/91	VfB Stuttgart	22	-			
91/92	VfB Stuttgart	28	1	UC	4	-

Guido BUCHWALD
24/01/61   Defender

		Apps	Gls			
87/88	VfB Stuttgart	30	1			
88/89	VfB Stuttgart	30	1	+UC	10	-
89/90	VfB Stuttgart	28	5	UC	5	1
90/91	VfB Stuttgart	21	3			
91/92	VfB Stuttgart	37	5	UC	4	2

★ Germany 55 caps, 1 goal

Alexander STREHMEL
20/03/68   Defender

		Apps	Gls			
87/88	VfB Stuttgart	26	1			
88/89	VfB Stuttgart	14	1	+UC	6	-
89/90	VfB Stuttgart	26	-	UC	4	-
90/91	VfB Stuttgart	16	1			
91/92	VfB Stuttgart	25	-	UC	2	1

Michael FRONTZECK
26/03/64   Defender

		Apps	Gls			
87/88	Borussia Mönchengladbach	33	3	UC	2	-
88/89	Borussia Mönchengladbach	32	1			
89/90	VfB Stuttgart	31	4	UC	6	1
90/91	VfB Stuttgart	32	5			
91/92	VfB Stuttgart	38	5	UC	4	-

★ Germany 18 caps, 0 goals

Uwe SCHNEIDER
28/08/71   Defender

		Apps	Gls			
90/91	VfB Stuttgart	14	-			
91/92	VfB Stuttgart	33	-	UC	3	-

Thomas SCHNEIDER
24/11/72   Midfield

		Apps	Gls			
91/92	VfB Stuttgart	2	-			

Thomas STRUNZ
25/04/68   Midfield

		Apps	Gls			
88/89	MSV Duisburg	Div 3				
89/90	FC Bayern München	20	5	CC	6	2
90/91	FC Bayern München	26	7	CC	6	1
91/92	FC Bayern München	13	-	UC	1	-

★ Germany 2 caps, 0 goals

Andreas BUCK
29/12/67   Midfield

		Apps	Gls			
88/89	SC Freiburg	Div 2				
89/90	SC Freiburg	Div 2				
90/91	VfB Stuttgart	21	1			
91/92	VfB Stuttgart	30	1	UC	3	-

GERMANY

FIVE YEAR RECORD	LEAGUE		EURO CUPS		
Birthdate/Playing position	Apps	Gls	Cup	Apps	Gls

Maurizio GAUDINO
12/12/66   Midfield

87/88	VfB Stuttgart	30	2		
88/89	VfB Stuttgart	30	8	+UC	12	4
89/90	VfB Stuttgart	27	4	UC	3	-
90/91	VfB Stuttgart	18	2		
91/92	VfB Stuttgart	38	8	UC	4	-

Ludwig KÖGL
07/03/66   Midfield

87/88	FC Bayern München	21	1	CC	6	1
88/89	FC Bayern München	32	-	UC	9	-
89/90	FC Bayern München	25	4	CC	7	2
90/91	VfB Stuttgart	22	3		
91/92	VfB Stuttgart	16	1		

★ Germany 2 caps, 0 goals

Fritz WALTER
21/07/60   Forward

87/88	VfB Stuttgart	33	17		
88/89	VfB Stuttgart	32	13	+UC	11	4
89/90	VfB Stuttgart	31	13	UC	6	2
90/91	VfB Stuttgart	26	12		
91/92	VfB Stuttgart	38	22	UC	3	2

Marc KIENLE
22/10/72   Forward

91/92	VfB Stuttgart	10	-	UC	2	1

Adrian KNUP (Sui)
02/07/68   Forward

87/88	FC Basel (Sui)	21	6		
88/89	FC Aarau (Sui)	21	6	UC	2	-
89/90	FC Luzern (Sui)	33	8		
90/91	FC Luzern (Sui)	35	6	UC	4	1
91/92	FC Luzern (Sui)	6	5		

★ Switzerland 20 caps, 14 goals

FIVE YEAR RECORD	LEAGUE		EURO CUPS		
Birthdate/Playing position	Apps	Gls	Cup	Apps	Gls

André GOLKE
15/08/64   Forward

87/88	FC St. Pauli	Div 2	
88/89	FC St. Pauli	33	9
89/90	FC St. Pauli	32	10
90/91	FC St. Pauli	33	6
91/92	1.FC Nürnberg	38	7

Eyjólfur SVERRISSON (Isl)
03/08/68   Forward

89	Tindastoll (Isl)	Div 2		
89/90	VfB Stuttgart	3	1		
90/91	VfB Stuttgart	20	5		
91/92	VfB Stuttgart	31	3	UC	2	1

★ Iceland 6 caps, 2 goals

EUROPEAN HONOURS
none

EUROPEAN CUPS RECORD

	Entries	Pd	W	D	L	F	A
Champions' Cup	1	2	0	2	0	3	3
Cup-winners' Cup	1	4	1	1	2	4	7
UEFA/Fairs' Cup	12	68	34	16	18	129	73
Total - All 3 Cups	14	74	35	19	20	136	83

AEK

FIVE YEAR RECORD	LEAGUE		EURO CUPS		
Birthdate/Playing position	Apps	Gls	Cup	Apps	Gls

Antonis MINOU
04/05/58   Goalkeeper

87/88 Panathinaikos	19	-	UC	6	-
88/89 AEK	-	-			
89/90 AEK	26	-			
90/91 AEK	32	-			
91/92 AEK	33	-	UC	6	-

★ Greece 6 caps, 0 goals

Ilias ATMATSERIS
1969   Goalkeeper

91/92 AE Pondii Veria	Div 3	

Vaios KARAYANNIS
25/06/68   Defender

89/90 Karditsas	Div 4				
90/91 AEK	23	-			
91/92 AEK	30	-	UC	6	-

★ Greece 2 caps, 0 goals

Stelios MANOLAS
13/07/61   Defender

87/88 AEK	21	4			
88/89 AEK	24	4	UC	2	-
89/90 AEK	33	3	CC	4	-
90/91 AEK	24	4			
91/92 AEK	31	4	UC	4	-

★ Greece 56 caps, 6 goals

Refik SABANADZOVIC (Yug)
02/08/65   Defender

87/88 Crvena zvezda Beograd (Yug)	11	-	UC	4	1
88/89 Crvena zvezda Beograd (Yug)	14	2	CC	4	1
89/90 Crvena zvezda Beograd (Yug)	11	-			
90/91 Crvena zvezda Beograd (Yug)	26	-	#CC	8	-
91/92 AEK	31	1	UC	6	1

★ Yugoslavia 8 caps, 0 goals

FIVE YEAR RECORD	LEAGUE		EURO CUPS		
Birthdate/Playing position	Apps	Gls	Cup	Apps	Gls

Yorgos AGOROYANNIS
03/05/66   Defender

87/88 Larissa	26	-			
88/89 Larissa	29	4	CC	2	-
89/90 Larissa	26	4			
90/91 Larissa	29	7			
91/92 Larissa	28	5			

★ Greece 6 caps, 0 goals

Yorgos KOUTOULAS
09/02/67   Defender

87/88 AEK	24	4			
88/89 AEK	28	-	UC	2	-
89/90 AEK	25	-	CC	4	-
90/91 AEK	3	-			
91/92 AEK	18	-	UC	5	-

★ Greece 11 caps, 0 goals

Hristos VASSILOPOULOS
12/11/62   Defender

87/88 AEK	13	-			
88/89 AEK	20	-	UC	2	-
89/90 AEK	29	1	CC	3	-
90/91 AEK	30	-			
91/92 AEK	28	1	UC	5	-

Dimitris KARAGIOZOPOULOS
04/02/61   Defender

87/88 AEK	14	1			
88/89 AEK	3	1			
89/90 AEK	21	1	CC	1	-
90/91 AEK	29	5			
91/92 AEK	13	1	UC	2	-

Lambros YORYADIS
11/06/63   Defender

87/88 AEK	19	1			
88/89 AEK	17	-			
89/90 AEK	11	2			
90/91 AEK	26	2			
91/92 AEK	5	-			

GREECE

FIVE YEAR RECORD *Birthdate/Playing position*	LEAGUE Apps Gls	EURO CUPS Cup Apps Gls

Manolis PAPADOPOULOS
22/04/68   Defender

88/89	Ionikos	Div 2		
89/90	Ionikos	28	-	
90/91	Ionikos	33	-	
91/92	Ionikos	Div 2		

★ Greece 1 cap, 0 goals

Pavlos PAPAIOANNOU
19/03/59   Midfield

87/88	AEK	17	-		
88/89	AEK	24	-	UC 1	-
89/90	AEK	30	-	CC 4	-
90/91	AEK	28	-		
91/92	AEK	32	-	UC 6	1

★ Greece 9 caps, 0 goals

Toni SAVEVSKI (Yug)
14/06/63   Midfield

87/88	Vardar Skoplje (Yug)	27	3	CC 2	-
88/89	Vardar Skoplje (Yug)	13	4		
	AEK	17	6		
89/90	AEK	34	5	CC 4	2
90/91	AEK	34	6		
91/92	AEK	29	3	UC 6	-

★ Yugoslavia 2 caps, 0 goals

Stavros STAMATIS
13/01/66   Midfield

88/89	Haravyiakos	Div 2			
	AEK	9	1		
89/90	AEK	24	-	CC 1	-
90/91	AEK	13	-		
91/92	AEK	21	2	UC 6	-

★ Greece 5 caps, 0 goals

Anastassios MITROPOULOS
23/08/57   Midfield

87/88	Olympiakos	19	1	CC 2	-
88/89	Olympiakos	24	7		
89/90	Olympiakos	19	5	UC 6	-
90/91	Olympiakos	13	1	CWC 4	1
91/92	Olympiakos	17	1		

★ Greece 61 caps, 6 goals

FIVE YEAR RECORD *Birthdate/Playing position*	LEAGUE Apps Gls	EURO CUPS Cup Apps Gls

Dimitris PATIKAS
18/10/68   Forward

87/88	AEK	15	5		
88/89	AEK	15	1	UC 2	-
89/90	AEK	29	11	CC 4	-
90/91	AEK	24	6		
91/92	AEK	20	-	UC 2	-

Vassilis DIMITRIADIS
01/02/66   Forward

87/88	Aris	29	12		
88/89	Aris	28	10		
89/90	Aris	27	7		
90/91	Aris	29	8		
91/92	AEK	34	28	UC 5	2

★ Greece 20 caps, 1 goal

Alexandros ALEXANDRIS
21/10/68   Forward

87/88	Veria	30	7		
88/89	Veria	Div 2			
89/90	Veria	Div 2			
90/91	Veria	Div 2			
91/92	AEK	26	11	UC 6	-

★ Greece 4 caps, 0 goals

EUROPEAN HONOURS
none

EUROPEAN CUPS RECORD

	Entries	Pd	W	D	L	F	A
Champions' Cup	6	20	6	4	10	33	42
Cup-winners' Cup	3	6	2	0	4	7	11
UEFA/Fairs' Cup	10	38	14	5	19	41	58
Total - All 3 Cups	19	64	22	9	33	81	111

PSV

FIVE YEAR RECORD	LEAGUE		EURO CUPS		
Birthdate/Playing position	Apps	Gls	Cup	Apps	Gls

Hans VAN BREUKELEN
04/10/56   Goalkeeper

87/88	PSV	33	-	#CC	9	-
88/89	PSV	22	-	CC	2	-
89/90	PSV	32	-	CC	6	-
90/91	PSV	32	-	CWC	2	-
91/92	PSV	32	-	CC	4	-

★ Holland 73 caps, 0 goals

Wim DE RON
23/08/69   Goalkeeper

91/92	PSV	2	-

Gheorghe POPESCU (Rom)
09/10/67   Defender

87/88	Universitatea Craiova (Rom)	14	1	UC	2	-
	Steaua Bucuresti (Rom)	13	1	CC	3	-
88/89	Universitatea Craiova (Rom)	33	8			
89/90	Universitatea Craiova (Rom)	26	7			
90/91	PSV	30	5	CWC	2	-
91/92	PSV	29	7	CC	3	-

★ Romania 35 caps, 1 goal

Adri VAN TIGGELEN
16/06/57   Defender

87/88	RSC Anderlecht (Bel)	32	1	CC	6	-
88/89	RSC Anderlecht (Bel)	29	3	CWC	4	1
89/90	RSC Anderlecht (Bel)	27	1	+CWC	6	-
90/91	RSC Anderlecht (Bel)	25	-	UC	6	-
91/92	PSV	26	-	CC	3	-

★ Holland 56 caps, 0 goals

Jan HEINTZE (Den)
17/08/63   Defender

87/88	PSV	28	1	#CC	9	-
88/89	PSV	28	-	CC	4	-
89/90	PSV	33	-	CC	6	-
90/91	PSV	33	-	CWC	2	-
91/92	PSV	29	-	CC	4	-

★ Denmark 24 caps, 1 goal

FIVE YEAR RECORD	LEAGUE		EURO CUPS		
Birthdate/Playing position	Apps	Gls	Cup	Apps	Gls

Jerry DE JONG
29/08/64   Defender

87/88	Telstar	Div 2				
88/89	SC Heerenveen	Div 2				
89/90	PSV	3	-	CC	1	-
90/91	PSV	29	2	CWC	2	-
91/92	PSV	10	-	CC	3	-

★ Holland 3 caps, 0 goals

Mitchel VAN DER GAAG
22/10/71   Defender

89/90	NEC	10	2
90/91	Sparta	22	2
91/92	Sparta	33	1

Berry VAN AERLE
08/12/62   Midfield

87/88	PSV	33	2	#CC	9	1
88/89	PSV	24	1	CC	2	-
89/90	PSV	28	4	CC	6	-
90/91	PSV	11	2			
91/92	PSV	26	-	CC	3	-

★ Holland 33 caps, 0 goals

Gerald VANENBURG
05/03/64   Midfield

87/88	PSV	34	12	#CC	9	-
88/89	PSV	34	10	CC	4	-
89/90	PSV	21	6	CC	4	-
90/91	PSV	29	11	CWC	2	-
91/92	PSV	19	7	CC	2	1

★ Holland 41 caps, 1 goal

Edward LINSKENS
06/11/68   Midfield

87/88	PSV	14	-	#CC	3	1
88/89	PSV	17	3	CC	2	-
89/90	PSV	18	-	CC	2	-
90/91	PSV	12	1			
91/92	PSV	24	2	CC	1	-

HOLLAND

FIVE YEAR RECORD *Birthdate/Playing position*	LEAGUE Apps Gls	EURO CUPS Cup Apps Gls

Erwin KOEMAN
20/09/61 Midfield

		Apps	Gls	Cup	Apps	Gls
87/88	KV Mechelen (Bel)	24	5	#CWC	9	-
88/89	KV Mechelen (Bel)	28	7	CWC	5	2
89/90	KV Mechelen (Bel)	16	3	CC	1	-
90/91	PSV	27	3	CWC	2	-
91/92	PSV	28	3	CC	4	-

★ Holland 28 caps, 2 goals

Ernest FABER
27/08/71 Midfield

		Apps	Gls
90/91	NEC	30	-
91/92	Sparta	31	-

KALUSHA Bwalya (Zam)
16/08/63 Forward

		Apps	Gls	Cup	Apps	Gls
87/88	KSV Cercle Brugge (Bel)	33	13			
88/89	KSV Cercle Brugge (Bel)	29	13			
89/90	PSV	12	2	CC	2	-
90/91	PSV	22	3	CWC	2	-
91/92	PSV	30	12	CC	3	1

★ Zambia

Wim KIEFT
12/11/62 Forward

		Apps	Gls	Cup	Apps	Gls
87/88	PSV	32	28	#CC	9	1
88/89	PSV	20	6	CC	2	1
8/90	PSV	30	21	CC	5	1
90/91	Girondins de Bordeaux (Fra)	26	3	UC	4	-
91/92	PSV	33	19	CC	2	-

★ Holland 41 caps, 11 goals

ROMÁRIO de Souza Faria (Bra)
29/01/66 Forward

		Apps	Gls	Cup	Apps	Gls
87/88	Vasco da Gama (Bra)					
88/89	PSV	24	19	CC	2	2
89/90	PSV	20	23	CC	4	6
90/91	PSV	25	25	CWC	2	-
91/92	PSV	14	9	CC	2	-

★ Brazil

FIVE YEAR RECORD *Birthdate/Playing position*	LEAGUE Apps Gls	EURO CUPS Cup Apps Gls

Juul ELLERMAN
07/10/65 Forward

		Apps	Gls	Cup	Apps	Gls
87/88	Sparta	28	14			
88/89	PSV	21	11	CC	3	1
89/90	PSV	25	6	CC	6	3
90/91	PSV	29	16	CWC	1	-
91/92	PSV	28	12	CC	4	1

★ Holland 5 caps, 0 goals

Dick SCHREUDER
02/08/71 Forward

		Apps	Gls
91/92	PSV	4	-

Peter HOEKSTRA
04/04/73 Forward

		Apps	Gls
91/92	PSV	14	3

EUROPEAN HONOURS
Champions' Cup - (1) 1988.
UEFA Cup - (1) 1978.

EUROPEAN CUPS RECORD

	Entries	Pd	W	D	L	F	A
Champions' Cup	10	49	20	14	15	82	46
Cup-winners' Cup	4	22	13	3	6	45	17
UEFA/Fairs' Cup	9	43	21	7	15	73	48
Total - All 3 Cups	23	114	54	24	36	200	111

FERENCVÁROS

FIVE YEAR RECORD Birthdate/Playing position	LEAGUE Apps	Gls	EURO CUPS Cup	Apps	Gls
Tamás BALOGH					
06/09/67 Goalkeeper					
90/91 Ferencváros	14	-			
91/92 Ferencváros	29	-	CWC	4	-
★ Hungary 1 cap, 0 goals					
József SZEILER					
03/11/65 Goalkeeper					
89/90 Ferencváros	-	-			
90/91 Ferencváros	1	-	UC	1	-
91/92 Ferencváros	1	-			
József KELLER					
25/09/65 Defender					
87/88 Ferencváros	29	-			
88/89 Ferencváros	29	1			
89/90 Ferencváros	28	-	CWC	4	1
90/91 Ferencváros	30	1	UC	4	-
91/92 Ferencváros	25	-	CWC	4	-
★ Hungary 23 caps, 0 goals					
Tibor SIMON					
12/09/67 Defender					
87/88 Ferencváros	13	-			
88/89 Ferencváros	24	-			
89/90 Ferencváros	28	1	CWC	3	-
90/91 Ferencváros	9	-	UC	4	-
91/92 Ferencváros	30	-	CWC	4	-
★ Hungary 10 caps, 0 goals					
Tamás SZEKERES					
18/09/72 Defender					
90/91 Ferencváros	2	-			
91/92 Ferencváros	8	-			
András TELEK					
10/12/70 Defender					
89/90 Ferencváros	10	-			
90/91 Ferencváros	14	-			
91/92 Ferencváros	30	-	CWC	4	-
★ Hungary 5 caps, 0 goals					

FIVE YEAR RECORD Birthdate/Playing position	LEAGUE Apps	Gls	EURO CUPS Cup	Apps	Gls
Gyula VASZIL					
31/05/64 Defender					
87/88 Ferencváros	16	2			
88/89 Ferencváros	17	-			
89/90 Ferencváros	21	-	CWC	3	-
90/91 Ferencváros	13	-	UC	3	-
91/92 Ferencváros	6	-			
Sergei KUZNETSOV (Ukr)					
01/01/63 Defender					
87 Metallist Kharkov (Urs)	30	-			
88 Chernomorets Odessa (Urs)	22	1			
89 Chernomorets Odessa (Urs)	30	-			
90 Chernomorets Odessa (Urs)	16	1	UC	2	-
91/92 Ferencváros	23	4	CWC	4	-
Flórián ALBERT					
12/12/67 Midfield					
87/88 Ferencváros	4	-			
88/89 Ferencváros	9	-			
89/90 Ferencváros	7	-	CWC	1	-
90/91 Ferencváros	14	2	UC	1	-
91/92 Ferencváros	24	8	CWC	4	1
Sándor SZENES					
11/11/67 Midfield					
88/89 FC Bihor Oradea (Rom)	28	5			
89/90 FC Inter Sibiu (Rom)	26	6			
90/91 Ferencváros	26	3	UC	3	-
91/92 Ferencváros	22	3	CWC	3	-
Zsolt PÁLING					
26/02/69 Midfield					
88/89 Ferencváros	10	2			
89/90 Ferencváros	13	2	CWC	4	-
90/91 Ferencváros	13	-	UC	2	-
91/92 Ferencváros	20	1	CWC	4	-

HUNGARY

FIVE YEAR RECORD Birthdate/Playing position	LEAGUE Apps Gls	•EURO CUPS Cup Apps Gls

Imre FODOR
16/03/63   Midfield

87/88	Budapesti Honvéd SE ·	30	9	UC 6	3
88/89	Budapesti Honvéd SE	20	11	CC 2	1
89/90	Budapesti Honvéd SE	27	8	CC 4	1
90/91	Budapesti Honvéd SE	17	3		
	Siófok	11	3		
91/92	Siófok	14	4		
	Ferencváros	15	7		

★ Hungary 4 caps, 0 goals

Péter LIPCSEI
28/03/72   Midfield

90/91	Ferencváros	19	1	UC 4	-
91/92	Ferencváros	30	9	CWC 4	6

★ Hungary 10 caps, 0 goals

Zsolt NAGY
04/06/68   Forward

87/88	Ferencváros	16	1		
88/89	Ferencváros	13	-		
89/90	Ferencváros	18	3		
90/91	Ferencváros	7	-	UC 1	-
91/92	Ferencváros	15	2	CWC 1	-

László WUKOVICS
22/01/70   Forward

87/88	Ferencváros	1	-		
88/89	Ferencváros	19	5		
89/90	Ferencváros	9	2		
90/91	Ferencváros	3	2		
91/92	Ferencváros	18	11	CWC 2	-

Gábor BALOGH
29/10/64   Forward

87/88	MTK-VM	15	1		
88/89	Váci Izzó MTE	25	9		
89/90	MTK-VM	21	5	UC 1	-
90/91	MTK-VM	7	3	UC 1	-
91/92	Ferencváros	21	7		

FIVE YEAR RECORD Birthdate/Playing position	LEAGUE Apps Gls	EURO CUPS Cup Apps Gls

József GREGOR
30/11/63   Forward

87/88	Epitök SC	Div 2			
88/89	Budapesti Honvéd SE	28	9	CC 2	-
89/90	Budapesti Honvéd SE	26	7	CC 4	-
90/91	Budapesti Honvéd SE	30	15		
91/92	Siófok	27	7		

★ Hungary 6 caps, 0 goals

Sorin CIGAN (Rom)
29/05/64   Forward

87/88	FCM Brasov (Rom)	15 ·	6		
88/89	FCM Brasov (Rom)	29	7		
89/90	Victoria Bucuresti (Rom)	12	2	UC 2	-
	FCM Brasov (Rom)	9	1		
90/91	FC Bihor Oradea (Rom)	14	1		
	Szeged SC	14	6		
91/92	Újpesti TE	24	5		

★ Romania 1 cap, 0 goals

EUROPEAN HONOURS
Fairs' Cup - (1) 1965.

EUROPEAN CUPS RECORD

	Entries	Pd	W	D	L	F	A
Champions' Cup	5	18	9	2	7	39	33
Cup-winners' Cup	6	27	12	6	9	49	35
UEFA/Fairs' Cup	12	67	31	11	25	109	79
Total - All 3 Cups	23	112	52	19	41	197	147

VÍKINGUR

FIVE YEAR RECORD	LEAGUE		EURO CUPS		
Birthdate/Playing position	Apps	Gls	Cup	Apps	Gls

Gudmundur HREIDARSSON
05/10/60   Goalkeeper

87	Valur	8	-
88	Víkingur	18	-
89	Víkingur	18	-
90	Víkingur	10	-
91	Víkingur	18	-

★ Iceland 2 caps, 0 goals

Baldvin GUDMUNDSSON
20/06/64   Goalkeeper

87	Thór	18	-
88	Thór	18	-
89	Thór	18	-
90	Víkingur	8	-
91	Víkingur	-	-

Helgi BJÖRGVINSSON
09/07/70   Defender

88	Fram	1	-
89	Fram	1	-
90	Víkingur	18	-
91	Víkingur	14	-

Janez ZILNIK (Yug)
30/04/64   Defender

90	Víkingur	16	-
91	Víkingur	16	-

Helgi BJARNASON
22/01/69   Defender

88	Fram	5	-			
89	Fram	11	-	CC	2	-
90	Víkingur	18	-			
91	Víkingur	18	2			

Holmsteinn JÓNSSON
31/03/70   Defender

90	Fram	-	-
91	Víkingur	12	3

FIVE YEAR RECORD	LEAGUE		EURO CUPS		
Birthdate/Playing position	Apps	Gls	Cup	Apps	Gls

Thorsteinn THORSTEINSSON
07/07/64   Defender

87	Fram	18	-	CC	2	-
88	Fram	16	-	CWC	2	-
89	Fram	17	-			
90	Fram	9	-	CWC	1	-
91	Víkingur	14	-			

★ Iceland 9 caps, 0 goals

Tomislav BOSNJAK (Slo)
19/10/63   Midfield

87/88	Olimpija Ljubljana (Yug)	Div 2	
88/89	Olimpija Ljubljana (Yug)	Div 2	
89/90	Rabat Ajax (Mlt)	Div 2	
90/91	Rabat Ajax (Mlt)	4	-
91	Víkingur	16	3

Gudmundur Ingi MAGNÚSSON
01/10/64   Midfield

91	Víkingur	18	1

★ Iceland 1 cap, 0 goals

Hördur THEÓDÓRSSON
13/11/67   Midfield

89	ÍR	Div 2	
90	Víkingur	16	1
91	Víkingur	16	3

Atli HELGASON
07/03/67   Midfield

87	Víkingur	Div 2	
88	Víkingur	18	-
89	Víkingur	18	-
90	Víkingur	17	1
91	Víkingur	18	3

★ Iceland 1 cap, 0 goals

ICELAND

FIVE YEAR RECORD *Birthdate/Playing position*	LEAGUE Apps Gls	EURO CUPS Cup Apps Gls

Adalsteinn ADALSTEINSSON
25/04/62   Midfield

87	Völsungur	11	2			
88	Völsungur	11	1			
89	Víkingur	15	-			
90	Víkingur	16	-			
91	Leiftur	Div 3				

Marteinn GUDGEIRSSON
09/07/66   Midfield

90	Fram	-	-			
91	Víkingur	5	-			

Ólafur ÁRNASON
·18/10/66   Midfield

89	ÍBV	Div 2				
90	ÍBV	7	-			
91	Víkingur	12	-			

Lárus HULDARSSON
31/03/73   Defender

Gudmundur STEINSSON
18/07/60   Forward

87	Fram	9	5			
88	Fram	17	12	CWC	2	-
89	Fram	18	9	CC	2	-
90	Fram	18	10			
91	Víkingur	15	13			

★ Iceland 19 caps, 8 goals

Atli EINARSSON
20/10/66   Forward

87	Víkingur	Div 2				
88	Víkingur	18	4			

89	Víkingur	17	5			
90	Víkingur	18	3			
91	Víkingur	18	5			

★ Iceland 2 caps, 0 goals

Helgi SIGURDSSON
17/09/74   Forward

90	Víkingur	1	-			
91	Víkingur	6	1			

EUROPEAN HONOURS
none

EUROPEAN CUPS RECORD

	Entries	Pd	W	D	L	F	A
Champions' Cup	2	4	0	0	4	3	8
Cup-winners' Cup	1	2	0	0	2	0	11
UEFA/Fairs' Cup	1	2	0	0	2	0	8
Total - All 3 Cups	4	8	0	0	8	3	27

MILAN

FIVE YEAR RECORD *Birthdate/Playing position*	LEAGUE Apps Gls	EURO CUPS Cup Apps Gls

Sebastiano ROSSI
20/07/64   Goalkeeper

87/88	Cesena	27	-			
88/89	Cesena	33	-			
89/90	Cesena	34	-			
90/91	Milan	9	-	CC	1	-
91/92	Milan	30	-			

Francesco ANTONIOLI
14/09/69   Goalkeeper

87/88	Monza	Div 3				
88/89	Milan	-	-			
89/90	Milan	-	-			
90/91	Cesena	-	-			
	Modena	Div 2				
91/92	Milan	4	-			

Mauro TASSOTTI
19/01/60   Defender

87/88	Milan	28	-	UC	4	-
88/89	Milan	30	2	#CC	9	-
89/90	Milan	29	3	#CC	7	-
90/91	Milan	28	-	CC	4	-
91/92	Milan	33	-			

Paolo MALDINI
26/06/68   Defender

87/88	Milan	26	2	UC	2	-
88/89	Milan	26	-	#CC	7	-
89/90	Milan	30	1	#CC	8	-
90/91	Milan	26	4	CC	4	-
91/92	Milan	31	3			

★ Italy 40 caps, 0 goals

Alessandro COSTACURTA
24/04/66   Defender

87/88	Milan	7	-			
88/89	Milan	26	-	#CC	7	-
89/90	Milan	26	1	#CC	7	-
90/91	Milan	25	-	CC	4	-
91/92	Milan	30	1			

★ Italy 6 caps, 1 goal

FIVE YEAR RECORD *Birthdate/Playing position*	LEAGUE Apps Gls	EURO CUPS Cup Apps Gls

Franco BARESI
08/05/60   Defender

87/88	Milan	27	1	UC	3	-
88/89	Milan	33	2	#CC	8	-
89/90	Milan	30	1	#CC	8	-
90/91	Milan	31	-	CC	3	-
91/92	Milan	33	-			

★ Italy 63 caps, 1 goal

Demetrio ALBERTINI
23/08/71   Midfield

88/89	Milan	1	-			
89/90	Milan	1	-			
90/91	Padova	Div 2				
91/92	Milan	28	3			

★ Italy 1 cap, 0 goals

Roberto DONADONI
09/09/63   Midfield

87/88	Milan	29	4	UC	3	-
88/89	Milan	21	1	#CC	9	1
89/90	Milan	24	4	#CC	3	-
90/91	Milan	26	2	CC	3	-
91/92	Milan	30	1			

★ Italy 41 caps, 4 goals

Stefano ERANIO
29/12/66   Midfield

87/88	Genoa	Div 2				
88/89	Genoa	Div 2				
89/90	Genoa	Div 2				
90/91	Genoa	31	4			
91/92	Genoa	29	2	UC	9	-

★ Italy 8 caps, 0 goals

Fernando DE NAPOLI
15/03/64   Midfield

87/88	Napoli	30	2	CC	2	-
88/89	Napoli	30	2	#UC	9	-
89/90	Napoli	32	-	UC	6	-
90/91	Napoli	27	1	CC	4	-
91/92	Napoli	29	1			

★ Italy 52 caps, 1 goal

ITALY

FIVE YEAR RECORD	LEAGUE		EURO CUPS		
Birthdate/Playing position	Apps	Gls	Cup	Apps	Gls

Frank RIJKAARD (Hol)
30/09/62   Midfield

		Apps	Gls	Cup	Apps	Gls
87/88	Ajax (Hol)	8	3	+CWC	1	1
	Real Zaragoza (Esp)	11	-			
88/89	Milan	31	4	#CC	9	1
89/90	Milan	29	2	#CC	9	2
90/91	Milan	30	3	CC	4	-
91/92	Milan	30	5			

★ Holland 56 caps, 6 goals

Ruud GULLIT (Hol)
01/09/62   Midfield

		Apps	Gls	Cup	Apps	Gls
87/88	Milan	29	9	UC	4	1
88/89	Milan	19	5	#CC	8	4
89/90	Milan	2	-	#CC	1	-
90/91	Milan	26	7	CC	4	1
91/92	Milan	26	7			

★ Holland 61 caps, 16 goals

Alberigo EVANI
01/01/63   Midfield

		Apps	Gls	Cup	Apps	Gls
87/88	Milan	27	2	UC	1	-
88/89	Milan	30	3	#CC	5	-
89/90	Milan	32	3	#CC	9	1
90/91	Milan	24	3	CC	4	-
91/92	Milan	27	1			

★ Italy 3 caps, 0 goals

Gianluigi LENTINI
27/03/69   Midfield

		Apps	Gls	Cup	Apps	Gls
87/88	Torino	11	-			
88/89	Ancona	Div 2				
89/90	Torino	Div 2				
90/91	Torino	34	5			
91/92	Torino	33	5	+UC	10	1

★ Italy 6 caps, 0 goals

Marco SIMONE
07/01/69   Forward

		Apps	Gls	Cup	Apps	Gls
87/88	Virescit	Div 3				
88/89	Como	34	6			
89/90	Milan	21	1	#CC	4	1
90/91	Milan	14	4	CC	2	-
91/92	Milan	15	7			

FIVE YEAR RECORD	LEAGUE		EURO CUPS		
Birthdate/Playing position	Apps	Gls	Cup	Apps	Gls

Dejan SAVICEVIC (Yug)
15/09/66   Midfield

		Apps	Gls	Cup	Apps	Gls
87/88	Buducnost Titograd (Yug)	29	10			
88/89	Crvena zvezda Beograd (Yug)	-	-	CC	3	1
89/90	Crvena zvezda Beograd (Yug)	25	10	UC	6	3
90/91	Crvena zvezda Beograd (Yug)	25	8	#CC	7	3
91/92	Crvena zvezda Beograd (Yug)	14*	3*	CC	4	2

★ Yugoslavia 27 caps, 10 goals
* first half of season figures only.

Marco VAN BASTEN (Hol)
31/10/64   Forward

		Apps	Gls	Cup	Apps	Gls
87/88	Milan	10	3	UC	3	-
88/89	Milan	33	19	#CC	9	9
89/90	Milan	26	19	#CC	7	3
90/91	Milan	31	11	CC	2	-
91/92	Milan	31	25			

★ Holland 55 caps, 24 goals

Jean-Pierre PAPIN (Fra)
05/11/63   Forward

		Apps	Gls	Cup	Apps	Gls
87/88	Olympique Marseille (Fra)	37	19	CWC	8	4
88/89	Olympique Marseille (Fra)	36	22			
89/90	Olympique Marseille (Fra)	36	30	CC	8	6
90/91	Olympique Marseille (Fra)	36	23	+CC	9	6
91/92	Olympique Marseille (Fra)	37	27	CC	4	7

★ France 38 caps, 22 goals

EUROPEAN HONOURS
Champions' Cup - (4) 1963, 1969, 1989, 1990.
Cup-winners' Cup - (2) 1968, 1973.
Super Cup - (2) 1989, 1990.

EUROPEAN CUPS RECORD

	Entries	Pd	W	D	L	F	A
Champions' Cup	11	68	38	13	17	150	70
Cup-winners' Cup	4	30	17	10	3	47	20
UEFA/Fairs' Cup	9	53	22	12	19	71	57
Total - All 3 Cups	24	151	77	35	39	268	147

UNION LUXEMBOURG

FIVE YEAR RECORD Birthdate/Playing position	LEAGUE Apps Gls	EURO CUPS Cup Apps Gls

John VAN RIJSWIJCK
16/01/62 Goalkeeper

87/88	Jeunesse Esch	28	-	CC	2	-
88/89	Jeunesse Esch	28	-	CC	2	-
89/90	Union Luxembourg	28	-	CWC	2	-
90/91	Union Luxembourg	24	-	CC	2	-
91/92	Union Luxembourg	28	-	CC	2	-

★ Luxembourg 40 caps, 0 goals

Alija BESIC
30/03/75 Goalkeeper

91/92	Union Luxembourg	-	-

Marc BIRSENS
17/09/66 Defender

87/88	Union Luxembourg	28	6			
88/89	Union Luxembourg	27	-	UC	2	-
89/90	Union Luxembourg	25	3	CWC	2	-
90/91	Union Luxembourg	28	-	CC	2	-
91/92	Union Luxembourg	25	2	CC	2	-

★ Luxembourg 15 caps, 0 goals

Patrick FENDER
25/10/71 Defender

88/89	Progrès Niedercorn	7	-
89/90	Progrès Niedercorn	Div 2	
90/91	Progrès Niedercorn	19	1
91/92	Union Luxembourg	4	-

Laurent SCHONCKERT
25/02/58 Defender

87/88	Union Luxembourg	28	1			
88/89	Union Luxembourg	28	-	UC	2	-
89/90	Union Luxembourg	28	-	CWC	2	-
90/91	Union Luxembourg	16	-	CC	2	-
91/92	Union Luxembourg	15	-			

★ Luxembourg 48 caps, 0 goals

FIVE YEAR RECORD Birthdate/Playing position	LEAGUE Apps Gls	EURO CUPS Cup Apps Gls

Thomas WOLF
28/01/63 Defender

87/88	Avenir Beggen	26	2	CWC	1	-
88/89	Union Luxembourg	25	2	UC	2	-
89/90	Union Luxembourg	27	-	CWC	2	-
90/91	Union Luxembourg	24	-	CC	2	-
91/92	Union Luxembourg	26	1	CC	2	-

★ Luxembourg 5 caps, 1 goal

David BORBICONI
17/01/69 Midfield

87/88	US Rumelange	21	3			
88/89	US Rumelange	Div 2				
89/90	US Rumelange	Div 2				
90/91	Union Luxembourg	28	5	CC	2	-
91/92	Union Luxembourg	24	4	CC	2	-

Luc FEIEREISEN
20/09/66 Midfield

87/88	Union Luxembourg	27	-			
88/89	Union Luxembourg	24	6	UC	2	-
89/90	Union Luxembourg	27	-	CWC	2	-
90/91	Union Luxembourg	27	2	CC	2	-
91/92	Union Luxembourg	25	-	CC	1	-

Joël GROFF
11/09/68 Midfield

87/88	Union Luxembourg	27	4			
88/89	Union Luxembourg	27	3	UC	2	-
89/90	Union Luxembourg	24	2	CWC	2	-
90/91	Union Luxembourg	23	3	CC	2	-
91/92	Union Luxembourg	28	3	CC	1	-

★ Luxembourg 11 caps, 0 goals

Fernand HEINISCH
23/07/65 Midfield

87/88	Union Luxembourg	20	-			
88/89	Union Luxembourg	28	6	UC	2	-
89/90	Union Luxembourg	16	1	CWC	1	-
90/91	Fola Esch	25	-			
91/92	Union Luxembourg	12	3	CC	1	-

LUXEMBOURG

FIVE YEAR RECORD *Birthdate/Playing position*	LEAGUE Apps	Gls	EURO CUPS Cup	Apps	Gls

Gérard JEITZ
10/03/61   Midfield

		Apps	Gls		Apps	Gls
87/88	Spora Luxembourg	26	6	UC	2	1
88/89	Union Luxembourg	28	9	UC	2	1
89/90	Union Luxembourg	28	5	CWC	2	-
90/91	Union Luxembourg	27	6	CC	1	-
91/92	Union Luxembourg	25	-	CC	2	-

★ Luxembourg 26 caps, 0 goals

Yves PICARD
16/10/71   Midfield

89/90	SC Bettembourg	Div 3				
90/91	Union Luxembourg	7	1			
91/92	Union Luxembourg	13	1			

Frank DEVILLE
12/08/70   Midfield

87/88	Swift Hesperange	20	-			
88/89	Swift Hesperange	26	1			
89/90	Swift Hesperange	27	3			
90/91	Swift Hesperange	27	4	CWC	2	-
91/92	Swift Hesperange	28	6			

Fabien MELLINGER
03/04/65   Forward

87/88	Union Luxembourg	22	4			
88/89	Union Luxembourg	22	4	UC	2	-
89/90	Union Luxembourg	17	8			
90/91	Union Luxembourg	18	2			
91/92	Union Luxembourg	12	-	CC	2	-

Denis MOGENOT
15/08/63   Forward

87/88	Jeunesse Esch	27	11	CC	2	-
88/89	Jeunesse Esch	9	3			
89/90	Union Luxembourg	28	11	CWC	2	-
90/91	Union Luxembourg	28	9	CC	2	-
91/92	Union Luxembourg	28	11	CC	2	-

FIVE YEAR RECORD *Birthdate/Playing position*	LEAGUE Apps	Gls	EURO CUPS Cup	Apps	Gls

Patrick MOROCUTTI
12/02/68   Forward

87/88	Union Luxembourg	28	26			
88/89	Union Luxembourg	28	17	UC	2	-
89/90	Union Luxembourg	25	26	CWC	2	-
90/91	Union Luxembourg	22	23	CC	2	1
91/92	Union Luxembourg	26	18	CC	2	-

★ Luxembourg 9 caps, 0 goals

Serge THILL
22/01/69   Forward

87/88	Progrès Niedercorn	15	1			
88/89	Progrès Niedercorn	28	16			
89/90	Progrès Niedercorn	Div 2				
90/91	Progrès Niedercorn	28	18			
91/92	Union Luxembourg	27	10	CC	2	-

★ Luxembourg 1 cap, 0 goals

Christian JOACHIM
13/09/70   Forward

88/89	Union Luxembourg	10	-			
89/90	Union Luxembourg	16	5	CWC	1	-
90/91	Union Luxembourg	23	5	CC	2	-
91/92	Red Boys Differdange	28	16			

EUROPEAN HONOURS
none

EUROPEAN CUPS RECORD

	Entries	Pd	W	D	L	F	A
Champions' Cup	4	8	0	0	8	2	34
Cup-winners' Cup	8	16	2	2	12	8	48
UEFA/Fairs' Cup	4	8	0	0	8	2	42
Total - All 3 Cups	16	32	2	2	28	12	124

VALLETTA

FIVE YEAR RECORD	LEAGUE		EURO CUPS		
Birthdate/Playing position	Apps	Gls	Cup	Apps	Gls

Reggie CINI
22/10/70   Goalkeeper

88/89	Valletta	16	-			
89/90	Valletta	16	-	UC	2	-
90/91	Valletta	15	-	CC	2	-
91/92	Valletta	18	-	CWC	2	-

★ Malta 16 caps, 0 goals

Christopher CALLEJA
03/04/68   Goalkeeper

87/88	Valletta	1	-			
88/89	St. Andrew's	Div 3				
89/90	St. Andrew's	Div 2				
90/91	Valletta	2	-			
91/92	Valletta	-	-			

William MACKAY
11/08/64   Defender

88/89	Valletta	16	-			
89/90	Valletta	16	1	UC	2	-
90/91	Valletta	14	-	CC	2	-
91/92	Valletta	13	-	CWC	1	-

★ Malta 1 cap, 0 goals

Charles MAGRI
13/02/69   Defender

90/91	Valletta	15	3			
91/92	Valletta	14	-	CWC	2	-

Raymond SCIBERRAS
03/12/66   Defender

88/89	Valletta	11	-			
89/90	Valletta	14	-	UC	2	-
90/91	Valletta	15	-	CC	2	-
91/92	Valletta	13	-	CWC	1	-

★ Malta 2 caps, 0 goals

Raymond BRIFFA
31/01/65   Defender

87/88	Valletta	13	-	UC	2	-
88/89	Valletta	-	-			
89/90	Valletta	15	-	UC	2	-
90/91	Valletta	7	-	CC	2	-
91/92	Valletta	18	1	CWC	2	-

Christian LAFERLA
23/05/67   Midfield

87/88	Valletta	14	-	UC	2	-
88/89	Valletta	15	2			
89/90	Valletta	16	1	UC	2	-
90/91	Valletta	16	2	CC	2	-
91/92	Valletta	17	1	CWC	2	-

★ Malta 29 caps, 1 goal

Joe CAMILLERI
23/12/66   Midfield

87/88	Valletta	12	1	UC	2	-
88/89	Valletta	14	1			
89/90	Valletta	16	1	UC	2	-
90/91	Valletta	14	3	CC	2	-
91/92	Valletta	14	1	CWC	2	-

★ Malta 13 caps, 0 goals

Gilbert AGIUS
21/02/74   Midfield

90/91	Valletta	12	1	CC	2	-
91/92	Valletta	16	2	CWC	2	-

Robert SPITERI
20/09/73   Midfield

91/92	Valletta	6	1			

Nicky SALIBA
26/08/66   Midfield

87/88	Valletta	14	1	UC	2	-
88/89	Valletta	16	2			
89/90	Valletta	15	-	UC	2	-
90/91	Valletta	16	2	CC	2	-
91/92	Valletta	17	4	CWC	2	-

★ Malta 10 caps, 1 goal

MALTA

FIVE YEAR RECORD	LEAGUE		EURO CUPS		
Birthdate/Playing position	Apps	Gls	Cup	Apps	Gls

Osnir POPULIN (Bra)
20/02/65   Midfield

90/91	Nacional Rolandia (Bra)				
91/92	Valletta	15	-	CWC	1	-

Carlos DIMECH
01/11/74   Midfield

91/92	Valletta	-	-		

Joe ZARB
17/11/64   Forward

87/88	Hamrun Spartans	6	1	CC	2	-
	Valletta	8	3			
88/89	Valletta	15	11			
89/90	Valletta	16	17	UC	2	1
90/91	Valletta	16	12	CC	2	-
91/92	Valletta	18	19	CWC	2	-

★ Malta 9 caps, 1 goal

Jesmond ZERAFA
03/08/65   Forward

87/88	Valletta	13	1	UC	2	-
88/89	Valletta	15	1			
89/90	Valletta	14	5	UC	2	-
90/91	Valletta	14	7	CC	2	-
91/92	Valletta	17	8	CWC	2	-

★ Malta 18 caps, 1 goal

Leo REFALO
24/11/62   Forward

87/88	Hamrun Spartans	12	5	CC	2	-
88/89	Hamrun Spartans	11	9	CC	2	2
89/90	Hamrun Spartans	11	12			
90/91	Birkirkara	14	-			
91/92	Valletta	17	6	CWC	1	-

★ Malta 1 cap, 0 goals

FIVE YEAR RECORD	LEAGUE		EURO CUPS		
Birthdate/Playing position	Apps	Gls	Cup	Apps	Gls

Charlo AGIUS
08/02/72   Forward

91/92	Valletta	4	-	

Tonio MACKAY
26/09/73   Forward

91/92	Valletta	-	-	

EUROPEAN HONOURS
none

EUROPEAN CUPS RECORD

	Entries	Pd	W	D	L	F	A
Champions's Cup	6	12	1	0	11	5	54
Cup-winners' Cup	6	12	0	1	11	3	48
UEFA/Fairs' Cup	4	8	0	0	8	2	28
Total - All 3 Cups	16	32	1	1	30	10	130

GLENTORAN

FIVE YEAR RECORD Birthdate/Playing position	LEAGUE Apps	Gls	EURO CUPS Cup	Apps	Gls
Alan PATERSON 1954 Goalkeeper					
87/88 Glentoran	20	-	CWC	2	-
88/89 Glentoran	24	-	CC	2	-
89/90 Glentoran	8	-			
90/91 Glentoran	26	-			
91/92 Glentoran	15	-			

Dean SMYTH 13/08/64 Goalkeeper					
87/88 Glentoran	6	-			
88/89 Glentoran	2	-			
89/90 Glentoran	18	-	UC	2	-
90/91 Glentoran	4	-	CWC	2	-
91/92 Glentoran	12	-			

Barney BOWERS 19/08/59 Defender					
87/88 Glentoran	1	-	CWC	2	-
88/89 Glentoran	18	1	CC	2	-
89/90 Glentoran	25	1	UC	2	-
90/91 Glentoran	22	1	CWC	2	-
91/92 Glentoran	22	3			

John DEVINE 27/01/69 Defender					
87/88 Glentoran	19	1			
88/89 Glentoran	21	1	CC	1	-
89/90 Glentoran	24	-	UC	2	-
90/91 Glentoran	16	-	CWC	2	-
91/92 Glentoran	30	2			

Seamus HEATH 06/12/61 Defender					
89/90 Glentoran	11	-			
90/91 Glentoran	14	-			
91/92 Glentoran	14	-			

FIVE YEAR RECORD Birthdate/Playing position	LEAGUE Apps	Gls	EURO CUPS Cup	Apps	Gls
Conor McCAFFREY 04/11/69 Defender					
88/89 Glentoran	2	-			
89/90 Glentoran	17	1	UC	2	-
90/91 Glentoran	15	-	CWC	2	-
91/92 Glentoran	17	-			

Terry MOORE 02/06/58 Defender					
87/88 Glentoran	26	-	CWC	2	-
88/89 Glentoran	15	-	CC	2	1
89/90 Glentoran	23	-	UC	2	-
90/91 Glentoran	27	-	CWC	2	-
91/92 Glentoran	6	1			

George NEILL 30/09/62 Defender					
87/88 Glentoran	24	-			
88/89 Glentoran	13	-	CC	2	-
89/90 Glentoran	18	-	UC	2	-
90/91 Glentoran	25	-	CWC	2	-
91/92 Glentoran	28	-			

Gary SMYTH 20/12/69 Defender					
89/90 Glentoran	1	-			
90/91 Glentoran	18	-			
91/92 Glentoran	15	1			

Raymond CAMPBELL 03/10/68 Midfield					
88/89 Glentoran	6	-			
89/90 Glentoran	19	1	UC	2	-
90/91 Glentoran	30	1	CWC	2	-
91/92 Glentoran	29	6			

Andy MATHIESON 09/07/67 Midfield					
87/88 Glentoran	9	-			
88/89 Glentoran	9	-			
89/90 Glentoran	3	-	UC	1	-
90/91 Glentoran	24	3			
91/92 Glentoran	29	11			

NORTHERN IRELAND

FIVE YEAR RECORD	LEAGUE		EURO CUPS		
Birthdate/Playing position	Apps	Gls	Cup	Apps	Gls

Raymond MORRISON
1961   Midfield

87/88	Glentoran	22	10			
88/89	Glentoran	25	6	CC	2	-
89/90	Glentoran	15	3			
90/91	Glentoran	27	4	CWC	2	-
91/92	Glentoran	27	11			

Billy CASKEY
12/10/54   Midfield

87/88	Glentoran	22	4	CWC	2	1
88/89	Glentoran	23	1	CC	2	-
89/90	Glentoran	25	2	UC	2	-
90/91	Glentoran	22	3	CWC	1	-
91/92	Glentoran	5	1			

Stephen DOUGLAS
25/01/64   Forward

87/88	Bangor	12	2			
88/89	Bangor	25	9			
89/90	Glentoran	22	6	UC	2	-
90/91	Glentoran	22	3	CWC	1	1
91/92	Glentoran	9	2			

Gary HILLIS
19/04/64   Forward

87/88	Crusaders	22	5			
88/89	Glentoran	15	6	CC	1	-
89/90	Glentoran	5	2			
90/91	Glentoran	25	7			
91/92	Glentoran	25	8			

FIVE YEAR RECORD	LEAGUE		EURO CUPS		
Birthdate/Playing position	Apps	Gls	Cup	Apps	Gls

Justin McBRIDE
16/10/71   Forward

90/91	Carrick Rangers	8	-			
91/92	Glentoran	27	15			

Gary McCARTNEY
1960   Forward

87/88	Glentoran	14	7	CWC	2	-
88/89	Glentoran	25	16	CC	2	-
89/90	Glentoran	24	17	UC	2	-
90/91	Glentoran	30	18	CWC	2	-
91/92	Glentoran	27	12			

David WEST
21/10/70   Forward

90/91	Glentoran	5	1
91/92	Glentoran	9	3

EUROPEAN HONOURS
none

EUROPEAN CUPS RECORD

	Entries	Pd	W	D	L	F	A
Champions' Cup	7	18	3	6	9	18	29
Cup-winners' Cup	7	18	3	7	8	16	33
UEFA/Fairs' Cup	11	22	2	4	16	16	61
Total - All 3 Cups	25	58	8	17	33	50	123

VIKING FK

FIVE YEAR RECORD	LEAGUE		EURO CUPS		
Birthdate/Playing position	Apps	Gls	Cup	Apps	Gls

Lars Gaute BØ
20/11/63   Goalkeeper

87	Bryne IL	22	-		
88	Bryne IL	22	-		
89	Viking FK	22	-		
90	Viking FK	22	-	CWC	2	-
91	Viking FK	22	-		

★ Norway 1 cap, 0 goals

Vidar GEITLE
15/10/69   Goalkeeper

89	Viking FK	-	-		
90	Viking FK	-	-		
91	Viking FK	-	-		

Ulf KARLSEN
08/03/66   Defender

87	Viking FK	Div 2			
88	Bryne IL	22	-		
89	Bryne IL	Div 2			
90	Bryne IL	Div 2			
91	Viking FK	21	-		

★ Norway 2 caps, 0 goals

Ingve Henrik BØE
29/09/64   Defender

87	Viking FK	Div 2			
88	Viking FK	Div 2			
89	Viking FK	21	-		
90	Viking FK	22	-	CWC	2	-
91	Viking FK	22	2		

Roger NILSEN
08/08/69   Defender

87	Tromsø IL	1	-		
88	Tromsø IL	2	-		
89	Viking FK	15	1		
90	Viking FK	22	8	CWC	2	-
91	Viking FK	21	-		

★ Norway 6 caps, 0 goals

Kent CHRISTIANSEN
09/02/64   Defender

87	Viking FK	Div 2			
88	Viking FK	Div 2			
89	Viking FK	22	-		
90	Viking FK	17	-	CWC	2	-
91	Viking FK	10	-		

Egil FJETLAND
12/08/62   Defender

88	Viking FK	Div 2			
89	Viking FK	14	4		
90	Viking FK	17	3	CWC	2	-
91	Viking FK	6	-		

Leif Rune SALTE
28/11/66   Defender

87	Bryne IL	22	-		
88	Bryne IL	22	-	CWC	2	-
89	Bryne IL	Div 2			
90	Bryne IL	Div 2			
91	Bryne IL	Div 2			

★ Norway 1 cap, 0 goals

Erik PEDERSEN
11/10/67   Midfield

87	Odds BK	Div 2			
88	Tromsø IL	18	1		
89	Tromsø IL	20	5		
90	Tromsø IL	21	3		
91	Viking FK	19	1		

★ Norway 10 caps, 0 goals

Børre MEINSETH
24/11/66   Midfield

87	Bryne IL	22	9		
88	Bryne IL	18	3		
89	Bryne IL	Div 2			
90	Bryne IL	Div 2			
91	Viking FK	22	8		

★ Norway 8 caps, 0 goals

NORWAY

FIVE YEAR RECORD	LEAGUE		EURO CUPS		
Birthdate/Playing position	Apps	Gls	Cup	Apps	Gls

Gaute JOHANNESSEN
19/08/67   Midfield

89	FK Vidar	Div 2				
90	Viking FK	15	3	CWC	2	-
91	Viking FK	17	2			

Gunnar AASE
29/09/71   Midfield

90	Viking FK	12	-	CWC	2	-
91	Viking FK	19	5			

Kenneth STORVIK
27/02/72   Midfield

90	Viking FK	17	4	CWC	2	-
91	Viking FK	17	3			

Øyvind MELLEMSTRAND
17/10/69   Midfield

89	Stord TIL	Div 2				
90	Viking FK	2	-	CWC	1	-
91	Viking FK	9	1			

Alf Kåre TVEIT
26/04/67   Forward

87	Viking FK	Div 2				
88	Viking FK	Div 2				
89	Viking FK	14	5			
90	Viking FK	20	8	CWC	1	-
91	Viking FK	19	7			

Mike McCABE (Sco)
21/08/64   Forward

88	Tromsø IL	19	5	
89	Tromsø IL	22	10	
90	Tromsø IL	21	13	
91	Viking FK	21	3	

Egil ØSTENSTAD
02/01/72   Forward

90	Viking FK	10	1
91	Viking FK	10	1

FIVE YEAR RECORD	LEAGUE		EURO CUPS		
Birthdate/Playing position	Apps	Gls	Cup	Apps	Gls

Atle HÅLAND
08/03/69   Forward

89	Viking FK	1	-
90	Viking FK	-	-
91	Viking FK	4	2

EUROPEAN HONOURS
none

EUROPEAN CUPS RECORD

	Entries	Pd	W	D	L	F	A
Champions' Cup	6	12	1	1	10	11	28
Cup-winners' Cup	1	2	0	0	2	0	5
UEFA/Fairs' Cup	4	12	3	4	5	9	23
Total - All 3 Cups	11	26	4	5	17	20	56

LECH POZNAN

FIVE YEAR RECORD *Birthdate/Playing position*	LEAGUE Apps Gls		EURO CUPS Cup Apps Gls	

Kazimierz SIDORCZUK
04/03/67   Goalkeeper

		Apps	Gls	Cup	Apps	Gls
88/89	Lech Poznan	1	-			
89/90	Lech Poznan	26	-			
90/91	Lech Poznan	25	-	CC	4	-
91/92	Lech Poznan	34	-			

★ Poland 6 caps, 0 goals

Grzegorz STENCEL
25/01/62   Goalkeeper

		Apps	Gls	Cup	Apps	Gls
87/88	Baltyk Gdynia	25	-			
88/89	Baltyk Gdynia	Div 2				
89/90	Baltyk Gdynia	Div 2				
	Olimpia Poznan	12	-			
90/91	Olimpia Poznan	22	-			
91/92	Olimpia Poznan	34	-			

★ Poland 1 cap, 0 goals

Marek RZEPKA
06/01/64   Defender

		Apps	Gls	Cup	Apps	Gls
87/88	Lech Poznan	24	-			
88/89	Lech Poznan	30	2	CWC	4	-
89/90	Lech Poznan	28	-			
90/91	Lech Poznan	27	-	CC	4	1
91/92	Lech Poznan	31	1			

★ Poland 7 caps, 1 goal

Michal GEBURA
10/11/64   Defender

		Apps	Gls	Cup	Apps	Gls
89/90	Siarka Tarnobrzeg	Div 2				
90/91	Lech Poznan	30	11	CC	4	-
91/92	Lech Poznan	23	4			

★ Poland 3 caps, 0 goals

Waldemar KRYGER
08/11/68   Defender

		Apps	Gls	Cup	Apps	Gls
87/88	Lech Poznan	1	-			
88/89	Lech Poznan	23	-	CWC	3	-
89/90	Lech Poznan	28	-			
90/91	Lech Poznan	23	-			
91/92	Lech Poznan	21	-			

Pawel WOJTALA
27/10/72   Defender

		Apps	Gls	Cup	Apps	Gls
90/91	Lech Poznan	5	-			
91/92	Lech Poznan	19	-			

Przemyslaw BERESZYNSKI
11/01/69   Defender

		Apps	Gls	Cup	Apps	Gls
88/89	Lech Poznan	17	-	CWC	4	-
89/90	Lech Poznan	6	-			
90/91	Lech Poznan	23	1	CC	3	-
91/92	Lech Poznan	30	-			

Ryszard REMIEN
10/04/68   Defender

		Apps	Gls	Cup	Apps	Gls
90/91	Lech Poznan	13	-			
91/92	Lech Poznan	30	1			

Jacek BAK
24/03/73   Defender

		Apps	Gls	Cup	Apps	Gls
89/90	Motor Lublin	3	-			
90/91	Motor Lublin	12	-			
91/92	Motor Lublin	31	2			

Dariusz KOFNYT
28/01/64   Midfield

		Apps	Gls	Cup	Apps	Gls
87/88	Lech Poznan	14	-			
88/89	Lech Poznan	27	-	CWC	3	-
89/90	Lech Poznan	28	1			
90/91	Lech Poznan	23	-	CC	4	-
91/92	Lech Poznan	26	-			

Dariusz SKRZYPCZAK
13/11/67   Midfield

		Apps	Gls	Cup	Apps	Gls
87/88	Lech Poznan	24	-			
88/89	Lech Poznan	22	2	CWC	2	-
89/90	Lech Poznan	27	2			
90/91	Lech Poznan	27	1	CC	3	-
91/92	Lech Poznan	34	10			

★ Poland 7 caps, 0 goals

POLAND

FIVE YEAR RECORD
Birthdate/Playing position

FIVE YEAR RECORD Birthdate/Playing position	LEAGUE Apps Gls	EURO CUPS Cup Apps Gls	FIVE YEAR RECORD Birthdate/Playing position	LEAGUE Apps Gls	EURO CUPS Cup Apps Gls

Kazimierz MOSKAL
09/01/67   Midfield

87/88	Wisla Kraków	Div 2		
88/89	Wisla Kraków	29	8	
89/90	Wisla Kraków	30	11	
90/91	Wisla Kraków	28	7	CC 4 1
91/92	Lech Poznan	31	1	

★ Poland 3 caps, 0 goals

Jerzy BRZECZEK
18/03/71   Midfield

88/89	Olimpia Poznan	19	-
89/90	Olimpia Poznan	29	1
90/91	Olimpia Poznan	28	2
91/92	Olimpia Poznan	31	5

★ Poland 1 cap, 0 goals

Grzegorz MIELCARSKI
19/03/71   Forward

88/89	Polonia Bydgoszcz	Div 3	
89/90	Olimpia Poznan	17	-
90/91	Olimpia Poznan	24	14
91/92	Olimpia Poznan	31	9

★ Poland 1 cap, 0 goals

Jerzy PODBROZNY
17/12/66   Forward

88/89	Resovia Rzeszów	Div 2	
89/90	Igloopol Debica	Div 2	
90/91	Pegrotour Debica	26	7
91/92	Lech Poznan	34	20

★ Poland 3 caps, 0 goals

Jaroslaw ARASZKIEWICZ
01/02/65   Forward

87/88	Lech Poznan	28	3	
88/89	Lech Poznan	29	10	CWC 4 2
89/90	Lech Poznan	27	7	
90/91	Bakirköyspor (Tur)	27	12	
91/92	Bakirköyspor (Tur)	23	8	

★ Poland 9 caps, 0 goals

Miroslaw TRZECIAK
11/04/68   Forward

87/88	Lech Poznan	5	-	
88/89	Lech Poznan	14	1	
89/90	Lech Poznan	22	2	
90/91	Lech Poznan	28	9	CC 4 -
91/92	Lech Poznan	34	14	

★ Poland 3 caps, 1 goal

Jacek DEMBINSKI
20/12/69   Forward

90/91	Polonia Poznan	Div 4	
91/92	Lech Poznan	13	2

EUROPEAN HONOURS
none

EUROPEAN CUPS RECORD

	Entries	Pd	W	D	L	F	A
Champions' Cup	3	8	4	0	4	11	18
Cup-winners' Cup	2	8	4	2	2	10	7
UEFA/Fairs' Cup	2	4	0	1	3	3	13
Total - All 3 Cups	7	20	8	3	9	24	38

FC PORTO

FIVE YEAR RECORD — *Birthdate/Playing position*

VÍTOR BAÍA
15/10/69   Goalkeeper

		Apps	Gls	Cup	Apps	Gls
88/89	FC Porto	15	-			
89/90	FC Porto	34	-	CWC	6	-
90/91	FC Porto	38	-	CC	6	-
91/92	FC Porto	34	-	CWC	4	-

★ Portugal 14 caps, 0 goals

VALENTE
13/03/65   Goalkeeper

		Apps	Gls	Cup	Apps	Gls
87/88	Académica Coimbra	1	-			
88/89	Académica Coimbra	Div 2				
89/90	CF União	16	-			
90/91	CF União	29	-			
91/92	FC Porto	1	-			

JOÃO PINTO
21/11/61   Defender

		Apps	Gls	Cup	Apps	Gls
87/88	FC Porto	34	1	CC	4	-
88/89	FC Porto	35	1	CC	3	-
89/90	FC Porto	30	-	CWC	6	-
90/91	FC Porto	29	-	CC	5	-
91/92	FC Porto	33	8	CWC	4	-

★ Portugal 52 caps, 1 goal

PAULO PEREIRA (Bra)
27/08/65   Defender

		Apps	Gls	Cup	Apps	Gls
88/89	FC Porto	18	1			
89/90	FC Porto	18	1	CWC	2	-
90/91	FC Porto	28	7	CC	3	-
91/92	FC Porto	23	4	CWC	2	-

ALOÍSIO (Bra)
16/08/63   Defender

		Apps	Gls	Cup	Apps	Gls
87/88	Internacional Porto Alegre (Bra)					
88/89	FC Barcelona (Esp)	27	-	#CWC	7	-
89/90	FC Barcelona (Esp)	21	-	CWC	3	-
90/91	FC Porto	37	1	CC	6	-
91/92	FC Porto	33	-	CWC	3	-

★ Brazil

FERNANDO COUTO
02/08/69   Defender

		Apps	Gls	Cup	Apps	Gls
87/88	FC Porto	1	-			
88/89	FC Famalicão	Div 2				
89/90	Academica Coimbra	Div 2				
90/91	FC Porto	25	3	CC	4	-
91/92	FC Porto	32	2	CWC	4	-

★ Portugal 10 caps, 0 goals

Lubomir VLK (Tch)
21/07/64   Defender

		Apps	Gls	Cup	Apps	Gls
87/88	TJ Vítkovice (Tch)	29	7	UC	5	1
88/89	TJ Vítkovice (Tch)	18	2			
89/90	TJ Vítkovice (Tch)	7	-			
90/91	FC Porto	9	3			
91/92	FC Porto	10	3	CWC	1	-

★ Czechoslovakia 11 caps, 2 goals

MORGADO
31/12/69   Defender

		Apps	Gls	Cup	Apps	Gls
88/89	Gil Vicente FC	Div 2				
89/90	CD Feirense	22	2			
90/91	FC Porto	6	-	CC	1	-
91/92	FC Porto	5	-	CWC	1	-

JAIME MAGALHÃES
10/07/62   Midfield

		Apps	Gls	Cup	Apps	Gls
87/88	FC Porto	35	5	CC	4	1
88/89	FC Porto	15	-	CC	2	-
89/90	FC Porto	26	2	CWC	4	1
90/91	FC Porto	22	1	CC	4	-
91/92	FC Porto	22	2	CWC	3	-

★ Portugal 18 caps, 0 goals

SEMEDO
05/03/65   Midfield

		Apps	Gls	Cup	Apps	Gls
87/88	FC Porto	22	6	CC	2	-
88/89	FC Porto	25	2	CC	1	-
89/90	FC Porto	32	4	CWC	6	-
90/91	FC Porto	35	3	CC	6	1
91/92	FC Porto	17	-	CWC	3	-

★ Portugal 13 caps, 1 goal

PORTUGAL

FIVE YEAR RECORD	LEAGUE		EURO CUPS		
Birthdate/Playing position	Apps	Gls	Cup	Apps	Gls

ANDRÉ
24/12/57   Midfield

87/88	FC Porto	31	1	CC	4	-
88/89	FC Porto	35	4	CC	3	-
89/90	FC Porto	30	2	CWC	6	-
90/91	FC Porto	33	-	CC	4	-
91/92	FC Porto	26	-	CWC	4	-

★ Portugal 18 caps, 1 goal

RUI FILIPE
21/04/72   Midfield

91/92	FC Porto	25	4	CWC	2	-

Ion TIMOFTE (Rom)
16/12/67   Midfield

88/89	Politehnica Timisoara (Rom) Div 2		
89/90	Politehnica Timisoara (Rom)	32	9
90/91	Politehnica Timisoara (Rom)	33	10	UC	4	-
91/92	FC Porto	25	9	CWC	4	2

★ Romania 7 caps, 1 goal

JORGE COUTO
01/07/70   Forward

88/89	Gil Vicente	Div 2	
89/90	FC Porto	26	2	CWC	3	2
90/91	FC Porto	33	2	CC	4	1
91/92	FC Porto	18	1		

★ Portugal 2 caps, 0 goals

Emil KOSTADINOV (Bul)
12/08/67   Forward

87/88	CFKA Sredets Sofia (Bul)	24	13	CC	2	-
88/89	CFKA Sredets Sofia (Bul)	29	12	CWC	8	3
89/90	CSKA Sofia (Bul)	26	6	CC	6	2
90/91	FC Porto	33	8	CC	4	3
91/92	FC Porto	29	9	CWC	4	2

★ Bulgaria 20 caps, 9 goals

FIVE YEAR RECORD	LEAGUE		EURO CUPS		
Birthdate/Playing position	Apps	Gls	Cup	Apps	Gls

DOMINGOS
02/01/69   Forward

87/88	FC Porto	8	1		
88/89	FC Porto	26	5	CC	1	1
89/90	FC Porto	12	1	CWC	6	-
90/91	FC Porto	34	24	CC	4	2
91/92	FC Porto	24	5	CWC	1	-

★ Portugal 7 caps, 1 goal

PAULINHO (Bra)
Forward

91/92	Santos (Bra)

★ Brazil

TOZÉ
04/09/65   Forward

87/88	Vitória Guimarães	12	-	UC	2	-
88/89	CS Marítimo	24	-		
89/90	Marítimo	21	1		
90/91	SC Beira Mar	38	2		
91/92	FC Porto	24	1	CWC	3	-

★ Portugal 1 cap, 0 goals

EUROPEAN HONOURS
Champions' Cup - (1) 1987.
Super Cup - (1) 1987.

EUROPEAN CUPS RECORD

	Entries	Pd	W	D	L	F	A
Champions' Cup	9	37	19	5	13	69	41
Cup-winners' Cup	7	35	17	7	11	48	41
UEFA/Fairs' Cup	14	50	23	8	19	70	61
Total - All 3 Cups	30	122	59	20	43	187	143

SHELBOURNE

FIVE YEAR RECORD	LEAGUE		EURO CUPS		
Birthdate/Playing position	Apps	Gls	Cup	Apps	Gls

Jody BYRNE
30/04/63   Goalkeeper

87/88	Shamrock Rovers	33	-	CC	2	-
88/89	Shamrock Rovers	33	-			
89/90	Shamrock Rovers	32	-			
90/91	Shelbourne	33	-			
91/92	Shelbourne	33	-			

Fred DAVIS
28/10/53   Goalkeeper

87/88	Shelbourne	33	-
88/89	Shelbourne	33	-
89/90	Shelbourne	30	-
90/91	Shelbourne	-	-
91/92	Shelbourne	-	-

Peter COYLE
24/09/63   Defender

87/88	Limerick City	14	-
88/89	Limerick City	20	1
89/90	Limerick City	26	-
90/91	Limerick City	5	-
	Shelbourne	10	1
91/92	Shelbourne	28	-

Mick NEVILLE
25/11/60   Defender

87/88	Shamrock Rovers	33	7	CC	2	-
88/89	Derry City	33	2	CWC	2	-
89/90	Derry City	33	5	CC	2	-
90/91	Shelbourne	30	2			
91/92	Shelbourne	30	3			

Ian HILL
Defender

88/89	Shelbourne	20	-
89/90	Shelbourne	32	1
90/91	Shelbourne	31	-
91/92	Shelbourne	1	-
	Limerick City	Div 2	

FIVE YEAR RECORD	LEAGUE		EURO CUPS		
Birthdate/Playing position	Apps	Gls	Cup	Apps	Gls

Anto WHELAN
23/11/59   Defender

87/88	Bray Wanderers	32	-
88/89	Shelbourne	33	1
89/90	Shelbourne	24	3
90/91	Shelbourne	30	3
91/92	Shelbourne	30	4

Brian FLOOD
22/06/71   Defender

89/90	Shelbourne	19	-
90/91	Shelbourne	1	-
91/92	Shelbourne	18	1

Kevin BRADY
02/12/62   Defender

87/88	Shamrock Rovers	32	1	CC	2	-
88/89	Derry City	32	-	CWC	2	-
89/90	Derry City	31	-	CC	2	-
90/91	Derry City	30	-	UC	2	-
91/92	Shelbourne	14	2			

Gary HOWLETT
02/04/63   Midfield

87/88	Aldershot (Eng)	Div 3	
	Chester City (Eng)	Div 3	
	York City (Eng)	Div 3	
88/89	York City (Eng)	Div 4	
89/90	York City (Eng)	Div 4	
90/91	York City (Eng)	Div 4	
	Shelbourne	6	1
91/92	Shelbourne	32	3

★ Republic of Ireland 1 cap, 0 goals

Joe SULLIVAN
Midfield

91/92	Shelbourne	1	-

REPUBLIC OF IRELAND

FIVE YEAR RECORD	LEAGUE		EURO CUPS		
Birthdate/Playing position	Apps	Gls	Cup	Apps	Gls

Greg COSTELLO
05/04/70   Midfield

89/90	Queen's Park Rangers (Eng)	-	-			
90/91	Shelbourne	11	-			
91/92	Shelbourne	24	2			

Bobby BROWNE
09/06/62   Midfield

87/88	Shelbourne	33	6			
88/89	Shelbourne	25	1			
89/90	Shelbourne	22	-			
90/91	Shelbourne	27	2			
91/92	Shelbourne	28	3			

Pat BYRNE
15/05/56   Midfield

87/88	Shamrock Rovers	28	1	CC	2	-
88/89	Shelbourne	30	1			
89/90	Shelbourne	28	3			
90/91	Shelbourne	24	-			
91/92	Shelbourne	9	2			

★ Republic of Ireland 9 caps, 0 goals

Paul DOOLIN
26/03/63   Midfield

87/88	Shamrock Rovers	21	3	CC	2	-
88/89	Derry City	31	6	CWC	2	-
89/90	Derry City	32	12	CC	2	-
90/91	Portadown (Nir)	28	9	CC	2	-
91/92	Portadown (Nir)	6	1	CC	2	-
	Shamrock Rovers	20	1			

Padraig DULLY
20/04/65   Forward

87/88	Athlone Town	Div 2				
88/89	Athlone Town	12	1			
89/90	Athlone Town	32	10			
90/91	Shelbourne	26	9			
91/92	Shelbourne	30	10			

FIVE YEAR RECORD	LEAGUE		EURO CUPS		
Birthdate/Playing position	Apps	Gls	Cup	Apps	Gls

Garry HAYLOCK
31/12/70   Forward

89/90	Huddersfield Town (Eng)	Div 3				
	Shelbourne	10	9			
90/91	Huddersfield Town (Eng)	Div 3				
	Shelbourne	11	8			
91/92	Shelbourne	23	13			

Mark RUTHERFORD (Eng)
25/03/72   Forward

89/90	Birmingham City (Eng)	Div 3				
90/91	Birmingham City (Eng)	Div 3				
91/92	Shelbourne	26	6			

Dessie GORMAN
13/12/64   Forward

87/88	Dundalk	31	14	CWC	2	-
88/89	Dundalk	26	8	CC	2	-
89/90	FC Bourges (Fra)	Div 3				
90/91	Derry City	28	7			
91/92	Shelbourne	30	6			

EUROPEAN HONOURS
none

EUROPEAN CUPS RECORD

	Entries	Pd	W	D	L	F	A
Champions' Cup	1	2	0	0	2	1	7
Cup-winners' Cup	1	2	0	0	2	1	5
UEFA/Fairs' Cup	2	7	1	3	3	4	6
Total - All 3 Cups	4	11	1	3	7	6	18

DINAMO BUCURESTI

Florin PRUNEA
08/08/68   Goalkeeper

FIVE YEAR RECORD	LEAGUE		EURO CUPS		
Birthdate/Playing position	Apps	Gls	Cup	Apps	Gls
87/88 Dinamo Bucuresti	2	-			
88/89 Universitatea Cluj	31	-			
89/90 Universitatea Cluj	25	-			
90/91 Universitatea Craiova	32	-	UC	4	-
91/92 Universitatea Craiova	16	-	CC	2	-

★ Romania 7 caps, 0 goals

Florin Alexandru TENE
10/11/68   Goalkeeper

88/89 Flacara Moreni	14	-			
89/90 Flacara Moreni	31	-			
90/91 Gloria Bistrita	33	-			
91/92 Gloria Bistrita	11	-			
Dinamo Bucuresti	21	-			

Iulian MIHAESCU
11/09/62   Defender

87/88 Dinamo Bucuresti	33	12	CWC	2	-
88/89 Dinamo Bucuresti	30	9	CWC	5	-
89/90 Dinamo Bucuresti	24	7	CWC	7	1
90/91 Dinamo Bucuresti	24	4	CC	4	-
91/92 Dinamo Bucuresti	27	1	UC	2	-

Gheorghe MIHALI
09/12/65   Defender

87/88 FC Olt Scornicesti	29	-			
88/89 FC Olt Scornicesti	31	-			
89/90 FC Olt Scornicesti	14	-			
FC Inter Sibiu	12	-			
90/91 FC Inter Sibiu	31	3			
91/92 Dinamo Bucuresti	30	-	UC	3	-

★ Romania 6 caps, 0 goals

Adrian MATEI
29/02/68   Defender

87/88 Rapid Bucuresti	28	-			
88/89 Rapid Bucuresti	15	-			
Dinamo Bucuresti	10	-			
89/90 Dinamo Bucuresti	10	-			
90/91 Dinamo Bucuresti	26	2	CC	3	-
91/92 Dinamo Bucuresti	16	-	UC	4	-

Marian PANA
24/12/68   Defender

FIVE YEAR RECORD	LEAGUE		EURO CUPS		
Birthdate/Playing position	Apps	Gls	Cup	Apps	Gls
87/88 Flacara Moreni	8	-			
88/89 Flacara Moreni	16	-			
Victoria Bucuresti	12	2	UC	2	-
89/90 Victoria Bucuresti	13	1			
Flacara Moreni	13	-			
90/91 FC Arges Pitesti	32	9			
91/92 Dinamo Bucuresti	24	-	UC	3	-

★ Romania 2 caps, 0 goals

Tudorel CRISTEA
22/04/64   Defender

87/88 Sportul Studentesc Bucuresti	28	1	UC	5	1
88/89 Sportul Studentesc Bucuresti	30	8			
89/90 Sportul Studentesc Bucuresti	30	2			
90/91 Sportul Studentesc Bucuresti	15	3			
Dinamo Bucuresti	16	4			
91/92 Dinamo Bucuresti	13	1	UC	2	1

★ Romania 9 caps, 0 goals

Tibor SELYMES
14/05/70   Defender

87/88 FCM Brasov	12	1			
88/89 FCM Brasov	21	1			
89/90 FCM Brasov	31	1			
90/91 Dinamo Bucuresti	26	2	CC	3	-
91/92 Dinamo Bucuresti	27	-	UC	1	-

Vasile JERCALAU
05/09/67   Defender

87/88 Dinamo Bucuresti	9	-			
88/89 SC Bacau	30	2			
89/90 Flacara Moreni	9	-	UC	1	-
SC Bacau	15	2			
90/91 FC Bacau	28	3			
91/92 FC Bacau	14	4			

Gabor GERSTENMAJER
13/09/67   Midfield

90/91 FC Brasov	31	15			
91/92 Dinamo Bucuresti	30	21	UC	4	3

★ Romania 2 caps, 0 goals

ROMANIA

FIVE YEAR RECORD *Birthdate/Playing position*	LEAGUE Apps Gls	EURO CUPS Cup Apps Gls

Constantin PANA
15/07/67   Midfield

87/88	Flacara Moreni	30	1			
88/89	Flacara Moreni	31	6			
89/90	Flacara Moreni	20	3			
90/91	Dinamo Bucuresti	24	3	CC	3	-
91/92	Dinamo Bucuresti	29	7	UC	4	-

★ Romania 1 cap, 1 goal

Dorinel MUNTEANU
25/06/68   Midfield

88/89	FC Olt Scornicesti	31	2			
89/90	FC Olt Scornicesti	2	-			
	FC Inter Sibiu	14	-			
90/91	FC Inter Sibiu	33	7			
91/92	Dinamo Bucuresti	33	12	UC	4	1

★ Romania 11 caps, 2 goals

Ioan Sebastian MOGA
18/12/71   Midfield

90/91	Gloria Bistrita	30	3			
91/92	Dinamo Bucuresti	32	4	UC	4	-

★ Romania 4 caps, 0 goals

Marius CHEREGI
04/10/67   Midfield

89/90	FC Bihor Oradea	28	7			
90/91	Dinamo Bucuresti	29	5	CC	4	1
91/92	Dinamo Bucuresti	28	4	UC	4	-

★ Romania 3 caps, 0 goals

Zoltán KÁDÁR
04/10/66   Forward

87/88	Universitatea Cluj	33	1			
88/89	Universitatea Cluj	30	9			
89/90	Universitatea Cluj	29	5			
90/91	Universitatea Cluj	31	1			
91/92	Dinamo Bucuresti	29	1	UC	4	-

★ Romania 5 caps, 0 goals

FIVE YEAR RECORD *Birthdate/Playing position*	LEAGUE Apps Gls	EURO CUPS Cup Apps Gls

Suleiman DEMOLLARI (Alb)
05/05/64   Forward

87/88	Dinamo Tiranë (Alb)	35	7			
88/89	Dinamo Tiranë (Alb)	28	10			
89/90	Dinamo Tiranë (Alb)	33	14	CWC	4	2
90/91	Dinamo Tiranë (Alb)	28	9	CC	2	-
91/92	Dinamo Bucuresti	30	18	UC	3	-

★ Albania 30 caps, 0 goals

Cristian SAVA
05/12/67   Forward

87/88	Dinamo Bucuresti	1	-			
	SC Bacau	11	2			
88/89	Universitatea Cluj	30	2			
89/90	Rapid Bucuresti	Div 2				
90/91	Rapid Bucuresti	31	5			
91/92	Rapid Bucuresti	15	2			
	Dinamo Bucuresti	14	1			

Ovidiu HANGANU
04/05/70   Forward

87/88	Corvinul Hunedoara	21	7			
88/89	Corvinul Hunedoara	30	9			
89/90	Victoria Bucuresti	16	2	UC	2	1
	Corvinul Hunedoara	14	3			
90/91	Corvinul Hunedoara	30	24			
91/92	Corvinul Hunedoara	22	6			

EUROPEAN HONOURS
none

EUROPEAN CUPS RECORD

	Entries	Pd	W	D	L	F	A
Champions' Cup	13	52	21	8	23	84	83
Cup-winners' Cup	5	20	8	4	8	25	18
UEFA/Fairs' Cup	7	26	10	5	11	44	31
Total - All 3 Cups	25	98	39	17	42	153	132

CSKA MOSKVA

Dmitry KHARIN
16/08/68   Goalkeeper

		Apps	Gls	Cup	Apps	Gls
87	Torpedo Moskva	27	-			
88	Dinamo Moskva	19	-			
89	Dinamo Moskva	20	-			
90	Dinamo Moskva	1	-			
91	CSKA Moskva	11	-	CWC	2	-

★ USSR/CIS 15 caps, 0 goals

Aleksandr GUTEYEV
18/06/67   Goalkeeper

89	CSKA Moskva	Div 2				
90	CSKA Moskva	6	-			
91	CSKA Moskva	6	-			

Dmitry BYSTROV
30/07/67   Defender

87	CSKA Moskva	12	-			
88	CSKA Moskva	Div 2				
89	CSKA Moskva	Div 2				
90	CSKA Moskva	23	1			
91	CSKA Moskva	21	-	CWC	2	-

Sergei KOLOTOVKIN
28/09/65   Defender

87	CSKA Moskva	27	-			
88	CSKA Moskva	Div 2				
89	CSKA Moskva	Div 2				
90	CSKA Moskva	20	-			
91	CSKA Moskva	25	1	CWC	2	-

Oleg MALYUKOV
30/10/65   Defender

87	CSKA Moskva	14	-			
88	CSKA Moskva	Div 2				
89	CSKA Moskva	Div 2				
90	CSKA Moskva	16	-			
91	CSKA Moskva	19	-			

Vasily IVANOV
21/03/70   Defender

87	Zenit Leningrad	1	-			
88	Zenit Leningrad	3	-			
89	Zenit Leningrad	25	1	UC	3	-
90	Zenit Leningrad	Div 2				
91	CSKA Moskva	15	-			

Vasily MINKO
08/08/71   Defender

89	Dinamo Branaul	Div 3				
90	CSKA Moskva	-	-			
91	CSKA Moskva	8	-			

Aleksei GUSCHIN
21/10/71   Defender

90	CSKA Moskva	-	-			
91	CSKA Moskva	-	-			

Denis MASHKARIN
17/05/70   Defender

90	Dinamo Leningrad	Div 3				
91	Zenit Sankt-Peterburg	Div 2				

Mikhail KOLESNIKOV
08/09/66   Midfield

87	CSKA Moskva	23	-			
88	CSKA Moskva	Div 2				
89	CSKA Moskva	Div 2				
90	CSKA Moskva	18	2			
91	CSKA Moskva	28	2	CWC	2	-

Sergei KRUTOV
18/04/69   Midfield

88	CSKA Moskva	Div 2				
89	CSKA Moskva	Div 2				
90	CSKA Moskva	2	-			
90/91	Vitesse (Hol)	-	-			
91/92	Vitesse (Hol)	1	-			

RUSSIA

FIVE YEAR RECORD	LEAGUE		EURO CUPS	
Birthdate/Playing position	Apps	Gls	Cup	Apps Gls

Lev MATEYEV
12/02/71   Midfield

91	CSKA Moskva	1	-	

Yury BAVYKIN
21/03/73   Midfield

91	CSKA Moskva	-	-	

Aleksei PODDUBSKI
13/06/72   Midfield

90	SKA Khabarovsk	Div 3		
91	CSKA Moskva	-	-	

Aleksandr GRISHIN
18/11/71   Midfield

88	CSKA Moskva	Div 2		
89	CSKA Moskva	Div 2		
90	CSKA Moskva	1	-	
91	CSKA Moskva	5	-	

Valery MASALITIN
27/09/66   Forward

87	CSKA Moskva	15	5		
88	CSKA Moskva	Div 2			
89	CSKA Moskva	Div 2			
89/90	Vitesse (Hol)	5	-		
90	CSKA Moskva	9	8		
91	CSKA Moskva	18	7	CWC 2	-

FIVE YEAR RECORD	LEAGUE		EURO CUPS	
Birthdate/Playing position	Apps	Gls	Cup	Apps Gls

Oleg SERGEEV
29/03/68   Forward

87	Rotor Volgograd	Div 2			
88	Rotor Volgograd	Div 2			
89	Rotor Volgograd	27	4		
90	CSKA Moskva	24	6		
91	CSKA Moskva	30	9	CWC 2	1

★ USSR/CIS 7 caps, 1 goal

Ilshat FAYZULLIN
05/03/73   Forward

90	CSKA Moskva	-	-	
91	CSKA Moskva	3	-	

EUROPEAN HONOURS
none

EUROPEAN CUPS RECORD

	Entries	Pd	W	D	L	F	A
Champions' Cup	1	4	2	1	1	5	3
Cup-winners' Cup	1	2	1	0	1	2	2
UEFA/Fairs' Cup	1	2	1	0	1	2	2
Total - All 3 Cups	3	8	4	1	3	9	7

RANGERS

Andy GORAM
13/04/64   Goalkeeper

		Apps	Gls	Cup	Apps	Gls
87/88	Hibernian	33	1			
88/89	Hibernian	36	-			
89/90	Hibernian	34	-	UC	4	-
90/91	Hibernian	35	-			
91/92	Rangers	44	-	CC	2	-

★ Scotland 23 caps, 0 goals

Ally MAXWELL
29/06/60   Goalkeeper

		Apps	Gls	Cup	Apps	Gls
87/88	Motherwell	1	-			
	Clydebank	Div 2				
88/89	Motherwell	17	-			
89/90	Motherwell	36	-			
90/91	Motherwell	36	-			
91/92	Motherwell	-	-			

Gary STEVENS (Eng)
27/03/63   Defender

		Apps	Gls	Cup	Apps	Gls
87/88	Everton (Eng)	31	-			
88/89	Rangers	35	1	CWC	4	-
89/90	Rangers	35	1	CC	2	-
90/91	Rangers	36	4	CC	4	-
91/92	Rangers	43	2	CC	2	-

★ England 46 caps, 0 goals

David ROBERTSON
17/10/68   Defender

		Apps	Gls	Cup	Apps	Gls
87/88	Aberdeen	23	-	UC	2	-
88/89	Aaberdeen	23	-	UC	2	-
89/90	Aberdeen	19	1	UC	1	-
90/91	Aberdeen	35	1	CWC	4	-
91/92	Rangers	42	1	CC	2	-

★ Scotland 2 caps, 0 goals

John BROWN
26/01/62   Defender

		Apps	Gls	Cup	Apps	Gls
87/88	Dundee	21	3			
	Rangers	9	2			
88/89	Rangers	29	1	CWC	1	-
89/90	Rangers	27	1			
90/91	Rangers	27	1	CC	4	-
91/92	Rangers	25	4	CC	2	-

Richard GOUGH
05/04/62   Defender

		Apps	Gls	Cup	Apps	Gls
87/88	Tottenham Hotspur (Eng)	9	-			
	Rangers	31	5	CC	2	1
88/89	Rangers	35	3	CWC	4	-
89/90	Rangers	26	-	CC	1	-
90/91	Rangers	26	-	CC	3	-
91/92	Rangers	33	2	CC	1	-

★ Scotland 59 caps, 6 goals

Oleg KUZNETSOV (Ukr)
02/03/63   Defender

		Apps	Gls	Cup	Apps	Gls
87	Dinamo Kiev (Urs)	24	3	CC	2	-
88	Dinamo Kiev (Urs)	26	1			
89	Dinamo Kiev (Urs)	29	4	UC	6	-
90	Dinamo Kiev (Urs)	20	2			
90/91	Rangers	2	-			
91/92	Rangers	18	-	CC	1	-

★ USSR/CIS 63 caps, 1 goal

Dave McPHERSON
28/01/64   Defender

		Apps	Gls	Cup	Apps	Gls
87/88	Heart of Midlothian	44	4			
88/89	Heart of Midlothian	32	4	UC	8	-
89/90	Heart of Midlothian	35	4			
90/91	Heart of Midlothian	34	2	UC	3	1
91/92	Heart of Midlothian	44	2			

★ Scotland 23 caps, 0 goals

Trevor STEVEN (Eng)
21/09/63   Midfield

		Apps	Gls	Cup	Apps	Gls
87/88	Everton (Eng)	36	6			
88/89	Everton (Eng)	29	6			
89/90	Rangers	34	3	CC	2	-
90/91	Rangers	19	2	CC	4	-
91/92	Olympique Marseille (Fra)	28	3	CC	3	-

★ England 36 caps, 4 goals

Dale GORDON (Eng)
09/01/67   Midfield

		Apps	Gls	Cup	Apps	Gls
87/88	Norwich City (Eng)	21	3			
88/89	Norwich City (Eng)	38	5			
89/90	Norwich City (Eng)	26	3			

SCOTLAND

FIVE YEAR RECORD *Birthdate/Playing position*	LEAGUE Apps Gls	EURO CUPS Cup Apps Gls

		LEAGUE		EURO CUPS		
90/91	Norwich City (Eng)	36	7			
91/92	Norwich City (Eng)	15	4			
	Rangers	23	5			

Stuart McCALL
10/06/64   Midfield

87/88	Bradford City (Eng)	Div 2				
88/89	Everton (Eng)	33	-			
89/90	Everton (Eng)	37	3			
90/91	Everton (Eng)	33	2			
91/92	Rangers	36	1	CC	2	2

★ Scotland 20 caps, 1 goal

Ian FERGUSON
13/05/67   Midfield

87/88	St. Mirren	22	6			
	Rangers	8	1			
88/89	Rangers	30	7	CWC	4	1
89/90	Rangers	23	-	CC	2	-
90/91	Rangers	11	1	CC	1	-
91/92	Rangers	16	1	CC	1	-

★ Scotland 3 caps, 0 goals

Aleksei MIKHAILICHENKO (Ukr)
30/03/63   Midfield

87	Dinamo Kiev (Urs)	28	9	CC	2	1
88	Dinamo Kiev (Urs)	23	6			
89	Dinamo Kiev (Urs)	15	3	UC	6	1
90	Dinamo Kiev (Urs)	8	-			
90/91	Sampdoria (Ita)	24	3	CWC	5	-
91/92	Rangers	27	10	CC	1	-

★ USSR/CIS 41 caps, 9 goals

Paul RIDEOUT (Eng)
14/08/64   Forward

87/88	Bari (Ita)	Div 2				
88/89	Southampton (Eng)	24	6			
89/90	Southampton (Eng)	31	7			
90/91	Southampton (Eng)	16	6			
91/92	Southampton (Eng)	4	-			
	Notts County (Eng)	11	3			
	Rangers	11	1			

FIVE YEAR RECORD *Birthdate/Playing position*	LEAGUE Apps Gls	EURO CUPS Cup Apps Gls

Pieter HUISTRA (Hol)
18/01/67   Midfield

87/88	FC Twente (Hol)	33	8			
88/89	FC Twente (Hol)	34	6			
89/90	FC Twente (Hol)	25	3	UC	2	-
90/91	Rangers	27	4	CC	2	-
91/92	Rangers	32	5	CC	1	-

★ Holland 8 caps, 0 goals

Iain DURRANT
29/10/66   Midfield

87/88	Rangers	40	10	CC	5	1
88/89	Rangers	8	2	CWC	2	1
89/90	Rangers	-	-			
90/91	Rangers	4	1			
91/92	Rangers	13	-	CC	2	-

★ Scotland 5 caps, 0 goals

Ally McCOIST
24/09/62   Forward

87/88	Rangers	40	31	CC	6	4
88/89	Rangers	19	10	CWC	2	-
89/90	Rangers	34	14			
90/91	Rangers	26	11	CC	4	3
91/92	Rangers	38	34	CC	2	-

★ Scotland 41 caps, 12 goals

Mark HATELEY (Eng)
07/11/61   Forward

87/88	AS Monaco (Fra)	28	14			
88/89	AS Monaco (Fra)	18	6	CC	2	-
89/90	AS Monaco (Fra)	13	2	CWC	2	-
90/91	Rangers	33	10	CC	2	1
91/92	Rangers	30	21	CC	1	-

★ England 32 caps, 9 goals

EUROPEAN HONOURS
Cup-winners' Cup : (1) 1972.

EUROPEAN CUPS RECORD

	Entries	Pd	W	D	L	F	A
Champions' Cup	13	57	26	8	23	94	92
Cup-winners' Cup	10	54	27	11	16	100	62
UEFA/Fairs' Cup	8	38	18	8	12	53	41
Total - All 3 Cups	31	149	71	27	51	247	195

FC BARCELONA

FIVE YEAR RECORD *Birthdate/Playing position*	LEAGUE Apps Gls		EURO CUPS Cup Apps Gls		

Andoni ZUBIZARRETA
23/10/61   Goalkeeper

87/88	FC Barcelona	38	-	UC	8	-
88/89	FC Barcelona	36	-	#CWC	9	-
89/90	FC Barcelona	35	-	CWC	4	-
90/91	FC Barcelona	38	-	+CWC	8	-
91/92	FC Barcelona	38	-	#CC	11	-

★ Spain 69 caps, 0 goals

Carlos BUSQUETS
19/07/67   Goalkeeper

90/91	FC Barcelona	-	-	+CWC	1	-
91/92	FC Barcelona	-	-			

Albert FERRER
06/06/70   Defender

89/90	CD Tenerife	17	-			
90/91	FC Barcelona	26	-	+CWC	7	-
91/92	FC Barcelona	12	1	#CC	4	-

★ Spain 1 cap, 0 goals

Ronald KOEMAN (Hol)
21/03/63   Defender

87/88	PSV (Hol)	32	20	#CC	8	1
88/89	PSV (Hol)	32	14	CC	4	2
89/90	FC Barcelona	36	14	CWC	4	1
90/91	FC Barcelona	21	6	+CWC	7	4
91/92	FC Barcelona	35	16	#CC	11	1

★ Holland 60 caps, 10 goals

Ricardo SERNA
21/01/64   Defender

87/88	Sevilla FC	36	1			
88/89	FC Barcelona	33	2	#CWC	8	-
89/90	FC Barcelona	20	-	CWC	3	-
90/91	FC Barcelona	33	-	+CWC	7	-
91/92	FC Barcelona	15	-	#CC	6	-

★ Spain 6 caps, 0 goals

FIVE YEAR RECORD *Birthdate/Playing position*	LEAGUE Apps Gls		EURO CUPS Cup Apps Gls		

PABLO Alfaro
26/04/69   Defender

89/90	Real Zaragoza	37	1	UC	4	1
90/91	Real Zaragoza	36	1			
91/92	Real Zaragoza	34	-			

JUAN CARLOS Rodríguez
19/01/65   Defender

87/88	Atlético Madrid	12	-			
88/89	Atlético Madrid	27	-			
89/90	Atlético Madrid	13	-			
90/91	Atlético Madrid	24	-			
91/92	FC Barcelona	22	-	#CC	5	-

★ Spain 1 cap, 0 goals

EUSEBIO Sacristán
13/04/64   Midfield

87/88	Atlético Madrid	27	3			
88/89	FC Barcelona	37	4	·#CWC	8	-
89/90	FC Barcelona	36	3	CWC	4	-
90/91	FC Barcelona	32	2	+CWC	8	1
91/92	FC Barcelona	30	4	#CC	10	-

★ Spain 15 caps, 0 goals

José María BAKERO
11/02/63   Midfield

87/88	Real Sociedad	32	17	CWC	4	-
88/89	FC Barcelona	22	10	#CWC	6	2
89/90	FC Barcelona	30	13	CWC	2	-
90/91	FC Barcelona	34	12	+CWC	6	1
91/92	FC Barcelona	33	11	#CC	9	3

★ Spain 17 caps, 4 goals

Guillermo AMOR
04/12/67   Midfield

88/89	FC Barcelona	27	8	#CWC	5	2
89/90	FC Barcelona	33	6	CWC	2	-
90/91	FC Barcelona	34	4	+CWC	8	2
91/92	FC Barcelona	36	6	#CC	3	1

★ Spain 9 caps, 1 goal

SPAIN

FIVE YEAR RECORD	LEAGUE		EURO CUPS		
Birthdate/Playing position	Apps	Gls	Cup	Apps	Gls

Aitor BEGUIRISTAIN
12/08/64   Midfield

		Apps	Gls	Cup	Apps	Gls
87/88	Real Sociedad	36	5	CWC	4	1
88/89	FC Barcelona	38	12	#CWC	9	2
89/90	FC Barcelona	37	10	CWC	4	1
90/91	FC Barcelona	33	6	+CWC	8	2
91/92	FC Barcelona	34	7	#CC	8	2

★ Spain 11 caps, 2 goals

Josep GUARDIOLA
18/01/71   Midfield

		Apps	Gls	Cup	Apps	Gls
90/91	FC Barcelona	4	-			
91/92	FC Barcelona	25	-	#CC	11	-

Richard WITSCHGE (Hol)
20/09/69   Midfield

		Apps	Gls	Cup	Apps	Gls
87/88	Ajax (Hol)	10	1	+CWC	3	-
88/89	Ajax (Hol)	14	-			
89/90	Ajax (Hol)	28	2	UC	2	-
90/91	Ajax (Hol)	33	-			
91/92	FC Barcelona	23	-	#CC	9	-

★ Holland 18 caps, 1 goal

Miguel Angel NADAL
28/07/66   Midfield

		Apps	Gls	Cup	Apps	Gls
87/88	RCD Mallorca	20	2			
88/89	RCD Mallorca	Div 2				
89/90	RCD Mallorca	34	7			
90/91	RCD Mallorca	38	6			
91/92	FC Barcelona	24	4	#CC	9	-

★ Spain 2 caps, 0 goals

Jon Andoni GOIKOETXEA
21/10/65   Midfield

		Apps	Gls	Cup	Apps	Gls
87/88	CA Osasuna	36	11			
88/89	Real Sociedad	37	5	UC	8	1
89/90	Real Sociedad	36	4			
90/91	FC Barcelona	37	3	+CWC	6	1
91/92	FC Barcelona	32	-	#CC	6	-

★ Spain 11 caps, 0 goals

FIVE YEAR RECORD	LEAGUE		EURO CUPS		
Birthdate/Playing position	Apps	Gls	Cup	Apps	Gls

Christo STOICHKOV (Bul)
08/02/66   Forward

		Apps	Gls	Cup	Apps	Gls
87/88	CFKA Sredets Sofia (Bul)	27	14	CC	2	-
88/89	CFKA Sredets Sofia (Bul)	26	23	CWC	8	7
89/90	CSKA Sofia (Bul)	30	38	CC	5	3
90/91	FC Barcelona	24	14	+CWC	8	6
91/92	FC Barcelona	32	17	#CC	9	4

★ Bulgaria 32 caps, 5 goals

Michael LAUDRUP (Den)
15/06/64   Forward

		Apps	Gls	Cup	Apps	Gls
87/88	Juventus (Ita)	27	-	UC	4	2
88/89	Juventus (Ita)	26	6	UC	8	3
89/90	FC Barcelona	33	3	CWC	3	1
90/91	FC Barcelona	30	9	+CWC	7	-
91/92	FC Barcelona	36	13	#CC	11	3

★ Denmark 64 caps, 27 goals

Julio SALINAS
11/09/62   Forward

		Apps	Gls	Cup	Apps	Gls
87/88	Atlético Madrid	37	16			
88/89	FC Barcelona	37	20	#CWC	7	2
89/90	FC Barcelona	34	15	CWC	4	1
90/91	FC Barcelona	33	11	+CWC	8	1
91/92	FC Barcelona	17	7	#CC	7	2

★ Spain 29 caps, 8 goals

EUROPEAN HONOURS
Champions' Cup - (1) 1992.
Cup-winners' Cup - (3) 1979, 1982, 1989.
Fairs' Cup - (3) 1958, 1960, 1966.

EUROPEAN CUPS RECORD

	Entries	Pd	W	D	L	F	A
Champions' Cup	6	46	26	9	11	87	42
Cup-winners' Cup	12	76	45	14	17	160	78
UEFA/Fairs' Cup	19	122	60	27	35	229	142
Total - All 3 Cups	37	244	131	50	63	476	262

IFK GÖTEBORG

| FIVE YEAR RECORD | LEAGUE | EURO CUPS |
| Birthdate/Playing position | Apps Gls | Cup Apps Gls |

Thomas RAVELLI
13/08/59   Goalkeeper

87	Östers IF	22	-			
88	Östers IF	22	-	UC	2	-
89	IFK Göteborg	22	-	UC	2	-
90	IFK Göteborg	26	-			
91	IFK Göteborg	28	-	CC	4	-

★ Sweden 92 caps, 0 goals

Dick LAST
02/03/69   Goalkeeper

90	IK Oddevold	Div 2	
91	IFK Göteborg	-	-

Ola SVENSSON
06/04/64   Defender

87	Halmstads BK	21	3			
88	IFK Göteborg	22	2	CC	6	-
89	IFK Göteborg	22	3	UC	2	-
90	IFK Göteborg	26	5			
91	IFK Göteborg	27	6	CC	4	1

Jonas OHLSSON
14/01/70   Defender

89	IFK Göteborg	7	-
90	IFK Göteborg	6	-
91	IFK Göteborg	-	-

Mikael NILSSON
28/09/68   Defender

88	IFK Göteborg	18	2	CC	4	-
89	IFK Göteborg	18	5	UC	2	1
90	IFK Göteborg	23	-			
91	IFK Göteborg	27	-	CC	4	-

★ Sweden 7 caps, 0 goals

Tore PEDERSEN (Nor)
29/09/69   Defender

89	Fredrikstad FK (Nor)	Div 2				
90	IFK Göteborg	18	-			
91	IFK Göteborg	25	-	CC	4	-

★ Norway 15 caps, 0 goals

Pontus KÅMARK
05/04/69   Defender

87	Västerås SK	Div 2				
88	Västerås SK	Div 2				
89	IFK Göteborg	18	3	UC	2	-
90	IFK Göteborg	8	-			
91	IFK Göteborg	26	-	CC	3	-

★ Sweden 2 caps, 0 goals

Magnus JOHANSSON
10/11/71   Defender

90	IFK Göteborg	24	2			
91	IFK Göteborg	22	-	CC	1	-

Stefan REHN
22/09/66   Midfield

87	Djurgårdens IF	Div 2				
88	Djurgårdens IF	20	8			
89	Djurgårdens IF	12	1			
89/90	Everton (Eng)	4	-			
90	IFK Göteborg	24	6			
91	IFK Göteborg	27	1	CC	3	-

★ Sweden 24 caps, 5 goals

Håkan MILD
14/06/71   Midfield

89	IFK Göteborg	1	-			
90	IFK Göteborg	19	-			
91	IFK Göteborg	28	2	CC	4	-

★ Sweden 9 caps, 1 goal

Peter ERIKSSON
18/05/69   Midfield

88	IFK Göteborg	10	1	CC	4	1
89	IFK Göteborg	12	2	UC	1	-
90	IFK Göteborg	22	5			
91	IFK Göteborg	27	4	CC	4	-

★ Sweden 1 cap, 0 goals

SWEDEN

FIVE YEAR RECORD *Birthdate/Playing position*	LEAGUE Apps Gls	EURO CUPS Cup Apps Gls

Per Edmund MORDT (Nor)
25/03/65   Midfield

87	IFK Göteborg	17	1	UC	2	-
88	IFK Göteborg	9	1	CC	4	-
89	IFK Göteborg	15	-	UC	2	-
90	IFK Göteborg	8	2			
91	IFK Göteborg	4	-	CC	3	-

★ Norway 31 caps, 1 goal

Thomas ANDERSSON
21/11/70   Midfield

90	IFK Göteborg	10	-			
91	IFK Göteborg	12	-	CC	4	-

Zoran STOJCEVSKI
04/03/71   Midfield

91	IFK Göteborg	6	-

Johnny EKSTRÖM
05/03/65   Forward

87/88	Empoli (Ita)	29	5			
88/89	FC Bayern München (Ger)	23	7	UC	8	2
89/90	AS Cannes (Fra)	22	4			
90/91	AS Cannes (Fra)	13	-			
91	IFK Göteborg	10	6	CC	4	2

★ Sweden 41 caps, 11 goals

Stefan LINDQVIST
18/03/67   Forward

87	Halmstads BK	22	-			
88	Halmstads BK	Div 2				
89	Halmstads BK	22	8			
90	Halmstads BK	6	-			
90/91	Neuchâtel Xamax FC (Sui)	9	-			
91	IFK Göteborg	28	8	CC	4	-

★ Sweden 5 caps, 1 goal

FIVE YEAR RECORD *Birthdate/Playing position*	LEAGUE Apps Gls	EURO CUPS Cup Apps Gls

Kaj ESKELINEN
21/02/69   Forward

87	Västra Frölunda IF	15	5			
88	Västra Frölunda IF	9	2			
89	Västra Frölunda IF	22	7			
90	IFK Göteborg	26	12			
91	IFK Göteborg	21	2	CC	4	-

Fredrik LEKSELL
16/02/71   Forward

91	IFK Göteborg	1	-	CC	1	-

EUROPEAN HONOURS
UEFA Cup - (2) 1982, 1987.

EUROPEAN CUPS RECORD

	Entries	Pd	W	D	L	F	A
Champions' Cup	9	40	17	7	16	78	67
Cup-winners' Cup	2	8	2	3	3	7	11
UEFA/Fairs' Cup	5	30	18	9	3	53	25
Total - All 3 Cups	16	78	37	19	22	138	103

FC SION

FIVE YEAR RECORD *Birthdate/Playing position*	LEAGUE Apps	Gls	EURO CUPS Cup	Apps	Gls

Stephan LEHMANN
15/08/63   Goalkeeper

87/88 FC Schaffhausen	Div 2				
88/89 FC Sion	34	-			
89/90 FC Sion	32	-	UC	3	-
90/91 FC Sion	36	-			
91/92 FC Sion	35	-	CWC	4	-

★ Switzerland 1 cap, 0 goals

Daniel OBRIST
20/04/65   Goalkeeper

91/92 FC Sion	1	-			

Alain GEIGER
05/11/60   Defender

87/88 Neuchâtel Xamax FC	35	3	CC	4	-
88/89 AS Saint-Etienne (Fra)	32	2			
89/90 AS Saint-Etienne (Fra)	38	-			
90/91 FC Sion	33	1			
91/92 FC Sion	36	1	CWC	4	-

★ Switzerland 74 caps, 2 goals

Michel SAUTHIER
17/02/66   Defender

87/88 FC Sion	18	-	UC	2	-
88/89 FC Sion	12	2			
89/90 FC Sion	34	-	UC	4	-
90/91 FC Sion	33	3			
91/92 FC Sion	31	2	CWC	4	-

★ Switzerland 1 cap, 0 goals

Jean-Paul BRIGGER
14/12/57   Defender

87/88 FC Sion	20	10	UC	2	1
88/89 FC Sion	32	6			
89/90 FC Sion	32	3	UC	3	1
90/91 FC Sion	32	2			
91/92 FC Sion	36	4	CWC	4	-

★ Switzerland 33 caps, 3 goals

Fabrice SCHULER
23/03/71   Defender

91/92 FC Sion	2	-			

Sébastien FOURNIER
27/06/71   Defender

89/90 FC Sion	23	1	UC	3	-
90/91 FC Sion	9	-			
91/92 FC Sion	27	1	CWC	4	-

Yvan QUENTIN
02/05/70   Defender

90/91 FC Sion	10	-			
91/92 FC Sion	26	-	CWC	2	-

Dominique HERR
25/10/65   Defender

87/88 FC Basel	21	-			
88/89 Lausanne-Sports	21	1			
89/90 Lausanne-Sports	33	1			
90/91 Lausanne-Sports	34	3	UC	2	-
91/92 Lausanne-Sports	32	2	UC	2	-

★ Switzerland 26 caps, 1 goal

Marc HOTTIGER
07/11/67   Defender

88/89 Lausanne-Sports	20	3			
89/90 Lausanne-Sports	35	1			
90/91 Lausanne-Sports	33	1	UC	2	2
91/92 Lausanne-Sports	35	-	UC	2	-

* Switzerland 22 caps, 2 goals

Blaise PIFFARETTI
09/03/66   Midfield

87/88 FC Sion	21	2	UC	2	-
88/89 FC Sion	36	3			
89/90 FC Sion	35	1	UC	4	1
90/91 FC Sion	34	1			
91/92 FC Sion	33	3	CWC	1	-

★ Switzerland 20 caps, 0 goals

Roberto ASSIS
10/01/71   Midfield

91/92 Internacional Porto Alegre (Bra)					

SWITZERLAND

FIVE YEAR RECORD	LEAGUE		EURO CUPS		
Birthdate/Playing position	Apps	Gls	Cup	Apps	Gls

Reto GERTSCHEN
07/02/65   Midfield

87/88	Lausanne-Sports	33	4		
88/89	Lausanne-Sports	9	-		
89/90	Lausanne-Sports	31	4		
90/91	FC Sion	35	7		
91/92	FC Sion	34	5	CWC	4	-

★ Switzerland 1 cap, 0 goals

Olivier BIAGGI
17/03/71   Midfield

89/90	FC Sion	8	1	UC	1	-
90/91	FC Sion	6	-			
91/92	FC Sion	4	-	CWC	1	-

LUIS CARLOS (Bra)
11/06/68   Midfield

91/92	Catuense (Bra)	

Umberto TULIO (Bra)
02/06/69   Forward

91/92	Goiás (Bra)	

FIVE YEAR RECORD	LEAGUE		EURO CUPS		
Birthdate/Playing position	Apps	Gls	Cup	Apps	Gls

David ORLANDO
13/10/71   Forward

89/90	FC Monthey	Div 3				
90/91	FC Sion	31	3			
91/92	FC Sion	26	5	CWC	3	1

Alexandre REY
22/09/72   Forward

90/91	FC Sion	14	3			
91/92	FC Sion	24	5	CWC	4	1

EUROPEAN HONOURS
none

EUROPEAN CUPS RECORD

	Entries	Pd	W	D	L	F	A
Champions' Cup	none						
Cup-winners' Cup	6	20	5	7	8	23	35
UEFA/Fairs' Cup	4	12	6	1	5	17	20
Total - All 3 Cups	10	32	11	8	13	40	55

BESIKTAS

FIVE YEAR RECORD Birthdate/Playing position	LEAGUE Apps	Gls	EURO CUPS Cup	Apps	Gls
Jaroslaw BAKO (Pol)					
12/08/64 Goalkeeper					
87/88 LKS Lódz (Pol)	30	-			
88/89 LKS Lódz (Pol)	28	-			
89/90 Zaglebie Lubin (Pol)	27	-			
90/91 Zaglebie Lubin (Pol)	22	-	UC	2	-
91/92 Besiktas	28	-	CC	2	-
★ Poland 27 caps, 0 goals					

METIN Akçevre					
03/03/67 Goalkeeper					
87/88 Orduspor	Div 2				
88/89 Besiktas	-	-			
89/90 Besiktas	1	-			
90/91 Besiktas	3	-			
91/92 Besiktas	2	-			

GÖKHAN Keskin					
01/02/66 Defender					
87/88 Besiktas	35	2	UC	2	-
88/89 Besiktas	35	1	UC	2	-
89/90 Besiktas	34	-	CWC	2	-
90/91 Besiktas	28	1	CC	2	-
91/92 Besiktas	27	2	CC	2	-
★ Turkey 27 caps, 0 goals					

ULVI Güvenipoglu					
26/07/60 Defender					
87/88 Besiktas	36	1	UC	2	-
88/89 Besiktas	34	3	UC	2	-
89/90 Besiktas	33	-	CWC	2	-
90/91 Besiktas	30	3	CC	2	-
91/92 Besiktas	23	-	CC	1	-

KADIR Akbulut					
08/05/60 Defender					
87/88 Besiktas	32	-	UC	2	-
88/89 Besiktas	35	1	UC	2	-
89/90 Besiktas	33	-	CWC	2	-
90/91 Besiktas	27	-	CC	2	-
91/92 Besiktas	27	-	CC	2	-
★ Turkey 1 caps, 0 goals					

FIVE YEAR RECORD Birthdate/Playing position	LEAGUE Apps	Gls	EURO CUPS Cup	Apps	Gls
HAMIT Yüksel					
02/09/67 Defender					
87/88 Zonguldakspor	37	3			
88/89 Ankaragücü	32	11			
89/90 Ankaragücü	32	2			
90/91 Besiktas	5	-			
91/92 Besiktas	18	1	CC	2	-

TURAN Uzun					
31/07/69 Defender					
87/88 Besiktas	21	-			
88/89 Besiktas	7	-			
89/90 Besiktas	3	-			
90/91 Besiktas	10	-			
91/92 Besiktas	23	2	CC	2	-

RECEP Cetin					
01/10/65 Defender					
87/88 Boluspor	35	1			
88/89 Besiktas	33	1	UC	2	-
89/90 Besiktas	31	1	CWC	2	-
90/91 Besiktas	24	1	CC	2	-
91/92 Besiktas	25	1	CC	2	-
★ Turkey 20 caps, 0 goals					

MUTLU Topcu					
16/11/70 Defender					
89/90 Inegölspor	Div 2				
90/91 Besiktas	9	-			
91/92 Besiktas	9	-			

RIZA Çalimbay					
02/02/63 Midfield					
87/88 Besiktas	35	6	UC	2	-
88/89 Besiktas	33	3	UC	2	-
89/90 Besiktas	34	3	CWC	2	-
90/91 Besiktas	30	5	CC	2	-
91/92 Besiktas	30	1	CC	2	-
★ Turkey 32 caps, 1 goal					

TURKEY

FIVE YEAR RECORD *Birthdate/Playing position*	LEAGUE Apps Gls	EURO CUPS Cup Apps Gls

ZEKI Önatli
30/10/68 Midfield

87/88	Besiktas	33	3	UC 1 -
88/89	Besiktas	30	2	UC 2 -
89/90	Besiktas	9	1	
90/91	Besiktas	20	-	
91/92	Besiktas	19	5	

★ Turkey 2 caps, 0 goals

MEHMET Özdilek
01/04/66 Midfield

87/88	Kahramanmarasspor	Div 2		
88/89	Besiktas	34	8	UC 2 -
89/90	Besiktas	30	3	CWC 2 -
90/91	Besiktas	27	10	CC 2 -
91/92	Besiktas	30	12	CC 2 1

★ Turkey 14 caps, 0 goals

Adam ZEJER (Pol)
03/11/63 Midfield

87/88	Zaglebie Lubin (Pol)	27	3	
88/89	Zaglebie Lubin (Pol)	Div 2		
89/90	Zaglebie Lubin (Pol)	30	2	
90/91	Zaglebie Lubin (Pol)	29	4	UC 2 -
91/92	Besiktas	12	-	CC 2 -

★ Poland 3 caps, 0 goals

Mitar MRKELA (Yug)
10/07/65 Forward

87/88	Crvena zvezda Beograd (Yug)	5	-	
88/89	Crvena zvezda Beograd (Yug)	21	4	CC 4 2
89/90	Crvena zvezda Beograd (Yug)	23	2	UC 5 1
90/91	FC Twente (Hol)	32	8	
91/92	FC Twente (Hol)	32	8	
91/92	FC Twente (Hol)	29	2	

★ Yugoslavia 5 caps, 1 goal

SERGEN Yolgin
05/11/72 Forward

91/92	Besiktas	14	2	CC 1 -

FIVE YEAR RECORD *Birthdate/Playing position*	LEAGUE Apps Gls	EURO CUPS Cup Apps Gls

ALI Gültiken
27/06/65 Forward

87/88	Besiktas	38	30	UC 2 -
88/89	Besiktas	34	15	UC 2 -
89/90	Besiktas	33	17	CWC 2 1
90/91	Besiktas	27	14	CC 2 1
91/92	Besiktas	20	5	CC 2 -

★ Turkey 9 caps, 0 goals

METIN Tekin
08/05/64 Forward

87/88	Besiktas	22	2	UC 2 -
88/89	Besiktas	13	-	
89/90	Besiktas	30	13	CWC 1 -
90/91	Besiktas	26	7	CC 2 -
91/92	Besiktas	19	7	CC 2 1

★ Turkey 33 caps, 2 goals

FEYYAZ Uçar
27/10/63 Forward

87/88	Besiktas	33	16	UC 2 1
88/89	Besiktas	33	22	UC 2 1
89/90	Besiktas	34	28	CWC 2 -
90/91	Besiktas	26	16	CC 2 3
91/92	Besiktas	28	19	CC 2 -

★ Turkey 20 caps, 4 goals

EUROPEAN HONOURS
none

EUROPEAN CUPS RECORD

	Entries	Pd	W	D	L	F	A
Champions' Cup	8	18	3	4	11	13	33
Cup-winners' Cup	4	8	1	1	6	5	19
UEFA/Fairs' Cup	4	8	2	1	5	5	13
Total - All 3 Cups	16	34	6	6	22	23	65

Werder Bremen's New Zealand striker Wynton Rufer holds aloft the Cup-winners' Cup trophy after victory over Monaco in Lisbon.

CUP-WINNERS' CUP

THE CUP-WINNERS' CUP is generally regarded as the least demanding of the three European trophies. With fewer matches to play than in the other two competitions and with the field often made up of mid-table and even lower-divisonn teams, this competition nevertheless offers the easiest route to continental glory for its participants.

Last season, for example, the final in Lisbon was contested by two teams which had never previously reached a European final of any description, with the German club Werder Bremen emerging 2-0 victors against a Monaco side which was still in a state of mourning following the stadium disaster in Corsica the previous evening.

These two teams return for this year's competition - Bremen as holders and Monaco as honorary representatives of a French Cup competition which was not concluded as a mark of respect towards the victims of Bastia - and both begin their campaigns against Second Division teams who won their domestic Cup on a penalty shoot-out!

Bremen feature in an all-German tie with Hannover, spot-kick conquerors of Borussia Mönchengladbach, while Monaco tackle European debutants Miedz Legnica, who snatched the Polish Cup from one-time Cup-winners' Cup finalists, Górnik Zabrze.

Other Division Two participants in this year's competition are Norway's Strømsgodset IF and Switzerland's FC Luzern, both of whom were relegated at the end of last season. And competing too are Cardiff City from the English Fourth Division, not to mention Liechtenstein's FC Vaduz, who compete in the Swiss amateur league!

The Italian representatives, Parma, a Second Division team barely two seasons ago, have enjoyed a meteoric rise over the past 24 months and, fortified with a new batch of foreign stars, enter the Cup-winners' Cup as one of the favourites to take the trophy.

There are also a number of more traditional big names taking part. FA Cup winners Liverpool will be strongly fancied to return the trophy to the North-West of England after Manchester United's triumph in 1991, while last year's

quarter-finalists Atlético Madrid and semi-finalists Feyenoord will both be hoping to go at least one step better this season.

The strongest of the outsiders could well be Czechoslovakia's Sparta Prague, who performed so well in the Champions' Cup last season, defeating Rangers and Olympique Marseille and also eventual winners Barcelona. Spartak Moscow could also pose a threat. Representing Russia, as opposed to the Soviet Union, for the first time, they have recruited most of the best former Soviet/CIS internationals who have not yet departed for the West and are unlikely to be significantly weakened from the team which reached the Champions' Cup semi-final two years ago.

With only five previous winners of a European trophy taking part in this year's competition - Liverpool, Atlético Madrid, Feyenoord, Steaua Bucharest and holders Werder Bremen - there is plenty of opportunity for one of the less favoured teams to steal the limelight. Antwerp, Olympiakos and Boavista might never have a better opportunity to make a name in European competition.

Like the Champions' Cup, the Cup-winners' Cup has a record entry of 36 teams this year, which means preliminary round ties for eight teams, including the newcomers from Slovenia, Liechtenstein, Israel and the Faeroe Isles. No places were found for the Cup winners from the three Baltic states, but that could well be rectified for the 1993/94 competition.

★ TEN TO WATCH ★

Jürgen Klinsmann (Monaco), Vassilis Karapialis (Olympiakos), Lumír Mistr (Sparta Prague), Tomas Brolin (Parma), Rob Jones (Liverpool), Paulo Futre (Atlético Madrid), Manolo (Atlético Madrid), Gaston Taument (Feyenoord), Hami Mandirali (Trabzonspor), Andreas Herzog (Werder Bremen).

CUP-WINNERS' CUP

PRELIMINARY ROUND

1st Leg - August 19, 1992; 2nd Leg - September 2, 1992

			1st Leg	2nd Leg	Agg.	Away gls	Pens
Maribor Branik (Slo)	v	Hamrun Spartans (Mlt)					
Strømsgodset IF (Nor)	v	Hapoel Petah-Tikvah (Isr)					
FC Vaduz (Lie)	v	Chernomorets Odessa (Ukr)					
B 36 (Far)	v	Avenir Beggen (Lux)					

FIRST ROUND

1st Leg - September 16, 1992; 2nd Leg - September 30, 1992

			1st Leg	2nd Leg	Agg.	Away gls	Pens
AS Monaco (Fra)	v	Miedz Legnica (Pol)					
Trabzonspor (Tur)	v	TPS (Fin)					
Bohemians (Irl)	v	Steaua Bucuresti (Rom)					
Olympiakos (Gre)	v	FC Vaduz or Chernomorets Odessa					
Valur (Isl)	v	Boavista FC (Por)					
Airdrieonians (Sco)	v	Sparta Praha (Tch)					
Glenavon (Nir)	v	Royal Antwerp FC (Bel)					
FC Admira Wacker (Aut)	v	Cardiff City (Wal)					
Parma (Ita)	v	Újpesti TE (Hun)					
AIK (Swe)	v	AGF (Den)					
B 36 or Avenir Beggen	v	Spartak Moskva (Rus)					
Liverpool (Eng)	v	Apollon Limassol (Cyp)					
Levski Sofia (Bul)	v	FC Luzern (Sui)					
Maribor Branik or Hamrun Spartans	v	Atlético Madrid (Esp)					
Feyenoord (Hol)	v	Strømsgodset IF or Hapoel Petah-Tikvah					
SV Werder Bremen (Ger)	v	Hannover 96 (Ger)					

1992-93

SECOND ROUND

1st Leg - October 21, 1992; 2nd Leg - November 4, 1992

	1st Leg	2nd Leg	Agg.	Away gls	Pens
v					
v					
v					
v					
v					
v					
v					
v					

QUARTER-FINAL

1st Leg - March 3, 1993; 2nd Leg - March 17, 1993

	1st Leg	2nd Leg	Agg.	Away gls	Pens
v					
v					
v					
v					

SEMI-FINAL

1st Leg - April 7, 1993; 2nd Leg - April 21, 1993

	1st Leg	2nd Leg	Agg.	Away gls	Pens
v					
v					

FINAL

May 12, 1993

v	

FC ADMIRA WACKER

FIVE YEAR RECORD Birthdate/Playing position	LEAGUE Apps	Gls	EURO CUPS Cup	Apps	Gls

Wolfgang KNALLER
09/10/61   Goalkeeper

	Apps	Gls	Cup	Apps	Gls
87/88 FC Admira Wacker	26	-	UC	1	-
88/89 FC Admira Wacker	35	-			
89/90 FC Admira Wacker	28	-	CWC	6	-
90/91 FC Admira Wacker	36	-	UC	6	-
91/92 FC Admira Wacker	36	-			

★ Austria 3 caps, 0 goals

Franz GRUBER
31/07/67   Goalkeeper

	Apps	Gls			
90/91 First Vienna FC	1	-			
91/92 First Vienna FC	-	-			

Gerald BACHER
08/10/68   Defender

	Apps	Gls	Cup	Apps	Gls
87/88 FC Admira Wacker	10	-			
88/89 FC Admira Wacker	10	-			
89/90 FC Admira Wacker	34	1	CWC	4	-
90/91 FC Admira Wacker	26	3	UC	2	-
91/92 FC Admira Wacker	31	-			

Alois DÖTZL
05/04/60   Defender

	Apps	Gls	Cup	Apps	Gls
87/88 FC Admira Wacker	33	1	UC	2	-
88/89 FC Admira Wacker	26	2			
89/90 FC Admira Wacker	12	-	CWC	2	-
90/91 FC Admira Wacker	30	-	UC	6	-
91/92 FC Admira Wacker	15	-			

Helmut GRAF
08/02/63   Defender

	Apps	Gls	Cup	Apps	Gls
87/88 FC Admira Wacker	25	-	UC	2	-
88/89 FC Admira Wacker	33	-			
89/90 FC Admira Wacker	35	-	CWC	5	-
90/91 FC Admira Wacker	31	-	UC	6	-
91/92 FC Admira Wacker	27	-			

Gerald MESSLENDER
01/10/61   Defender

	Apps	Gls	Cup	Apps	Gls
87/88 FC Swarovski Tirol	10	3	CWC	2	-
88/89 FC Swarovski Tirol	-	-			
89/90 VfB Mödling	Div 2				
90/91 VfB Mödling	Div 2				
91/92 FC Admira Wacker	31	4			

★ Austria 14 caps, 0 goals

Thomas ZINGLER
21/08/70   Defender

	Apps	Gls	Cup	Apps	Gls
89/90 FC Admira Wacker	19	-	CWC	4	-
90/91 FC Admira Wacker	17	-			
91/92 FC Admira Wacker	18	1			

Peter ARTNER
20/05/66   Midfield

	Apps	Gls	Cup	Apps	Gls
87/88 FC Admira Wacker	35	4	UC	2	-
88/89 FC Admira Wacker	28	1			
89/90 FC Admira Wacker	31	2	CWC	6	-
90/91 FC Admira Wacker	33	2	UC	6	-
91/92 FC Admira Wacker	31	4			

★ Austria 35 caps, 1 goal

Gerald GLATZMAYER
13/12/68   Midfield

	Apps	Gls	Cup	Apps	Gls
87/88 First Vienna FC	25	2			
88/89 First Vienna FC	34	7	UC	4	2
89/90 First Vienna FC	30	12	UC	4	-
90/91 FC Admira Wacker	25	4	UC	2	-
91/92 FC Admira Wacker	20	2			

★ Austria 6 caps, 1 goal

Michael GRUBER
05/02/66   Midfield

	Apps	Gls	Cup	Apps	Gls
87/88 FC Admira Wacker	21	1	UC	1	-
88/89 FC Admira Wacker	30	2			
89/90 FC Admira Wacker	23	2	CWC	5	-
90/91 SK Sturm Graz	30	2			
91/92 FC Admira Wacker	30	2			

AUSTRIA

FIVE YEAR RECORD	LEAGUE		EURO CUPS		
Birthdate/Playing position	Apps	Gls	Cup	Apps	Gls

Andreas GUTLEDERER
24/03/73   Midfield

91/92	FC Admira Wacker	25	1		

Kurt TEMM
30/07/67   Midfield

87/88	SK Sturm Graz	31	1			
88/89	SK Sturm Graz	21	1	UC	2	-
89/90	SK Sturm Graz	24	2			
90/91	SK Sturm Graz	29	8			
91/92	SK Sturm Graz	22	1	UC	2	-

Roger LJUNG (Swe)
08/01/66   Midfield

87	Malmö FF (Swe)	20	1	CC	2	-
88	Malmö FF (Swe)	20	-	UC	4	1
89	Malmö FF (Swe)	12	3			
89/90	BSC Young Boys (Sui)	29	4			
90/91	FC Zürich (Sui)	21	-			
91/92	FC Admira Wacker	35	10			

★ Sweden 31 caps, 2 goals

Uwe MÜLLER (Ger)
16/10/63   Midfield

87/88	Eintracht Frankfurt (Ger)	16	-			
88/89	FC Admira Wacker	36	3			
89/90	FC Admira Wacker	36	4	CWC	6	-
90/91	FC Admira Wacker	18	-	UC	5	1
91/92	FC Admira Wacker	29	2			

Johannes ABFALTERER
26/12/62   Forward

87/88	Wiener Sport-Club	32	9			
88/89	Wiener Sport-Club	34	11			
89/90	FC Admira Wacker	10	1	CWC	2	-
90/91	FC Admira Wacker	19	2			
91/92	FC Admira Wacker	30	8			

Tino JESSENITSCHNIG
02/08/65   Forward

87/88	First Vienna FC	18	1		
88/89	GAK	12	2		
89/90	GAK	9	1		
90/91	GAK	Div 2			
91/92	Kremser SC	16	3		

Olaf MARSCHALL (Ger)
19/03/66   Forward

87/88	1.FC Lokomotive Leipzig (Gdr)	25	8	CWC	2	-
88/89	1.FC Lokomotive Leipzig (Gdr)	23	12	UC	4	1
89/90	1.FC Lokomotive Leipzig (Gdr)	25	7			
90/91	FC Admira Wacker	27	7	UC	6	2
91/92	FC Admira Wacker	36	14			

★ East Germany 4 caps, 0 goals

Ernst OGRIS
09/12/67   Forward

87/88	FK Austria	12	1	UC	2	-
88/89	VSE St. Pölten	31	7			
89/90	VSE St. Pölten	33	11			
90/91	FC Admira Wacker	32	6	UC	6	1
91/92	FC Admira Wacker	9	2			

★ Austria 1 cap, 1 goal

EUROPEAN HONOURS
none

EUROPEAN CUPS RECORD

	Entries	Pd	W	D	L	F	A
Champions' Cup	1	2	0	1	1	0	1
Cup-winners' Cup	2	8	3	1	4	7	8
UEFA/Fairs' Cup	4	14	7	1	6	15	19
Total - All 3 Cups	7	24	10	3	11	22	28

ROYAL ANTWERP FC

FIVE YEAR RECORD	LEAGUE		EURO CUPS		
Birthdate/Playing position	Apps	Gls	Cup	Apps	Gls

Wim DE CONINCK
23/06/59   Goalkeeper

87/88	Royal Antwerp FC	33	-		
88/89	Royal Antwerp FC	30	-	UC	2	-
89/90	Royal Antwerp FC	14	-	UC	3	-
90/91	Royal Antwerp FC	23	-	UC	2	-
91/92	Royal Antwerp FC	17	-		

Stevan STOJANOVIC (Yug)
29/10/64   Goalkeeper

87/88	Crvena zvezda Beograd (Yug)	23	-	UC	4	-
88/89	Crvena zvezda Beograd (Yug)	12	-	CC	3	-
89/90	Crvena zvezda Beograd (Yug)	29	-	UC	5	-
90/91	Crvena zvezda Beograd (Yug)	33	-	#CC	9	-
91/92	Royal Antwerp FC	6	-		

Wim KIEKENS
26/02/68   Defender

87/88	RWD Molenbeek	24	-		
88/89	RWD Molenbeek	31	2		
89/90	Royal Antwerp FC	28	1	UC	8	-
90/91	Royal Antwerp FC	27	-	UC	1	-
91/92	Royal Antwerp FC	33	2		

Nico BROECKAERT
23/11/60   Defender

87/88	KV Kortrijk	32	2		
88/89	KV Kortrijk	31	-		
89/90	Royal Antwerp FC	34	4	UC	7	1
90/91	Royal Antwerp FC	30	2	UC	2	-
91/92	Royal Antwerp FC	32	-		

★ Belgium 2 caps, 0 goals

Rudy SMIDTS
12/08/63   Defender

87/88	Royal Antwerp FC	33	2		
88/89	Royal Antwerp FC	24	1	UC	2	-
89/90	Royal Antwerp FC	30	1	UC	8	-
90/91	Royal Antwerp FC	34	-	UC	1	-
91/92	Royal Antwerp FC	34	2		

FIVE YEAR RECORD	LEAGUE		EURO CUPS		
Birthdate/Playing position	Apps	Gls	Cup	Apps	Gls

Geert EMMERECHTS
05/05/68   Defender

87/88	RWD Molenbeek	26	-		
88/89	Royal Antwerp FC	9	1	UC	1	-
89/90	Royal Antwerp FC	24	1	UC	6	-
90/91	Royal Antwerp FC	31	2	UC	2	-
91/92	Royal Antwerp FC	32	-		

★ Belgium 1 cap, 0 goals

Patrick VAN VEIRDEGHEM
09/01/63   Defender

87/88	KSC Lokeren	33	2		
88/89	KSC Lokeren	31	-		
89/90	Royal Antwerp FC	17	3	UC	2	-
90/91	Royal Antwerp FC	1	-		
91/92	Royal Antwerp FC	22	-		

Ronny VAN RETHY
21/11/61   Defender

87/88	Royal Antwerp FC	23	2		
88/89	Royal Antwerp FC	32	2	UC	2	-
89/90	Royal Antwerp FC	-	-		
90/91	Royal Antwerp FC	10	-		
91/92	Royal Antwerp FC	30	2		

Didier SEGERS
21/02/65   Defender

87/88	K Lierse SK	Div 2			
88/89	K Lierse SK	27	1		
89/90	K Lierse SK	26	3		
90/91	K Lierse SK	32	1		
91/92	K Lierse SK	34	4		

Kari UKKONEN (Fin)
19/02/61   Midfield

87/88	RSC Anderlecht	14	1		
88/89	RSC Anderlecht	15	-	CWC	3	-
89/90	RSC Anderlecht	8	2	+CWC	2	1
90/91	RSC Anderlecht	-	-		
91/92	Royal Antwerp FC	27	-		

★ Finland 50 caps, 4 goals

BELGIUM

| FIVE YEAR RECORD | LEAGUE | | EURO CUPS | | |
| *Birthdate/Playing position* | Apps | Gls | Cup | Apps | Gls |

Zsolt MUSZNAY (Rom)
20/06/65   Midfield

87/88	FC Bihor Oradea (Rom)	Div 2				
88/89	FC Bihor Oradea (Rom)	31	9			
89/90	Steaua Bucuresti (Rom)	25	1	CC	4	1
90/91	Videoton-Waltham (Hun)	23	5			
91/92	Royal Antwerp FC	15	-			

★ Romania 6 caps, 0 goals

Hans-Peter LEHNHOFF (Ger)
12/07/63   Midfield

87/88	Royal Antwerp FC	27	8			
88/89	Royal Antwerp FC	34	8	UC	2	-
89/90	Royal Antwerp FC	33	9	UC	8	2
90/91	Royal Antwerp FC	30	10	UC	2	-
91/92	Royal Antwerp FC	34	11			

Ronny VAN GENEUGDEN
17/08/68   Midfield

87/88	Waterschei Thor	Div 2				
88/89	RKC (Hol)	5	-			
89/90	Royal Antwerp FC	16	1			
90/91	Royal Antwerp FC	10	1	UC	1	-
91/92	Royal Antwerp FC	11	-			

Mario KROHM (Ger)
02/06/67   Forward

87/88	Alemannia Aachen (Ger)	Div 2				
88/89	Alemannia Aachen (Ger)	Div 2				
89/90	KRC Mechelen	32	13			
90/91	Royal Antwerp FC	13	2			
91/92	SC Eendracht Aalst	21	6			

Christopher N'WOSU (Nig)
06/10/71   Forward

89/90	K St-Truidense VV	9	3
90/91	K St-Truidense VV	25	5
91/92	K St-Truidense VV	Div 2	

| FIVE YEAR RECORD | LEAGUE | | EURO CUPS | | |
| *Birthdate/Playing position* | Apps | Gls | Cup | Apps | Gls |

Dragan JAKOVLJEVIC (Yug)
23/02/62   Forward

87/88	FK Sarajevo (Yug)	30	12			
88/89	FK Sarajevo	-	-			
89/90	FC Nantes (Fra)	28	5			
90/91	FC Nantes (Fra)	19	2			
91/92	Royal Antwerp FC	22	3			

★ Yugoslavia 8 caps, 3 goals

Alex CZERNIATYNSKI
27/07/60   Forward

87/88	R Standard Liège	28	14			
88/89	R Standard Liège	25	10			
89/90	Royal Antwerp FC	27	5	UC	8	-
90/91	Royal Antwerp FC	33	9			
91/92	Royal Antwerp FC	32	16			

★ Belgium 21 caps, 5 goals

Nico CLAESEN
01/10/62   Forward

87/88	Tottenham Hotspur (Eng)	24	10			
88/89	Royal Antwerp FC	29	7	UC	2	-
89/90	Royal Antwerp FC	33	16	UC	7	4
90/91	Royal Antwerp FC	26	10	UC	2	-
91/92	Royal Antwerp FC	31	6			

★ Belgium 31 caps, 12 goals

EUROPEAN HONOURS
none

EUROPEAN CUPS RECORD

	Entries	Pd	W	D	L	F	A
Champions' Cup	1	2	0	0	2	1	8
Cup-winners' Cup	none						
UEFA/Fairs' Cup	10	38	14	8	16	53	55
Total - All 3 Cups	11	40	14	8	18	54	63

LEVSKI SOFIA

FIVE YEAR RECORD Birthdate/Playing position	LEAGUE Apps Gls		EURO CUPS Cup Apps Gls	

Zdravko ZDRAVKOV
04/10/70   Goalkeeper

88/89	Vitosha Sofia	10	-		
89/90	Levski Sofia	19	-	UC 1	-
90/91	Levski Sofia	19	-		
91/92	Levski Sofia	6	-	CWC 1	-

Ivko GANCHEV
21/07/65   Goalkeeper

87/88	Beroe Stara Zagora	27	-	
88/89	Beroe Stara Zagora	26	-	
89/90	Beroe Stara Zagora	23	-	
90/91	Slavia Sofia	30	-	UC 2 -
91/92	Slavia Sofia	29	1	

Stoian PUMPALOV
28/10/68   Defender

88/89	Lokomotiv Ruse	Div 2			
89/90	Chernomortes Bourgas	30	1	CWC 1	1
90/91	Chernomorets Bourgas	23	-		
91/92	Levski Sofia	28	-	CWC 2	-

Valentin DARTILOV
26/02/67   Defender

87/88	Pirin Blagoevgrad	22	-		
88/89	Pirin Blagoevgrad	30	1		
89/90	Pirin Blagoevgrad	28	3		
90/91	Levski Sofia	11	-		
91/92	Levski Sofia	30	1	CWC 2	1

Kalin BANKOV
12/05/65   Defender

88/89	Etar Veliko Tarnovo	28	2		
89/90	Etar veliko Tarnovo	27	7		
90/91	Levski Sofia	11	-		
91/92	Levski Sofia	14	-	CWC 2	1

★ Bulgaria 7 caps, 1 goal

Plamen PASKOV
10/09/70   Defender

90/91	Akademik Sofia	Div 2	
91/92	Levski Sofia	2	-

Petar KHUBCHEV
26/02/64   Defender

89/90	Levski Sofia	27	-	UC 1	-
90/91	Levski Sofia	27	1		
91/92	Levski Sofia	29	2	CWC 2	-

★ Bulgaria 5 caps, 0 goals

Daniel BORIMIROV
16/01/70   Defender

89/90	Bdin Vidin	Div 2		
90/91	Levski Sofia	28	3	
91/92	Levski Sofia	14	-	

Krasimir KOEV
27/08/63   Defender

87/88	Vitosha Sofia	30	1		
88/89	Vitosha Sofia	27	-	CC 2	-
89/90	Levski Sofia	23	-	UC 2	-
90/91	Slavia Sofia	4	-		
91/92	Levski Sofia	5	-		

Aleksandr MARKOV
17/08/61   Defender

87/88	Spartak Pleven	20	-		
88/89	Slavia Sofia	27	1	UC 1	-
89/90	Slavia Sofia	23	-		
90/91	Slavia Sofia	22	1	UC 2	-
91/92	Levski Sofia	15	-		

★ Bulgaria 21 caps, 0 goals

Valeri VALKOV
18/08/67   Midfield

87/88	Sliven	20	1		
88/89	Sliven	23	5		
89/90	Sliven	25	7		
90/91	Sliven	25	5	CWC 1	-
91/92	Levski Sofia	10	1	CWC 2	-

★ Bulgaria 1 cap, 0 goals

BULGARIA

FIVE YEAR RECORD	LEAGUE		EURO CUPS		
Birthdate/Playing position	Apps	Gls	Cup	Apps	Gls

Yasen PETROV
23/06/68   Midfield

89/90	Pirin Goche Delchev	Div 3			
90/91	Botev Plovdiv	27	11		
91/92	Levski Sofia	26	1	CWC	2	-

Ilian ILIEV
02/07/68   Midfield

87/88	Cherno More Varna	Div 2			
88/89	Cherno More Varna	11	2		
89/90	Cherno More Varna	29	3		
90/91	Cherno More Varna	Div 2			
91/92	Levski Sofia	30	4	CWC	2	-

★ Bulgaria 1 cap, 0 goals

Zlatko YANKOV
07/08/66   Midfield

87/88	Chernomorets Bourgas	22	-		
88/89	Chernomorets Bourgas	Div 2			
89/90	Chernomorets Bourgas	30	2	CWC	2	-
90/91	Levski Sofia	29	-		
91/92	Levski Sofia	29	3	CWC	2	-

★ Bulgaria 12 caps, 1 goal

Emil MITSANSKI
02/07/64   Midfield

88/89	Vichren Sandanski	Div 2			
89/90	Pirin Blagoevgrad	29	-		
90/91	Pirin Blagoevgrad	28	4		
91/92	Pirin Blagoevgrad	11	-		

Georgi DONKOV
02/06/70   Forward

87/88	Vitosha Sofia	1	-		
88/89	Vitosha Sofia	25	6	CC	1	-
89/90	Levski Sofia	24	5	UC	2	1
90/91	Levski Sofia	26	3		
91/92	Levski Sofia	15	-		

Velko YOTOV
26/08/70   Forward

88/89	Vitosha Sofia	18	2		
89/90	Levski Sofia	16	6	UC	1	-
90/91	Levski Sofia	29	9		
91/92	Levski Sofia	26	4	CWC	2	-

★ Bulgaria 2 caps, 0 goals

Ilia GRUEV
30/10/69   Forward

88/89	Vitosha Sofia	13	-		
89/90	Levski Sofia	20	-	UC	2	-
90/91	Levski Sofia	16	-		
91/92	Levski Sofia	4	-		

EUROPEAN HONOURS
none

EUROPEAN CUPS RECORD

	Entries	Pd	W	D	L	F	A
Champions' Cup	7	20	4	4	12	30	40
Cup-winners' Cup	7	26	11	3	12	55	47
UEFA/Fairs' Cup	8	30	10	7	13	44	57
Total - All 3 Cups	22	76	25	14	37	129	144

APOLLON LIMASSOL

Michalis CHRISTOPHI
24/07/67   Goalkeeper

FIVE YEAR RECORD	LEAGUE		EURO CUPS		
	Apps	Gls	Cup	Apps	Gls
89/90 Apollon Limassol	12	-	UC	1	-
90/91 Apollon Limassol	26	-			
91/92 Apollon Limassol	24	-	CC	4	-

★ Cyprus 8 caps, 0 goals

George NICOLAOU
22/10/63   Goalkeeper

	Apps	Gls	Cup	Apps	Gls
87/88 Aris Limassol	18	-			
88/89 Aris Limassol	8	-			
89/90 Aris Limassol	1	-			
90/91 Aris Limassol	18	-			
91/92 Apollon Limassol	2	-			

Andonis ELIA "ANDRELIS"
04/12/63   Defender

	Apps	Gls	Cup	Apps	Gls
87/88 Apollon Limassol	28	1			
88/89 Apollon Limassol	26	-			
89/90 Apollon Limassol	24	2	UC	2	-
90/91 Apollon Limassol	25	-			
91/92 Apollon Limassol	26	-	CC	4	-

★ Cyprus 25 caps, 0 goals

Charalambos PITTAS
26/07/66   Defender

	Apps	Gls	Cup	Apps	Gls
87/88 Apollon Limassol	30	8			
88/89 Apollon Limassol	26	11			
89/90 Apollon Limassol	24	3	UC	2	1
90/91 Apollon Limassol	19	2			
91/92 Apollon Limassol	26	7	CC	3	-

★ Cyprus 26 caps, 4 goals

Dimitris IOANNOU
08/12/68   Defender

	Apps	Gls	Cup	Apps	Gls
87/88 Apop Paphos	28	-			
88/89 Apop Paphos	26	-			
89/90 Apollon Limassol	25	5	UC	2	-
90/91 Apollon Limassol	25	6			
91/92 Apollon Limassol	25	1	CC	4	-

★ Cyprus 6 caps, 0 goals

Pambos CHRISTOPHI
10/05/68   Defender

	Apps	Gls	Cup	Apps	Gls
87/88 Apep Limassol	23	1			
88/89 Apollon Limassol	24	-			
89/90 Apollon Limassol	25	1	UC	2	-
90/91 Apollon Limassol	25	4			
91/92 Apollon Limassol	25	1	CC	4	-

★ Cyprus 3 caps, 0 goals

Andreas SOFOCLEOUS
07/09/73   Defender

	Apps	Gls	Cup	Apps	Gls
90/91 Apollon Limassol	12	-			
91/92 Apollon Limassol	3	-	CC	2	-

Dimitris ORPHANIDES
26/09/68   Defender

	Apps	Gls	Cup	Apps	Gls
88/89 Apollon Limassol	3	-			
89/90 Apollon Limassol	10	-			
90/91 Apollon Limassol	14	1			
91/92 Apollon Limassol	23	3	CC	1	-

Yiannakis YIANGOUDAKIS
17/01/59   Midfield

	Apps	Gls	Cup	Apps	Gls
87/88 Apollon Limassol	28	3			
88/89 Apollon Limassol	27	8			
89/90 Apollon Limassol	21	-	UC	2	-
90/91 Apollon Limassol	25	-			
91/92 Apollon Limassol	18	1	CC	3	-

★ Cyprus 55 caps, 1 goal

Marios CHARALAMBOUS
18/06/69   Midfield

	Apps	Gls	Cup	Apps	Gls
87/88 Apollon Limassol	24	-			
88/89 Apollon Limassol	1	-			
89/90 Apollon Limassol	6	1			
90/91 Apollon Limassol	25	-			
91/92 Apollon Limassol	23	3	CC	4	-

★ Cyprus 6 caps, 0 goals

CYPRUS

FIVE YEAR RECORD	LEAGUE		EURO CUPS		
Birthdate/Playing position	Apps	Gls	Cup	Apps	Gls

George IOSIPHIDES
08/01/68   Midfield

88/89	Apollon Limassol	25	2			
89/90	Apollon Limassol	14	2	UC	2	-
90/91	Apollon Limassol	26	5			
91/92	Apollon Limassol	17	4	CC	4	-

★ Cyprus 1 cap, 0 goals

Lakis ATHANASIOU
08/12/68   Midfield

88/89	Apollon Limassol	20	2			
89/90	Apollon Limassol	14	6			
90/91	Apollon Limassol	12	-			
91/92	Apollon Limassol	7	-	CC	1	-

David KENNY (Sco)
16/11/62   Midfield

87/88	Apoel Nicosia	30	11			
88/89	Aris Limassol	26	1			
89/90	Aris Limassol	25	1			
90/91	Apop Paphos	16	4			
91/92	Apollon Limassol	25	2	CC	4	-

Chrysostomous CHRISTODOULOU
29/06/66   Midfield

91/92	Apollon Limassol	1	-			

Christos IOSIPHIDES
08/01/68   Forward

87/88	Apollon Limassol	20	-			
88/89	Keravnos Strovolos	11	-			
89/90	Keravnos Strovolos	Div 2				
90/91	Apollon Limassol	18	1			
91/92	Apollon Limassol	16	4			

FIVE YEAR RECORD	LEAGUE		EURO CUPS		
Birthdate/Playing position	Apps	Gls	Cup	Apps	Gls

Angelos TSOLAKIS
23/08/69   Forward

87/88	Apollon Limassol	17	2			
88/89	Apollon Limassol	18	4			
89/90	Apollon Limassol	25	5	UC	2	-
90/91	Apollon Limassol	26	11			
91/92	Apollon Limassol	3	-	CC	2	-

★ Cyprus 5 caps, 1 goal

Suad BESIREVIC (Yug)
04/03/63   Forward

87/88	Borac Banja Luka (Yug)	Div 2				
88/89	Borac Banja Luka (Yug)	Div 2		CWC	2	-
89/90	Rijeka (Yug)	14	3			
90/91	Apollon Limassol	26	19			
91/92	Apollon Limassol	25	15	CC	4	2

Milenko SPOLJARIC (Yug)
24/01/67   Forward

89/90	OFK Beograd (Yug)	Div 2				
90/91	OFK Beograd (Yug)	Div 2				
91/92	OFK Beograd (Yug)	16**	5**			

* first half of season figures only.

EUROPEAN HONOURS
none

EUROPEAN CUPS RECORD

	Entries	Pd	WW	D	L	F	A
Champions' Cup	2	6	1	0	5	4	19
Cup-winners' Cup	4	8	1	1	6	4	31
UEFA/Fairs' Cup	2	4	0	2	2	4	12
Total - All 3 Cups	8	18	2	3	13	12	62

SPARTA PRAHA

FIVE YEAR RECORD	LEAGUE		EURO CUPS		
Birthdate/Playing position	Apps	Gls	Cup	Apps	Gls

Petr KOUBA
28/01/69   Goalkeeper

88/89 Bohemians Praha	13	-			
89/90 Bohemians Praha	27	-			
90/91 Bohemians Praha	15	-			
Sparta Praha	15	-			
91/92 Sparta Praha	30	-	CC	10	-

★ Czechoslovakia 7 caps, 0 goals

Milan SOVA
09/05/62   Goalkeeper

89/90 VTZ Chomutov	Div 2				
90/91 Sparta Praha	8	-	CC	1	-
91/92 Sparta Praha	-	-			

Michal HORNÁK
26/04/70   Defender

88/89 Sparta Praha	5	-			
89/90 RH Cheb	15	1			
90/91 SKP Union Cheb	14	1			
Sparta Praha	9	-			
91/92 Sparta Praha	24	1	CC	10	-

Jiří NOVOTNY
07/04/70   Defender

87/88 Sparta Praha	1	-			
88/89 Sparta Praha	16	-	CC	1	-
89/90 Sparta Praha	30	1	CC	3	-
90/91 Sparta Praha	27	4	CC	2	-
91/92 Sparta Praha	30	6	CC	9	1

★ Czechoslovakia 4 caps, 0 goals

Jan SOPKO
17/10/68   Defender

87/88 RH Cheb	1	-			
88/89 RH Cheb	14	-			
89/90 RH Cheb	14	1			
90/91 SKP Union Cheb	23	4			
91/92 Sparta Praha	13	-	CC	4	-

FIVE YEAR RECORD	LEAGUE		EURO CUPS		
Birthdate/Playing position	Apps	Gls	Cup	Apps	Gls

Petr VRABEC
05/06/62   Defender

87/88 Sparta Praha	19	-	CC	3	-
88/89 Sparta Praha	25	3	CC	2	-
89/90 Sparta Praha	14	-	CC	4	-
90/91 Sparta Praha	18	1	CC	1	-
91/92 Sparta Praha	28	8	CC	10	3

Jozef CHOVANEC
07/03/60   Defender

87/88 Sparta Praha	30	12	CC	4	1
88/89 Sparta Praha	14	2	CC	2	-
PSV (Hol)	8	1			
89/90 PSV (Hol)	12	3	CC	2	-
90/91 PSV (Hol)	13	-	CWC	1	-
91/92 PSV (Hol)	1	-			
Sparta Praha	21	4	CC	4	1

★ Czechoslovakia 50 caps, 3 goals

Jiří NEMEC
16/05/66   Midfield

87/88 Dukla Praha	24	2			
88/89 Dukla Praha	28	-	UC	2	1
89/90 Dukla Praha	29	3			
90/91 Sparta Praha	28	3	CC	1	-
91/92 Sparta Praha	29	-	CC	9	1

★ Czechoslovakia 13 caps, 0 goals

Martin FRYDEK
09/03/69   Midfield

89/90 Tatra Kolín	Div 4				
90/91 Sparta Praha	20	4			
91/92 Sparta Praha	27	4	CC	10	1

★ Czechoslovakia 7 caps, 0 goals

Vitezslav LAVICKA
30/04/63   Midfield

87/88 Sparta Praha	15	4			
88/89 Sparta Praha	16	1	CC	2	-
89/90 Spartak Hradec Králové	Div 2				
Sparta Praha	6	-			
90/91 Sparta Praha	18	3			
91/92 Sparta Praha	16	2	CC	6	-

CZECHOSLOVAKIA

FIVE YEAR RECORD Birthdate/Playing position	LEAGUE Apps Gls	EURO CUPS Cup Apps Gls

Michal BÍLEK
13/04/65 Midfield

		Apps	Gls	Cup	Apps	Gls
87/88	Sparta Praha	29	4	CC	4	-
88/89	Sparta Praha	30	8	CC	2	2
89/90	Sparta Praha	26	10	CC	4	3
90/91	Sparta Praha	11	1	CC	2	-
	Real Betis (Esp)	22	1			
91/92	Real Betis (Esp)	Div 2				

★ Czechoslovakia 31 caps, 11 goals

Lumír MISTR
12/01/69 Midfield

		Apps	Gls	Cup	Apps	Gls
89/90	RH Cheb	6	-			
90/91	SKP Union Cheb	30	4			
91/92	Sparta Praha	26	2	CC	9	-

Rudolf MATTA
20/07/68 Midfield

		Apps	Gls	Cup	Apps	Gls
87/88	Tatran Presov	26	3			
88/89	Tatran Presov	Div 2				
89/90	Sparta Praha	6	-			
90/91	Sparta Praha	5	-	CC	1	-
91/92	Dukla Praha	9	-			
	Sparta Praha	4	-	CC	7	-

Pavel CERNY
11/10/62 Forward

		Apps	Gls	Cup	Apps	Gls
87/88	Spartak Hradec Králové	29	11			
88/89	Spartak Hradec Králové	30	13			
89/90	Spartak Hradec Králové	Div 2				
	Sparta Praha	15	7			
90/91	Sparta Praha	22	11	CC	2	-
91/92	Sparta Praha	29	12	CC	8	-

★ Czechoslovakia 4 caps, 0 goals

Horst SIEGL
15/02/69 Forward

		Apps	Gls	Cup	Apps	Gls
87/88	Sparta Praha	2	1			
88/89	Sparta Praha	5	-	CC	2	-
	RH Cheb	12	5			
89/90	RH Cheb	26	2			
90/91	Sparta Praha	25	8	CC	1	-
91/92	Sparta Praha	27	13	CC	10	2

★ Czechoslovakia 3 caps, 0 goals

Marek TRVAL
14/08/67 Forward

		Apps	Gls	Cup	Apps	Gls
88/89	TJ Vítkovice	3	-			
89/90	TJ Vítkovice	13	-			
90/91	TJ Vítkovice	21	10			
91/92	TJ Vítkovice	14	7			
	Sparta Praha	10	2	CC	2	-

Dejan JOKSIMOVIC (Yug)
10/01/65 Forward

		Apps	Gls	Cup	Apps	Gls
87/88	Crvena zvezda Beograd (Yug)	17	3	UC	1	-
88/89	Vojvodina Novi Sad (Yug)	23	5			
89/90	Partizan Beograd (Yug)	12	3			
90/91	Crvena zvezda Beograd (Yug)	5	-			
91/92	Sparta Praha	8	-	CC	2	-

Viktor DVIRNIK (Ukr)
1969 Forward

		Apps	Gls	Cup	Apps	Gls
90/91	Inter Bratislava	18	9			
91/92	Inter Bratislava	27	13			

EUROPEAN HONOURS
none

EUROPEAN CUPS RECORD

	Entries	Pd	W	D	L	F	A
Champions' Cup	9	42	19	9	14	67	60
Cup-winners' Cup	4	18	9	2	7	43	17
UEFA/Fairs' Cup	5	20	8	4	8	31	33
Total - All 3 Cups	18	80	36	15	29	141	110

AGF

FIVE YEAR RECORD *Birthdate/Playing position*	LEAGUE Apps Gls	EURO CUPS Cup Apps Gls

Troels RASMUSSEN
07/04/61   Goalkeeper

87	AGF	26	-	CC	4	-
88	AGF	26	-	CWC	6	-
89	AGF	26	-			
90	AGF	25	1			
91	AGF	18	-			
91/92	AGF	32	-			

★ Denmark 35 caps, 0 goals

Tony HENRIKSEN
25/04/73   Goalkeeper

91	Randers Freja FC	Div 3	
91/92	AGF	-	-

Lasse SKOV
30/08/62   Defender

88	OB	19	-
89	OB	25	-
90	AGF	25	-
91	AGF	15	-
91/92	AGF	14	-

Kent NIELSEN
28/12/61   Defender

87	Brøndby IF	26	2	UC	4	-
88	Brøndby IF	22	1	CC	2	-
89	Brøndby IF	11	-			
89/90	Aston Villa (Eng)	36	2			
90/91	Aston Villa (Eng)	37	2	UC	4	1
91/92	Aston Villa (Eng)	6	-			
	AGF	14	2			

★ Denmark 54 caps, 3 goals

Claus THOMSEN
31/05/70   Defender

88	AGF	5	1	CWC	2	-
89	AGF	23	6			
90	AGF	25	5			
91	AGF	18	1			
91/92	AGF	22	-			

FIVE YEAR RECORD *Birthdate/Playing position*	LEAGUE Apps Gls	EURO CUPS Cup Apps Gls

Claus CHRISTIANSEN
27/03/72   Defender

90	AGF	3	-
91	AGF	4	-
91/92	AGF	31	3

Jan-Halvor HALVORSEN (Nor)
08/03/63   Defender

87	SK Brann (Nor)	22	-
88	SK Brann (Nor)	20	1
89	IK Start (Nor)	8	-
89/90	Hertha BSC (Ger)	Div 2	
90/91	Hertha BSC (Ger)	28	-
91/92	Hertha BSC (Ger)	Div 2	
	AGF	13	-

★ Norway 5 caps, 0 goals

Erik MADSEN
20/08/68   Midfield

90	AGF	11	-
91	AGF	17	2
91/92	AGF	20	4

Stig TØFTING
14/08/69   Midfield

88	AGF	-	-
89	AGF	1	-
90	AGF	22	2
91	AGF	18	-
91/92	AGF	24	2

Jan BARTRAM
06/03/62   Midfield

87	AGF	21	4	CC	3	1
87/88	Rangers (Sco)	11	3			
88	Brøndby IF	14	2	CC	2	-
88/89	Bayer 05 Uerdingen (Ger)	19	1			
89/90	Bayer 05 Uerdingen (Ger)	33	4			
90/91	Bayer 05 Uerdingen (Ger)	22	4			
91	AGF	14	6			

★ Denmark 32 caps, 5 goals

DENMARK

FIVE YEAR RECORD *Birthdate/Playing position*	LEAGUE Apps Gls	EURO CUPS Cup Apps Gls

Lars KLAUSEN
10/04/68   Midfield

91	AGF	2	-
91/92	AGF	1	-

Ole MORTENSEN
14/06/69   Midfield

89	Horsens FS	Div 2	
90	Horsens FS	Div 3	
91	Horsens FS	Div 3	
91/92	AGF	28	2

Jesper SØRENSEN
10/06/73   Midfield

91/92	AGF	21	-

Bo HARDER
05/03/68   Midfield

87	AGF	4	-
88	AGF	9	-
89	AGF	-	-
90	AGF	9	-
91	AGF	4	1
91/92	AGF	29	2

Palle SØRENSEN
04/04/72   Forward

91/92	AGF	12	1

Torben CHRISTENSEN
14/07/63   Forward

87	Ikast FS	20	8
88	Ikast FS	10	1
88/89	FC St. Gallen (Sui)	9	-
89	AGF	16	2
90	AGF	25	7
91	AGF	18	6
91/92	AGF	28	6

★ Denmark 3 caps, 0 goals

FIVE YEAR RECORD *Birthdate/Playing position*	LEAGUE Apps Gls	EURO CUPS Cup Apps Gls

Søren ANDERSEN
31/01/70   Forward

88	Hvidorre IF	Div 2	
89	AGF	17	4
90	AGF	20	10
91	AGF	18	8
91/92	AGF	29	11

Mads IVERSEN
15/11/70   Forward

88	Randers Freja FC	4	-
89	Randers Freja FC	Div 2	
90	Randers Freja FC	Div 3	
91	Randers Freja FC	Div 3	
91/92	AGF	7	-

EUROPEAN HONOURS
none

EUROPEAN CUPS RECORD

	Entries	Pd	W	D	L	F	A
Champions' Cup	5	18	6	4	8	22	25
Cup-winners' Cup	3	12	6	1	5	19	14
UEFA/Fairs' Cup	4	10	2	1	7	8	19
Total - All 3 Cups	12	40	14	6	20	49	58

LIVERPOOL

FIVE YEAR RECORD	LEAGUE		EURO CUPS		
Birthdate/Playing position	Apps	Gls	Cup	Apps	Gls

Bruce GROBBELAAR (Zim)
06/10/57   Goalkeeper

87/88	Liverpool	38	-			
88/89	Liverpool	21	-			
89/90	Liverpool	38	-			
90/91	Liverpool	31	-			
91/92	Liverpool	37	-	UC	5	-

★ Zimbabwe

David JAMES
01/08/70   Goalkeeper

90/91	Watford	Div 2	
91/92	Watford	Div 2	

David BURROWS
25/10/68   Defender

87/88	West Bromwich Albion	Div 2				
88/89	West Bromwich Albion	Div 2				
	Liverpool	21	-			
89/90	Liverpool	26	-			
90/91	Liverpool	35	-			
91/92	Liverpool	30	1	UC	7	-

Steve NICOL (Sco)
11/12/61   Defender

87/88	Liverpool	40	6			
88/89	Liverpool	38	2			
89/90	Liverpool	23	6			
90/91	Liverpool	35	3			
91/92	Liverpool	34	1	UC	7	-

★ Scotland 27 caps, 0 goals

Nicky TANNER
24/05/65   Defender

87/88	Bristol Rovers	Div 3				
88/89	Liverpool	-	-			
89/90	Liverpool	4	-			
	Norwich City	6	-			
90/91	Liverpool	-	-			
	Swindon Town	Div 2				
91/92	Liverpool	32	1	UC	6	-

Mark WRIGHT
01/08/63   Defender

87/88	Derby County	38	3			
88/89	Derby County	33	1			
89/90	Derby County	36	6			
90/91	Derby County	37	-			
91/92	Liverpool	21	-	UC	4	-

★ England 42 caps, 1 goal

Rob JONES
05/11/71   Defender

87/88	Crewe Alexandra	Div 4				
88/89	Crewe Alexandra	Div 3				
89/90	Crewe Alexandra	Div 3				
90/91	Crewe Alexandra	Div 3				
91/92	Crewe Alexandra	Div 4				
	Liverpool	28	-	UC	2	-

★ England 1 cap, 0 goals

Mike MARSH
21/07/69   Midfield

88/89	Liverpool	1	-			
89/90	Liverpool	2	-			
90/91	Liverpool	2	-			
91/92	Liverpool	34	-	UC	8	1

Jan MØLBY (Den)
04/07/63   Midfield

87/88	Liverpool	7	-			
88/89	Liverpool	13	2			
89/90	Liverpool	17	1			
90/91	Liverpool	25	9			
91/92	Liverpool	26	3	UC	5	1

★ Denmark 33 caps, 2 goals

Paul STEWART
07/10/64   Midfield

87/88	Manchester City	Div 2				
88/89	Tottenham Hotspur	30	12			
89/90	Tottenham Hotspur	28	8			
90/91	Tottenham Hotspur	35	3			
91/92	Tottenham Hotspur	38	5	CWC	8	-

★ England 3 caps, 0 goals

ENGLAND

FIVE YEAR RECORD *Birthdate/Playing position*	LEAGUE Apps Gls	EURO CUPS Cup Apps Gls

Michael THOMAS
24/08/67   Midfield

87/88	Arsenal	37	9		
88/89	Arsenal	37	7		
89/90	Arsenal	36	5		
90/91	Arsenal	31	2		
91/92	Arsenal	10	2	CC	2	-
	Liverpool	17	3		

★ England 2 caps, 0 goals

István KOZMA (Hun)
03/12/64   Midfield

87/88	Újpesti Dózsa SC (Hun)	30	2	CWC	2	-
88/89	Újpesti Dózsa SC (Hun)	29	5	UC	4	-
89/90	Girondins de Bordeaux (Fra)	-	-		
	Dunfermline Athletic (Sco)	33	6		
90/91	Dunfermline Athletic (Sco)	34	2		
91/92	Dunfermline Athletic (Sco)	23	-		
	Liverpool	5	-		

★ Hungary 29 caps, 1 goal

John BARNES
07/11/63   Midfield

87/88	Liverpool	38	15		
88/89	Liverpool	33	8		
89/90	Liverpool	34	22		
90/91	Liverpool	35	16		
91/92	Liverpool	12	1	UC	1	-

★ England 67 caps, 10 goals

Dean SAUNDERS (Wal)
21/06/64   Forward

87/88	Oxford United	37	12		
88/89	Oxford United	Div 2			
	Derby County	30	14		
89/90	Derby County	38	11		
90/91	Derby County	38	17		
91/92	Liverpool	36	10	UC	5	9

* Wales 33 caps, 10 goals

Mark WALTERS
12/01/61   Forward

87/88	Aston Villa	Div 2	

	Rangers (Sco)	18	7		
88/89	Rangers (Sco)	31	8	CWC	4	1
89/90	Rangers (Sco)	27	5	CC	2	1
90/91	Rangers (Sco)	30	12	CC	4	-
91/92	Liverpool	25	3	UC	5	1

★ England 1 cap, 0 goals

Ian RUSH (Wal)
20/10/61   Forward

87/88	Juventus (Ita)	29	8	UC	3	1
88/89	Liverpool	24	7		
89/90	Liverpool	36	18		
90/91	Liverpool	37	16		
91/92	Liverpool	18	3	UC	4	1

★ Wales 54 caps, 20 goals

Steve McMANAMAN
11/02/72   Forward

90/91	Liverpool	2	-		
91/92	Liverpool	30	5	UC	8	-

Ronny ROSENTHAL (Isr)
11/10/63   Forward

87/88	Club Brugge KV (Bel)	15	4	UC	8	-
88/89	R Standard Liège (Bel)	30	14		
89/90	R Standrad Liège (Bel)	14	6		
	Liverpool	8	7		
90/91	Liverpool	16	5		
91/92	Liverpool	20	3	UC	1	-

★ Israel

EUROPEAN HONOURS
Champions' Cup - (4) 1977, 1978, 1981, 1984.
UEFA Cup - (2) 1973, 1976.
Super Cup - (1) 1977.

EUROPEAN CUPS RECORD

	Entries	Pd	W	D	L	F	A
Champions' Cup	12	77	48	13	16	159	64
Cup-winners' Cup	**3**	**17**	**8**	**4**	**5**	**29**	**12**
UEFA/Fairs' Cup	7	54	32	9	13	106	38
Total - All 3 Cups	22	148	88	26	34	294	114

TPS

FIVE YEAR RECORD *Birthdate/Playing position*	LEAGUE Apps Gls	EURO CUPS Cup Apps Gls

Petri JAKONEN
09/06/67   Goalkeeper

87	Reipas	17	-	
88	Reipas	3	-	
89	HJK	25	-	CC 2 -
90	HJK	9	-	
91	Helsingborgs IF (Swe)	Div 2		

Tuomas BRUMMER
19/03/66   Goalkeeper

89	TuPa	Div 2
90	TuPa	Div 3
91	TuPa	Div 3

Ari HEIKKINEN
08/04/64   Defender

87	TPS	22	-	UC 4	-
88	TPS	26	1	UC 6	-
89	TPS	27	-		
90	TPS	12	-	UC 2	-
91	TPS	33	4		

★ Finland 32 caps, 0 goals

Esa JOHANSSON
01/05/67   Defender

87	TPS	19	-	UC 3	-
88	TPS	23	-	UC 6	-
89	TPS	19	-		
90	TPS	19	-	UC 2	-
91	TPS	25	-		

Juha LAAKSONEN
24/09/63   Defender

87	TPS	19	-	UC 4	-
88	TPS	13	-	UC 4	-
89	TPS	22	-		
90	TPS	19	-	UC 1	-
91	TPS	23	-		

★ Finland 6 caps, 0 goals

FIVE YEAR RECORD *Birthdate/Playing position*	LEAGUE Apps Gls	EURO CUPS Cup Apps Gls

Jyrki HÄNNIKÄINEN
30/03/65   Defender

87	FC Kuusysi	15	-		
88	TPS	26	-	UC 6	-
89	TPS	20	1		
90	TPS	10	-		
91	TPS	14	-		

Janne LEHTINEN
17/08/72   Defender

91	TPS	20	-

Petteri VILJANEN
22/01/72   Defender

90	TPS	1	-
91	TPS	16	-

Petri SULONEN
20/06/63   Defender

87	TPS	22	-	UC 4	-
88	TPS	26	2	UC 6	1
89	TPS	26	2		
90	TPS	25	1	UC 2	-
91	TPS	31	2		

★ Finland 9 caps, 0 goals

Kim LEHTONEN
10/02/73   Midfield

91	TPS	-	-

Mika AALTONEN
16/11/65   Midfield

87	TPS	20	8	UC 4	3
87/88	AC Bellinzona (Sui)	2	-		
88/89	Bologna (Ita)	3	-		
89/90	Hertha BSC (Ger)	Div 2			
90	TPS	11	2	UC 2	-
91	TPS	32	2		

★ Finland 6 caps, 0 goals

FINLAND

FIVE YEAR RECORD	LEAGUE		EURO CUPS		
Birthdate/Playing position	Apps	Gls	Cup	Apps	Gls

Juha HALONEN
29/06/63   Midfield

87	TPS	20	5	UC	4	-
88	TPS	25	-	UC	6	1
89	TPS	27	4			
90	TPS	25	4	UC	2	-
91	TPS	-	-			

Riku RISSANEN
24/10/69   Midfield

90	TPS	1	-
91	TPS	-	-

Tommi VIRTANEN
25/01/71   Midfield

91	TuPa	Div 3

Olli KANGASLAHTI
02/02/72   Forward

90	P-Iirot	Div 3
91	TPS	12	2

Mika LIPPONEN
09/05/64   Forward

87/88	FC Twente (Hol)	27	10
88/89	FC Twente (Hol)	24	3
89/90	FC Aarau (Sui)	7	2
90/91	FC Aarau (Sui)	13	-
91/92	FC Aarau (Sui)	6	-

★ Finland 47 caps, 11 goals

FIVE YEAR RECORD	LEAGUE		EURO CUPS		
Birthdate/Playing position	Apps	Gls	Cup	Apps	Gls

Marko RAJAMÄKI
03/10/68   Forward

87	TPS	21	4	UC	4	-
88	TPS	26	9	UC	6	1
89	TPS	27	11			
90	TPS	25	14	UC	2	-
91	TPS	33	10			

György KAJDY (Hun)
23/07/64   Forward

87/88	Ferencváros (Hun)	5	-
88/89	Budapesti Volán (Hun)	Div 2	
89/90	Budapesti Volán	Div 2	
90/91	Volán FC (Hun)	28	2
91/92	Volán FC	Div 2	

EUROPEAN HONOURS
none

EUROPEAN CUPS RECORD

	Entries	Pd	W	D	L	F	A
Champions' Cup	4	10	1	0	9	4	28
Cup-winners' Cup	none						
UEFA/Fairs' Cup	4	14	4	2	8	9	17
Total - All 3 Cups	8	24	5	2	17	13	45

AS MONACO

FIVE YEAR RECORD	LEAGUE		EURO CUPS		
Birthdate/Playing position	Apps	Gls	Cup	Apps	Gls

Jean-Luc ETTORI
29/07/58   Goalkeeper

87/88	AS Monaco	37	-			
88/89	AS Monaco	37	-	CC	6	-
89/90	AS Monaco	38	-	CWC	8	-
90/91	AS Monaco	38	-	UC	6	-
91/92	AS Monaco	34	-	+CWC	9	-

★ France 17 caps, 0 goals

Angelo HUGUES
03/09/66   Goalkeeper

87/88	AS Monaco	1	-	
88/89	AS Monaco	1	-	
89/90	AS Monaco	-	-	
90/91	AS Monaco	-	-	
91/92	AS Monaco	2	-	

John SIVEBAEK (Den)
25/10/61   Defender

87/88	AS Saint-Etienne	30	-			
88/89	AS Saint-Etienne	34	-			
89/90	AS Saint-Etienne	35	-			
90/91	AS Saint-Etienne	30	1			
91/92	AS Monaco	23	-	+CWC	2	-

★ Denmark 82 caps, 1 goal

Luc SONOR
15/09/62   Defender

87/88	AS Monaco	31	1			
88/89	AS Monaco	35	1	CC	6	1
89/90	AS Monaco	32	-	CWC	7	-
90/91	AS Monaco	29	1	UC	5	-
91/92	AS Monaco	32	-	+CWC	9	-

★ France 9 caps, 0 goals

Emmanuel PETIT
22/09/70   Defender

88/89	AS Monaco	9	-			
89/90	AS Monaco	28	-	CWC	7	-
90/91	AS Monaco	27	1	UC	5	-
91/92	AS Monaco	28	-	+CWC	7	-

★ France 4 caps, 0 goals

FIVE YEAR RECORD	LEAGUE		EURO CUPS		
Birthdate/Playing position	Apps	Gls	Cup	Apps	Gls

Franck DUMAS
09/01/68   Defender

87/88	SM Caen	Div 2		
88/89	SM Caen	38	3	
89/90	SM Caen	36	2	
90/91	SM Caen	38	2	
91/92	SM Caen	36	2	

Patrick VALERY
03/07/69   Defender

87/88	AS Monaco	11	-			
88/89	AS Monaco	28	-	CC	6	-
89/90	AS Monaco	19	-	CWC	4	-
90/91	AS Monaco	32	-	UC	6	-
91/92	AS Monaco	14	-	+CWC	5	1

Patrick REVELLES
20/09/68   Midfield

88/89	SC Toulon	10	1
89/90	SC Toulon	28	3
90/91	SC Toulon	27	6
91/92	SC Toulon	27	8

Christian PEREZ
13/05/63   Midfield

87/88	Montpellier PSC	32	12			
88/89	Paris-Saint-Germain FC	35	7			
89/90	Paris-Saint-Germain FC	33	1	UC	4	-
90/91	Paris-Saint-Germain FC	22	2			
91/92	Paris-Saint-Germain FC	37	12			

★ France 22 caps, 2 goals

Claude PUEL
02/09/61   Midfield

87/88	AS Monaco	33	-			
88/89	AS Monaco	17	1	CC	5	-
89/90	AS Monaco	35	-	CWC	7	-
90/91	AS Monaco	36	-	UC	4	-
91/92	AS Monaco	33	2	+CWC	8	-

FRANCE

FIVE YEAR RECORD	LEAGUE		EURO CUPS		
Birthdate/Playing position	Apps	Gls	Cup	Apps	Gls

RUI BARROS (Por)
24/11/65   Midfield

87/88	FC Porto (Por)	34	12	CC	4	-
88/89	Juventus (Ita)	29	12	UC	8	2
89/90	Juventus (Ita)	31	2	#UC	12	2
90/91	AS Monaco	34	7	UC	6	-
91/92	AS Monaco	34	6	+CWC	9	4

★ Portugal 23 caps, 1 goal

Marcel DIB
10/08/60   Midfield

87/88	AS Monaco	33	4			
88/89	AS Monaco	36	2	CC	3	-
89/90	AS Monaco	38	3	CWC	7	-
90/91	AS Monaco	35	1	UC	5	1
91/92	AS Monaco	32	-	+CWC	9	-

★ France 6 caps, 0 goals

Gérald PASSI
21/01/64   Midfield

87/88	Toulouse FC	21	8	UC	1	1
88/89	Toulouse FC	29	3			
89/90	Toulouse FC	26	8			
90/91	AS Monaco	29	4	UC	6	3
91/92	AS Monaco	30	6	+CWC	9	3

★ France 11 caps, 2 goals

Youri DJORKAEFF
09/03/68   Midfield

87/88	FC Grenoble	Div 2				
88/89	FC Grenoble	Div 2				
89/90	RC Strasbourg	Div 2				
90/91	RC Strasbourg	Div 2				
	AS Monaco	20	5			
91/92	AS Monaco	35	9	+CWC	6	1

Christophe ROBERT
30/03/64   Forward

87/88	FC Nantes	6	2			
88/89	FC Nantes	29	6			
89/90	FC Nantes	28	5			
90/91	FC Nantes	32	9			
91/92	AS Monaco	21	3	+CWC	3	1

FIVE YEAR RECORD	LEAGUE		EURO CUPS		
Birthdate/Playing position	Apps	Gls	Cup	Apps	Gls

Jürgen KLINSMANN (Ger)
30/07/64   Forward

87/88	VfB Stuttgart (Ger)	34	19			
88/89	VfB Stuttgart (Ger)	25	13	+UC	8	4
89/90	Internazionale (Ita)	31	13	CC	2	-
90/91	Internazionale (Ita)	33	14	#UC	12	3
91/92	Internazionale (Ita)	31	7	UC	1	-

★ Germany 41 caps, 10 goals

Youssouf FOFANA (Civ)
26/07/66   Forward

87/88	AS Monaco	23	6			
88/89	AS Monaco	25	7	CC	6	3
89/90	AS Monaco	30	-	CWC	4	-
90/91	AS Monaco	20	2	UC	1	-
91/92	AS Monaco	27	4	+CWC	7	1

★ Ivory Coast

Jérôme GNAKO
17/02/68   Forward

87/88	Girondins de Bordeaux	1	-			
88/89	Girondins de Bordeaux	4	-			
89/90	SCO Angers	Div 2				
90/91	SCO Angers	Div 2				
91/92	AS Monaco	21	3	+CWC	7	-

EUROPEAN HONOURS
none

EUROPEAN CUPS RECORD

	Entries	Pd	W	D	L	F	A
Champions' Cup	5	18	4	4	10	25	23
Cup-winners' Cup	5	23	7	11	5	31	26
UEFA/Fairs' Cup	4	14	6	2	6	23	23
Total - All 3 Cups	14	55	17	17	21	79	72

SV WERDER BREMEN

FIVE YEAR RECORD Birthdate/Playing position	LEAGUE Apps	Gls	EURO CUPS Cup	Apps	Gls

Oliver RECK
27/02/65　Goalkeeper

		Apps	Gls	Cup	Apps	Gls
87/88	SV Werder Bremen	32	-	UC	10	-
88/89	SV Werder Bremen	34	-	CC	6	-
89/90	SV Werder Bremen	32	-	UC	8	-
90/91	SV Werder Bremen	34	-			
91/92	SV Werder Bremen	33	-	#CWC	8	-

Hans Jürgen GRUNDELACH
29/11/63　Goalkeeper

		Apps	Gls
87/88	Eintracht Frankfurt	14	-
88/89	Eintracht Frankfurt	1	-
89/90	FC Homburg	34	-
90/91	FC Homburg	Div 2	
91/92	FC Homburg	Div 2	

Manfred BOCKENFELD
23/07/60　Defender

		Apps	Gls	Cup	Apps	Gls
87/88	SV Waldhof Mannheim	32	5			
88/89	SV Waldhof Mannheim	32	7			
89/90	SV Werder Bremen	30	2	UC	9	1
90/91	SV Werder Bremen	14	-			
91/92	SV Werder Bremen	25	-	#CWC	8	1

★ Germany 1 cap, 0 goals

Ulrich BOROWKA
19/05/62　Defender

		Apps	Gls	Cup	Apps	Gls
87/88	SV Werder Bremen	31	1	UC	8	-
88/89	SV Werder Bremen	28	1	CC	5	-
89/90	SV Werder Bremen	28	2	UC	10	-
90/91	SV Werder Bremen	32	1			
91/92	SV Werder Bremen	36	1	#CWC	8	-

★ Germany 6 caps, 0 goals

Rune BRATSETH (Nor)
19/03/61　Defender

		Apps	Gls	Cup	Apps	Gls
87/88	SV Werder Bremen	31	-	UC	10	-
88/89	SV Werder Bremen	32	5	CC	6	-
89/90	SV Werder Bremen	29	2	UC	10	-
90/91	SV Werder Bremen	31	1			
91/92	SV Werder Bremen	34	-	#CWC	8	2

★ Norway 42 caps, 4 goals

Dietmar BEIERSDORFER
16/11/63　Defender

		Apps	Gls	Cup	Apps	Gls
87/88	Hamburger SV	30	3	CWC	4	-
88/89	Hamburger SV	21	-			
89/90	Hamburger SV	31	3	UC	8	1
90/91	Hamburger SV	33	6			
91/92	Hamburger SV	34	1	UC	5	-

★ Germany 1 cap, 0 goals

Thomas SCHAAF
30/04/61　Defender

		Apps	Gls	Cup	Apps	Gls
87/88	SV Werder Bremen	29	2	UC	9	1
88/89	SV Werder Bremen	23	2	CC	4	1
89/90	SV Werder Bremen	19	-	UC	5	-
90/91	SV Werder Bremen	13	-			
91/92	SV Werder Bremen	17	-	#CWC	6	-

Thomas WOLTER
04/10/63　Defender

		Apps	Gls	Cup	Apps	Gls
87/88	SV Werder Bremen	16	-	UC	5	1
88/89	SV Werder Bremen	33	1	CC	5	1
89/90	SV Werder Bremen	22	-	UC	8	-
90/91	SV Werder Bremen	29	-			
91/92	SV Werder Bremen	26	1	#CWC	6	-

Dieter EILTS
13/12/64　Midfield

		Apps	Gls	Cup	Apps	Gls
87/88	SV Werder Bremen	2	-			
88/89	SV Werder Bremen	13	-			
89/90	SV Werder Bremen	31	1	UC	9	2
90/91	SV Werder Bremen	32	-			
91/92	SV Werder Bremen	37	1	#CWC	7	1

Andreas HERZOG (Aut)
10/09/68　Midfield

		Apps	Gls	Cup	Apps	Gls
87/88	SK Rapid Wien (Aut)	5	-			
	First Vienna FC (Aut)	7	3			
88/89	SK Rapid Wien (Aut)	34	8	CC	2	-
89/90	SK Rapid Wien (Aut)	27	8	UC	6	-
90/91	SK Rapid Wien (Aut)	30	6	UC	2	-
91/92	SK Rapid Wien (Aut)	33	11			

★ Austria 32 caps, 3 goals

GERMANY

FIVE YEAR RECORD *Birthdate/Playing position*	LEAGUE Apps	Gls	EURO CUPS Cup	Apps	Gls

Günter HERMANN
05/12/60   Midfield

		Apps	Gls	Cup	Apps	Gls
87/88	SV Werder Bremen	30	-	UC	9	-
88/89	SV Werder Bremen	34	-	CC	6	1
89/90	SV Werder Bremen	27	1	UC	7	1
90/91	SV Werder Bremen	29	1			
91/92	SV Werder Bremen	24	1	#CWC	6	-

★ Germany 2 caps, 0 goals

Thorsten LEGAT
07/11/68   Midfield

		Apps	Gls	Cup	Apps	Gls
87/88	VfL Bochum	17	1			
88/89	VfL Bochum	26	-			
89/90	VfL Bochum	28	1			
90/91	VfL Bochum	31	7			
91/92	SV Werder Bremen	25	2	#CWC	6	-

Mirko VOTAVA
25/04/56

		Apps	Gls	Cup	Apps	Gls
87/88	SV Werder Bremen	32	3	UC	10	-
88/89	SV Werder Bremen	33	1	CC	6	-
89/90	SV Werder Bremen	30	3	UC	10	-
90/91	SV Werder Bremen	31	2			
91/92	SV Werder Bremen	32	-	#CWC	8	1

★ Germany 5 caps, 0 goals

Klaus ALLOFS
05/12/56   Forward

		Apps	Gls	Cup	Apps	Gls
87/88	Olympique Marseille (Fra)	31	13	CWC	8	4
88/89	Olympique Marseille (Fra)	22	7			
89/90	Girondins de Bordeaux (Fra)	37	14			
90/91	SV Werder Bremen	30	10			
91/92	SV Werder Bremen	32	8	#CWC	6	2

★ Germany 56 caps, 17 goals

Marco BODE
23/07/69   Forward

		Apps	Gls	Cup	Apps	Gls
89/90	SV Werder Bremen	19	4	UC	4	2
90/91	SV Werder Bremen	25	3			
91/92	SV Werder Bremen	32	12	#CWC	9	3

Stefan KOHN
09/10/65   Forward

		Apps	Gls	Cup	Apps	Gls
87/88	Hannover 96	23	5			
88/89	Hannover 96	26	7			
89/90	VfL Bochum	29	6			
90/91	VfL Bochum	26	11			
91/92	SV Werder Bremen	26	6	#CWC	5	3

Frank NEUBARTH
29/07/62   Forward

		Apps	Gls	Cup	Apps	Gls
87/88	SV Werder Bremen	23	7	UC	6	4
88/89	SV Werder Bremen	27	13	CC	4	-
89/90	SV Werder Bremen	19	6	UC	8	3
90/91	SV Werder Bremen	23	5			
91/92	SV Werder Bremen	30	5	#CWC	7	3

★ Germany 1 cap, 0 goals

Wynton RUFER (Nzl)
29/12/62   Forward

		Apps	Gls	Cup	Apps	Gls
87/88	FC Aarau (Sui)	36	21			
88/89	Grasshopper-Club (Sui)	36	18	CWC	2	-
89/90	SV Werder Bremen	34	10	UC	10	4
90/91	SV Werder Bremen	33	15			
91/92	SV Werder Bremen	29	5	#CWC	8	4

★ New Zealand

EUROPEAN HONOURS
Cup-winners' Cup - (1) 1992.

EUROPEAN CUPS RECORD

	Entries	Pd	W	D	L	F	A
Champions' Cup	2	10	5	2	3	17	7
Cup-winners' Cup	2	13	9	2	2	28	10
UEFA/Fairs' Cup	7	36	17	8	11	65	42
Total - All 3 Cups	11	59	31	12	16	110	59

HANNOVER 96

FIVE YEAR RECORD	LEAGUE		EURO CUPS		
Birthdate/Playing position	Apps	Gls	Cup	Apps	Gls

Jörg SIEVERS
22/09/65   Goalkeeper

88/89	VfL Wolfsburg	Div 3				
89/90	Hannover 96	Div 2				
90/91	Hannover 96	Div 2				
91/92	Hannover 96	Div 2				

Carsten KRUSE
02/05/73   Goalkeeper

91/92	Hannover 96	-	-			

Roman WOJCICKI (Pol)
08/01/58   Defender

87/88	FC Homburg	29	2			
88/89	FC Homburg	Div 2				
89/90	Hannover 96	Div 2				
90/91	Hannover 96	Div 2				
91/92	Hannover 96	Div 2				

★ Poland 59 caps, 2 goals

Jörg-Uwe KLÜTZ
21/07/68   Defender

89/90	VfL Herzlake	Div 3				
90/91	Hannover 96	Div 2				
91/92	Hannover 96	Div 2				

Axel SUNDERMANN
23/01/68   Defender

88/89	Hannover 96	7	-			
89/90	Hannover 96	Div 2				
90/91	Hannover 96	Div 2				
91/92	Hannover 96	Div 2				

Bernd HEEMSOTH
10/10/66   Defender

88/89	VfB Oldenburg	Div 3				
89/90	Hannover 96	Div 2				
90/91	Hannover 96	Div 2				
91/92	Hannover 96	Div 2				

FIVE YEAR RECORD	LEAGUE		EURO CUPS		
Birthdate/Playing position	Apps	Gls	Cup	Apps	Gls

Matthias KUHLMEY
28/02/66   Defender

87/88	Hannover 96	28	-			
88/89	Hannover 96	26	1			
89/90	Hannover 96	Div 2				
90/91	Hannover 96	Div 2				
91/92	Hannover 96	Div 2				

Jörg KRETSCHMAR
09/12/64   Midfield

87/88	VfL Wolfsburg	Div 3				
88/89	Borussia Mönchengladbach	8	-			
89/90	SV Meppen	Div 2				
90/91	Hannover 96	Div 2				
91/92	Hannover 96	Div 2				

Reinhold DASCHNER
16/10/69   Midfield

89/90	FC Bayern München	-	-			
90/91	1.FC Köln	6	-			
91/92	1.FC Köln	-	-			

André SIROCKS
18/09/66   Midfield

87/88	1.FC Union Berlin	14	2			
88/89	1.FC Union Berlin	19	4			
89/90	1.FC Union Berlin	Div 2				
90/91	1.FC Union Berlin	Div 2				
91/92	1.FC Union Berlin	Div 3				

Michael SCHÖNBERG
19/01/67   Midfield

90	Esbjerg FB (Den)	Div 2				
90/91	Hannover 96	Div 2				
91/92	Hannover 96	Div 2				

Milos DJELMAS (Yug)
04/06/60   Forward

87/88	OGC Nice (Fra)	27	-			
88/89	OGC Nice (Fra)	27	1			
89/90	OGC Nice (Fra)	21	2			
91/92	Hannover 96	Div 2				

★ Yugoslavia 1 cap, 0 goals

GERMANY

FIVE YEAR RECORD *Birthdate/Playing position*	LEAGUE Apps Gls	EURO CUPS Cup Apps Gls

Martin GROTH
20/10/69   Midfield

87/88	Hannover 96	1	-
88/89	Hannover 96	16	2
89/90	Hannover 96	Div 2
90/91	Hannover 96	Div 2
91/92	Hannover 96	Div 2

Michael KOCH
27/09/69   Forward

89/90	FC Altona 93	Div 3
90/91	Hamburger SV	-	-
91/92	Hannover 96	Div 2

Niclas WEILAND
22/07/72   Forward

89/90	Hannover 96	Div 2
90/91	Hannover 96	Div 2
91/92	Hannover 96	Div 2

Reinhold MATHY
12/04/62   Forward

87/88	Bayer 05 Uerdingen	24	8
88/89	Bayer 05 Uerdingen	31	4
89/90	Bayer 05 Uerdingen	23	1
90/91	FC Wettingen (Sui)	7	2
91/92	FC Wettingen (Sui)	15	2

FIVE YEAR RECORD *Birthdate/Playing position*	LEAGUE Apps Gls	EURO CUPS Cup Apps Gls

Patrick GRÜN
20/03/68   Forward

89/90	VfL Marburg	Div 4
90/91	Hannover 96	Div 2
91/92	Hannover 96	Div 2

Uwe JURSCH
20/06/63   Forward

87/88	VfL Osnabrück	Div 2
88/89	VfL Osnabrück	Div 2
89/90	VfL Osnabrück	Div 2
90/91	VfL Osnabrück	Div 2
91/92	Hannover 96	Div 2

EUROPEAN HONOURS
none

EUROPEAN CUPS RECORD

	Entries	P	W	D	L	F	A
Champions' Cup	none						
Cup-winners' Cup	**none**						
UEFA/Fairs' Cup	7	21	6	3	12	30	50
Total - All 3 Cups	7	21	6	3	12	30	50

OLYMPIAKOS

FIVE YEAR RECORD	LEAGUE		EURO CUPS		
Birthdate/Playing position	Apps	Gls	Cup	Apps	Gls

Ilias TALIKRIADIS
10/07/65   Goalkeeper

87/88 Xanthi	Div 2				
Olympiakos	10	-			
88/89 Olympiakos	30	-			
89/90 Olympiakos	26	-	UC	5	-
90/91 Olympiakos	21	-	CWC	4	-
91/92 Olympiakos	33	-			

★ Greece 5 caps, 0 goals

Yorgos MIRTSOS
12/12/64   Goalkeeper

89/90 APS Patras	Div 4	
90/91 Panahaiki	30	-
91/92 Panahaiki	31	-

Theodoros PAHATOURIDIS
04/09/67   Defender

87/88 Doxa	Div 2				
Olympiakos	11	1			
88/89 Olympiakos	17	-			
89/90 Olympiakos	28	1	UC	4	-
90/91 Olympiakos	32	2	CWC	4	-
91/92 Olympiakos	25	2			

★ Greece 1 cap, 0 goals

Kiriakos KARATAIDIS
04/07/65   Defender

87/88 Kastoria	Div 2				
88/89 Olympiakos	26	1			
89/90 Olympiakos	30	-	UC	5	-
90/91 Olympiakos	32	-	CWC	4	-
91/92 Olympiakos	32	-			

★ Greece 7 caps, 0 goals

Sotiris MAVROMATIS
21/02/66   Defender

87/88 PAOK	25	5			
88/89 Olympiakos	7	-			
89/90 Olympiakos	27	1	UC	5	-
90/91 Olympiakos	31	7	CWC	4	-
91/92 Olympiakos	18	-			

★ Greece 1 caps, 0 goals

FIVE YEAR RECORD	LEAGUE		EURO CUPS		
Birthdate/Playing position	Apps	Gls	Cup	Apps	Gls

Mihalis VLAHOS
20/09/67   Defender

87/88 Apollon	Div 2	
88/89 Apollon	22	4
89/90 Apollon	29	6
90/91 Apollon	29	-
91/92 Olympiakos	27	1

Yorgos HRISTODOULOU (Cyp)
22/08/65   Defender

87/88 Omonia Nicosia (Cyp)	25	-	CC	4	-
88/89 Omonia Nicosia (Cyp)	27	5	CWC	2	-
89/90 Omonia Nicosia (Cyp)	24	1	CC	2	-
90/91 Olympiakos	24	2	CWC	3	1
91/92 Olympiakos	10	1			

★ Cyprus 14 caps, 1 goals

Yorgos MITSIBONAS
01/11/62   Defender

87/88 Larissa	25	8			
88/89 Larissa	29	5	CC	2	1
89/90 PAOK	32	2			
90/91 PAOK	32	1	UC	2	-
91/92 PAOK	31	-	UC	4	-

★ Greece 25 caps, 1 goal

Panayiotis TSALOUHIDIS
30/03/63   Midfield

87/88 Veria	9	3			
Olympiakos	17	1			
88/89 Olympiakos	30	4			
89/90 Olympiakos	33	6	UC	6	2
90/91 Olympiakos	31	8	CWC	4	-
91/92 Olympiakos	33	16			

★ Greece 44 caps, 9 goals

Ilias SAVVIDIS
03/11/67   Midfield

87/88 Panserraikos	29	8			
88/89 Olympiakos	15	1			
89/90 Olympiakos	22	2	UC	5	-
90/91 Olympiakos	8	2	CWC	1	-
91/92 Olympiakos	16	1			

★ Greece 6 caps, 0 goals

GREECE

FIVE YEAR RECORD	LEAGUE		EURO CUPS		
Birthdate/Playing position	Apps	Gls	Cup	Apps	Gls

Gennady LITOVCHENKO (Ukr)
11/09/63   Midfield

87	Dnepr Dnepropetrovsk (Urs)	28	6			
88	Dinamo Kiev (Urs)	29	7			
89	Dinamo Kiev (Urs)	29	7	UC	6	1
90	Dinamo Kiev (Urs)	24	6	CWC	4	3
90/91	Olympiakos	23	1			
91/92	Olympiakos	30	6			

★ USSR 57 caps, 14 goals

Vassilis KARAPIALIS
13/06/65   Midfield

87/88	Larissa	30	4			
88/89	Larissa	26	8	CC	2	1
89/90	Larissa	24	8		-	
90/91	Larissa	30	8			
91/92	Olympiakos	27	6			

★ Greece 17 caps, 2 goals

Nikos TSIANTAKIS
20/10/63   Midfield

87/88	Panionios	9	-	UC	2	-
	Olympiakos	17	3			
88/89	Olympiakos	30	4			
89/90	Olympiakos	30	3	UC	6	-
90/91	Olympiakos	28	2	CWC	4	-
91/92	Olympiakos	30	3			

★ Greece 32 caps, 2 goals

Savvas KOFIDIS
01/03/61   Midfield

87/88	Iraklis	29	2			
88/89	Olympiakos	16	2			
89/90	Olympiakos	26	3	UC	2	-
90/91	Olympiakos	33	4	CWC	4	-
91/92	Olympiakos	19	-			

★ Greece 57 caps, 1 goal

Minas HANTZIDIS
04/07/66   Midfield

87/88	Bayer 04 Leverkusen (Ger)	3	-	#UC	1	-
	Olympiakos	12	3			
88/89	Olympiakos	21	4			
89/90	Olympiakos	10	-	UC	3	-
90/91	Olympiakos	19	2	CWC	4	1
91/92	Olympiakos	25	2			

FIVE YEAR RECORD	LEAGUE		EURO CUPS		
Birthdate/Playing position	Apps	Gls	Cup	Apps	Gls

Daniel BATISTA (Hol)
09/09/64   Forward

87/88	Ethnikos	28	7			
88/89	Ethnikos	25	3			
89/90	AEK	29	15	CC	4	-
90/91	AEK	31	13			
91/92	AEK	30	10	UC	5	3

Oleg PROTASOV (Ukr)
14/02/64   Forward

87	Dnepr Dnepropetrovsk (Urs)	30	18			
88	Dinamo Kiev (Urs)	29	11			
89	Dinamo Kiev (Urs)	26	7	UC	3	1
90	Dinamo Kiev (Urs)	16	12			
90/91	Olympiakos	29	11			
91/92	Olympiakos	21	15			

★ USSR 68 caps, 29 goals

Apostolos SOFIANOPOULOS
12/12/66   Forward

87/88	Panserraikos	9	1			
	Olympiakos	13	1			
88/89	Olympiakos	17	3			
89/90	Olympiakos	8	-			
90/91	Olympiakos	13	7	CWC	1	-
91/92	Olympiakos	14	5			

★ Greece 2 caps, 1 goals

EUROPEAN HONOURS
none

EUROPEAN CUPS RECORD

	Entries	Pd	W	D	L	F	A
Champions' Cup	11	28	7	6	15	25	43
Cup-winners' Cup	**8**	**27**	**12**	**4**	**11**	**37**	**42**
UEFA/Fairs' Cup	7	22	9	5	8	24	31
Total - All 3 Cups	26	77	28	15	34	86	116

FEYENOORD

FIVE YEAR RECORD	LEAGUE		EURO CUPS		
Birthdate/Playing position	Apps	Gls	Cup	Apps	Gls

Ed DE GOEY
20/12/66   Goalkeeper

87/88	Sparta	34	-			
88/89	Sparta	31	-			
89/90	Sparta	34	-			
90/91	Feyenoord	34	-			
91/92	Feyenoord	34	-	CWC	8	-

Harold WAPENAAR
10/04/70   Goalkeeper

91/92	Feyenoord	-	-

John DE WOLF
10/12/62   Defender

87/88	FC Groningen	30	1			
88/89	FC Groningen	23	2	UC	5	-
89/90	Feyenoord	-	-			
90/91	Feyenoord	22	-			
91/92	Feyenoord	22	2	CWC	6	-

★ Holland 1 cap, 0 goals

Henk FRÄSER
07/07/66   Defender

87/88	FC Utrecht	28	2	UC	4	-
88/89	Roda JC	31	3	CWC	6	-
89/90	Roda JC	27	3			
90/91	Feyenoord	23	2			
91/92	Feyenoord	26	6	CWC	8	-

★ Holland 5 caps, 0 goals

Ruud HEUS
24/02/61   Defender

87/88	Feyenoord	25	1	UC	4	1
88/89	Feyenoord	29	-			
89/90	Feyenoord	29	-			
90/91	Feyenoord	19	-			
91/92	Feyenoord	30	1	CWC	8	-

John METGOD
27/02/58   Defender

87/88	Tottenham Hotspur (Eng)	12	-			
88/89	Feyenoord	30	3			
89/90	Feyenoord	27	4	UC	2	-
90/91	Feyenoord	32	-			
91/92	Feyenoord	34	3	CWC	8	-

★ Holland 21 caps, 4 goals

Erol REFOS
19/03/70   Defender

87/88	Excelsior	Div 2				
88/89	Excelsior	Div 2				
89/90	SVV	Div 2				
90/91	SVV	16	-			
91/92	SVV/Dordrecht '90	28	-			

Ulrich VAN GOBBEL
16/01/71   Defender

88/89	Willem II	16	3			
89/90	Willem II	18	-			
	Feyenoord	2	-			
90/91	Feyenoord	19	-			
91/92	Feyenoord	20	1	CWC	5	-

Orlando TRUSTFULL
04/08/70   Defender

89/90	Haarlem	15	-			
90/91	SVV	28	-			
91/92	SVV/Dordrecht '90	22	1			

Arnold SCHOLTEN
05/12/62   Midfield

87/88	Ajax	18	2	+CWC	7	-
88/89	Ajax	28	2	UC	2	-
89/90	Ajax	6	-			
	Feyenoord	16	2			
90/91	Feyenoord	33	1			
91/92	Feyenoord	33	1	CWC	8	-

HOLLAND

FIVE YEAR RECORD	LEAGUE		EURO CUPS		
Birthdate/Playing position	Apps	Gls	Cup	Apps	Gls

Peter BOSZ
21/11/63   Midfield

87/88	RKC	Div 2			
88/89	SC Toulon (Fra)	24	•	-	
89/90	SC Toulon (Fra)	34		-	
90/91	SC Toulon (Fra)	35		-	
91/92	Feyenoord	33	1	CWC	6	1

★ Holland 6 caps, 0 goals

Rob WITSCHGE
22/08/66   Midfield

87/88	Ajax	32	3	CWC	8	2
88/89	Ajax	30	7	UC	2	-
89/90	AS Saint-Etienne (Fra)	38	9			
90/91	AS Saint-Etienne (Fra)	13	2			
	Feyenoord	19	2			
91/92	Feyenoord	31	1	CWC	8	2

★ Holland 12 caps, 1 goal

Dean GORRÉ
10/09/70   Midfield

87/88	SVV	Div 2	
88/89	SVV	Div 2	
89/90	SVV	Div 2	
90/91	SVV	16	1
91/92	SVV/Dordrecht '90	32	8

Regi BLINKER
04/06/69   Forward

87/88	Feyenoord	24	2	UC	5	1
88/89	BVV Den Bosch	25	6			
	Feyenoord	1	-			
89/90	Feyenoord	31	2	UC	2	-
90/91	Feyenoord	26	1			
91/92	Feyenoord	28	5	CWC	8	-

Mike OBIKOU (Nig)
24/09/68   Forward

89/90	Anorthosis Famagusta (Cyp)	24	6			
90/91	Anorthosis Famagusta (Cyp)	21	11			
91/92	Anorthosis Famagusta (Cyp)	24	16	UC	2	2

FIVE YEAR RECORD	LEAGUE		EURO CUPS		
Birthdate/Playing position	Apps	Gls	Cup	Apps	Gls

Marian DAMASCHIN (Rom)
01/05/61   Forward

87/88	Dinamo Bucuresti (Rom)	11	3	CWC	2	-
	Victoria Bucuresti (Rom)	15	8			
88/89	Victoria Bucuresti (Rom)	27	9	UC	8	-
89/90	Dinamo Bucuresti (Rom)	5	1	CWC	1	-
90/91	Dinamo Bucuresti (Rom)	32	15	CC	4	1
91/92	Feyenoord	29	9	CWC	5	1

★ Romania 5 caps, 0 goals

József KIPRICH (Hun)
06/09/63   Forward

87/88	Tatabánya (Hun)	24	14			
88/89	Tatabánya (Hun)	22	10	UC	2	-
89/90	Feyenoord	23	5	UC	2	-
90/91	Feyenoord	25	7			
91/92	Feyenoord	23	9	CWC	6	1

★ Hungary 54 caps, 22 goals

Gaston TAUMENT
01/10/70   Forward

88/89	Feyenoord	1	-		
89/90	Feyenoord	2	-		
	Excelsior	Div 2			
90/91	Feyenoord	29	3		
91/92	Feyenoord	32	7	CWC	8	-

★ Holland 1 cap, 0 goals

EUROPEAN HONOURS
Champions' Cup - (1) 1970.
UEFA Cup - (1) 1974.

EUROPEAN CUPS RECORD

	Entries	Pd	W	D	L	F	A
Champions' Cup	8	39	20	10	9	90	41
Cup-winners' Cup	2	16	8	6	2	23	13
UEFA/Fairs' Cup	12	58	30	9	19	110	71
Total - All 3 Cups	22	113	58	25	30	223	125

ÚJPESTI TE

FIVE YEAR RECORD Birthdate/Playing position	LEAGUE Apps	Gls	EURO CUPS Cup	Apps	Gls
István BROCKHAUSER					
03/05/64 Goalkeeper					
87/88 Váci Izzó MTE	30	-			
88/89 Újpesti Dózsa SC	25	-	UC	3	-
89/90 Újpesti Dózsa SC	30	-			
90/91 Újpesti TE	30	-	CC	2	-
91/92 Újpesti TE	30	-			
★ Hungary 8 caps, 0 goals					

Vilmos BORSOS
16/11/67   Goalkeeper

91/92 Újpesti TE	-	-			

János TOMKA
31/01/67   Defender

87/88 Pécsi MSC	5	-			
88/89 Pécsi MSC	9	-			
89/90 Pécsi MSC	6	1			
90/91 Pécsi MSC	18	-	CWC	1	-
91/92 Újpesti TE	21	-			

Zoltán ACZÉL
13/03/67   Defender

87/88 Újpesti Dózsa SC	1	-			
88/89 Siófok	19	-			
89/90 Siófok	28	-			
90/91 Siófok	14	1			
91/92 Daewoo Royals (Kor)					
Újpesti TE	13	-			
★ Hungary 2 caps, 0 goals					

Tamás SZÖNYI
23/07/72   Defender

90/91 Újpesti TE	16	-			
91/92 Újpesti TE	16	-			

Zoltán SZLEZÁK
26/12/67   Defender

87/88 Újpesti Dózsa SC	8	-			
88/89 Újpesti Dózsa SC	18	-	UC	3	-
89/90 Újpesti Dózsa SC	28	-			
90/91 Újpesti TE	29	4	CC	2	-
91/92 Újpesti TE	28	2			

FIVE YEAR RECORD Birthdate/Playing position	LEAGUE Apps	Gls	EURO CUPS Cup	Apps	Gls
Zoltán KECSKÉS					
24/11/65 Defender					
87/88 Újpesti Dózsa SC	18	-	CWC	2	-
88/89 Újpesti Dózsa SC	18	-	UC	2	-
89/90 Újpesti Dózsa SC	3	-			
90/91 Újpesti TE	15	5	CC	2	-
Volán FC	10	-			
91/92 MTK-VM	28	-			
★ Hungary 1 cap, 0 goals					

János TÓTH
13/11/70   Defender

90/91 Újpesti TE	4	-			
91/92 Újpesti TE	4	-			

Imre MILISITS
31/10/70   Defender

91/92 Újpesti TE	7	-			

Zoltán MIOVECZ
09/09/67   Midfield

87/88 Kaposvári Rákóczi SC	3	1			
88/89 Rákóczi FC	Div 2				
89/90 Újpesti Dózsa SC	24	3			
90/91 Újpesti TE	25	2	CC	2	-
91/92 Újpesti TE	30	5			

György VÉBER
25/07/69   Midfield

88/89 Újpesti Dózsa SC	4	-			
89/90 Újpesti Dózsa SC	8	1			
90/91 Újpesti TE	10	-	CC	1	-
91/92 Újpesti TE	29	3			

Zoltán BALÁZS
11/04/70   Midfield

90/91 Újpesti TE	5	-	CC	1	-
91/92 Újpesti TE	18	1			

HUNGARY

FIVE YEAR RECORD *Birthdate/Playing position*	LEAGUE Apps Gls	EURO CUPS Cup Apps Gls

Attila VARGA
06/06/69   Midfield

89/90	Újpesti Dózsa SC	6	-	
90/91	Újpesti TE	11	-	CC 2 -
91/92	Újpesti TE	4	-	

Sándor BÁCSI
26/11/69   Forward

87/88	Budapesti Volán SC	Div 2		
88/89	Újpesti Dózsa SC	8	4	
89/90	Újpesti Dózsa SC	22	8	
90/91	Újpesti TE	14	3	CC 1 -
91/92	Újpesti TE	20	3	

★ Hungary 2 caps, 0 goals

Petr KASPAR (Tch)
26/06/60   Midfield

87/88	DAC Dunajská Streda (Tch)	21	1	CWC 4 1
88/89	DAC Dunajská Streda (Tch)	29	6	UC 4 -
89/90	DAC Dunajská Streda (Tch)	29	1	
90/91	DAC Dunajská Streda (Tch)	27	-	
90/91	Újpesti TE	20	-	

Tamás TIEFENBACH
25/12/72   Midfield

91/92	Újpesti TE	17	1

Ferenc LOVÁSZ
24/01/67   Forward

87/88	Pécsi MSC	21	5	
88/89	Pécsi MSC	17	2	
89/90	Pécsi MSC	27	8	
90/91	Pécsi MSC	25	5	CWC 2 -
91/92	Újpesti TE	15	1	

★ Hungary 1 cap, 0 goals

Dénes ESZENYI
09/01/68   Forward

87/88	Újpesti Dózsa SC	8	1	
88/89	Újpesti Dózsa SC	11	3	UC 2 -
89/90	Újpesti Dózsa SC	19	4	
90/91	Újpesti TE	17	6	CC 2 -
91/92	Újpesti TE	29	12	

★ Hungary 9 caps, 0 goals

EUROPEAN HONOURS
none

EUROPEAN CUPS RECORD

	Entries	Pd	W	D	L	F	A
Champions' Cup	10	40	17	8	15	65	63
Cup-winners' Cup	5	25	11	4	10	50	38
UEFA/Fairs' Cup	10	44	19	6	19	79	66
Total - All 3 Cups	25	109	47	18	44	194	167

VALUR

FIVE YEAR RECORD	LEAGUE		EURO CUPS		
Birthdate/Playing position	Apps	Gls	Cup	Apps	Gls

Bjarni SIGURDSSON
16/10/60   Goalkeeper

87	SK Brann (Nor)	21	-			
88	SK Brann (Nor)	21	-			
89	Valur	18	-	CWC	2	-
90	Valur	17	-			
91	Valur	18	-	CWC	2	-

★ Iceland 4 caps, 0 goals

Saevar Thór GYLFASON
21/05/69   Goalkeeper

Jón S. HELGASON
05/02/69   Defender

90	Leiftur	Div 2				
91	Valur	10	-	CWC	2	-

Bergthór MAGNÚSSON
29/12/62   Defender

88	Valur	2	-	
89	Arvallur	Div 4		
90	Valur	11	1	
91	Skallagrimur	Div 3		

Einar Páll TÓMASSON
18/10/68   Defender

88	Valur	6	-			
89	Valur	17	-	CWC	2	-
90	Valur	17	-			
91	Valur	17	-	CWC	2	-

★ Iceland 4 caps, 0 goals

Saevar JÓNSSON
22/07/58   Defender

87	Valur	18	-	UC	2	-
88	Valur	12	3	CC	2	-
89	Valur	18	4	CWC	2	-
90	Valur	17	4			
91	Valur	18	2	CWC	2	-

★ Iceland 66 caps, 1 goal

Magni Blöndal PÉTURSSON
19/03/57   Midfield

87	Valur	16	4	UC	2	-
88	Valur	18	1	CC	2	-
89	Valur	18	1	CWC	2	-
90	Valur	18	-			
91	Valur	16	-			

Ágúst GYLFASON
01/08/71   Midfield

90	Valur	7	1
91	Valur	16	-

Steinar ADÓLFSSON
25/01/70   Midfield

88	Valur	8	1	CC	1	-
89	Valur	12	1	CWC	2	-
90	Valur	14	1			
91	Valur	18	2	CWC	2	-

★ Iceland 1 cap, 0 goals

Izudin DERVIC (Slo)
22/02/63   Midfield

89/90	Olimpija Ljubljana (Yug)	6	-
90	Selfoss	Div 2	
91	FH	17	1

Gunnlaugur EINARSSON
05/01/70   Midfield

88	Valur	1	-			
89	Valur	7	1			
90	Grindavík	Div 2				
91	Valur	13	1	CWC	2	1

Amaldur LOFTSSON
21/06/70   Midfield

90	Valur	5	-			
91	Valur	9	-	CWC	2	-

ICELAND

| FIVE YEAR RECORD | LEAGUE | | EURO CUPS | | |
| Birthdate/Playing position | Apps | Gls | Cup | Apps | Gls |

Antony Karl GREGORY
06/07/66 Forward

87	Valur	7	-			
88	KA	18	6			
89	KA	18	8			
90	Valur	18	8			
91	Valur	13	5	CWC	2	-

★ Iceland 5 caps, 2 goals

Jón Grétar JÓNSSON
25/02/66 Forward

87	Valur	18	2	UC	2	1
88	Valur	11	3	CC	1	-
89	KA	17	3			
90	KA	18	2	CC	2	-
91	Valur	18	7	CWC	2	-

Baldur BRAGASON
29/05/68 Forward

88	Valur	2	-			
89	Valur	10	1	CWC	1	-
90	Valur	18	1			
91	Valur	18	3	CWC	2	-

★ Iceland 1 cap, 0 goals

Salih PORCA (Yug)
30/11/65 Forward

90	Selfoss	Div 2				-
91	Selfoss	Div 2				

| FIVE YEAR RECORD | LEAGUE | | EURO CUPS | | |
| Birthdate/Playing position | Apps | Gls | Cup | Apps | Gls |

Arnljótur DAVÍDSSON
03/09/68 Forward

87	Fram	11	-	CC	1	-
88	Fram	17	6	CWC	2	-
89	Fram	3	1			
90	Fram	7	1			
91	ÍBV	18	5			

★ Iceland 3 caps, 0 goals

Gunnar GUNNARSSON
16/11/72 Forward

91	Valur	5	2			

EUROPEAN HONOURS
none

EUROPEAN CUPS RECORD

	Entries	Pd	W	D	L	F	A
Champions' Cup	7	16	2	3	11	9	50
Cup-winners' Cup	5	10	0	3	7	6	29
UEFA/Fairs' Cup	4	8	1	3	4	4	15
Total - All 3 Cups	16	34	3	9	22	19	94

PARMA

FIVE YEAR RECORD	LEAGUE		EURO CUPS		
Birthdate/Playing position	Apps	Gls	Cup	Apps	Gls

Claudio TAFFAREL (Bra)
08/05/66   Goalkeeper

89/90	Internacional Porto Alegre (Bra)					
90/91	Parma	34	-			
91/92	Parma	34	-	UC	2	-
★ Brazil						

Marco BALLOTTA
03/04/64   Goalkeeper

87/88	Modena	Div 2	
88/89	Modena	Div 3	
89/90	Modena	Div 3	
90/91	Modena	Div 2	
	Cesena	5	-
91/92	Parma	-	-

Lorenzo MINOTTI
08/02/67   Defender

87/88	Cesena		-	-		
	Parma	Div 2				
88/89	Parma	Div 2				
89/90	Parma	Div 2				
90/91	Parma	33	4			
91/92	Parma	33	4	UC	2	-

Luigi APOLLONI
02/05/67   Defender

87/88	Parma	Div 2				
88/89	Parma	Div 2				
89/90	Parma	Div 2				
90/91	Parma	32	-			
91/92	Parma	32	-	UC	2	-

Georges GRÜN (Bel)
25/01/62   Defender

87/88	RSC Anderlecht (Bel)	33	2	CC	6	-
88/89	RSC Anderlecht (Bel)	30	4	CWC	4	-
89/90	RSC Anderlecht (Bel)	23	4	+CWC	7	-
90/91	Parma	33	2			
91/92	Parma	33	4	UC	2	-
★ Belgium 60 caps, 3 goals						

Antonio BENARRIVO
21/08/68   Defender

87/88	Brindisi	Div 3				
88/89	Brindisi	Div 3				
89/90	Padova	Div 2				
90/91	Padova	Div 2				
91/92	Parma	30	-	UC	2	-

Salvatore MATRECANO
05/10/70   Defender

90/91	Turris	Div 4	
91/92	Foggia	28	-

Alberto DI CHIARA
29/03/64   Defender

87/88	Fiorentina	28	3			
88/89	Fiorentina	31	1			
89/90	Fiorentina	21	2			
90/91	Fiorentina	27	2			
91/92	Parma	31	1	UC	1	-
★ Italy 2 caps, 0 goals						

Gabriele PIN
21/01/62   Midfield

87/88	Lazio	Div 2	
88/89	Lazio	27	2
89/90	Lazio	31	6
90/91	Lazio	32	2
91/92	Lazio	32	1

Fausto PIZZI
21/07/67   Midfield

87/88	Vicenza	Div 3				
88/89	Vicenza	Div 3				
89/90	Parma	Div 2				
90/91	Internazionale	27	3	#UC	7	-
91/92	Internazionale	12	3	UC	1	-

ITALY

FIVE YEAR RECORD *Birthdate/Playing position*	LEAGUE Apps Gls	EURO CUPS Cup Apps Gls

Ivo PULGA
20/06/64   Midfield

87/88	Cagliari	Div 3			
88/89	Cagliari	Div 3			
89/90	Cagliari	Div 2			
90/91	Cagliari	30	-		
91/92	Parma	15	-	UC 2	-

Daniele ZORATTO
15/11/61   Midfield

87/88	Brescia	Div 2			
88/89	Brescia	Div 2			
89/90	Parma	Div 2			
90/91	Parma	32	-		
91/92	Parma	32	-		

Stefano CUOGHI
08/08/59   Midfield

87/88	Pisa	24	1		
88/89	Pisa	26	-		
89/90	Pisa	Div 2			
90/91	Parma	29	-		
91/92	Parma	31	1	UC 2	-

Tomas BROLIN (Swe)
29/11/69   Forward

87	GIF Sundsvall (Swe)	13	3		
88	GIF Sundsvall (Swe)	21	6		
89	GIF Sundsvall (Swe)	21	4		
90	IFK Norrköping (Swe)	9	7		
90/91	Parma	33	7		
91/92	Parma	34	4	UC 2	-

★ Sweden 20 caps, 12 goals

Marco OSIO
13/01/66   Forward

87/88	Parma	Div 2			
88/89	Parma	Div 2			
89/90	Parma	Div 2			
90/91	Parma	30	6		
91/92	Parma	25	2	UC 1	-

FIVE YEAR RECORD *Birthdate/Playing position*	LEAGUE Apps Gls	EURO CUPS Cup Apps Gls

Alessandro MELLI
11/12/69   Forward

87/88	Parma	Div 2			
88/89	Modena	Div 3			
	Parma	Div 2			
89/90	Parma	Div 2			
90/91	Parma	29	13		
91/92	Parma	30	6	UC 2	-

Sergio Angel BERTI (Arg)
17/02/69   Forward

91/92	River Plate (Arg)	

★ Argentina

Faustino ASPRILLA (Col)
10/11/69   Forward

91/92	Nacional Medellín (Col)	

★ Colombia

EUROPEAN HONOURS
none

EUROPEAN CUPS RECORD

	Entries	Pd	W	D	L	F	A
Champions' Cup	none						
Cup-winners' Cup	**none**						
UEFA/Fairs' Cup	1	2	0	2	0	1	1
Total - All 3 Cups	1	2	0	2	0	1	1

AVENIR BEGGEN

FIVE YEAR RECORD	LEAGUE		EURO CUPS		
Birthdate/Playing position	Apps	Gls	Cup	Apps	Gls

Paul KOCH
07/06/66   Goalkeeper

		Apps	Gls	Cup	Apps	Gls
87/88	Avenir Beggen	27	-	CWC	2	-
88/89	Red Boys Differdange	28	-			
89/90	Red Boys Differdange	28	-			
90/91	Red Boys Differdange	29	-			
91/92	Avenir Beggen	25	-			

★ Luxembourg 2 caps, 0 goals

Georges EIDEN
02/05/68   Goalkeeper

		Apps	Gls	Cup	Apps	Gls
90/91	Avenir Beggen	3	-	UC	2	-
91/92	Avenir Beggen	3	-			

Ralph FERRON
13/05/72   Defender

		Apps	Gls			
89/90	Etzella Ettelbrück	Div 2				
90/91	Etzella Ettelbrück	Div 2				
91/92	Avenir Beggen	25	1			

Rolf JENTGEN
17/09/62   Defender

		Apps	Gls	Cup	Apps	Gls
87/88	Avenir Beggen	24	-	CWC	2	-
88/89	Avenir Beggen	25	-	CWC	2	-
89/90	Avenir Beggen	22	-			
90/91	Avenir Beggen	20	-	UC	2	-
91/92	Avenir Beggen	27	-			

Jean VANEK
19/01/69   Defender

		Apps	Gls			
88/89	Etzella Ettelbrück	Div 2				
89/90	Etzella Ettelbrück	Div 2				
90/91	Etzella Ettelbrück	Div 2				
91/92	Avenir Beggen	25	1			

Alex WILHELM
30/04/68   Defender

		Apps	Gls	Cup	Apps	Gls
87/88	Avenir Beggen	28	2			
88/89	Avenir Beggen	23	1	CWC	2	-
89/90	Avenir Beggen	27	1			
90/91	Avenir Beggen	18	1	UC	1	-
91/92	Avenir Beggen	22	1			

Frank GOERGEN
27/07/68   Midfield

		Apps	Gls	Cup	Apps	Gls
87/88	Aris Bonnevoie	22	9			
88/89	Avenir Beggen	17	3	CWC	2	-
89/90	Avenir Beggen	27	4			
90/91	Avenir Beggen	28	7	UC	2	-
91/92	Avenir Beggen	28	2			

★ Luxembourg 1 cap, 0 goals

Serge JENTGEN
28/01/62   Midfield

		Apps	Gls	Cup	Apps	Gls
87/88	Avenir Beggen	27	8			.
88/89	Avenir Beggen	26	1	CWC	1	-
89/90	Avenir Beggen	23	-			
90/91	Avenir Beggen	22	1	UC	2	-
91/92	Avenir Beggen	24	-			

Jaba MOREIRA
02/10/68   Midfield

		Apps	Gls	Cup	Apps	Gls
90/91	Avenir Beggen	19	-	UC	2	-
91/92	Avenir Beggen	15	2			

Théo SCHOLTEN
04/01/63   Midfield

		Apps	Gls	Cup	Apps	Gls
87/88	Jeunesse Esch	28	9			
88/89	Jeunesse Esch	27	21	CC	2	-
89/90	Jeunesse Esch	28	12	UC	2	-
90/91	Avenir Beggen	27	7	UC	2	-
91/92	Avenir Beggen	28	8			

★ Luxembourg 21 caps, 0 goals

Carlo WEIS
04/12/58   Midfield

		Apps	Gls	Cup	Apps	Gls
87/88	Spora Luxembourg	26	7			
88/89	FC Thionville (Fra)	Div 4				
89/90	Avenir Beggen	27	9			
90/91	Avenir Beggen	27	6	UC	2	-
91/92	Avenir Beggen	28	3			

★ Luxembourg 63 caps, 1 goal

LUXEMBOURG

FIVE YEAR RECORD *Birthdate/Playing position*	LEAGUE Apps Gls	EURO CUPS Cup Apps Gls

Luc HOLTZ
14/06/69   Midfield

88/89	FC Montceau (Fra)	Div 3				
89/90	Red Boys Differdange	24	10			
90/91	Red Boys Differdange	29	7			
91/92	Red Boys Differdange	27	18			

★ Luxembourg 3 caps, 0 goals

Eugenio CABRAL
13/02/61   Forward

90/91	Avenir Beggen	5	-			
91/92	Avenir Beggen	7	1			

Markus KRAHEN
11/03/65   Forward

87/88	Borussia M'gladbach (Ger)	-	-			
88/89	Avenir Beggen	27	21	CWC	2	-
89/90	Avenir Beggen	28	30			
90/91	Avenir Beggen	20	6	UC	2	2
91/92	Avenir Beggen	28	19			

Armin KRINGS
22/11/62   Forward

87/88	Avenir Beggen	26	20			
88/89	Avenir Beggen	28	21	CWC	2	1
89/90	Avenir Beggen	19	17			
90/91	Avenir Beggen	26	12	UC	1	-
91/92	Avenir Beggen	28	12			

★ Luxembourg 14 caps, 1 goal

FIVE YEAR RECORD *Birthdate/Playing position*	LEAGUE Apps Gls	EURO CUPS Cup Apps Gls

Mario NOVAK
14/05/68   Forward

87/88	Olympique Eischen	22	8			
88/89	Olympique Eischen	14	-			
89/90	Olympique Eischen	Div 2				
90/91	Avenir Beggen	17	5			
91/92	Avenir Beggen	23	2			

Joey MATTGEN
29/12/70   Forward

91/92	Avenir Beggen	1	-			

Gilles GRICCA
22/05/73   Forward

EUROPEAN HONOURS
none

EUROPEAN CUPS RECORD

	Entries	Pd	W	D	L	F	A
Champions' Cup	4	8	0	0	8	0	44
Cup-winners' Cup	4	8	0	0	8	4	36
UEFA/Fairs' Cup	3	6	1	0	5	2	22
Total - All 3 Cups	11	22	1	0	21	6	102

HAMRUN SPARTANS

Ian LEIGH (Eng)
11/06/62   Goalkeeper

FIVE YEAR RECORD *Birthdate/Playing position*	LEAGUE Apps	Gls	EURO CUPS Cup	Apps	Gls
87/88 Hamrun Spartans	14	-	CC	2	-
88/89 Hamrun Spartans	16	-	CC	2	-
89/90 Hamrun Spartans	15	-	CWC	2	-
90/91 Hamrun Spartans	14	5			
91/92 Hamrun Spartans	9	1	CC	2	-

Anthony MALLIA
31/01/72   Goalkeeper

	Apps	Gls		Apps	Gls
89/90 Valletta	1	-			
90/91 Hamrun Spartans	-	-			
91/92 Hamrun Spartans	10	-			

Alex AZZOPARDI
24/03/61   Defender

	Apps	Gls		Apps	Gls
87/88 Hamrun Spartans	13	-	CC	1	-
88/89 Hamrun Spartans	16	-	CC	2	-
89/90 Hamrun Spartans	11	-	CWC	2	-
90/91 Hamrun Spartans	15	1			
91/92 Hamrun Spartans	10	-	CC	2	-

★ Malta 43 caps, 0 goals

Marco GRECH
28/10/62   Defender

	Apps	Gls		Apps	Gls
87/88 Hamrun Spartans	14	-	CC	2	-
88/89 Hamrun Spartans	15	-	CC	2	-
89/90 Hamrun Spartans	16	-	CWC	2	-
90/91 Hamrun Spartans	15	-			
91/92 Hamrun Spartans	16	-	CC	2	-

John MICALLEF
17/12/62   Defender

	Apps	Gls		Apps	Gls
87/88 Hamrun Spartans	14	-	CC	2	-
88/89 Hamrun Spartans	15	3	CC	2	-
89/90 Hamrun Spartans	16	1	CWC	2	-
90/91 Hamrun Spartans	5	-			
91/92 Hamrun Spartans	16	2	CC	2	-

★ Malta 1 cap, 0 goals

Ivan ZAMMIT
17/03/72   Defender

FIVE YEAR RECORD *Birthdate/Playing position*	LEAGUE Apps	Gls	EURO CUPS Cup	Apps	Gls
88/89 Valletta	12	1			
89/90 Floriana	11	-			
90/91 Hamrun Spartans	16	3			
91/92 Hamrun Spartans	18	-	CC	1	-

David CAMILLERI
1970   Defender

	Apps	Gls		Apps	Gls
91/92 Hamrun Spartans	8	-			

Joe BRINCAT
05/03/70   Midfield

	Apps	Gls		Apps	Gls
87/88 Hamrun Spartans	14	-	CC	2	-
88/89 Hamrun Spartans	10	4	CC	2	-
89/90 Hamrun Spartans	-	-			
90/91 Hamrun Spartans	15	4			
91/92 Hamrun Spartans	17	6	CC	2	-

★ Malta 22 caps, 2 goals

James CUTAJAR
07/07/72   Midfield

	Apps	Gls		Apps	Gls
89/90 Hamrun Spartans	5	-			
90/91 Hamrun Spartans	6	-			
91/92 Hamrun Spartans	2	-			

Noel FENECH
30/08/68   Midfield

	Apps	Gls		Apps	Gls
87/88 Hamrun Spartans	6	-			
88/89 Hamrun Spartans	11	1			
89/90 Hamrun Spartans	14	-	CWC	2	-
90/91 Hamrun Spartans	12	1			
91/92 Hamrun Spartans	13	-	CC	1	-

Brian MUNDEE (Eng)
12/01/64   Midfield

	Apps	Gls		Apps	Gls
89/90 Hamrun Spartans	1	1	CWC	2	-
90/91 Hamrun Spartans	14	1			
91/92 Hamrun Spartans	5	-	CC	2	-

MALTA

FIVE YEAR RECORD *Birthdate/Playing position*	LEAGUE Apps Gls	EURO CUPS Cup Apps Gls

Raymond VELLA
11/01/59   Midfield

87/88	Hamrun Spartans	14	2	
88/89	Hamrun Spartans	15	1	CC 2 -
89/90	Hamrun Spartans	13	2	CWC 2 -
90/91	Hamrun Spartans	16	1	
91/92	Hamrun Spartans	17	-	CC 2 -

★ Malta 55 caps, 1 goals

Julian MICALLEF
02/06/67   Midfield

87/88	Birkirkara	13	1	
88/89	Birkirkara	10	-	
89/90	Hamrun Spartans	14	1	CWC 2 -
90/91	Hamrun Spartans	12	2	
91/92	Hamrun Spartans	16	4	CC 1 -

Emanuel BRINCAT
27/12/64   Forward

89/90	Marsa	Div 3		
90/91	Hamrun Spartans	16	6	
91/92	Hamrun Spartans	13	2	CC 2 -

Michael DEGIORGIO
15/11/62   Forward

87/88	Hamrun Spartans	13	-	CC 2 -
88/89	Hamrun Spartans	16	1	CC 2 -
89/90	Hamrun Spartans	16	2	CWC 2 -
90/91	Hamrun Spartans	16	4	
91/92	Hamrun Spartans	18	7	CC 2 -

★ Malta 72 caps, 4 goals

Engelbert MAMO
17/05/72   Forward

89/90	Sliema Wanderers	1	-
90/91	Sliema Wanderers	1	-
91/92	Hamrun Spartans	3	-

FIVE YEAR RECORD *Birthdate/Playing position*	LEAGUE Apps Gls	EURO CUPS Cup Apps Gls

Dennis MIZZI
19/05/64   Forward

87/88	Zurrieq	10	4	
88/89	Zurrieq	12	3	
89/90	Zurrieq	8	3	
90/91	Zurrieq	10	1	
91/92	Hamrun Spartans	14	5	CC 2 -

★ Malta 11 caps, 2 goals

Stefan SULTANA
18/07/68   Forward

87/88	Hamrun Spartans	13	5	CC 2 -
88/89	Hamrun Spartans	16	2	CC 2 -
89/90	Hamrun Spartans	15	11	CWC 2 -
90/91	Hamrun Spartans	14	2	
91/92	Hamrun Spartans	17	22	CC 2 -

★ Malta 5 caps, 2 goals

EUROPEAN HONOURS
none

EUROPEAN CUPS RECORD
	Entries	Pd	W	D	L	F	A
Champions' Cup	4	8	1	0	7	2	26
Cup-winners' Cup	2	6	2	0	4	3	13
UEFA/Fairs' Cup	1	2	0	1	1	0	1
Total - All 3 Cups	7	16	3	1	12	5	40

GLENAVON

FIVE YEAR RECORD Birthdate/Playing position	LEAGUE Apps Gls		EURO CUPS Cup Apps Gls		

Robbie BECK
1964 Goalkeeper

		Apps	Gls	Cup	Apps	Gls
87/88	Glenavon	26	-			
88/89	Glenavon	9	-	CWC	2	-
89/90	Glenavon	25	-			
90/91	Glenavon	18	-	UC	2	-
91/92	Glenavon	30	-	CWC	2	-

Craig ROBSON
1972 Goalkeeper

90/91	Glenavon	12	-			
91/92	Glenavon	-	-			

Paul BYRNE
1963 Defender

87/88	Glenavon	26	3			
88/89	Glenavon	25	1	CWC	2	-
89/90	Glenavon	25	3			
90/91	Glenavon	30	3	UC	2	-
91/92	Glenavon	28	1	CWC	2	-

Dean McCULLOUGH
01/12/63 Defender

88/89	Carrick Rangers	22	-			
89/90	Carrick Rangers	24	-			
90/91	Glenavon	28	1	UC	1	-
91/92	Glenavon	20	1	CWC	2	-

Michael McKEOWN
1969 Defender

87/88	Glenavon	26	2			
88/89	Glenavon	16	1			
89/90	Glenavon	12	1			
90/91	Glenavon	20	-			
91/92	Glenavon	18	-	CWC	2	-

Tony SCAPPATICI
1969 Defender

88/89	Glenavon	9	-			
89/90	Glenavon	24	2			
90/91	Glenavon	27	-	UC	2	-
91/92	Glenavon	23	-	CWC	2	-

FIVE YEAR RECORD Birthdate/Playing position — LEAGUE Apps Gls — EURO CUPS Cup Apps Gls

Andy RUSSELL
14/04/70 Defender

87/88	Glenavon	14	-			
88/89	Glenavon	8	1	CWC	2	-
89/90	Glenavon	-	-			
90/91	Glenavon	15	2			
91/92	Glenavon	12	1	CWC	1	-

Alan McCANN
1966 Defender

87/88	Portadown	11	1			
88/89	Portadown	5	-			
89/90	Glenavon	11	-			
90/91	Glenavon	6	-			
91/92	Glenavon	8	-	CWC	2	-

Stevie CONVILLE
1958 Midfield

87/88	Ballymena United	25	7			
88/89	Glenavon	18	4			
89/90	Glenavon	25	3			
90/91	Glenavon	17	3	UC	2	-
91/92	Glenavon	27	7	CWC	2	1

Michael CROWE
21/04/71 Midfield

88/89	Portadown	2	-			
89/90	Portadown	-	-			
90/91	Portadown	-	-			
91/92	Glenavon	28	2	CWC	2	-

Brian KENNEDY
13/07/70 Midfield

87/88	Linfield	15	-	CC	2	-
88/89	Glenavon	17	-			
89/90	Glenavon	7	1			
90/91	Glenavon	11	-			
91/92	Glenavon	19	1			

NORTHERN IRELAND

FIVE YEAR RECORD *Birthdate/Playing position*	LEAGUE Apps Gls	EURO CUPS Cup Apps Gls	FIVE YEAR RECORD *Birthdate/Playing position*	LEAGUE Apps Gls	EURO CUPS Cup Apps Gls

Trevor McMULLAN
22/11/65 Midfield

87/88	Larne	7	-
88/89	Larne	26	-
89/90	Larne	21	4
90/91	Larne	29	1
91/92	Larne	28	2

Colin CRAWFORD
18/02/60 Midfield

87/88	Carrick Rangers	25	1
88/89	Carrick Rangers	24	6
89/90	Carrick Rangers	26	4
90/91	Carrick Rangers	21	3
91/92	Glenavon	16	1

Fintan McCONVILLE
1964 Midfield

87/88	Glenavon	23	1		
88/89	Glenavon	22	1	CWC 2	1
89/90	Glenavon	16	3		
90/91	Glenavon	19	3	UC 2	-
91/92	Glenavon	9	-		

Glenn FERGUSON
10/07/69 Forward

87/88	Ards	8	1		
88/89	Ards	22	5		
89/90	Ards	21	8		
90/91	Glenavon	30	13	UC 2	-
91/92	Glenavon	17	6	CWC 2	1

Geoff FERRIS
1962 Forward

88/89	Glenavon	26	12	CWC 2	-
89/90	Glenavon	22	5		
90/91	Glenavon	8	1		
91/92	Glenavon	12	4	CWC 1	-

Stephen McBRIDE
02/05/64 Forward

87/88	Glenavon	26	5		
88/89	Glenavon	19	5	CWC 2	-
89/90	Glenavon	25	12		
90/91	Glenavon	29	22	UC 2	-
91/92	Glenavon	26	18	CWC 2	2

★ Northern Ireland 4 caps, 0 goals

Raymond McCOY
1964 Forward

87/88	Coleraine	23	9		
88/89	Coleraine	21	5		
89/90	Coleraine	25	9		
90/91	Glenavon	21	6		
91/92	Glenavon	24	6	CWC 2	-

EUROPEAN HONOURS
none

EUROPEAN CUPS RECORD

	Entries	Pd	W	D	L	F	A
Champions' Cup	1	2	0	1	1	0	3
Cup-winners' Cup	3	6	1	0	5	8	18
UEFA/Fairs' Cup	3	6	0	1	5	2	15
Total - All 3 Cups	7	14	1	2	11	10	36

STRØMSGODSET IF

FIVE YEAR RECORD	LEAGUE		EURO CUPS		
Birthdate/Playing position	Apps	Gls	Cup	Apps	Gls

Lasse Jørn FREDRIKSEN
18/03/71   Goalkeeper

91	Tromsø IL	-	-			

Ronny HVAMBSAL
04/10/67   Goalkeeper

89	Strømsgodset IF	Div 2				
90	Strømsgodset IF	10	-			
91	Strømsgodset IF	-	-			

Frode JOHANNESSEN
15/04/67   Defender

89	Strømsgodset IF	Div 2				
90	Strømsgodset IF	14	-			
91	Strømsgodset IF	22	-			

Vegard HANSEN
08/08/69   Defender

89	Strømsgodset IF	Div 2				
90	Strømsgodset IF	14	-			
91	Strømsgodset IF	16	-			

Jan WENDELBORG
26/01/67   Defender

89	Strømsgodset IF	Div 2				
90	Strømsgodset IF	21	-			
91	Strømsgodset IF	17	-			

Espen HORSRUD
27/08/72   Defender

91	Strømsgodset IF	1	-			

Robert PEDERSEN
12/08/66   Defender

91	Strømsgodset IF	13	2			

Ole Viggo WALSETH
27/07/57   Defender

89	Strømsgodset IF	Div 2				
90	Strømsgodset IF	18	2			

Ulf CAMITZ
25/10/60   Midfield

89	Strømsgodset IF	Div 2				
90	Strømsgodset IF	22	1			
91	Strømsgodset IF	11	-			

Eirik ARILDSET
12/04/67   Midfield

90	Strømmen IF	Div 2				
91	Strømmen IF	Div 2				

Trond NORDEIDE
18/04/64   Midfield

87	SK Brann	19	1			
88	SK Brann	17	1			
89	SK Brann	17	-	CWC	2	-
90	Strømsgodset IF	21	1			
91	Strømsgodset IF	18	1			

Glenn KNUTSEN
01/05/70   Midfield

90	Strømsgodset IF	18	2			
91	Strømsgodset IF	18	1			

Geir ANDERSEN
06/06/63   Midfield

87	Mjøndalen IF	22	3	UC	2	-
88	Mjøndalen IF	Div 2				
89	Strømsgodset IF	Div 2				
90	Strømsgodset IF	11	-			
91	Strømsgodset IF	22	4			

Juro KUVICEK
15/12/67   Midfield

90	Strømsgodset IF	8	-			
91	Strømsgodset IF	21	1			

Krister IKAKSEN
15/04/70   Forward

89	IK Start	15	1			
90	IK Start	8	1			
91	Strømsgodset IF	2	-			

NORWAY

FIVE YEAR RECORD *Birthdate/Playing position*	LEAGUE Apps Gls	EURO CUPS Cup Apps Gls

Odd JOHNSEN
19/03/63   Forward

87	SK Brann	20	3	
88	SK Brann	20	6	
89	Strømsgodset IF	Div 2		
90	Strømsgodset IF	21	5	
91	Strømsgodset IF	22	9	

Halvor STORSKOGEN
23/04/61   Forward

87	SK Brann	18	5	
88	SK Brann	18	3	
89	SFK Lyn	Div 2		
90	Strømsgodset IF	19	12	
91	Strømsgodset IF	22	8	

FIVE YEAR RECORD *Birthdate/Playing position*	LEAGUE Apps Gls	EURO CUPS Cup Apps Gls

Ståle SKAU
05/01/68   Forward

91	Strømsgodset IF	6	-	

EUROPEAN HONOURS
none

EUROPEAN CUPS RECORD

	Entries	Pd	W	D	L	F	A
Champions' Cup	1	2	0	0	2	1	7
Cup-winners' Cup	2	4	1	0	3	3	19
UEFA/Fairs' Cup	1	2	0	1	1	2	7
Total - All 3 Cups	4	8	1	1	6	6	33

MIEDZ LEGNICA

FIVE YEAR RECORD	LEAGUE	EURO CUPS
Birthdate/Playing position	Apps Gls	Cup Apps Gls

Dariusz PLACZKIEWICZ
07/10/62   Goalkeeper

87/88	Zaglebie Lubin	- -
88/89	Zaglebie Lubin	Div 2
89/90	Zaglebie Lubin	- -
90/91	Miedz Legnica	Div 2
91/92	Miedz Legnica	Div 2

Pawel PRIMEL
06/11/69   Goalkeeper

87/88	Zaglebie Lubin	- -
88/89	Miedz Legnica	Div 3
89/90	Miedz Legnica	Div 2
90/91	Miedz Legnica	Div 2
91/92	Miedz Legnica	Div 2

Andrzej CYMBALA
1970   Defender

87/88	Lechia Zielona Góra	Div 3
88/89	Miedz Legnica	Div 3
89/90	Miedz Legnica	Div 2
90/91	Miedz Legnica	Div 2
91/92	Miedz Legnica	Div 2

Grzegorz KOCHANEK
1960   Defender

87/88	Celuloza Kostrzyn	Div 3
88/89	Miedz Legnica	Div 3
89/90	Miedz Legnica	Div 2
90/91	Miedz Legnica	Div 2
91/92	Miedz Legnica	Div 2

Cezary MICHALSKI
1964   Defender

87/88	Miedz Legnica	Div 3
88/89	Miedz Legnica	Div 3
89/90	Miedz Legnica	Div 2
90/91	Miedz Legnica	Div 2
91/92	Miedz Legnica	Div 2

FIVE YEAR RECORD	LEAGUE	EURO CUPS
Birthdate/Playing position	Apps Gls	Cup Apps Gls

Piotr PRZERYWACZ
1972   Defender

| 90/91 | Kuznia Jawór | Div 3 |
| 91/92 | Miedz Legnica | Div 2 |

Krzysztof WOJTOWSKI
01/10/68   Defender

88/89	Zaglebie Lubin	Div 2
89/90	Zaglebie Lubin	- -
90/91	Miedz Legnica	Div 2
91/92	Miedz Legnica	Div 2

Jaroslaw GIEREJKIEWICZ
03/09/65   Midfield

87/88	Zaglebie Lubin	27 -
88/89	Jagiellonia Bialystok	13 1
89/90	Jagiellonia Bialystok	21 -
90/91	Miedz Legnica	Div 2
91/92	Miedz Legnica	Div 2
★ Poland 1 cap, 0 goals		

Tadeusz GAJDZIS
1967   Midfield

87/88	Miedz Legnica	Div 3
88/89	Miedz Legnica	Div 3
89/90	Miedz Legnica	Div 2
90/91	Miedz Legnica	Div 2
91/92	Miedz Legnica	Div 2

Artur WÓJCIK
1967   Midfield

87/88	Miedz Legnica	Div 3
88/89	Miedz Legnica	Div 3
89/90	Miedz Legnica	Div 2
90/91	Miedz Legnica	Div 2
91/92	Miedz Legnica	Div 2

POLAND

FIVE YEAR RECORD	LEAGUE		EURO CUPS		
Birthdate/Playing position	Apps	Gls	Cup	Apps	Gls

Marcin CILINSKI
10/04/68   Midfield

87/88	Zaglebie Lubin	13	-			
88/89	Zaglebie Lubin	Div 2				
89/90	Zaglebie Lubin	16	-			
90/91	Zaglebie Lubin	5	-	UC	1	-
91/92	Miedz Legnica	Div 2				

Robert STYK
1968   Midfield

90/91	Lechia Zielona Góra	Div 3				
91/92	Miedz Legnica	Div 2				

Bogdan PISZ
07/08/63   Midfield

91/92	Zaglebie Lubin	23	-	CC	2	-

Daniel DYLUS
03/12/64   Forward

87/88	Zaglebie Lubin	27	5			
88/89	Zaglebie Lubin	Div 2				
89/90	Zaglebie Lubin	1	-			
90/91	Miedz Legnica	Div 2				
91/92	Miedz Legnica	Div 2				

Dariusz DZIARMAGA
20/09/68   Forward

87/88	Piast Nowa Ruda	Div 2				
88/89	Piast Nowa Ruda	Div 2				
89/90	Piast Nowa Ruda	Div 3				
	Slask Wroclaw	15	-			
90/91	Slask Wroclaw	7	1			
91/92	Miedz Legnica	Div 2				

Wojciech GÓRSKI
1972   Forward

90/91	Miedz Legnica	Div 2				
91/92	Miedz Legnica	Div 2				

Mariusz OLBINSKI
26/02/64   Forward

89/90	Chrobry Glogów	Div 3				
	Zaglebie Lubin	6	-			
90/91	Zaglebie Lubin	18	1			
91/92	Zaglebie Lubin	9	2	CC	2	-
	Chrobry Glogów	Div 2				

Krzysztof KEDZIA
1972   Forward

91/92	Miedz Legnica	Div 2				

EUROPEAN HONOURS
none

EUROPEAN CUPS RECORD

	Entries	Pd	W	D	L	F	A
Champions' Cup	none						
Cup-winners' Cup	none						
UEFA/Fairs' Cup	none						
Total - All 3 Cups	none						

BOAVISTA FC

FIVE YEAR RECORD	LEAGUE		EURO CUPS		
Birthdate/Playing position	Apps	Gls	Cup	Apps	Gls

Zoran LEMAJIC (Yug)
08/11/60   Goalkeeper

87/88	FK Pristina (Yug)	26	-		
88/89	FK Pristina (Yug)	Div 2			
90/91	SC Farense	38	-		
91/92	SC Farense	31	-		

ALFREDO
05/10/62   Goalkeeper

87/88	Boavista FC	36	-		
88/89	Boavista FC	5	-		
89/90	Boavista FC	18	-		
90/91	Boavista FC	25	-		
91/92	Boavista FC	13	-		

SAMUEL
03/08/66   Defender

87/88	SL Benfica	7	-			
88/89	SL Benfica	14	-			
89/90	SL Benfica	26	-	+CC	4	-
90/91	SL Benfica	10	-	UC	1	-
91/92	Boavista FC	34	-	UC	4	-

★ Portugal 5 caps, 0 goals

PAULO SOUSA
31/03/67   Defender

89/90	FC Maia	Div 2				
90/91	Boavista FC	3	-			
91/92	Boavista FC	32	-	UC	4	-

★ Portugal 3 caps, 0 goals

RUI BENTO
14/10/72   Defender

91/92	SL Benfica	24	-	CC	7	-

★ Portugal 2 caps, 0 goals

CAETANO
05/07/66   Defender

87/88	Boavista FC	3	-		
88/89	CF Estrela Amadora	30	-		
89/90	CF Estrela Amadora	28	1		
90/91	Boavista FC	29	-		
91/92	Vitória Guimarães	31	-		

FIVE YEAR RECORD	LEAGUE		EURO CUPS		
Birthdate/Playing position	Apps	Gls	Cup	Apps	Gls

TAVARES
23/04/65   Defender

89/90	Infesta	Div 2				
90/91	FC Porto	7	1	CC	2	-
91/92	Boavista FC	22	3	UC	3	-

VENÂNCIO
21/11/63   Defender

87/88	Sporting CP	21	3	CWC	4	-
88/89	Sporting CP	24	-	UC	4	-
89/90	Sporting CP	29	-	UC	2	-
90/91	Sporting CP	29	2	UC	9	-
91/92	Sporting CP	18	-	UC	2	-

★ Portugal 21 caps, 0 goals

NOGUEIRA
21/09/63   Midfield

87/88	Saravanense	Div 2				
88/89	Académico Viseu	34	1			
89/90	AD Fafe	Div 2				
90/91	FC Penafiel	36	2			
91/92	Boavista FC	28	1	UC	3	-

★ Portugal 1 cap, 1 goal

CASACA
18/10/59   Midfield

87/88	Boavista FC	15	2			
88/89	Boavista FC	34	1			
89/90	Boavista FC	32	1	UC	2	-
90/91	Boavista FC	36	1			
91/92	Boavista FC	32	1	UC	4	-

NELO
25/08/67   Midfield

87/88	SC Farense	25	-			
88/89	Boavista FC	1	-			
89/90	Boavista FC	-	-			
90/91	Boavista FC	35	-			
91/92	Boavista FC	29	1	UC	3	-

★ Portugal 7 caps, 0 goals

PORTUGAL

FIVE YEAR RECORD Birthdate/Playing position	LEAGUE Apps	Gls	EURO CUPS Cup	Apps	Gls

BOBÓ
09/02/63   Midfield

		Apps	Gls	Cup	Apps	Gls
87/88	CS Marítimo	18	2			
88/89	CF Estrela Amadora	31	3			
89/90	CF Estrela Amadora	27	1			
90/91	Boavista FC	31	1			
91/92	Boavista FC	28	-	UC	1	-

JAIME CERQUEIRA
24/12/67   Midfield

		Apps	Gls	Cup	Apps	Gls
87/88	CF Estrela Amadora	Div 2				
88/89	CF Estrela Amadora	12	-			
89/90	CF Estrela Amadora	4	-			
90/91	Boavista FC	6	-			
91/92	Boavista FC	12	-			

JAIME ALVES
28/03/65   Midfield

		Apps	Gls	Cup	Apps	Gls
87/88	Boavista FC	13	1			
88/89	Boavista FC	34	7			
89/90	Boavista FC	28	4	UC	2	-
90/91	Boavista FC	33	4			
91/92	Vitória Guimarães	24	1			

★ Portugal 3 caps, 0 goals

MARLON (Bra)
01/09/63   Forward

		Apps	Gls	Cup	Apps	Gls
87/88	Sporting CP	17	4	CWC	3	-
88/89	CF Estrela Amadora	34	8			
89/90	Sporting CP	29	3	UC	2	-
90/91	Boavista FC	31	11			
91/92	Boavista FC	23	-	UC	3	1

Richard OWUBOKIRI "RICKY" (Nig)
16/07/61   Forward

		Apps	Gls	Cup	Apps	Gls
87/88	FC Metz (Fra)	33	8			
88/89	FC Metz (Fra)	1	-			
	SL Benfica	4	-			
89/90	CF Estrela Amadora	30	13			
90/91	CF Estrela Amadora	38	15	CWC	4	1
91/92	Boavista FC	34	30	UC	3	-

★ Nigeria

FIVE YEAR RECORD Birthdate/Playing position	LEAGUE Apps	Gls	EURO CUPS Cup	Apps	Gls

TOZÉ
24/01/69   Forward

		Apps	Gls	Cup	Apps	Gls
89/90	SC Salgueiros	Div 2				
90/91	SC Salgueiros	36	11			
91/92	Sporting CP	9	2			

Erwin SANCHEZ (Bol)
19/10/69   Forward

		Apps	Gls	Cup	Apps	Gls
89/90	Bolivia					
90/91	SL Benfica	16	1			
91/92	GD Estoril Praia	28	8			

★ Bolivia

EUROPEAN HONOURS
none

EUROPEAN CUPS RECORD

	Entries	Pd	W	D	L	F	A
Champions' Cup	none						
Cup-winners' Cup	3	12	5	4	3	22	11
UEFA/Fairs' Cup	7	22	7	4	11	22	31
Total - All 3 Cups	10	34	12	8	14	44	42

BOHEMIANS

FIVE YEAR RECORD *Birthdate/Playing position*	LEAGUE Apps	Gls	EURO CUPS Cup	Apps	Gls

Dave HENDERSON
02/12/60   Goalkeeper

87/88 St. Patrick's Athletic	29	-			
88/89 St. Patrick's Athletic	25	-	UC	2	-
89/90 St. Patrick's Athletic	27	-			
90/91 St. Patrick's Athletic	23	-			
91/92 Shamrock Rovers	31	-			

John CONNOLLY
28/12/71   Goalkeeper

90/91 Bohemians	2	-			
91/92 Bohemians	11	-			

Robbie BEST
12/09/67   Defender

88/89 St. Patrick's Athletic	5	-			
89/90 St. Patrick's Athletic	6	-			
90/91 Athlone Town	22	-			
91/92 Bohemians	31	-			

Paul BYRNE
25/11/65   Defender

87/88 St. Patrick's Athletic	19	2			
88/89 St. Patrick's Athletic	23	1	UC	2	-
89/90 Athlone Town	23	3			
90/91 Bohemians	31	3			
91/92 Bohemians	31	-			

Tommy BYRNE
30/08/69   Defender

90/91 Boom FC (Bel)	Div 2				
91/92 Bohemians	8	-			

Donal BROUGHAN
28/11/72   Defender

91/92 Bohemians	8	-			

Paul WHELAN
10/05/64   Defender

89/90 Bohemians	28	1			
90/91 Bohemians	27	-			
91/92 Bohemians	30	3			

Declan GEOGHEGAN
29/08/64   Defender

88/89 Drogheda United	Div 2				
89/90 Drogheda United	23	2			
90/91 Drogheda United	Div 2				
91/92 Drogheda United	33	1			

Tony O'CONNOR
15/11/66   Midfield

89/90 St. Patrick's Athletic	31	6			
90/91 St. Patrick's Athletic	30	4	CC	2	-
91/92 St. Patrick's Athletic	33	2			

Alan BYRNE
12/05/69   Midfield

87/88 Bohemians	7	1			
88/89 Bohemians	12	-			
89/90 Bohemians	19	-			
90/91 Bohemians	27	-			
91/92 Bohemians	29	1			

Paul McDERMOTT
07/07/61   Midfield

87/88 Shelbourne	32	1			
88/89 Shelbourne	31	1			
89/90 Shelbourne	7	-			
90/91 Shelbourne	12	2			
Limerick City	7	1			
91/92 Bohemians	31	1			

David TILSON
17/05/68   Midfield

89/90 Bohemians	23	5			
90/91 Bohemians	26	3			
91/92 Bohemians	31	10			

Maurice O'DRISCOLL
02/08/66   Midfield

87/88 St. Patrick's Athletic	32	3			
88/89 St. Patrick's Athletic	31	3	UC	2	-
89/90 St. Patrick's Athletic	20	3			
90/91 St. Patrick's Athletic	29	-	CC	2	-
91/92 St. Patrick's Athletic	28	-			

REPUBLIC OF IRELAND

FIVE YEAR RECORD *Birthdate/Playing position*	LEAGUE Apps Gls	EURO CUPS Cup Apps Gls

Ian DOUGLAS
13/02/71   Forward

89/90	Drogheda United	24	2
90/91	Bohemians	31	11
91/92	Bohemians	16	1

Pat FENLON
15/03/69   Forward

87/88	St. Patrick's Athletic	13	4			
88/89	St. Patrick's Athletic	31	8	UC	2	-
89/90	St. Patrick's Athletic	8	-			
90/91	St. Patrick's Athletic	32	12	CC	2	1
91/92	Bohemians	31	10			

Lee KING
11/11/69   Forward

88/89	Bohemians	7	-
89/90	Bohemians	12	-
90/91	Bohemians	21	1
91/92	Bohemians	24	6

Joe LAWLESS
13/02/62   Forward

87/88	Bohemians	28	9	UC	2	-
88/89	Bohemians	27	2			
89/90	St. Patrick's Athletic	29	5			
90/91	St. Patrick's Athletic	23	4	CC	2	-
91/92	Bohemians	31	9			

FIVE YEAR RECORD *Birthdate/Playing position*	LEAGUE Apps Gls	EURO CUPS Cup Apps Gls

Tommy FITZGERALD
02/01/70   Forward

89/90	Shelbourne	20	6
90/91	Limerick City	9	3
91/92	Limerick City	Div 2	

EUROPEAN HONOURS
none

EUROPEAN CUPS RECORD

	Entries	Pd	W	D	L	F	A
Champions' Cup	2	6	1	2	3	4	13
Cup-winners' Cup	2	6	2	1	3	6	9
UEFA/Fairs' Cup	7	14	1	4	9	8	27
Total - All 3 Cups	11	26	4	7	15	18	49

STEAUA BUCURESTI

FIVE YEAR RECORD *Birthdate/Playing position*	LEAGUE Apps	Gls	EURO CUPS Cup	Apps	Gls

Dumitru STINGACIU
09/08/64   Goalkeeper

87/88	Steaua Bucuresti	12	-	CC 3	-
88/89	FC Olt Scornicesti	16	-		
89/90	Steaua Bucuresti	3	-		
90/91	Steaua Bucuresti	33	-	CWC 3	-
91/92	Steaua Bucuresti	25	-	UC 6	-

★ Romania 1 cap, 0 goals

Daniel GHERASIM
02/11/64   Goalkeeper

87/88	FC Olt Scornicesti	16	-		
88/89	Universitatea Craiova	1	-		
	FC Olt Scornicesti	13	-		
89/90	FC Olt Scornicesti	17	-		
	Steaua Bucuresti	1	-		
90/91	Steaua Bucuresti	4	-	CWC 1	-
91/92	Steaua Bucuresti	9	-		

Nicolae UNGUREANU
11/10/56   Defender

87/88	Steaua Bucuresti	24	4	CC 7	-
88/89	Steaua Bucuresti	31	1	+CC 9	-
89/90	Steaua Bucuresti	25	2		
90/91	Steaua Bucuresti	26	2	CWC 2	-
91/92	Steaua Bucuresti	30	1	UC 6	-

★ Romania 57 caps, 1 goal

Aurel PANAIT
27/08/68   Defender

87/88	Petrolul Ploiesti	27	1		
88/89	Petrolul Ploiesti	Div 2			
89/90	Petrolul Ploiesti	26	-		
90/91	Petrolul Ploiesti	28	1	UC 2	-
91/92	Steaua Bucuresti	23	1	UC 4	-

★ Romania 1 cap, 0 goals

Bogdan BUCUR
21/04/70   Defender

88/89	Dinamo Bucuresti	11	-		
89/90	FC Inter Sibiu	29	-		
90/91	FC Inter Sibiu	17	1		
	Dinamo Bucuresti	8	-		
91/92	Steaua Bucuresti	29	-	UC 6	-

Cornel MIREA
20/08/63   Defender

87/88	Victoria Bucuresti	32	2		
88/89	Victoria Bucuresti	29	-	UC 7	-
89/90	Victoria Bucuresti	15	1		
	Dinamo Bucuresti	12	-		
90/91	Steaua Bucuresti	10	-	CWC 2	-
91/92	Steaua Bucuresti	23	1	UC 6	-

Anton DOBOS
13/10/65   Defender

87/88	Universitatea Cluj	16	1		
88/89	Universitatea Cluj	30	4		
89/90	Dinamo Bucuresti	21	1	CWC 2	-
90/91	Dinamo Bucuresti	22	1	CC 4	1
91/92	Dinamo Bucuresti	4	-	UC 2	-
	Steaua Bucuresti	13	2		

Cornel CRISTESCU
25/08/68   Midfield

91/92	Steaua Bucuresti	23	-	UC 1	-

Constantin GALCA
08/03/72   Midfield

89/90	FC Arges Pitesti	4	-		
90/91	FC Arges Pitesti	31	2		
91/92	Steaua Bucuresti	26	5	UC 5	-

Nica Basarab PANDURU
11/07/70   Midfield

89/90	CSM Resita	Div 2			
90/91	CSM Resita	Div 2			
	Steaua Bucuresti	16	4		
91/92	Steaua Bucuresti	29	8	UC 6	-

★ Romania 1 cap, 0 goals

ROMANIA

FIVE YEAR RECORD *Birthdate/Playing position*	LEAGUE Apps Gls	EURO CUPS Cup Apps Gls

Ilie DUMITRESCU
06/01/69   Midfield

		Apps	Gls	Cup	Apps	Gls
87/88	FC Olt Scornicesti	32	1			
88/89	Steaua Bucuresti	29	8	+CC	7	4
89/90	Steaua Bucuresti	25	7	CC	4	-
90/91	Steaua Bucuresti	_25	6	CWC	4	2
91/92	Steaua Bucuresti	30	9	UC	6	2

★ Romania 18 caps, 0 goals

Iulian MINEA
06/12/69   Midfield

		Apps	Gls	Cup	Apps	Gls
88/89	ASA Tirgu Mures	9	-			
89/90	ASA Tirgu Mures	Div 2				
90/91	Steaua Bucuresti	22	2	CWC	3	-
91/92	Steaua Bucuresti	17	2	UC	3	-

Cristian MUSTACA
31/01/67   Midfield

		Apps	Gls
88/89	FC Farul Constanta	23	2
89/90	FC Farul Constanta	26	8
90/91	FC Farul Constanta	22	3
91/92	Steaua Bucuresti	21	2

Ilie STAN
17/10/67   Midfield

		Apps	Gls	Cup	Apps	Gls
87/88	Steaua Bucuresti	2	-			
88/89	Steaua Bucuresti	14	2	+CC	1	-
89/90	Steaua Bucuresti	18	3	CC	2	-
90/91	Steaua Bucuresti	33	10	CWC	3	2
91/92	Steaua Bucuresti	29	12	UC	6	3

Alexandru ANDRASI
13/05/65   Forward

		Apps	Gls	Cup	Apps	Gls
87/88	FCM Brasov	27	4			
88/89	FCM Brasov	33	3			
89/90	FCM Brasov	30	8			
90/91	FC Brasov	34	6			
91/92	Steaua Bucuresti	22	5	UC	3	-

FIVE YEAR RECORD *Birthdate/Playing position*	LEAGUE Apps Gls	EURO CUPS Cup Apps Gls

Marian POPA
03/02/67   Forward

		Apps	Gls	Cup	Apps	Gls
87/88	FC Constanta	Div 2				
88/89	FC Farul Constanta	31	8			
89/90	FC Farul Constanta	28	15			
90/91	Steaua Bucuresti	22	9	CWC	1	-
91/92	Steaua Bucuresti	27	11	UC	6	2

★ Romania 1 cap, 0 goals

Ion VLADOIU
05/11/68   Forward

		Apps	Gls	Cup	Apps	Gls
87/88	FC Arges Pitesti	9	2			
88/89	FC Arges Pitesti	25	3			
89/90	FC Arges Pitesti	24	3			
90/91	FC Arges Pitesti	17	5			
	Steaua Bucuresti	16	9			
91/92	Steaua Bucuresti	18	4	UC	4	-

Adrian STATE
28/06/68   Forward

		Apps	Gls	Cup	Apps	Gls
87/88	Otelul Galati	3	-			
88/89	Otelul Galati	-	-			
89/90	Otelul Galati	Div 2				
90/91	Otelul Galati	Div 2				
91/92	Steaua Bucuresti	14	4	UC	3	-

EUROPEAN HONOURS
Champions' Cup - (1) 1986.
Super Cup - (1) 1986.

EUROPEAN CUPS RECORD

	Entries	Pd	W	D	L	F	A
Champions' Cup	10	43	20	8	15	68	52
Cup-winners' Cup	**10**	**34**	**12**	**9**	**13**	**42**	**43**
UEFA/Fairs' Cup	3	10	2	3	5	11	18
Total - All 3 Cups	23	87	34	20	33	121	113

SPARTAK MOSKVA

FIVE YEAR RECORD *Birthdate/Playing position*	LEAGUE Apps Gls	EURO CUPS Cup Apps Gls

Stanislav CHERCHESOV
02/09/63   Goalkeeper

87	Spartak Moskva	2	-		
88	Lokomotiv Moskva	30	-		
89	Spartak Moskva	30	-	UC	4	-
90	Spartak Moskva	24	-	CC	8	-
91	Spartak Moskva	30	-	UC	4	-

★ USSR/CIS 11 caps, 0 goals

Gintaras STAUCHE (Lit)
24/12/69   Goalkeeper

91	CSKA Moskva	-	-		
	Spartak Moskva	-	-	UC	1	-

★ Lithuania

Andrey IVANOV
06/04/67   Defender

88	Spartak Moskva	12	-	CC	4	1
89	Spartak Moskva	10	-	UC	3	-
90	Spartak Moskva	2	-		
91	Spartak Moskva	23	-	UC	4	-

★ USSR/CIS 4 caps, 0 goals

Kakhaber TSKHADADZE
07/09/68   Defender

88	Dinamo Tbilisi	14	1		
89	Dinamo Tbilisi	27	-		
90	GIF Sundsvall (Swe)	Div 2			
91	GIF Sundsvall (Swe)	4	-		

★ CIS 6 caps, 1 goal

Dmitry KHLESTOV
21/01/71   Defender

89	Spartak Moskva	-	-		
90	Spartak Moskva	4	-		
91	Spartak Moskva	14	-	UC	4	-

★ CIS 3 caps, 0 goals

FIVE YEAR RECORD *Birthdate/Playing position*	LEAGUE Apps Gls	EURO CUPS Cup Apps Gls

Yevgeny BUSHMANOV
02/11/71   Defender

88	Shinnik Yaroslavl	Div 2			
89	Spartak Moskva	-	-		
90	Spartak Moskva	2	-	CC	2	-
91	Spartak Moskva	8	1	UC	2	-

Andrey CHERNYSHOV
07/01/68   Defender

88	Dinamo Moskva	-	-		
89	Dinamo Moskva	25	-		
90	Dinamo Moskva	22	2		
91	Dinamo Moskva	26	-	UC	5	-

★ USSR/CIS 26 caps, 0 goals

Dmitry GRADILENKO
12/08/69   Defender

88	Spartak Moskva	6	-	CC	2	-
89	Spartak Moskva	1	-		
90	Spartak Moskva	8	-	CC	4	-
91	Spartak Moskva	6	-	UC	1	-

Igor LEDYAKHOV
22/05/68   Midfield

88	SKA Rostov	Div 2			
89	SKA Rostov	Div 2			
	Dnepr Dnepropetrovsk	-	-	CC	1	-
90	Dnepr Dnepropetrovsk	5	1		
91	Rotor Volgograd	Div 2			

★ CIS 7 caps, 1 goal

Valery KARPIN
02/02/69   Midfield

87	Sport Tallinn (Est)	Div 3			
88	CSKA Moskva (II)	Div 3			
89	Fakel Voronezh	Div 2			
90	Spartak Moskva	21	-	CC	8	-
91	Spartak Moskva	28	3	UC	4	1

★ CIS 1 cap, 0 goals

RUSSIA

FIVE YEAR RECORD *Birthdate/Playing position*	LEAGUE Apps Gls	EURO CUPS Cup Apps Gls

Viktor ONOPKO
14/10/69   Midfield

88	Shakhtyor Donetsk	3	-
89	Shakhtyor Donetsk	-	-
90	Shakhtyor Donetsk	21	-
91	Shakhtyor Donetsk	24	1

★ CIS 4 caps, 0 goals

Rashid RAKHIMOV
18/03/63   Midfield

87	Pamir Dushanbe	Div 2	
88	Pamir Dushanbe	Div 2	
89	Pamir Dushanbe	26	2
90	Pamir Dushanbe	23	4
91	Pamir Dushanbe	25	4

Andrey PYATNITSKY
27/09/67   Midfield

87	CSKA Moskva	3	-
88	Pakhtakor Tashkent	Div 2	
89	Pakhtakor Tashkent	Div 2	
90	Pakhtakor Tashkent	Div 2	
91	Pakhtakor Tashkent	28	10

★ USSR/CIS 6 caps, 2 goals

Fyodor CHERENKOV
25/07/59   Midfield

87	Spartak Moskva	27	12	UC	4	2
88	Spartak Moskva	30	3	CC	4	2
89	Spartak Moskva	28	7	UC	4	2
89/90	AS Red Star (Fra)	Div 2				
90	Spartak Moskva	11	1			
91	Spartak Moskva	22	3	UC	3	1

★ USSR 40 caps, 16 goals

Dmitry RADCHENKO
02/02/70   Forward

88	Dinamo Leningrad	Div 3				
89	Zenit Leningrad	26	4			
90	Zenit Leningrad	Div 2				
	Spartak Moskva			UC	4	2
91	Spartak Moskva	29	13	UC	4	1

★ USSR 2 caps, 0 goals

Vladimir BESCHASTNYKH
01/04/74   Forward

Aleksandr TATARKIN
04/07/66   Forward

88	SKA Rostov	Div 2
89	SKA Rostov	Div 2
90	Rotselmash	Div 2
91	Rotselmash	Div 2

Mikhail RUSYAYEV
15/11/64   Forward

87	Spartak Moskva	2	-
88	Lokomotiv Moskva	29	15
89	Lokomotiv Moskva	29	9
90/91	Alemannia Aachen (Ger)	Div 2	
91/92	VfB Oldenburg (Ger)	Div 2	

EUROPEAN CUPS RECORD

	Entries	Pd	W	D	L	F	A
Champions' Cup	4	20	8	5	7	29	20
Cup-winners' Cup	2	10	4	3	3	14	10
UEFA/Fairs' Cup	12	60	34	11	15	97	65
Total - All 3 Cups	18	90	46	19	25	140	95

AIRDRIEONIANS

FIVE YEAR RECORD	LEAGUE		EURO CUPS	
Birthdate/Playing position	Apps	Gls	Cup Apps	Gls

John MARTIN
27/10/58   Goalkeeper

87/88	Airdrieonians	Div 2		
88/89	Airdrieonians	Div 2		
89/90	Airdrieonians	Div 2		
90/91	Airdrieonians	Div 2		
91/92	Airdrieonians	41	-	

Allen McKNIGHT (Nir)
27/01/64   Goalkeeper

87/88	Celtic	12	-	UC	2	-
88/89	West Ham United (Eng)	23	-		
89/90	West Ham United (Eng)	Div 2			
90/91	West Ham United (Eng)	Div 2			
91/92	Airdrieonians	2	-		

★ Northern Ireland 10 caps, 0 goals

Walter KIDD
10/03/58   Defender

87/88	Heart of Midlothian	18	-			
88/89	Heart of Midlothian	20	-	UC	6	-
89/90	Heart of Midlothian	17	1			
90/91	Heart of Midlothian	4	-	UC	1	-
91/92	Airdrieonians	32	-			

Paul JACK
15/05/65   Defender

87/88	Arbroath	Div 3		
88/89	Arbroath	Div 3		
89/90	Airdrieonians	Div 2		
90/91	Airdrieonians	Div 2		
91/92	Airdrieonians	23	1	

Jimmy SANDISON
22/06/65   Defender

87/88	Heart of Midlothian	2	-			
88/89	Heart of Midlothian	14	-	UC	1	-
89/90	Heart of Midlothian	12	2			
90/91	Heart of Midlothian	25	1	UC	1	-
91/92	Airdrieonians	40	-			

FIVE YEAR RECORD	LEAGUE		EURO CUPS	
Birthdate/Playing position	Apps	Gls	Cup Apps	Gls

Chris HONOR (Eng)
05/06/68   Defender

87/88	Bristol City (Eng)	Div 3		
88/89	Bristol City (Eng)	Div 3		
89/90	Bristol City (Eng)	Div 3		
	Hereford United (Eng)	Div 4		
90/91	Swansea City (Wal)	Div 3		
91/92	Airdrieonians	30	-	

Jim SMITH
14/05/61   Defender

87/88	Dundee	40	1	
88/89	Dundee	7	-	
89/90	Dundee	4	-	
90/91	Airdrieonians	Div 2		
91/92	Airdrieonians	1	-	

Sandy STEWART
14/10/65   Defender

88/89	Kilmarnock	Div 2		
89/90	Airdrieonians	Div 2		
90/91	Airdrieonians	Div 2		
91/92	Airdrieonians	41	1	

Gus CAESAR (Eng)
05/03/66   Defender

87/88	Arsenal (Eng)	22	-	
88/89	Arsenal (Eng)	2	-	
89/90	Arsenal (Eng)	3	-	
90/91	Queen's Park Rangers (Eng)	5	-	
91/92	Bristol City (Eng)	Div 2		
	Airdrieonians	12	-	

Kenny BLACK
29/11/63   Midfield

87/88	Heart of Midlothian	42	4	UC	8	1
88/89	Heart of Midlothian	33	1			
89/90	Portsmouth (Eng)	Div 2				
90/91	Portsmouth (Eng)	Div 2				
91/92	Airdrieonians	33	2			

SCOTLAND

FIVE YEAR RECORD Birthdate/Playing position	LEAGUE Apps Gls	EURO CUPS Cup Apps Gls	FIVE YEAR RECORD Birthdate/Playing position	LEAGUE Apps Gls	EURO CUPS Cup Apps Gls

Sammy CONN
26/10/61   Midfield

87/88	Falkirk	36	2
88/89	Airdrieonians	Div 2	
89/90	Airdrieonians	Div 2	
90/91	Airdrieonians	Div 2	
91/92	Airdrieonians	27	5

Evan BALFOUR
09/09/65   Midfield

89/90	Airdrieonians	Div 2	
90/91	Airdrieonians	Div 2	
91/92	Airdrieonians	41	2

Davie KIRKWOOD
27/08/67   Midfield

87/88	Rangers	4	-		
88/89	Rangers	2	-		
89/90	Heart of Midlothian	19	-		
90/91	Heart of Midlothian	9	1	UC 4	-
	Airdrieonians	Div 2			
91/92	Airdrieonians	36	9		

Jimmy BOYLE
19/02/67   Midfield

87/88	Queen's Park	Div 3	
88/89	Queen's Park	Div 3	
89/90	Airdrieonians	Div 2	
90/91	Airdrieonians	Div 2	
91/92	Airdrieonians	37	3

John WATSON
13/02/59   Midfield

87/88	Dunfermline Athletic	25	3
88/89	Dunfermline Athletic	Div 2	
89/90	Fulham (Eng)	Div 3	
	Airdrieonians	Div 2	
90/91	Airdrieonians	Div 2	
91/92	Airdrieonians	22	4

Alan LAWRENCE
19/08/62   Forward

87/88	Dundee	22	1
88/89	Dundee	10	1
	Airdrieonians	Div 2	
89/90	Airdrieonians	Div 2	
90/91	Airdrieonians	Div 2	
91/92	Airdrieonians	31	7

Owen COYLE
14/07/66   Forward

87/88	Dumbarton	Div 3	
88/89	Clydebank	Div 2	
89/90	Clydebank	Div 2	
90/91	Aadr	Div 2	
91/92	Airdrieonians	43	11

Andy SMITH
22/11/68   Forward

90/91	Airdrieonians	Div 2	
91/92	Airdrieonians	29	4

EUROPEAN HONOURS
none

EUROPEAN CUPS RECORD

	Entries	Pd	W	D	L	F	A
Champions' Cup	none						
Cup-winners' Cup	none						
UEFA/Fairs' Cup	none						
Total - All 3 Cups	none						

ATLETICO MADRID

FIVE YEAR RECORD	LEAGUE		EURO CUPS		
Birthdate/Playing position	Apps	Gls	Cup	Apps	Gls

ABEL Resino
02/02/60   Goalkeeper

87/88	Atlético Madrid	32	-		
88/89	Atlético Madrid	37	-	UC	2	-
89/90	Atlético Madrid	34	-	UC	2	-
90/91	Atlético Madrid	33	-	UC	2	-
91/92	Atlético Madrid	32	-	CWC	6	-

★ Spain 2 caps, 0 goals

Diego DIEGO Garrido
30/12/68   Goalkeeper

90/91	Sporting Gijón	5	-
91/92	Atlético Madrid	6	-

TOMAS Reñones
09/08/60   Defender

87/88	Atlético Madrid	37	-			
88/89	Atlético Madrid	37	1	UC	2	-
89/90	Atlético Madrid	31	-	UC	2	-
90/91	Atlético Madrid	33	1	UC	2	-
91/92	Atlético Madrid	32	-	CWC	6	-

★ Spain 18 caps, 0 goals

Miguel SOLER
13/03/65   Defender

87/88	RCD Español	33	-	+UC	12	1
88/89	FC Barcelona	23	1	#CWC	5	-
89/90	FC Barcelona	27	-	CWC	1	-
90/91	FC Barcelona	26	1	+CWC	5	-
91/92	Atlético Madrid	25	1	CWC	5	1

★ Spain 9 caps, 0 goals

Roberto SOLOZABAL
15/09/69   Defender

88/89	Atlético Madrileño	Div 3				
89/90	Atlético Madrid	10	-			
90/91	Atlético Madrid	36	2	UC	1	-
91/92	Atlético Madrid	37	-	CWC	6	-

★ Spain 5 caps, 0 goals

DONATO Gama da Silva (Bra)
30/12/62   Defender

87/88	Vasco da Gama (Bra)					
88/89	Atlético Madrid	37	4			
89/90	Atlético Madrid	34	2	UC	2	-
90/91	Atlético Madrid	24	-	UC	1	-
91/92	Atlético Madrid	36	1	CWC	2	-

Juan Francisco Rodríguez "JUANITO"
10/05/65   Defender

87/88	Real Zaragoza	28	1			
88/89	Real Zaragoza	34	6			
89/90	Real Zaragoza	33	6	UC	4	1
90/91	Atlético Madrid	36	5	UC	1	1
91/92	Atlético Madrid	28	2	CWC	6	-

★ Spain 5 caps, 1 goal

Antonio Muñoz "TONI"
01/09/69   Defender

89/90	Atlético Madrileño	Div 2				
90/91	Atlético Madrid	11	-	UC	1	-
91/92	Atlético Madrid	30	-	CWC	3	1

★ Spain 1 cap, 0 goals

Francisco FERREIRA
22/05/67   Defender

87/88	Athletic Bilbao	35	6			
88/89	Athletic Bilbao	36	4	UC	4	-
89/90	Atlético Madrid	36	1	UC	2	-
90/91	Atlético Madrid	21	1	UC	1	-
91/92	Atlético Madrid	21	1	CWC	3	-

★ Spain 1 cap, 0 goals

Bernd SCHUSTER (Ger)
22/12/59   Midfield

87/88	FC Barcelona	30	9	UC	8	1
88/89	Real Madrid	33	7	CC	8	-
89/90	Real Madrid	28	6	CC	2	-
90/91	Atlético Madrid	29	4			
91/92	Atlético Madrid	34	6	CWC	6	4

★ West Germany 21 caps, 4 goals

SPAIN

FIVE YEAR RECORD	LEAGUE		EURO CUPS		
Birthdate/Playing position	Apps	Gls	Cup	Apps	Gls

Juan VIZCAINO
06/08/66   Midfield

		Apps	Gls	Cup	Apps	Gls
87/88	Real Zaragoza	13	2			
88/89	Real Zaragoza	37	6			
89/90	Real Zaragoza	36	2	UC	3	-
90/91	Atlético Madrid	34	3			
91/92	Atlético Madrid	36	9	CWC	6	-

★ Spain 12 caps, 0 goals

Gabriel MOYA
30/03/66   Midfield

		Apps	Gls	Cup	Apps	Gls
87/88	Real Valladolid	35	6			
88/89	Real Valladolid	19	1			
89/90	Real Valladolid	32	8	CWC	4	1
90/91	Real Valladolid	35	6			
91/92	Atlético Madrid	31	5	CWC	6	-

★ Spain 5 caps, 1 goal

ALFREDO Santaelena
13/10/67   Midfield

		Apps	Gls	Cup	Apps	Gls
88/89	Atlético Madrid	9	-			
89/90	Atlético Madrid	33	1	UC	1	-
90/91	Atlético Madrid	32	3	UC	2	-
91/92	Atlético Madrid	9	-			

Manuel Sánchez "MANOLO"
17/01/65   Forward

		Apps	Gls	Cup	Apps	Gls
87/88	CR Murcia	37	9			
88/89	Atlético Madrid	35	10	UC	2	-
89/90	Atlético Madrid	34	12	UC	2	-
90/91	Atlético Madrid	37	16	UC	2	-
91/92	Atlético Madrid	36	27	CWC	6	5

★ Spain 27 caps, 9 goals

Carlos AGUILERA
22/05/69   Forward

		Apps	Gls	Cup	Apps	Gls
87/88	Atlético Madrid	6	-			
88/89	Atlético Madrid	20	4	UC	2	-
89/90	Atlético Madrid	22	-			
90/91	Atlético Madrid	4	-			
91/92	Atlético Madrid	23	3	CWC	2	-

FIVE YEAR RECORD	LEAGUE		EURO CUPS		
Birthdate/Playing position	Apps	Gls	Cup	Apps	Gls

Paulo Jorge dos Santos "FUTRE" (Por)
28/02/66   Forward

		Apps	Gls	Cup	Apps	Gls
87/88	Atlético Madrid	35	8			
88/89	Atlético Madrid	28	5	UC	2	1
89/90	Atlético Madrid	27	10	UC	2	-
90/91	Atlético Madrid	26	3	UC	2	-
91/92	Atlético Madrid	31	6	CWC	6	5

★ Portugal 30 caps, 4 goals

Juan SABAS
13/04/67   Forward

		Apps	Gls	Cup	Apps	Gls
88/89	CD Pegaso Madrid	Div 3				
89/90	AD Rayo Vallecano	34	6			
90/91	Atlético Madrid	20	3			
91/92	Atlético Madrid	15	3	CWC	1	-

Sebastián LOSADA
03/09/67   Forward

		Apps	Gls	Cup	Apps	Gls
87/88	RCD Español	28	8	+UC	5	3
88/89	Real Madrid	9	3	CC	1	1
89/90	Real Madrid	14	8	CC	3	1
90/91	Real Madrid	12	2	CC	4	5
91/92	Atlético Madrid	9	1	CWC	1	-

EUROPEAN HONOURS
Cup-winners' Cup - (1) 1962.

EUROPEAN CUPS RECORD

	Entries	Pd	W	D	L	F	A
Champions' Cup	5	39	21	7	11	65	39
Cup-winners' Cup	8	54	33	11	10	101	52
UEFA/Fairs' Cup	14	43	19	4	20	60	59
Total - All 3 Cups	27	136	73	22	41	226	150

AIK

FIVE YEAR RECORD	LEAGUE		EURO CUPS		
Birthdate/Playing position	Apps	Gls	Cup	Apps	Gls

Bernt LJUNG
08/05/58 Goalkeeper

87	Vasalunds IF	Div 2				
88	Vasalunds IF	Div 2				
89	Vasalunds IF	Div 2				
90	Vasalunds IF	Div 2				
91	AIK	26	-			

★ Sweden 8 caps, 0 goals

Magnus HEDMAN
19/03/73 Goalkeeper

90	AIK	2	-
91	AIK	2	-

Peter LARSSON
08/03/61 Defender

87	IFK Göteborg	20	2	UC	2	-
87/88	Ajax (Hol)	15	2	CWC	5	2
88/89	Ajax (Hol)	14	1	UC	2	-
89/90	Ajax (Hol)	26	1	UC	2	-
90/91	Ajax (Hol)	3	-			
91	AIK	27	-			

★ Sweden 47 caps, 4 goals

Johan MJÄLLBY
09/02/71 Defender

89	AIK	1	-
90	AIK	14	-
91	AIK	26	-

Björn KINDLUND
25/01/62 Defender

87	AIK	21	1	UC	1	-
88	AIK	21	1			
89	AIK	15	3			
90	AIK	15	3			
91	AIK	28	5			

★ Sweden 1 cap, 0 goals

Anders HJELM
11/11/66 Defender

88	Råsunda IS	Div 3	
89	AIK	14	-
90	AIK	12	-
91	AIK	25	2

Karl STÅHL
02/08/73 Defender

91	AIK	-	-

Björn RYDBERG-RUNDGREN
01/01/73 Defender

91	AIK	-	-

Thomas LAGERLÖF
15/11/71 Defender

90	AIK	1	-
91	AIK	6	-

Peter HALLSTRÖM
29/07/71 Midfield

90	AIK	9	1
91	AIK	12	1

Vadim YEVTUSHENKO (Ukr)
01/01/58 Midfield

87	Dinamo Kiev (Urs)	28	3	CC	2	-
88	Dnepr Dnepropetrovsk (Urs)	20	-	UC	1	-
89	AIK	21	2			
90	AIK	21	3			
91	AIK	27	8			

★ USSR 12 caps, 1 goal

Michael BORGQVIST
17/12/67 Midfield

89	Jonsereds IF	Div 2	
90	Spårvägens IF	Div 2	
91	AIK	28	1

SWEDEN

FIVE YEAR RECORD *Birthdate/Playing position*	LEAGUE Apps Gls	EURO CUPS Cup Apps Gls

Krister NORDIN
25/02/68   Midfield

87	Djurgårdens IF	Div 2			
88	Djurgårdens IF	21	2		
89	Djurgårdens IF	22	3	CWC	4	-
90	Djurgårdens IF	19	2	CWC	2	-
91	Djurgårdens IF	25	6		

Pascal SIMPSON
04/05/71   Midfield

90	BP	Div 2	
91	AIK	24	3

Stefan JONSSON
06/10/66   Midfield

91	Hudiksvalls ABK	Div 3

Gary SUNDGREN
25/10/67   Forward

87	IK Franke	Div 4	
88	AIK	17	-
89	AIK	20	2
90	AIK	20	1
91	AIK	28	2

Kim BERGSTRAND
18/04/68   Forward

87	AIK	16	1	UC	2	-
88	AIK	20	3			
89	AIK	18	3			
90	AIK	12	2			
91	AIK	24	3			

FIVE YEAR RECORD *Birthdate/Playing position*	LEAGUE Apps Gls	EURO CUPS Cup Apps Gls

Dick LIDMAN
24/01/67   Forward

87	Skellefteå AIK	Div 2	
88	Skellefteå AIK	Div 2	
89	GIF Sundsvall	19	7
90	GIF Sundsvall	Div 2	
91	GIF Sundsvall	7	1

EUROPEAN HONOURS
none

EUROPEAN CUPS RECORD

	Entries	Pd	W	D	L	F	A
Champions' Cup	none						
Cup-winners' Cup	2	6	2	2	2	17	6
UEFA/Fairs' Cup	6	16	5	5	6	20	26
Total - All 3 Cups	8	22	7	7	8	37	32

FC LUZERN

FIVE YEAR RECORD Birthdate/Playing position	LEAGUE Apps Gls	EURO CUPS Cup Apps Gls

Giorgio MELLACINA
15/01/61   Goalkeeper

		Apps	Gls	Cup	Apps	Gls
87/88	AC Bellinzona	21	-			
88/89	FC Luzern	7	-			
89/90	FC Luzern	7	-	CC	1	-
90/91	FC Luzern	16	-	UC	3	-
91/92	FC Luzern	22	-			

Beat MUTTER
22/07/62   Goalkeeper

		Apps	Gls	Cup	Apps	Gls
87/88	Servette FC Genève	20	-			
88/89	AC Bellinzona	35	-			
89/90	AC Bellinzona	21	-			
90/91	FC Luzern	22	-	UC	1	-
91/92	FC Luzern	-	-			

René VAN ECK (Hol)
18/02/66   Defender

		Apps	Gls	Cup	Apps	Gls
87/88	FC Den Bosch (Hol)	34	-			
88/89	BVV Den Bosch (Hol)	30	-			
89/90	BVV Den Bosch (Hol)	32	-			
90/91	FC Luzern	33	-	UC	4	1
91/92	FC Luzern	20	1			

Martin RUEDA
09/01/63   Defender

		Apps	Gls	Cup	Apps	Gls
87/88	FC Wettingen	Div 2				
88/89	FC Wettingen	34	7			
89/90	FC Wettingen	21	1	UC	4	-
90/91	FC Wettingen	21	2			
91/92	FC Luzern	21	1			

Urs BIRRER
04/09/61   Defender

		Apps	Gls	Cup	Apps	Gls
87/88	FC Luzern	34	-			
88/89	FC Luzern	32	1			
89/90	FC Luzern	22	-	CC	1	-
90/91	FC Luzern	32	-	UC	4	-
91/92	FC Luzern	19	1			

★ Switzerland 3 caps, 0 goals

FIVE YEAR RECORD Birthdate/Playing position	LEAGUE Apps Gls	EURO CUPS Cup Apps Gls

Patrick HUSER
18/04/71   Defender

		Apps	Gls	Cup	Apps	Gls
90/91	FC Luzern	10	-	UC	1	-
91/92	SC Zug	Div 2				

Christoph GILLI
17/06/63   Defender

		Apps	Gls	Cup	Apps	Gls
87/88	AC Bellinzona	19	-			
88/89	FC Zürich	Div 2				
89/90	FC Zürich	Div 2				
90/91	FC Zürich	21	-			
91/92	FC Zürich	27	-			

Stephan WOLF
31/01/71   Defender

		Apps	Gls	Cup	Apps	Gls
90/91	FC Luzern	18	-	UC	1	-
91/92	FC Luzern	20	-			

Peter GMÜR
15/05/67   Defender

		Apps	Gls	Cup	Apps	Gls
87/88	FC Luzern	1	-			
88/89	FC Luzern	9	-			
89/90	FC Luzern	24	-	CC	1	-
90/91	FC Luzern	26	-	UC	4	-
91/92	FC Luzern	13	-			

Stefan MARINI
23/06/65   Defender

		Apps	Gls	Cup	Apps	Gls
87/88	FC Luzern	26	1			
88/89	FC Luzern	21	-			
89/90	FC Luzern	14	-	CC	2	-
90/91	FC Luzern	13	-	UC	4	1
91/92	FC Luzern	3	-			

★ Switzerland 19 caps, 0 goals

Arno ARTS (Hol)
23/06/69   Midfield

		Apps	Gls	Cup	Apps	Gls
87/88	NEC (Hol)	Div 2				
88/89	NEC (Hol)	Div 2				
89/90	NEC (Hol)	34	7			
90/91	NEC (Hol)	34	7			
91/92	FC Luzern	20	-			

SWITZERLAND

FIVE YEAR RECORD *Birthdate/Playing position*	LEAGUE Apps Gls	EURO CUPS Cup Apps Gls

Hanspeter BURRI
22/12/63   Midfield

87/88	FC Luzern	27	2	
88/89	FC Luzern	33	3	
89/90	FC Luzern	26	2	CC 1 -
90/91	FC Luzern	26	-	UC 3 -
91/92	FC Luzern	12	-	

★ Switzerland 1 cap, 0 goals

Urs SCHÖNENBERGER
21/02/59   Midfield

87/88	FC Luzern	33	3	
88/89	FC Luzern	30	2	
89/90	FC Luzern	33	1	CC 2 -
90/91	FC Luzern	33	-	UC 4 -
91/92	FC Luzern	18	-	

Herbert BAUMANN
16/09/64   Midfield

87/88	FC Luzern	20	-	
88/89	FC Luzern	34	-	
89/90	FC Luzern	33	1	CC 2 -
90/91	FC Luzern	27	3	UC 1 -
91/92	FC Luzern	20	1	

★ Switzerland 15 caps, 0 goals

Roberto FREGNO (Ita)
23/02/59   Midfield

87/88	AC Bellinzona	22	1
88/89	AC Bellinzona	34	2
89/90	AC Bellinzona	20	3
90/91	FC Zürich	18	2
91/92	FC Zürich	33	5

FIVE YEAR RECORD *Birthdate/Playing position*	LEAGUE Apps Gls	EURO CUPS Cup Apps Gls

Brian BERTELSEN (Den)
19/04/63   Forward

87/88	FC Wettingen	Div 2		
88/89	FC Wettingen	31	10	
89/90	FC Wettingen	19	2	UC 4 1
90/91	FC Basel	Div 2		
91/92	FC St. Gallen	25	3	

Semir TUCE (Yug)
11/02/64   Forward

87/88	Velez Mostar (Yug)	27	13	UC 4 4
88/89	Velez Mostar (Yug)	25	12	UC 6 2
89/90	FC Luzern	8	4	
90/91	FC Luzern	18	5	UC 4 -
91/92	FC Luzern	22	2	

★ Yugoslavia 7 caps, 2 goals

André KUNZ
14/06/73   Forward

90/91	FC Luzern	2	-
91/92	FC Luzern	3	-

EUROPEAN HONOURS
none

EUROPEAN CUPS RECORD

	Entries	Pd	W	D	L	F	A
Champions' Cup	1	2	0	0	2	0	5
Cup-winners' Cup	1	2	0	0	2	2	9
UEFA/Fairs' Cup	2	6	1	3	2	4	5
Total - All 3 Cups	4	10	1	3	6	6	19

TRABZONSPOR

FIVE YEAR RECORD *Birthdate/Playing position*	LEAGUE Apps Gls	EURO CUPS Cup Apps Gls

Viktor GRISHKO (Ukr)
02/11/61   Goalkeeper

87	Chernomorets Odessa (Urs)	Div 2			
88	Chernomorets Odessa (Urs)	20	-		
89	Chernomorets Odessa (Urs)	25	1		
90	Chernomorets Odessa (Urs)	24	-	UC	4	-
91	Chernomorets Odessa (Urs)	30	-		

LEVENT Zorluer
25/03/67   Goalkeeper

87/88	Yeni Salihlispor	Div 2			
88/89	Trabzonspor	2	-		
89/90	Trabzonspor	9	-		
90/91	Trabzonspor	12	-	CWC	2	-
91/92	Trabzonspor	4	-		

ERKAN Sozeri
09/10/67   Defender

89/90	Gaziantepspor	Div 2			
90/91	Gaziantepspor	29	-		
91/92	Trabzonspor	8	-	UC	1	-

KEMAL Serdar
08/05/62   Defender

87/88	Trabzonspor	31	1		
88/89	Trabzonspor	34	2		
89/90	Trabzonspor	34	3		
90/91	Trabzonspor	28	4	CWC	4	-
91/92	Trabzonspor	28	1	UC	6	-

★ Turkey 10 caps, 0 goals

OGÜN Temizkanoglu
14/04/68   Defender

89/90	Trabzonspor	5	-		
90/91	Trabzonspor	17	-	CWC	4	-
91/92	Trabzonspor	26	5	UC	6	-

★ Turkey 8 caps, 0 goals

FIVE YEAR RECORD *Birthdate/Playing position*	LEAGUE Apps Gls	EURO CUPS Cup Apps Gls

SEYHMUZ Suna
10/02/65   Defender

87/88	Inegölspor	Div 2			
88/89	Maltayaspor	32	2		
89/90	Malatyaspor	32	3		
90/91	Trabzonspor	28	-	CWC	4	-
91/92	Trabzonspor	25	-	UC	5	1

ISMAIL Gökçek
10/09/63   Defender

87/88	Bakirköyspor	Div 2			
88/89	Trabzonspor	34	1		
89/90	Trabzonspor	33	1		
90/91	Trabzonspor	22	-	CWC	2	-
91/92	Trabzonspor	21	-	UC	5	-

MEHMET Arslan
07/06/68   Midfield

87/88	Ankaragücü	16	1		
88/89	Ankaragücü	27	1		
89/90	Ankaragücü	32	-		
90/91	Trabzonspor	23	-	CWC	3	-
91/92	Trabzonspor	27	1	UC	5	-

ÜNAL Karaman
01/08/66   Midfield

87/88	Malatyaspor	35	7		
88/89	Malatyaspor	33	8		
89/90	Malatyaspor	23	8		
90/91	Trabzonspor	19	3	CWC	3	-
91/92	Trabzonspor	19	11	UC	5	1

★ Turkey 27 caps, 2 goals

Yury SHELEPNITSKY (Ukr)
31/07/65   Midfield

89	Chernomorets Odessa (Urs)	21	2		
90	Chernomorets Odessa (Urs)	20	-	UC	4	1
91	Chernomorets Odessa (Urs)	24	2		

TURKEY

FIVE YEAR RECORD *Birthdate/Playing position*	LEAGUE Apps Gls	EURO CUPS Cup Apps Gls

ABDULLAH Ercan
13/03/72   Midfield

90/91	Trabzonspor	20	-		
91/92	Trabzonspor	15	-	UC 2	-

★ Turkey 2 caps, 0 goals

SONER Boz
11/01/68   Midfield

87/88	Trabzonspor	7	2		
88/89	Trabzonspor	30	3		
89/90	Trabzonspor	8	-		
90/91	Trabzonspor	28	4	CWC 4	1
91/92	Trabzonspor	20	1	UC 5	-

TURGUT Uçar
10/03/64   Midfield

87/88	Altay	33	2		
88/89	Trabzonspor	25	-		
89/90	Trabzonspor	22	1		
90/91	Trabzonspor	27	-	CWC 3	-
91/92	Trabzonspor	16	-	UC 2	-

Jacek CYZIO (Pol)
06/08/68   Forward

87/88	Pogon Szcecin (Pol)	23	3	UC 2	-
88/89	Pogon Szcecin (Pol)	23	10		
89/90	Legia Warszawa (Pol)	26	5	CWC 1	-
90/91	Legia Warszawa (Pol)	24	2	CWC 7	1
91/92	Trabzonspor	26	6	UC 6	1

HAMI Mandirali
06/06/68   Forward

87/88	Trabzonspor	37	17		
88/89	Trabzonspor	33	22		
89/90	Trabzonspor	33	6		
90/91	Trabzonspor	30	13	CWC 3	-
91/92	Trabzonspor	28	18	UC 6	5

★ Turkey 13 caps, 4 goals

FIVE YEAR RECORD *Birthdate/Playing position*	LEAGUE Apps Gls	EURO CUPS Cup Apps Gls

ORHAN Çikirçi
15/04/67   Forward

87/88	Eskisehirspor	7	-		
88/89	Eskisehirspor	30	3		
89/90	Trabzonspor	33	11		
90/91	Trabzonspor	30	5	CWC 4	-
91/92	Trabzonspor	28	4	UC 6	2

★ Turkey 8 caps, 1 goal

HAMDI Aslan
06/09/67   Forward

87/88	Trabzonspor	26	4		
88/89	Trabzonspor	33	5		
89/90	Trabzonspor	33	21		
90/91	Trabzonspor	29	15	CWC 4	3
91/92	Trabzonspor	27	8	UC 5	3

LEMI Çelik
09/03/66   Midfield

87/88	Trabzonspor	29	-		
88/89	Trabzonspor	31	-		
89/90	Trabzonspor	33	6		
90/91	Trabzonspor	29	3	CWC 3	-
91/92	Trabzonspor	6	1		

EUROPEAN HONOURS
none

EUROPEAN CUP RESULTS

	Entries	Pd	W	D	L	F	A
Champions' Cup	6	14	6	1	7	12	19
Cup-winners' Cup	1	4	2	1	1	6	8
UEFA/Fairs' Cup	3	10	4	2	4	14	17
Total - All 3 Cups	10	28	12	4	12	32	44

CARDIFF CITY

FIVE YEAR RECORD	LEAGUE		EURO CUPS	
Birthdate/Playing position	Apps	Gls	Cup	Apps Gls

Mark GREW (Eng)
15/02/58 Goalkeeper

87/88	Port Vale	Div 3
88/89	Port Vale	Div 3
89/90	Port Vale	Div 2
90/91	Port Vale	Div 2
	Blackburn Rovers	Div 2
91/92	Port Vale	Div 2

Gavin WARD (Eng)
30/06/70 Goalkeeper

88/89	Shrewsbury Town	Div 2
89/90	West Bromwich Albion	Div 2
	Cardiff City	Div 3
90/91	Cardiff City	Div 4
91/92	Cardiff City	Div 4

Neil MATTHEWS (Eng)
03/12/67 Defender

87/88	Blackpool	Div 3
88/89	Blackpool	Div 3
89/90	Blackpool	Div 3
90/91	Cardiff City	Div 4
91/92	Cardiff City	Div 4

Damon SEARLE
26/10/71 Defender

90/91	Cardiff City	Div 4
91/92	Cardiff City	Div 4

Jason PERRY
02/04/70 Defender

87/88	Cardiff City	Div 4		
88/89	Cardiff City	Div 3	CWC	1 -
89/90	Cardiff City	Div 3		
90/91	Cardiff City	Div 4		
91/92	Cardiff City	Div 4		

Lee BADDELEY
12/07/74 Defender

90/91	Cardiff City	Div 4
91/92	Cardiff City	Div 4

Gareth ABRAHAM
13/02/69 Defender

87/88	Cardiff City	Div 4		
88/89	Cardiff City	Div 3	CWC	1 -
89/90	Cardiff City	Div 3		
90/91	Cardiff City	Div 4		
91/92	Cardiff City	Div 4		

Allan LEWIS
31/05/71 Defender

89/90	Cardiff City	Div 3
90/91	Cardiff City	Div 4
91/92	Cardiff City	Div 4

Andy GORMAN
06/08/73 Midfield

91/92	Cardiff City	Div 4

Eddie NEWTON (Eng)
13/12/71 Midfield

91/92	Cardiff City	Div 4	
	Chelsea		1 1

Paul RAMSEY (Nir)
03/09/62 Midfield

87/88	Leicester City	Div 2
88/89	Leicester City	Div 2
89/90	Leicester City	Div 2
90/91	Leicester City	Div 2
91/92	Cardiff City	Div 4

★ Northern Ireland 14 caps, 0 goals

Nathan BLAKE
27/01/72 Midfield

89/90	Cardiff City	Div 3
90/91	Cardiff City	Div 4
91/92	Cardiff City	Div 4

WALES

FIVE YEAR RECORD	LEAGUE	EURO CUPS
Birthdate/Playing position	Apps Gls	Cup Apps Gls

Roger GIBBINS (Eng)
06/09/55   Midfield

87/88	Newport County	Div 4
	Torquay United	Div 4
88/89	Torquay United	Div 4
	Cardiff City	Div 3
89/90	Cardiff City	Div 3
90/91	Cardiff City	Div 4
91/92	Cardiff City	Div 4

Paul MILLAR (Nir)
16/11/66   Midfield

88/89	Port Vale	Div 3
89/90	Port Vale	Div 2
90/91	Port Vale	Div 2
	Hereford United	Div 4
91/92	Cardiff City	Div 4

Cohen GRIFFITH
26/12/62   Forward

89/90	Cardiff City	Div 3
90/91	Cardiff City	Div 4
91/92	Cardiff City	Div 4

Carl DALE
29/04/66   Forward

87/88	Chester City	Div 3
88/89	Chester City	Div 3
89/90	Chester City	Div 3
90/91	Chester City	Div 3
91/92	Cardiff City	Div 4

FIVE YEAR RECORD	LEAGUE	EURO CUPS
Birthdate/Playing position	Apps Gls	Cup Apps Gls

Chris PIKE
19/10/61   Forward

87/88	Fulham	Div 3
88/89	Fulham	Div 3
89/90	Cardiff City	Div 4
90/91	Cardiff City	Div 4
91/92	Cardiff City	Div 4

Jason DONOVAN
22/04/74   Forward

91/92	Cardiff City	Div 4

EUROPEAN HONOURS
none

EUROPEAN CUPS RECORD

	Entries	Pd	W	D	L	F	A
Champions' Cup	none						
Cup-winners' Cup	12	45	16	13	16	63	50
UEFA/Fairs' Cup	none						
Total - All 3 Cups	12	45	16	13	16	63	50

Ajax captain Danny Blind celebrates his team's success against Torino, thus completing the Dutch club's collection of European trophies.

UEFA CUP

UNLIKE the other two competitions, the UEFA Cup goes straight into first round action without the need for any preliminaries. Of all the new countries granted admission to the European competitions this season, only Slovenia and the Ukraine have been allowed entries to the UEFA Cup. With Yugoslavia excluded and Russia entering only two teams instead of their permitted three, the competition is left with its usual starting line-up of 64.

Holders Ajax and last year's runners-up Torino are amongst a clutch of prestigious clubs taking part in what is a very strong field containing no fewer than 14 previous European trophy winners.

Torino's away goals defeat in last year's final denied Italy a fourth successive victory in the competition after wins for Napoli in 1989, Juventus in 1990 and Internazionale in 1991. But the Italian contingent is as strong as ever in 1992/93, with two of those former winners, Juventus and Napoli, joining Torino and the 1991 runners-up, Roma, in a four-pronged assault on the trophy.

Of the quartet, Juventus appear to be the team best equipped to reach the final. They tracked Milan all the way in last year's Italian championship and have since signed a number of top-class internationals including England's David Platt, Germany's Andreas Möller and Italy's very own star striker Gianluca Vialli. With the brilliant Roberto Baggio still on hand to provide ingenuity in midfield, the Turin team will be extremely difficult to beat.

Torino may have lost star forward Lentini to Milan, but they can still count on the marvellous strategic skills of Belgian Enzo Scifo in midfield. Roma, with Euro '92 star Thomas Hässler joined by Red Star Belgrade's Sinisa Mihajlovic and Argentinian World Cup hero Claudio Caniggia, and Napoli, with new Italian sensation Gianfranco Zola, now paired in midfield with Sweden's Jonas Thern, will provide a formidable test for anyone.

But the big names in this year's UEFA Cup are not exclusively Italian. The most successful European club of all time, Real Madrid, will be aiming to regain the trophy they won back-to-back in the mid-'80s, and after Barcelona's Champions' Cup triumph last year the men in white will be anxious to match their great rivals with another European trophy to add to their impressive roll of honour.

Another win for Ajax cannot be discounted either. The

Amsterdam club have lost midfielders Winter and Van 't Schip to Italy during the summer, but there are still enough gifted young players in the side to mount another serious challenge. Anderlecht, too, have enormous potential. They have bought Belgian internationals Marc Emmers and Philippe Albert to reinforce their squad, and with top strikers such as Nilis, Bosman and Degryse to call upon, they should not be short of firepower up front. And of course the German challenge is as strong as ever, with Borussia Dortmund and Eintracht Frankfurt probably the Bundesliga's best bets for European success this year.

1991 Cup-winners' Cup victors Manchester United lead a relatively strong British challenge, although Celtic, who only qualified for the competition as a result of the Yugoslav ban, will be hard pressed to get past UEFA Cup perennials Cologne. This tie rivals the Valencia-Napoli encounter as the most exciting confrontation of the first round, but there should also be plenty of entertainment in the matches between Dinamo Kiev and Rapid Vienna and Paris-Saint-Germain and PAOK.

Two teams which have enjoyed recent success in the UEFA Cup enter the competition this season under a different guise. The Austrian side FC Swarovski Tirol, which reached the semi-finals in 1987, have changed their name back to FC Wacker Innsbruck, while last year's quarter-finalists B 1903 have merged with another Danish club, KB, to form FC København.

There are also some genuine newcomers to European competition in the starting line-up - Caen of France, Electroputere Craiova of Romania and Slovenia's Belvedur Izola, who find themselves thrown in at the deep end to take on Portuguese giants Benfica!

★ TEN TO WATCH ★

Miodrag Belodedic (Valencia), Luc Nilis (Anderlecht), Dennis Bergkamp (Ajax), Ryan Giggs (Manchester United), Roberto Baggio (Juventus), Aleksandr Mostovoy (Benfica), Ivan Zamorano (Real Madrid), Stéphane Chapuisat (Borussia Dortmund), Gianfranco Zola (Napoli), Thomas Hässler (Roma).

UEFA CUP 1992-93

FIRST ROUND

1st Leg - September 16, 1992; 2nd Leg - September 30, 1992

		1st Leg	2nd Leg	Agg.	Away gls	Pens
Hibernian (Sco)	v RSC Anderlecht (Bel)					
Valencia CF (Esp)	v Napoli (Ita)					
Vitesse (Hol)	v Derry City (Irl)					
Neuchâtel Xamax FC (Sui)	v BK Frem (Den)					
SV Casino Salzburg (Aut)	v Ajax (Hol)					
Real Sociedad (Esp)	v Vitória Guimarães (Por)					
Sheffield Wednesday (Eng)	v Spora Luxembourg (Lux)					
Paris-Saint-Germain FC (Fra)	v PAOK (Gre)					
Örebro SK (Swe)	v KV Mechelen (Bel)					
SM Caen (Fra)	v Real Zaragoza (Esp)					
Vác FC (Hun)	v FC Groningen (Hol)					
Fram (Isl)	v 1.FC Kaiserslautern (Ger)					
Manchester United (Eng)	v Torpedo Moskva (Rus)					
1.FC Köln (Ger)	v Celtic (Sco)					
Portadown (Nir)	v R Standard Liège (Bel)					
MP (Fin)	v FC København (Den)					
Widzew Lódz (Pol)	v Eintracht Frankfurt (Ger)					
IFK Norrköping (Swe)	v Torino (Ita)					
Heart of Midlothian (Sco)	v Slavia Praha (Tch)					
Dinamo Moskva (Rus)	v Rosenborg BK (Nor)					
Juventus (Ita)	v Anorthosis Famagusta (Cyp)					
Lokomotiv Plovdiv (Bul)	v AJ Auxerre (Fra)					
Dinamo Kiev (Urs)	v SK Rapid Wien (Aut)					
Panathinaikos (Gre)	v Electroputere Craiova (Rom)					
SL Benfica (Por)	v Belvedur Izola (Slo)					
Wacker Innsbruck (Aut)	v Roma (Ita)					
Sigma Olomouc (Tch)	v Universitatea Craiova (Rom)					
GKS Katowice (Pol)	v Galatasaray (Tur)					
Floriana (Mlt)	v Borussia Dortmund (Ger)					
Real Madrid (Esp)	v Politehnica Timisoara (Rom)					
Botev Plovdiv (Bul)	v Fenerbahce (Tur)					
Grasshopper-Club Zürich (Sui)	v Sporting CP (Por)					

SECOND ROUND
1st Leg - October 21, 1992; 2nd Leg - November 4, 1992

	1st Leg	2nd Leg	Agg.	Away gls	Pens
v					
v					
v					
v					
v					
v					
v					
v					
v					
v					
v					
v					
v					
v					
v					
v					

THIRD ROUND
1st Leg - November 25, 1992; 2nd Leg - December 9, 1992

	1st Leg	2nd Leg	Agg.	Away gls	Pens
v					
v					
v					
v					
v					
v					
v					
v					

QUARTER-FINALS
1st Leg - March 3, 1993; 2nd Leg - March 17, 1993

	1st Leg	2nd Leg	Agg.	Away gls	Pens
v					
v					
v					
v					

SEMI-FINALS
1st Leg - April 7, 1993; 2nd Leg - April 21, 1993

	1st Leg	2nd Leg	Agg.	Away gls	Pens
v					
v					

FINAL
1st Leg - May 5, 1993; 2nd Leg - May 19, 1993

	1st Leg	2nd Leg	Agg.	Away gls	Pens
v					

SV CASINO SALZBURG

FIVE YEAR RECORD	LEAGUE		EURO CUPS		
Birthdate/Playing position	Apps	Gls	Cup	Apps	Gls

Herbert ILSANKER
24/05/67   Goalkeeper

89/90	SV Casino Salzburg	10	-			
90/91	SV Casino Salzburg	31	-			
91/92	SV Casino Salzburg	31	-			

Otto KONRAD
01/11/64   Goalkeeper

87/88	SK Sturm Graz	21	-			
88/89	SK Sturm Graz	20	-	UC	2	-
89/90	SK Sturm Graz	36	-			
90/91	SK Sturm Graz	36	1			
91/92	SK Sturm Graz	19	-	UC	2	-

★ Austria 6 caps, 0 goals

Christian FÜRSTALLER
30/12/64   Defender

87/88	SV Casino Salzburg	Div 2				
88/89	SV Casino Salzburg	Div 2				
89/90	SV Casino Salzburg	24	-			
90/91	SV Casino Salzburg	11	-			
91/92	SV Casino Salzburg	30	-			

Kurt GARGER
15/09/60   Defender

87/88	SK Rapid Wien	34	1	CC	4	-
88/89	FC Swarovski Tirol	33	3			
89/90	FC Swarovski Tirol	19	1	CC	3	-
90/91	SV Casino Salzburg	34	2			
91/92	SV Casino Salzburg	33	2			

★ Austria 1 cap, 0 goals

Leo LAINER
10/09/60   Defender

87/88	SV Casino Salzburg	Div 2				
88/89	FC Swarovski Tirol	32	7			
89/90	Fc Swarovski Tirol	34	4	CC	4	-
90/91	SV Casino Salzburg	33	2			
91/92	SV Casino Salzburg	28	2			

★ Austria 23 caps, 1 goal

FIVE YEAR RECORD	LEAGUE		EURO CUPS		
Birthdate/Playing position	Apps	Gls	Cup	Apps	Gls

Heribert WEBER
28/06/55   Defender

87/88	SK Rapid Wien	28	7	CC	4	1
88/89	SK Rapid Wien	30	1	CC	2	-
89/90	SV Casino Salzburg	30	3			
90/91	SV Casino Salzburg	31	2			
91/92	SV Casino Salzburg	27	3			

★ Austria 68 caps, 1 goal

Thomas WINKLHOFER
30/12/70   Defender

91/92	FC Swarovski Tirol	1	-	
	WSG Wattens	Div 2		

Andreas LIPA
26/04/71   Midfield

89/90	First Vienna FC	3	-	
90/91	First Vienna FC	12	1	
91/92	First Vienna FC	20	4	

Wolfgang FEIERSINGER
30/01/65   Midfield

87/88	SV Casino Salzburg	Div 2		
88/89	SV Casino Salzburg	Div 2		
89/90	SV Casino Salzburg	31	1	
90/91	SV Casino Salzburg	34	2	
91/92	SV Casino Salzburg	29	-	

★ Austria 2 caps, 0 goals

Peter HRSTIC
24/09/61   Midfield

87/88	SK Rapid Wien	25	4	CC	1	-
88/89	FC Swarovski Tirol	11	-			
89/90	SV Casino Salzburg	18	5			
90/91	FC Salzburg	Div 2				
91/92	SV Casino Salzburg	36	9			

★ Austria 1 cap, 0 goals

Johann PINWINKLER
15/08/68   Midfield

90/91	SV Casino Salzburg	12	1	
91/92	SV Casino Salzburg	10	-	

AUSTRIA

FIVE YEAR RECORD *Birthdate/Playing position*	LEAGUE Apps Gls	EURO CUPS Cup Apps Gls	FIVE YEAR RECORD *Birthdate/Playing position*	LEAGUE Apps Gls	EURO CUPS Cup Apps Gls

Andreas REISINGER
14/10/63   Midfield

87/88	Wiener Sport-Club	34	2		
88/89	Wiener Sport-Club	36	6		
89/90	SK Rapid Wien	29	3	UC	6 -
90/91	SK Rapid Wien	29	3	UC	2 -
91/92	SV Casino Salzburg	23	1		

★ Austria 10 caps, 0 goals

Robert SCHEIBER
07/07/60   Midfield

87/88	Wiener Sport-Club	30	1
88/89	Wiener Sport-Club	21	1
89/90	SV Casino Salzburg	34	5
90/91	SV Casino Salzburg	34	2
91/92	SV Casino Salzburg	25	2

Hermann STADLER
21/05/61   Midfield

87/88	SV Casino Salzburg	Div 2	
88/89	SV Casino Salzburg	Div 2	
89/90	SV Casino Salzburg	26	2
90/91	SV Casino Salzburg	27	1
91/92	SV Casino Salzburg	33	5

Gerald WILLFURTH
06/11/62   Midfield

87/88	SK Rapid Wien	35	9	CC	3 1
88/89	SK Rapid Wien	35	5	CC	2 -
89/90	SV Casino Salzburg	34	4		
90/91	SV Casino Salzburg	33	7		
91/92	SV Casino Salzburg	25	3		

★ Austria 30 caps, 3 goals

Nikola JURCEVIC (Cro)
14/09/66   Forward

89/90	NK Zagreb (Yug)	Div 3	
90/91	NK Zagreb (Yug)	Div 2	
91/92	SV Casino Salzburg	35	11

Heimo PFEIFENBERGER
29/12/66   Forward

87/88	SV Casino Salzburg	Div 2			
88/89	SK Rapid Wien	19	10		
89/90	SK Rapid Wien	35	13	UC	6 2
90/91	SK Rapid Wien	29	10	UC	2 1
91/92	SK Rapid Wien	34	9		

★ Austria 7 caps, 2 goals

Herfried SABITZER
19/10/69   Forward

87/88	DSV Alpine	Div 2	
88/89	DSV Alpine	Div 2	
89/90	DSV Alpine	Div 2	
90/91	DSV Alpine	32	9
91/92	SV Casino Salzburg	29	7

★ Austria 1 cap, 0 goals

EUROPEAN HONOURS
none

EUROPEAN CUPS RECORD

	Entries	Pd	W	D	L	F	A
Champions' Cup	none						
Cup-winners' Cup	1	2	0	0	2	0	8
UEFA/Fairs' Cup	2	6	3	0	3	11	9
Total - All 3 Cups	3	8	3	0	5	11	17

FC WACKER INNSBRUCK

FIVE YEAR RECORD Birthdate/Playing position	LEAGUE Apps	Gls	EURO CUPS Cup	Apps	Gls

Walter DEVORA
17/09/70   Goalkeeper

Milan ORAZE
29/03/67   Goalkeeper

		LEAGUE Apps	Gls	EURO CUPS Cup	Apps	Gls
90/91	SK Austria Klagenfurt	Div 2				
91/92	FC Swarovski Tirol	18	-	UC	4	-

Michael BAUR
16/04/69   Defender

		LEAGUE Apps	Gls	EURO CUPS Cup	Apps	Gls
89/90	FC Swarovski Tirol	22	2	CC	1	1
90/91	FC Swarovski Tirol	36	1	CC	4	-
91/92	FC Swarovski Tirol	33	3	UC	4	-

★ Austria 12 caps, 1 goal

Harald SCHNEIDER
08/06/66   Defender

		LEAGUE Apps	Gls	EURO CUPS Cup	Apps	Gls
87/88	SC Mittersill	Div 3				
88/89	Linzer ASK	20	2			
89/90	Linzer ASC	Div 2				
	FK Austria	7	-			
90/91	FK Austria	20	1	CWC	1	-
91/92	FK Austria	15	1	CC	1	-

★ Austria 1 cap, 0 goals

Kurt RUSS
23/11/64   Defender

		LEAGUE Apps	Gls	EURO CUPS Cup	Apps	Gls
87/88	First Vienna FC	13	3			
88/89	First Vienna FC	35	6	UC	4	-
89/90	First Vienna FC	34	3	UC	4	-
90/91	FC Swarovski Tirol	32	1	CC	4	-
91/92	FC Swarovski Tirol	32	-	UC	4	-

★ Austria 28 caps, 0 goals

Michael STREITER
19/01/66   Defender

		LEAGUE Apps	Gls	EURO CUPS Cup	Apps	Gls
87/88	FC Swarovski Tirol	24	-	CWC	1	-
88/89	FC Swarovski Tirol	32	-			
89/90	FC Swarovski Tirol	28	-	CC	4	-
90/91	FC Swarovski Tirol	28	-	CC	2	-
91/92	FC Swarovski Tirol	27	-	UC	5	-

★ Austria 17 caps, 1 goal

Robert WAZINGER
23/08/66   Defender

		LEAGUE Apps	Gls	EURO CUPS Cup	Apps	Gls
87/88	FC Swarovski Tirol	29	1	CWC	2	-
88/89	FC Swarovski Tirol	18	1			
89/90	FC Swarovski Tirol	17	-	CC	3	-
90/91	FC Swarovski Tirol	22	-			
91/92	FC Swarovski Tirol	25	4	UC	4	-

Andrzej LESIAK (Pol)
21/05/66   Defender

		LEAGUE Apps	Gls	EURO CUPS Cup	Apps	Gls
87/88	GKS Katowice (Pol)	8	-	UC	2	-
88/89	GKS Katowice (Pol)	17	-	UC	2	-
89/90	GKS Katowice (Pol)	29	-	UC	2	-
90/91	GKS Katowice (Pol)	26	-	UC	4	-
91/92	GKS Katowice (Pol)	31	6	CWC	4	-

★ Poland 12 caps, 1 goal

Jürgen HARTMANN
28/08/70   Midfield

		LEAGUE Apps	Gls	EURO CUPS Cup	Apps	Gls
88/89	DSV Alpine	Div 2				
89/90	DSV Alpine	Div 2				
90/91	FC Swarovski Tirol	32	-	CC	4	-
91/92	FC Swarovski Tirol	33	-	UC	6	-

★ Austria 7 caps, 0 goals

Alfred HÖRTNAGL
24/09/66   Midfield

		LEAGUE Apps	Gls	EURO CUPS Cup	Apps	Gls
87/88	FC Swarovski Tirol	24	-	CWC	1	-
88/89	FC Swarovski Tirol	20	4			
89/90	FC Swarovski Tirol	34	2	CC	4	1
90/91	FC Swarovski Tirol	32	4	CC	4	1
91/92	FC Swarovski Tirol	30	3	UC	6	1

★ Austria 19 caps, 1 goal

Roland KIRCHLER
29/09/70   Midfield

		LEAGUE Apps	Gls	EURO CUPS Cup	Apps	Gls
89/90	WSG Wattens	Div 2				
90/91	FC Swarovski Tirol	5	3			
91/92	FC Swarovski Tirol	18	3	UC	5	-

AUSTRIA

FIVE YEAR RECORD	LEAGUE		EURO CUPS		
Birthdate/Playing position	Apps	Gls	Cup	Apps	Gls

Manfred LINZMAIER
27/08/62   Midfield

87/88	FC Swarovski Tirol	33	2	CWC	2	1
88/89	FC Swarovski Tirol	32	7			
89/90	FC Swarovski Tirol	29	3	CC	4	-
90/91	FC Swarovski Tirol	28	4	CC	4	1
91/92	FC Swarovski Tirol	27	3	UC	6	-

★ Austria 25 caps, 2 goals

Mario BEEN (Hol)
11/12/63   Midfield

87/88	Feyenoord (Hol)	30	13	UC	4	1
88/89	Pisa (Ita)	27	3			
89/90	Pisa (Ita)	Div 2				
90/91	Roda JC (Hol)	12	1			
91/92	SC Heerenveen (Hol)	Div 2				

★ Holland 1 cap, 0 goals

Andreas SPIELMANN
26/03/65   Midfield

87/88	FC Swarovski Tirol	20	1			
88/89	FC Swarovski Tirol	3	-			
	VSE St. Pölten	16	-			
89/90	VSE St. Pölten	13	1			
90/91	First Vienna FC	19	2			
91/92	Apollon Kalamarias (Gre)	Div 2				

★ Austria 1 cap, 0 goals

Rudolf GUSSNIG
19/06/69   Forward

| 90/91 | FC Swarovski Tirol | 5 | 1 | | | |
| 91/92 | FC Swarovski Tirol | 16 | 3 | | | |

Václav DANEK (Tch)
22/12/60   Forward

87/88	Baník Ostrava (Tch)	26	23			
88/89	Baník Ostrava (Tch)	23	13			
89/90	FC Swarovski Tirol	25	15	CC	1	-
90/91	FC Swarovski Tirol	32	29	CC	4	-
91/92	AC Le Havre (Fra)	17	3			

* Czechoslovakia 22 caps, 9 goals

Christoph WESTERTHALER
11/01/65   Forward

87/88	LASK	21	5	UC	1	-
88/89	FC Swarovski Tirol	35	13			
89/90	FC Swarovski Tirol	31	13	CC	4	3
90/91	FC Swarovski Tirol	31	14	CC	2	-
91/92	FC Swarovski Tirol	35	17	UC	6	5

★ Austria 5 caps, 0 goals

Helmut LORENZ
02/02/69

90/91	FC Swarovski Tirol	-	-			
	WSG Wattens	Div 2				
91/92	WSG Wattens	Div 2				

EUROPEAN CUPS RECORD

	Entries	Pd	W	D	L	F	A
Champions' Cup	7	22	7	3	12	34	46
Cup-winners' Cup	5	14	6	2	6	18	26
UEFA/Fairs' Cup	7	28	11	4	13	34	42
Total - All 3 Cups	19	64	24	9	31	86	114

SK RAPID WIEN

FIVE YEAR RECORD	LEAGUE		EURO CUPS		
Birthdate/Playing position	Apps	Gls	Cup	Apps	Gls

Michael KONSEL
06/03/62   Goalkeeper

87/88	SK Rapid Wien	34	-			
88/89	SK Rapid Wien	32	-	CC	2	-
89/90	SK Rapid Wien	34	-	UC	5	-
90/91	SK Rapid Wien	36	-	UC	2	-
91/92	SK Rapid Wien	27	-			

★ Austria 16 caps, 0 goals

Roland SCHRAMMEL
11/09/68   Goalkeeper

88/89	First Vienna FC	-	-
89/90	First Vienna FC	-	-
90/91	SC Red Star	Div 3	
91/92	SK Rapid Wien	10	-

Michael HATZ
17/11/70   Defender

90/91	SK Rapid Wien	11	-
91/92	SK Rapid Wien	18	-

Robert PECL
15/11/65   Defender

87/88	SK Rapid Wien	31	1	CC	3	-
88/89	SK Rapid Wien	25	2	CC	2	-
89/90	SK Rapid Wien	22	1	UC	4	-
90/91	SK Rapid Wien	19	4	UC	2	-
91/92	SK Rapid Wien	23	3			

★ Austria 26 caps, 1 goal

Martin PUZA
23/01/70   Defender

88/89	SK Rapid Wien	5	-
89/90	SK Rapid Wien	3	-
90/91	SK Rapid Wien	-	-
91/92	SK Rapid Wien	14	-

Franz RESCH
04/05/69   Defender

89/90	SK Rapid Wien	12	-
90/91	SK Rapid Wien	16	-
91/92	SK Rapid Wien	22	-

★ Austria 2 caps, 0 goals

Andreas POIGER
04/04/68   Defender

87/88	Wiener Sport-Club	30	1			
88/89	Wiener Sport-Club	35	1			
89/90	SK Rapid Wien	18	-	UC	2	-
90/91	SK Rapid Wien	33	2	UC	2	-
91/92	SK Rapid Wien	15	-			

★ Austria 1 cap, 0 goals

Dietmar KÜHBAUER
04/04/71   Midfield

87/88	FC Admira Wacker	12	-			
88/89	FC Admira Wacker	23	-			
89/90	FC Admira Wacker	26	1	CWC	3	-
90/91	FC Admira Wacker	25	-	UC	4	-
91/92	FC Admira Wacker	35	6			

★ Austria 2 caps, 0 goals

Herbert GAGER
18/09/69   Midfield

88/89	SK Rapid Wien	11	-	CC	1	-
89/90	SK Rapid Wien	3	-			
	Wiener Sport-Club	14	2			
90/91	Wiener Sport-Club	21	2			
91/92	SK Rapid Wien	32	4			

★ Austria 4 caps, 0 goals

Franz BLIZENEC
30/01/66   Midfield

87/88	SK Rapid Wien	4	-			
88/89	SK Rapid Wien	21	1			
89/90	SK Rapid Wien	30	-	UC	6	-
90/91	SK Rapid Wien	7	-			
91/92	VfB Mödling	Div 2				

Sergei MANDREKO (Cis)
01/08/71   Midfield

90	Pamir Dushanbe (Urs)	14	-
91	Pamir Dushanbe (Urs)	24	2

★ CIS 4 caps, 0 goals

AUSTRIA

FIVE YEAR RECORD	LEAGUE		EURO CUPS		
Birthdate/Playing position	Apps	Gls	Cup	Apps	Gls

Aleksandr METLITSKY (Cis)
22/04/64 Midfield

		Apps	Gls	Cup	Apps	Gls
87	Dinamo Minsk (Urs)	24	3	CWC	1	-
88	Dinamo Minsk (Urs)	16	1	UC	4	-
89	Dinamo Minsk (Urs)	26	5			
90	Dinamo Minsk (Urs)	17	2			
90/91	Osijek (Yug)	18	4			
91/92	SK Rapid Wien	34	4			

Peter SCHÖTTEL
26/03/67 Midfield

		Apps	Gls	Cup	Apps	Gls
87/88	SK Rapid Wien	24	-	CC	1	-
88/89	SK Rapid Wien	29	-	CC	2	-
89/90	SK Rapid Wien	33	1	UC	6	-
90/91	SK Rapid Wien	33	-	UC	2	-
91/92	SK Rapid Wien	25	1			

★ Austria 24 caps, 0 goals

Franz WEBER
25/05/65 Midfield

		Apps	Gls	Cup	Apps	Gls
87/88	SK Rapid Wien	13	2	CC	3	-
88/89	SK Rapid Wien	23	4	CC	1	-
89/90	SK Rapid Wien	29	2	UC	5	-
90/91	SK Rapid Wien	9	-	UC	2	1
91/92	SK Rapid Wien	33	2			

Horst STEIGER
04/04/70 Forward

		Apps	Gls	Cup	Apps	Gls
88/89	SC Eisenstadt	Div 3				
89/90	SK Rapid Wien	26	1			
90/91	SK Rapid Wien	9	1	UC	1	-
91/92	SK Rapid Wien	12	-			

Jan Åge FJØRTOFT (Nor)
10/01/67 Forward

		Apps	Gls	Cup	Apps	Gls
87	Hamarkameratene (Nor)	22	10			
88	Lillestrøm SK (Nor)	24	14			
89	Lillestrøm SK (Nor)	11	6			
89/90	SK Rapid Wien	33	17	UC	6	3
90/91	SK Rapid Wien	33	16	UC	2	-
91/92	SK Rapid Wien	34	16			

★ Norway 34 caps, 10 goals

FIVE YEAR RECORD	LEAGUE		EURO CUPS		
Birthdate/Playing position	Apps	Gls	Cup	Apps	Gls

Stanislav GRIGA (Tch)
04/11/61 Forward

		Apps	Gls	Cup	Apps	Gls
87/88	Sparta Praha (Tch)	30	22	CC	4	1
88/89	Sparta Praha (Tch)	29	15			
89/90	Sparta Praha (Tch)	15	6	CC	2	-
	Feyenoord (Hol)	16	3			
90/91	Feyenoord (Hol)	19	6			
91/92	Feyenoord (Hol)	8	-	CWC	1	-

★ Czechoslovakia 34 caps, 8 goals

Gerhard RODAX
29/08/65 Forward

		Apps	Gls	Cup	Apps	Gls
87/88	FC Admira Wacker	30	14	UC	2	1
88/89	FC Admira Wacker	33	13			
89/90	FC Admira Wacker	36	35	CWC	6	3
90/91	Atlético Madrid (Esp)	26	9	UC	2	-
91/92	Atlético Madrid (Esp)					
	SK Rapid Wien	12	4			

★ Austria 20 caps, 3 goals

EUROPEAN HONOURS
none

EUROPEAN CUPS RECORD

	Entries	Pd	W	D	L	F	A
Champions' Cup	11	49	24	4	21	89	69
Cup-winners' Cup	9	43	14	15	14	72	68
UEFA/Fairs' Cup	**11**	**36**	**13**	**7**	**16**	**40**	**49**
Total - All 3 Cups	31	128	51	26	51	201	186

RSC ANDERLECHT

Filip DE WILDE
05/07/64   Goalkeeper

FIVE YEAR RECORD	LEAGUE		EURO CUPS		
	Apps	Gls	Cup	Apps	Gls
88/89 RSC Anderlecht	26	-	CWC	3	-
89/90 RSC Anderlecht	34	-	+CWC	9	-
90/91 RSC Anderlecht	34	-	UC	8	-
91/92 RSC Anderlecht	23	-	CC	6	-

★ Belgium 2 caps, 0 goals

Peter MAES
01/06/64   Goalkeeper

	LEAGUE		EURO CUPS		
	Apps	Gls	Cup	Apps	Gls
89/90 KRC Mechelen	-	-			
90/91 RSC Anderlecht	-	-			
91/92 RSC Anderlecht	12	-	CC	4	-

Bertrand CRASSON
05/10/71   Defender

	LEAGUE		EURO CUPS		
	Apps	Gls	Cup	Apps	Gls
89/90 RSC Anderlecht	1	-			
90/91 RSC Anderlecht	28	1	UC	8	-
91/92 RSC Anderlecht	20	2	CC	5	-

★ Belgium 2 caps, 0 goals

Jean-François DE SART
18/12/61   Defender

	LEAGUE		EURO CUPS		
	Apps	Gls	Cup	Apps	Gls
87/88 RFC Liège	31	1			
88/89 RFC Liège	28	3	UC	5	1
89/90 RFC Liège	32	1	UC	8	2
90/91 RFC Liège	25	-	CWC	6	-
91/92 RSC Anderlecht	14	-	CC	5	-

★ Belgium 2 caps, 0 goals

Michel DE WOLF
19/01/58   Defender

	LEAGUE		EURO CUPS		
	Apps	Gls	Cup	Apps	Gls
87/88 KAA Gent	24	1			
88/89 KV Kortrijk	33	2			
89/90 KV Kortrijk	34	-			
90/91 RSC Anderlecht	33	1	UC	8	-
91/92 RSC Anderlecht	33	1	CC	10	-

★ Belgium 34 caps, 1 goal

Philippe ALBERT
10/08/67   Defender

	LEAGUE		EURO CUPS		
	Apps	Gls	Cup	Apps	Gls
87/88 RSC Charleroi	32	5			
88/89 RSC Charleroi	33	2			
89/90 KV Mechelen	21	-	CC	5	-
90/91 KV Mechelen	32	4	UC	2	1
91/92 KV Mechelen	33	2	UC	2	-

★ Belgium 19 caps, 2 goals

Wim KOOIMAN (Hol)
09/09/60   Defender

	LEAGUE		EURO CUPS		
	Apps	Gls	Cup	Apps	Gls
87/88 KSV Cercle Brugge	33	5			
88/89 RSC Anderlecht	34	5	CC	4	-
89/90 RSC Anderlecht	22	2	+CWC	5	-
90/91 RSC Anderlecht	33	3	UC	8	1
91/92 RSC Anderlecht	25	1	CC	7	-

Graeme RUTJES (Hol)
26/03/60   Defender

	LEAGUE		EURO CUPS		
	Apps	Gls	Cup	Apps	Gls
87/88 KV Mechelen	32	1	#CWC	9	1
88/89 KV Mechelen	32	2	CWC	8	-
89/90 KV Mechelen	32	2	CC	6	-
90/91 RSC Anderlecht	33	3	UC	8	1
91/92 RSC Anderlecht	31	3	CC	10	-

★ Holland 13 caps, 1 goal

Danny BOFFIN
10/07/65   Midfield

	LEAGUE		EURO CUPS		
	Apps	Gls	Cup	Apps	Gls
87/88 RFC Liège	32	-			
88/89 RFC Liège	32	3	UC	4	1
89/90 RFC Liège	34	3	UC	8	2
90/91 RFC Liège	30	2	CWC	6	4
91/92 RSC Anderlecht	31	4	CC	10	1

★ Belgium 8 caps, 0 goals

Jean-Marie HOUBEN
24/11/66   Midfield

	LEAGUE		EURO CUPS		
	Apps	Gls	Cup	Apps	Gls
87/88 RFC Liège	20	1			
88/89 RFC Liège	30	3	UC	6	1
89/90 RFC Liège	31	2	UC	6	-
90/91 RFC Liège	24	-	CWC	5	1
91/92 RSC Anderlecht	15	-	CC	5	-

★ Belgium 2 caps, 0 goals

BELGIUM

FIVE YEAR RECORD *Birthdate/Playing position*	LEAGUE Apps Gls	EURO CUPS Cup Apps Gls

Nii LAMPTEY (Gha)
10/12/74   Midfield

90/91	RSC Anderlecht	14	7	UC	2	1
91/92	RSC Anderlecht	15	2	CC	4	1

★ Ghana

Marc EMMERS
25/02/66   Midfield

87/88	KV Mechelen	27	6	#CWC	5	1
88/89	KV Mechelen	33	9	CWC	8	-
89/90	KV Mechelen	34	9	CC	6	-
90/91	KV Mechelen	30	4	UC	2	-
91/92	KV Mechelen	31	5	UC	2	-

★ Belgium 28 caps, 2 goals

Bruno VERSAVEL
17/08/67   Midfield

87/88	KSC Lokeren	34	10	UC	2	-
88/89	KV Mechelen	34	2	CWC	8	-
89/90	KV Mechelen	33	10	CC	6	-
90/91	KV Mechelen	34	13	UC	2	-
91/92	KV Mechelen	4	-			
	RSC Anderlecht	17	3	CC	3	-

★ Belgium 25 caps, 3 goals

Johan WALEM
01/02/72   Midfield

91/92	RSC Anderlecht	29	-	CC	9	-

★ Belgium 4 caps, 0 goals

Johnny BOSMAN (Hol)
01/02/65   Forward

87/88	Ajax (Hol)	32	25	+CWC	9	1
88/89	KV Mechelen	30	18	CWC	7	3
89/90	KV Mechelen	31	16	CC	6	3
90/91	PSV (Hol)	30	11	CWC	2	-
91/92	RSC Anderlecht	32	16	CC	6	1

★ Holland 22 caps, 13 goals

FIVE YEAR RECORD *Birthdate/Playing position*	LEAGUE Apps Gls	EURO CUPS Cup Apps Gls

Marc DEGRYSE
04/09/65   Forward

87/88	Club Brugge KV	34	22	UC	10	1
88/89	Club Brugge KV	28	12	CC	2	-
89/90	RSC Anderlecht	31	18	+CWC	9	4
90/91	RSC Anderlecht	32	12	UC	7	-
91/92	RSC Anderlecht	28	5	CC	9	4

★ Belgium 39 caps, 12 goals

Luc NILIS
25/05/67   Forward

87/88	RSC Anderlecht	32	14	CC	6	1
88/89	RSC Anderlecht	33	19	CWC	4	-
89/90	RSC Anderlecht	27	10	+CWC	9	4
90/91	RSC Anderlecht	30	19	UC	6	3
91/92	RSC Anderlecht	27	16	CC	9	6

★ Belgium 18 caps, 0 goals

Peter VAN VOSSEN (Hol)
21/04/68   Forward

88/89	Vlissingen (Hol)	Div 3				
89/90	KSK Beveren	27	5			
90/91	KSK Beveren	Div 2				
91/92	KSK Beveren	29	13			

★ Holland 1 cap, 0 goals

EUROPEAN HONOURS
Cup-winners' Cup - (2) 1976, 1978.
UEFA Cup - (1) 1983.
Super Cup - (2) 1976, 1978.

EUROPEAN CUPS RECORD

	Entries	Pd	W	D	L	F	A
Champions' Cup	16	80	35	16	29	135	125
Cup-winners' Cup	7	44	29	3	12	86	34
UEFA/Fairs' Cup	9	62	35	11	16	129	75
Total - All 3 Cups	32	186	99	30	57	350	234

R STANDARD LIEGE

FIVE YEAR RECORD *Birthdate/Playing position*	LEAGUE Apps Gls	EURO CUPS Cup Apps Gls

Gilbert BODART
02/09/62   Goalkeeper

		LEAGUE Apps	Gls	EURO CUPS Cup	Apps	Gls
87/88	R Standard Liège	28	-			
88/89	R Standard Liège	34	-			
89/90	R Standard Liège	34	-			
90/91	R Standard Liège	31	-			
91/92	R Standard Liège	34	-			

★ Belgium 5 caps, 0 goals

Jacky MUNARON
08/09/56   Goalkeeper

		Apps	Gls	Cup	Apps	Gls
87/88	RSC Anderlecht	34	-	CC	6	-
88/89	RSC Anderlecht	8	-	CWC	1	-
89/90	RFC Liège	31	-	UC	8	-
90/91	RFC Liège	27	-	CWC	6	-
91/92	RFC Liège	29	-			

★ Belgium 8 caps, 0 goals

Mircea REDNIC (Rom)
09/04/62   Defender

		Apps	Gls	Cup	Apps	Gls
87/88	Dinamo Bucuresti (Rom)	30	5	CWC	2	-
88/89	Dinamo Bucuresti (Rom)	32	7	CWC	6	-
89/90	Dinamo Bucuresti (Rom)	19	1	CWC	8	1
90/91	Dinamo Bucuresti (Rom)	15	-	CC	4	-
	Bursaspor (Tur)	14	-			
91/92	R Standard Liège	17	-			

★ Romania 83 caps, 2 goals

ANDRE CRUZ (Bra)
20/09/68   Defender

		Apps	Gls	Cup	Apps	Gls
88/89	Flamengo (Bra)					
90/91	R Standard Liège	28	2			
91/92	R Standard Liège	30	5			

★ Brazil

Ljubomir RADANOVIC (Yug)
21/07/60   Defender

		Apps	Gls	Cup	Apps	Gls
87/88	Partizan Beograd (Yug)	31	2	UC	2	-
88/89	R Standard Liège	30	2			
89/90	R Standard Liège	32	1			
90/91	OGC Nice (Fra)	33	3			
91/92	R Standard Liège	4	-			

★ Yugoslavia 34 caps, 3 goals

Régis GENAUX
31/08/73   Defender

		Apps	Gls	Cup	Apps	Gls
90/91	R Standard Liège	4	-			
91/92	R Standard Liège	31	1			

★ Belgium 1 cap, 0 goals

Stéphane DEMOL
11/03/66   Defender

		Apps	Gls	Cup	Apps	Gls
87/88	RSC Anderlecht	8	-	CC	2	-
88/89	Bologna (Ita)	21	2			
89/90	FC Porto (Por)	31	11	UC	6	-
90/91	Toulouse FC (Fra)	27	1			
91/92	Toulouse FC (Fra)	6	1			
	R Standard Liège	27	3			

★ Belgium 38 caps, 1 goal

Patrick VERVOORT
17/01/65   Midfield

		Apps	Gls	Cup	Apps	Gls
87/88	RSC Anderlecht	31	4	CC	6	3
88/89	RSC Anderlecht	23	4	CWC	4	-
89/90	RSC Anderlecht	33	2	+CWC	9	2
90/91	Girondins de Bordeaux (Fra)	32	7			
91/92	Ascoli (Ita)	17	-			

★ Belgium 32 caps, 3 goals

Benoît THANS
20/08/64   Midfield

		Apps	Gls	Cup	Apps	Gls
87/88	RC Lens (Fra)	20	3			
88/89	R Standard Liège	32	3			
89/90	R Standard Liège	32	7			
90/91	R Standard Liège	19	3			
91/92	Royal Antwerp FC	2	-			

Thierry PISTER (Fra)
02/09/65   Midfield

		Apps	Gls	Cup	Apps	Gls
87/88	Royal Antwerp FC	30	2			
88/89	Royal Antwerp FC	31	6	UC	2	-
89/90	SC Toulon (Fra)	24	1			
90/91	R Standard Liège	22	-			
91/92	R Standard Liège	30	1			

BELGIUM

FIVE YEAR RECORD *Birthdate/Playing position*	LEAGUE Apps Gls	EURO CUPS Cup Apps Gls

Mohammed LASHAF (Mar)
07/10/67   Midfield

89/90	Racing Jet Wavre	Div 2			
90/91	Royal Antwerp FC	28	7	UC	2 -
91/92	R Standard Liège	8	2		

Frans VAN ROOY (Hol)
03/07/63   Midfield

87/88	Royal Antwerp FC	32	8		
88/89	Royal Antwerp FC	34	6	UC	2 1
89/90	Royal Antwerp FC	29	10	UC	8 2
90/91	Royal Antwerp FC	34	11	UC	2 1
91/92	R Standard Liège	30	6		

Patrick ASSELMAN
30/10/68   Midfield

87/88	KRC Mechelen	Div 2	-
88/89	KRC Mechelen	29	5
89/90	KRC Mechelen	27	6
90/91	R Standard Liège	27	6
91/92	R Standard Liège	27	5

Alain BETTAGNO
09/11/68   Midfield

87/88	FC Seraing	Div 2			
88/89	Club Brugge KV	11	2	CC	3 1
89/90	R Standard Liège	-	-		
90/91	R Standard Liège	22	2		
91/92	R Standard Liège	28	10		

Guy HELLERS (Lux)
10/10/64   Midfield

87/88	R Standard Liège	24	2
88/89	R Standard Liège	23	-
89/90	R Standard Liège	32	3
90/91	R Standard Liège	32	4
91/92	R Standard Liège	25	1

★ Luxembourg 34 caps, 1 goal

FIVE YEAR RECORD *Birthdate/Playing position*	LEAGUE Apps Gls	EURO CUPS Cup Apps Gls

Marc WILMOTS
22/02/69   Forward

87/88	K St-Truidense VV	30	9		
88/89	KV Mechelen	30	4	CWC	6 3
89/90	KV Mechelen	26	10	CC	4 -
90/91	KV Mechelen	32	8	UC	2 -
91/92	R Standard Liège	33	10		

★ Belgium 14 caps, 4 goals

Michael GOOSSENS
30/11/73   Forward

90/91	R Standard Liège	8	3
91/92	R Standard Liège	16	1

Henk VOS (Hol)
05/06/68   Forward

88/89	KFC Germinal Ekeren	Div 2	
89/90	KFC Germinal Ekeren	15	9
	R Standard Liège	14	3
90/91	R Standard Liège	10	1
	FC Metz (Fra)	16	2
91/92	R Standard Liège	26	13

EUROPEAN HONOURS
none

EUROPEAN CUPS RECORD

	Entries	Pd	W	D	L	F	A
Champions' Cup	8	40	23	3	14	72	47
Cup-winners' Cup	5	32	17	5	10	60	36
UEFA/Fairs' Cup	8	40	17	10	13	61	51
Total - All 3 Cups	21	112	57	18	37	193	134

KV MECHELEN

FIVE YEAR RECORD *Birthdate/Playing position*	LEAGUE Apps Gls	EURO CUPS Cup Apps Gls

Michel PREUD'HOMME
24/01/59   Goalkeeper

		Apps	Gls	Cup	Apps	Gls
87/88	KV Mechelen	30	-	#CWC	9	-
88/89	KV Mechelen	34	-	CWC	8	-
89/90	KV Mechelen	34	-	CC	6	-
90/91	KV Mechelen	34	-	UC	2	-
91/92	KV Mechelen	34	-	UC	2	-

★ Belgium 40 caps, 0 goals

Frédéric HALLEUX
07/12/69   Goalkeeper

		Apps	Gls
88/89	FC Seraing	Div 2	
89/90	KV Mechelen	-	-
90/91	KV Mechelen	-	-
91/92	KV Mechelen	-	-

Koen SANDERS
17/12/62   Defender

		Apps	Gls	Cup	Apps	Gls
87/88	KV Mechelen	33	3	#CWC	9	-
88/89	KV Mechelen	33	-	CWC	6	-
89/90	KV Mechelen	31	1	CC	6	-
90/91	KV Mechelen	32	1	UC	2	-
91/92	KV Mechelen	32	-	UC	2	-

★ Belgium 4 caps, 0 goals

Bart MAUROO
08/04/68   Defender

		Apps	Gls	Cup	Apps	Gls
87/88	KSV Waregem	8	-			
88/89	KSV Waregem	28	-	UC	2	-
89/90	KSV Waregem	31	-			
90/91	KSV Waregem	33	2			
91/92	KSV Waregem	31	-			

Geert DEFERM
06/05/63   Defender

		Apps	Gls	Cup	Apps	Gls
87/88	KV Mechelen	8	-	#CWC	2	-
88/89	KV Mechelen	20	1	CWC	7	1
89/90	KV Mechelen	14	-	CC	4	-
90/91	KV Mechelen	10	-	UC	1	-
91/92	KV Mechelen	25	1	UC	1	-

FIVE YEAR RECORD *Birthdate/Playing position*	LEAGUE Apps Gls	EURO CUPS Cup Apps Gls

Adri BOGERS (Hol)
04/05/65   Defender

		Apps	Gls	Cup	Apps	Gls
87/88	RKC (Hol)	Div 2				
88/89	RKC (Hol)	30	1			
89/90	RKC (Hol)	34	1			
90/91	KV Mechelen	26	-	UC	1	-
91/92	KV Mechelen	5	-	UC	2	-

Davy GIJSBRECHTS
20/09/72   Defender

		Apps	Gls
90/91	KV Mechelen	7	-
91/92	KV Mechelen	24	1

Joël BARTHOLOMEEUSSEN
02/03/66   Midfield

		Apps	Gls	Cup	Apps	Gls
87/88	KFC Germinal Ekeren	Div 3				
88/89	KFC Germinal Ekeren	Div 2				
89/90	KFC Germinal Ekeren	33	2			
90/91	KFC Germinal Ekeren	34	2			
91/92	KV Mechelen	27	1	UC	2	-

Klas INGESSON (Swe)
20/08/68   Midfield

		Apps	Gls	Cup	Apps	Gls
88	IFK Göteborg (Swe)	21	3	CC	6	2
89	IFK Göteborg (Swe)	21	5	UC	2	-
90	IFK Göteborg (Swe)	8	1			
90/91	KV Mechelen	32	6	UC	2	-
91/92	KV Mechelen	34	9	UC	2	1

★ Sweden 26 caps, 7 goals

Patrick VERSAVEL
07/01/61   Midfield

		Apps	Gls	Cup	Apps	Gls
87/88	KSC Lokeren	34	5	UC	2	-
88/89	KSC Lokeren	32	16			
89/90	KV Mechelen	33	2	CC	5	1
90/91	KV Mechelen	26	2	UC	1	-
91/92	KV Mechelen	25	2	UC	2	-

Glen DE BOECK
22/08/71   Midfield

		Apps	Gls
91/92	Boom FC	Div 2	

BELGIUM

FIVE YEAR RECORD *Birthdate/Playing position*	LEAGUE Apps Gls	EURO CUPS Cup Apps Gls

Frank LEEN
04/10/70   Midfield

87/88	K Lommel SK	Div 2				
88/89	KV Mechelen	16	-	CWC	2	-
89/90	KV Mechelen	5	-			
90/91	KV Mechelen	10	-			
91/92	KV Mechelen	23	1	UC	2	-

Alain PEETERMANS
05/12/67   Midfield

87/88	K St-Truidense VV	34	1
88/89	K St-Truidense VV	24	1
89/90	K St-Truidense VV	20	-
90/91	K St-Truidense VV	32	-
91/92	K St-Truidense VV	Div 2	

Stan VAN DEN BUYS
08/06/57   Midfield

87/88	K Lierse SK	Div 2	
88/89	K Lierse SK	29	-
89/90	K Lierse SK	27	1
90/91	RWD Molenbeek	16	2
91/92	RWD Molenbeek	29	3

Francis SEVEREYNS
08/01/68   Forward

87/88	Royal Antwerp FC	33	24			
88/89	Pisa (Ita)	26	-			
89/90	KV Mechelen	12	4	CC	3	1
90/91	KV Mechelen	28	13	UC	2	-
91/92	KV Mechelen	29	4	UC	1	-

★ Belgium 6 caps, 1 goal

René EYKELKAMP (Hol)
06/04/64   Forward

87/88	FC Groningen (Hol)	28	9			
88/89	FC Groningen (Hol)	30	15	UC	5	-
89/90	FC Groningen (Hol)	32	16	CWC	4	1
90/91	KV Mechelen	29	6	UC	2	-
91/92	KV Mechelen	31	13	UC	2	-

★ Holland 4 caps, 0 goals

Kennet ANDERSSON (Swe)
06/10/67   Forward

87	IFK Eskilstuna (Swe)	Div 2				
88	IFK Eskilstuna (Swe)	Div 2				
89	IFK Göteborg (Swe)	22	7	UC	2	-
90	IFK Göteborg (Swe)	25	9			
91	IFK Göteborg (Swe)	16	13			
91/92	KV Mechelen	25	6	UC	2	-

★ Sweden 17 caps, 10 goals

Zlatko ARAMBASIC (Aus)
20/09/69   Forward

89/90	Sydney SC (Aus)		
90/91	KV Mechelen	-	-
91/92	KV Mechelen	3	-

EUROPEAN HONOURS
Cup-winners' Cup - (1) 1988.
Super Cup - (1) 1989.

EUROPEAN CUPS RECORD

	Entries	Pd	W	D	L	F	A
Champions' Cup	1	6	2	3	1	9	3
Cup-winners' Cup	2	17	13	3	1	26	8
UEFA/Fairs' Cup	2	4	0	2	2	3	5
Total - All 3 Cups	5	27	15	8	4	38	16

LOKOMOTIV PLOVDIV

FIVE YEAR RECORD	LEAGUE		EURO CUPS	
Birthdate/Playing position	Apps	Gls	Cup Apps	Gls

Vasil VASILEV
05/06/62   Goalkeeper

87/88	Khebar Pazardshik	Div 2		
88/89	Khebar Pazardshik	Div 2		
89/90	Khebar Pazardshik	30	-	
90/91	Lokomotiv Plovdiv	27	-	
91/92	Lokomotiv Plovdiv	28	-	

Vladimir CHERNEV
13/01/65   Goalkeeper

88/89	Torpedo Karlovo	Div 3		
89/90	Botev Plovdiv	12	-	
90/91	Botev Plovdiv	15	-	
91/92	Lokomotiv Plovdiv	3	-	

Rumen DIMITROV
20/02/67   Defender

89/90	Gorubso Madan	Div 3		
90/91	Lokomotiv Plovdiv	25	-	
91/92	Lokomotiv Plovdiv	27	4	

Ivan GOVEDAROV
30/05/61   Defender

88/89	Trakia Plovdiv	12	-	UC 2	-
89/90	Spartak Plovdiv	Div 3			
90/91	Slanchev Briag	Div 2			
91/92	Lokomotiv Plovdiv	29	1		

Ivan MARINOV
21/08/61   Defender

88/89	Spartak Plovdiv	Div 2		
89/90	Spartak Varna	Div 2		
90/91	Lokomotiv Plovdiv	19	2	
91/92	Lokomotiv Plovdiv	29	3	

Petar PASHEV
16/07/70   Defender

90/91	Lokomotiv Plovdiv	10	-	
91/92	Lokomotiv Plovdiv	21	-	

Radi RAIKOVSKI
30/03/72   Defender

90/91	Lokomotiv Plovdiv	17	-
91/92	Lokomotiv Plovdiv	19	-

Mikahil YUMERSKI
22/02/71   Defender

89/90	Lokomotiv Plovdiv	15	-
90/91	Lokomotiv Plovdiv	26	-
91/92	Lokomotiv Plovdiv	8	-

Stoian KARAPETROV
18/06/68   Midfield

90/91	Pirin Goche Delchev	Div 3	
91/92	Lokomotiv Plovdiv	30	1

Valentin VALCHEV
09/09/66   Midfield

88/89	Dimitrovgrad	Div 3	
89/90	Lokomotiv Plovdiv	23	-
90/91	Lokomotiv Plovdiv	23	1
91/92	Lokomotiv Plovdiv	30	4

Kostadin VIDOLOV
02/05/70   Midfield

88/89	Maritsa Plovdiv	Div 3	
89/90	Lokomotiv Plovdiv	29	4
90/91	Lokomotiv Plovdiv	29	4
91/92	Lokomotiv Plovdiv	27	6

Yordan GEVEZOV
20/10/65   Midfield

89/90	Asenovets Asenovgrad	Div 3	
90/91	Lokomotiv Plovdiv	11	-
91/92	Lokomotiv Plovdiv	5	-

Stefan MILUSHEV
30/05/69   Forward

89/90	Pirin Goche Delchev	Div 3	
90/91	Lokomotiv Plovdiv	15	2
91/92	Lokomotiv Plovdiv	21	2

BULGARIA

FIVE YEAR RECORD Birthdate/Playing position	LEAGUE Apps Gls	EURO CUPS Cup Apps Gls

Lazar VACHKOV
05/01/69   Forward

90/91	Spartak Plovdiv	Div 3	
91/92	Lokomotiv Plovdiv	25	4

Stefan DRAGANOV
13/08/66   Forward

87/88	Lokomotiv Plovdiv	27	12
88/89	Lokomotiv Plovdiv	29	10
89/90	Lokomotiv Plovdiv	24	7
90/91	Lokomotiv Plovdiv	30	14
91/92	Lokomotiv Plovdiv	7	1

Yulian DZEVIZHOV
14/11/70   Forward

87/88	Lokomotiv Plovdiv	13	-
88/89	Lokomotiv Plovdiv	23	1
89/90	Lokomotiv Plovdiv	21	1
90/91	Lokomotiv Plovdiv	25	-
91/92	Lokomotiv Plovdiv	10	-

Aleksandar RADEV
24/04/70   Forward

90/91	Spartak Plovdiv	Div 3	
91/92	Lokomotiv Plovdiv	27	13

Dimitar RADEV
10/02/72   Forward

87/88	Lokomotiv Plovdiv	1	-
88/89	Lokomotiv Plovdiv	-	-
89/90	Lokomotiv Plovdiv	-	-
90/91	Lokomotiv Plovdiv	-	-
91/92	Lokomotiv Plovdiv	5	-

EUROPEAN HONOURS
none

EUROPEAN CUPS RECORD

	Entries	Pd	W	D	L	F	A
Champions' Cup	none						
Cup-winners' Cup	none						
UEFA/Fairs' Cup	10	30	10	6	14	40	50
Total - All 3 Cups	10	30	10	6	14	40	50

BOTEV PLOVDIV

FIVE YEAR RECORD *Birthdate/Playing position*	LEAGUE Apps Gls	EURO CUPS Cup Apps Gls

Igor KULISH
27/06/64   Goalkeeper

90/91	Slanchev Briag	Div 2		
91/92	Botev Plovdiv	15	-	

Christo TENEV
09/06/69   Goalkeeper

90/91	Botev Plovdiv	16	-	
91/92	Botev Plovdiv	16	-	

Trenko DUDOV
21/12/61   Defender

90/91	Yavorov Chirpan	Div 3		
91/92	Botev Plovdiv	26	-	

Ivan KOCHEV
14/10/65   Defender

87/88	Trakia Plovdiv	29	2	UC	2	-
88/89	Trakia Plovdiv	29	-	UC	2	-
89/90	Botev Plovdiv	30	1			
90/91	Botev Plovdiv	30	1			
91/92	Botev Plovdiv	21	1			

★ Bulgaria 2 caps, 0 goals

Dimitar MLADENOV
12/03/62   Defender

87/88	Trakia Plovdiv	23	-			
88/89	Trakia Plovdiv	30	2	UC	2	-
89/90	CSKA Sofia	28	1	CC	6	-
90/91	CSKA Sofia	29	-	CC	3	-
91/92	Botev Plovdiv	30	1			

★ Bulgaria 13 caps, 0 goals

Trifon PACHEV
28/09/59   Defender

87/88	Trakia Plovdiv	30	-	UC	1	-
88/89	Trakia Plovdiv	29	-	UC	2	-
89/90	Botev Plovdiv	25	-			
90/91	Botev Plovdiv	28	-			
91/92	Botev Plovdiv	28	-			
91/92	Botev Plovdiv	19	-			

★ Bulgaria 2 caps, 0 goals

FIVE YEAR RECORD *Birthdate/Playing position*	LEAGUE Apps Gls	EURO CUPS Cup Apps Gls

Zaprian RAKOV
04/01/62   Defender

87/88	Trakia Plovdiv	30	-	UC	2	-
88/89	Trakia Plovdiv	30	1	UC	2	-
89/90	Botev Plovdiv	29	-			
90/91	Botev Plovdiv	28	-			
91/92	Botev Plovdiv	30	-			

★ Bulgaria 19 caps, 0 goals

Petar SHOPOV
25/05/67   Midfield

88/89	Asenovets Asenovgrad	Div 3		
89/90	Botev Plovdiv	17	-	
90/91	Botev Plovdiv	17	-	
91/92	Botev Plovdiv	5	-	

Marin BAKALOV
18/04/62   Midfield

87/88	Trakia Plovdiv	26	6	UC	2	-
88/89	Trakia Plovdiv	29	7	UC	1	-
89/90	CSKA Sofia	26	5	CC	6	1
90/91	CSKA Sofia	21	3	CC	4	-
91/92	Botev Plovdiv	26	9			

★ Bulgaria 3 caps, 0 goals

Blagovest BOCHUKOV
13/09/70   Midfield

91/92	Botev Plovdiv	12	2

Geno DOBREVSKI
12/05/70   Midfield

88/89	Trakia Plovdiv	2	-
89/90	Botev Plovdiv	-	-
90/91	Botev Plovdiv	15	4
91/92	Botev Plovdiv	30	4

★ Bulgaria 1 cap, 0 goals

BULGARIA

FIVE YEAR RECORD *Birthdate/Playing position*	LEAGUE Apps Gls	EURO CUPS Cup Apps Gls

Todor ZAITSEV
30/05/67   Midfield

		Apps	Gls		Cup	Apps	Gls
87/88	Trakia Plovdiv	30	4	UC	2	-	
88/89	Trakia Plovdiv	29	2	UC	2	1	
89/90	Botev Plovdiv	29	4				
90/91	Botev Plovdiv	29	10				
91/92	Botev Plovdiv	28	9				

Ognean YOSIFOV
23/03/68   Midfield

		Apps	Gls
89/90	Botev Plovdiv	4	-
90/91	Botev Plovdiv	21	1
91/92	Botev Plovdiv	6	-

Bozhidar ISKRENOV
01/08/62   Forward

		Apps	Gls		Cup	Apps	Gls
87/88	Vitosha Sofia	27	6	CWC	2	-	
88/89	Vitosha Sofia	11	3	CC	1	-	
	Real Zaragoza (Esp)	10	1				
89/90	Levski Sofia	9	1	UC	2	-	
	Lausanne-Sports (Sui)	17	4				
90/91	Lausanne-Sports (Sui)	24	3	UC	2	-	
91/92	Botev Plovdiv	25	3				

★ Bulgaria 50 caps, 5 goals

Kostadin KOSTADINOV
25/06/59   Forward

		Apps	Gls		Cup	Apps	Gls
87/88	Trakia Plovdiv	1	-				
	SC Braga (Por)	20	1				
88/89	Trakia Plovdiv	11	2	UC	2	-	
	Doxa (Gre)	11	1				
89/90	Doxa (Gre)	-	-				
90/91	Botev Plovdiv	24	7				
91/92	Botev Plovdiv	24	3				

★ Bulgaria 44 caps, 7 goals

FIVE YEAR RECORD *Birthdate/Playing position*	LEAGUE Apps Gls	EURO CUPS Cup Apps Gls

Mincho MINCHEV
Forward

		Apps	Gls
88/89	Etar Veliko Tarnovo	18	4
89/90	Etar Veliko Tarnovo	19	2
90/91	Lokomotiv Plovdiv	7	-
91/92	Botev Plovdiv	12	2

Christo KOILOV
23/09/68   Forward

		Apps	Gls
89/90	Botev Plovdiv	25	3
90/91	Botev Plovdiv	15	-
91/92	Botev Plovdiv	26	1

Ivan DOBREVSKI
12/05/70   Forward

		Apps	Gls
90/91	Botev Plovdiv	12	1
91/92	Botev Plovdiv	3	-

EUROPEAN HONOURS
none

EUROPEAN CUPS RECORD

	Entries	Pd	W	D	L	F	A
Champions' Cup	3	8	2	1	5	8	11
Cup-winners' Cup	3	12	6	2	4	23	18
UEFA/Fairs' Cup	**6**	**14**	**3**	**4**	**7**	**21**	**23**
Total - All 3 Cups	12	34	11	7	16	52	52

ANORTHOSIS FAMAGUSTA

FIVE YEAR RECORD Birthdate/Playing position	LEAGUE Apps	Gls	EURO CUPS Cup	Apps	Gls

Michalis KAVELIS
29/09/66 Goalkeeper

87/88	Ethnikos Akhnas	27	-		
88/89	Anorthosis Famagusta	21	-		
89/90	Anorthosis Famagusta	18	-		
90/91	Anorthosis Famagusta	13	-		
91/92	Anorthosis Famagusta	19	-	UC	1	-

★ Cyprus 1 cap, 0 goals

Nicos PANAYIOTOU
06/12/70 Goalkeeper

87/88	Anorthosis Famagusta	5	-		
88/89	Anorthosis Famagusta	-	-		
89/90	Anorthosis Famagusta	7	-		
90/91	Anorthosis Famagusta	13	-		
91/92	Anorthosis Famagusta	10	-	UC	1	-

Spyros KASTANAS
12/12/62 Defender

87/88	Ethnikos Akhnas	30	1		
88/89	Ethnikos Akhnas	28	3		
89/90	Anorthosis Famagusta	23	-		
90/91	Anorthosis Famagusta	22	1		
91/92	Anorthosis Famagusta	24	1	UC	2	-

★ Cyprus 11 caps, 0 goals

Andreas PANAYIOTOU
27/12/66 Defender

87/88	Anorthosis Famagusta	15	-		
88/89	Anorthosis Famagusta	24	2		
89/90	Anorthosis Famagusta	24	-		
90/91	Anorthosis Famagusta	23	1		
91/92	Anorthosis Famagusta	24	-	UC	2	-

Kokos PANAYI
09/07/66 Defender

87/88	Alki Larnaca	29	-		
88/89	Alki Larnaca	Div 2			
89/90	Alki Larnaca	26	-		
90/91	Anorthosis Famagusta	25	1		
91/92	Anorthosis Famagusta	26	-	UC	2	-

★ Cyprus 4 caps, 0 goals

Dimitris KYRIAKOU
22/08/71 Defender

91/92	Anorthosis Famagusta	3	-		

Zacharias CHARALAMBOUS
25/03/71 Midfield

89/90	Anorthosis Famagusta	7	-		
90/91	Anorthosis Famagusta	19	2		
91/92	Anorthosis Famagusta	15	1	UC	2	-

Andreas IOANNOU
06/10/66 Midfield

87/88	Anorthosis Famagusta	16	-		
88/89	Anorthosis Famagusta	28	1		
89/90	Anorthosis Famagusta	26	-		
90/91	Anorthosis Famagusta	23	-		
91/92	Anorthosis Famagusta	26	-	UC	2	-

Temur KETSBAIA (Geo)
18/03/68 Midfield

87	Dinamo Tbilisi (Urs)	14	4	UC	4	-
88	Dinamo Tbilisi (Urs)	13	-		
89	Dinamo Tbilisi (Urs)	27	4		
90	Dinamo Tbilisi (Geo)				
91/92	Anorthosis Famagusta	26	13	UC	2	1

Nicos PAPALOIZOU
11/07/68 Midfield

90/91	Anorthosis Famagusta	11	-		
91/92	Anorthosis Famagusta	5	-		

Vassos TSAGARIS
18/05/66 Midfield

87/88	Alki Larnaca	1	-		
88/89	Alki Larnaca	Div 2			
89/90	Alki Larnaca	24	5		
90/91	Alki Larnaca	23	1		
91/92	Anorthosis Famagusta	21	2	UC	2	-

★ Cyprus 1 cap, 0 goals

CYPRUS

FIVE YEAR RECORD	LEAGUE		EURO CUPS	
Birthdate/Playing position	Apps	Gls	Cup	Apps Gls

Christos KITTOS
12/02/63   Midfield

		Apps	Gls	Cup	Apps Gls
89/90	Anorthosis Famagusta	21	1		
90/91	Anorthosis Famagusta	25	-		
91/92	Anorthosis Famagusta	24	1	UC	2 -

Christakis KASSIANOS
12/09/65   Forward

		Apps	Gls	Cup	Apps Gls
90/91	Anorthosis Famagusta	21	3		
91/92	Anorthosis Famagusta	21	7	UC	2 -

★ Cyprus 2 caps, 0 goals

Dimitris ASHIOTIS
31/03/71   Forward

		Apps	Gls	Cup	Apps Gls
87/88	Olympiakos Nicosia	5	-		
88/89	Olympiakos Nicosia	12	-		
89/90	Olympiakos Nicosia	26	4		
90/91	Olympiakos Nicosia	26	4		
91/92	Olympiakos Nicosia	14	3		

★ Cyprus 1 cap, 0 goals

Panayiotis POUNNAS
14/08/69   Forward

		Apps	Gls	Cup	Apps Gls
88/89	Anorthosis Famagusta	26	3		
89/90	Anorthosis Famagusta	18	1		
90/91	Anorthosis Famagusta	18	2		
91/92	Anorthosis Famagusta	24	2	UC	1 -

★ Cyprus 2 caps, 0 goals

FIVE YEAR RECORD	LEAGUE		EURO CUPS	
Birthdate/Playing position	Apps	Gls	Cup	Apps Gls

Costas RIZOS
01/01/68   Forward

		Apps	Gls	Cup	Apps Gls
90/91	Anorthosis Famagusta	20	7		
91/92	Anorthosis Famagusta	22	7	UC	2 -

Nikolai KOSTOV (Bul)
02/07/63   Forward

		Apps	Gls	Cup	Apps Gls
88/89	Vitosha Sofia (Bul)	6	-	CC	1 -
	Vratsa (Bul)	8	2		
89/90	Slavia Sofia (Bul)	29	9		
90/91	Anorthosis Famagusta	16	7		
91/92	Onisillos Sotiras	Div 2			

Marios MARKOU
15/06/69   Forward

		Apps	Gls	Cup	Apps Gls
91/92	AEK Kakopetrias	Div 3			

EUROPEAN HONOURS
none

EUROPEAN CUPS RECORD

	Entries	Pd	W	D	L	F	A
Champions' Cup	1	2	0	0	2	1	6
Cup-winners' Cup	3	6	0	1	5	1	34
UEFA/Fairs' Cup	2	4	0	1	3	3	15
Total - All 3 Cups	6	12	0	2	10	5	55

SIGMA OLOMOUC

FIVE YEAR RECORD *Birthdate/Playing position*	LEAGUE Apps Gls	EURO CUPS Cup Apps Gls

Lubos PRIBYL
16/10/61   Goalkeeper

87/88 RH Cheb	4	-
88/89 Slavia Praha	18	-
89/90 Slavia Praha	1	-
90/91 Slavia Praha	3	-
Sigma Olomouc	15	-
91/92 Sigma Olomouc	30	-	UC 8 -

Martin VANIAK
04/10/70   Goalkeeper

91/92 Sigma Olomouc	

Milos SLABY
18/08/65   Defender

87/88 Bohemians Praha	18	2
88/89 Bohemians Praha	29	3
89/90 Sigma Olomouc	22	-
90/91 Sigma Olomouc	28	3
91/92 Sigma Olomouc	29	1	UC 8 -

Roman PIVARNÍK
17/02/67   Defender

87/88 ZTS Kosice	Div 2	
88/89 Dukla Praha	7	-
89/90 Dukla Praha	17	-
90/91 Dukla Praha	22	-	CWC 2 -
91/92 Dukla Praha	29	1	

Martin KOTULEK
11/09/69   Defender

88/89 Sigma Olomouc	19	-
89/90 Dukla Banská Bystrica	24	-
90/91 Dukla Banská Bystrica	15	-
Sigma Olomouc	15	-
91/92 Sigma Olomouc	26	-	UC 8 -

★ Czechoslovakia 1 cap, 0 goals

Jirí VADURA
04/03/65   Defender

87/88 Sigma Olomouc	13	-
88/89 Sigma Olomouc	17	-
89/90 Sigma Olomouc	29	2
90/91 Sigma Olomouc	29	3
91/92 Sigma Olomouc	27	2	UC 8 -

Michal KOVAR
08/09/73   Defender

91/92 Sigma Olomouc	16	-	UC 3 -

Jiri BARBORÍK
17/03/72   Midfield

91/92 Sigma Olomouc	12	-	UC 1 -

Jan MAROSI
04/11/65   Midfield

87/88 Sigma Olomouc	30	5
88/89 Sigma Olomouc	29	7
89/90 Sigma Olomouc	29	9
90/91 Sigma Olomouc	30	9
91/92 Sigma Olomouc	30	9	UC 8 1

★ Czechoslovakia 2 caps, 0 goals

Roman HANUS
07/06/66   Midfield

89/90 Sigma Olomouc	27	2
90/91 Sigma Olomouc	26	3
91/92 Sigma Olomouc	29	14	UC 8 1

Radoslav LÁTAL
06/01/70   Midfield

87/88 Sigma Olomouc	9	-
88/89 Sigma Olomouc	26	1
89/90 Dukla Praha	28	1
90/91 Dukla Praha	13	1	CWC 4 -
Sigma Olomouc	6	-
91/92 Sigma Olomouc	29	4	UC 7 2

★ Czechoslovakia 3 caps, 0 goals

CZECHOSLOVAKIA

FIVE YEAR RECORD *Birthdate/Playing position*	LEAGUE Apps Gls	EURO CUPS Cup Apps Gls

Michal GOTTWALD
17/09/69   Midfield

90/91	Sigma Olomouc	8	-		
91/92	Sigma Olomouc	19	-	UC	7	1

Jirí KABYL
11/01/65   Midfield

87/88	RH Cheb	1	-
88/89	RH Cheb	9	2
89/90	RH Cheb	29	2
90/91	SKP Union Cheb	30	10
91/92	Sigma Olomouc	9	1

Robert FIALA
11/01/65   Forward

89/90	RH Cheb	23	3
90/91	SK Union Cheb	22	5
91/92	SK Union Cheb	27	4

Milan KERBR
09/06/67   Forward

90/91	FC Svit Zlín	Div 2				
91/92	Sigma Olomouc	27	11	UC	8	3

Tomás CAPKA
28/03/71   Forward

89/90	Sigma Olomouc	4	-
90/91	Sigma Olomouc	1	-
91/92	Sigma Olomouc	2	-

FIVE YEAR RECORD *Birthdate/Playing position*	LEAGUE Apps Gls	EURO CUPS Cup Apps Gls

Radek SINDELAR
29/05/64   Forward

87/88	VTZ Chomutov	Div 2				
88/89	VTZ Chomutov	Div 2				
	Bohemians Praha	12	6			
89/90	Bohemians Praha	25	6			
90/91	Zbrojovka Brno	14	1			
	Sigma Olomouc	10	2			
91/92	Sigma Olomouc	16	4	UC	7	3

Martin GUZÍK
07/04/74   Forward

91/92	Sigma Olomouc	7	-	UC	1	-

EUROPEAN HONOURS
none

EUROPEAN CUPS RECORD

	Entries	Pd	W	D	L	F	A
Champions' Cup	none						
Cup-winners' Cup	none						
UEFA/Fairs' Cup	2	10	5	3	2	16	9
Total - All 3 Cups	2	10	5	3	2	16	9

SLAVIA PRAHA

FIVE YEAR RECORD	LEAGUE		EURO CUPS	
Birthdate/Playing position	Apps	Gls	Cup Apps	Gls

Zdenek JÁNOS
11/05/67 Goalkeeper

88/89	Slavia Praha	12	-		
89/90	Slavia Praha	29	-		
90/91	Slavia Praha	22	-		
91/92	Slavia Praha	17	-		

Stanislav VAHALA
26/11/60 Goalkeeper

87/88	DAC Dunajská Streda	30	-	CWC	4	-
88/89	DAC Dunajská Streda	29	-	UC	4	-
89/90	DAC Dunajská Streda	30	-			
90/91	DAC Dunajská Streda	30	-			
91/92	Slavia Praha	10	-			

Petr HOLOTA
28/01/69 Defender

88/89	Bohemians Praha	20	2		
89/90	Bohemians Praha	26	5		
90/91	Bohemians Praha	21	6		
91/92	Slavia Praha	25	1		

★ Czechoslovakia 1 cap, 0 goals

Bartolomej JURASKO
31/08/62 Defender

87/88	Slavoj Trebisov	Div 2				
88/89	Inter Bratislava	24	4	CWC	2	-
89/90	Inter Bratislava	27	4			
89/90	Inter Bratislava	29	8	UC	4	2
91/92	Slavia Praha	24	1			

★ Czechoslovakia 4 caps, 0 goals

Michal PETROUS
06/12/69 Defender

88/89	Bohemians Praha	21	-		
89/90	Bohemians Praha	22	-		
90/91	Bohemians Praha	28	1		
91/92	Bohemians Praha	6	1		
	Slavia Praha	19	-		

Karol PRAZENICA
15/01/70 Defender

89/90	Dukla Banská Bystrica	27	-		
90/91	Dukla Banská Bystrica	25	-		
91/92	Slavia Praha	27	2		

Jaroslav SILHAVY
03/11/61 Defender

87/88	RH Cheb	25	1		
88/89	RH Cheb	29	1		
89/90	RH Cheb	14	-		
	Slavia Praha	14	1		
90/91	Slavia Praha	23	-		
91/92	Slavia Praha	18	1		

★ Czechoslovakia 4 caps, 0 goals

Jan SUCHOPÁREK
23/09/69 Defender

88/89	Dukla Praha	3	1			
89/90	Dukla Praha	24	-			
90/91	Dukla Praha	29	6	CWC	4	-
91/92	Slavia Praha	29	4			

★ Czechoslovakia 5 caps, 0 goals

Radek BEJBL
29/08/72 Midfield

90/91	Slavia Praha	22	1		
91/92	Slavia Praha	28	9		

Radim NECAS
26/08/69 Midfield

87/88	Baník Ostrava	27	3			
88/89	Baník Ostrava	28	9			
89/90	Baník Ostrava	29	5	UC	3	1
90/91	Baník Ostrava	23	11	UC	2	1
91/92	Baník Ostrava	26	13	CWC	4	-

Martin PENICKA
10/12/69 Midfield

89/90	Slovan Liberec	Div 2			
90/91	Slavia Praha	26	4		
91/92	Slavia Praha	28	6		

CZECHOSLOVAKIA

FIVE YEAR RECORD	LEAGUE		EURO CUPS		
Birthdate/Playing position	Apps	Gls	Cup	Apps	Gls

Jiří POVISER
1970   Midfield

90/91	Dynamo Ceske Budejovice	Div 2		
	Slavia Praha	15	2	
91/92	Slavia Praha	14	1	

Vladimir TATARCHUK (Cis)
25/04/66   Midfield

87	CSKA Moskva (Urs)	27	6			
88	CSKA Moskva (Urs)	Div 2				
89	CSKA Moskva	Div 2				
90	CSKA Moskva (Urs)	21	3			
91	CSKA Moskva (Urs)	24	5	CWC	2	-
91/92	Slavia Praha	11	1			

★ USSR 9 caps, 1 goal

Dragisa BINIC (Yug)
20/10/61   Forward

87/88	Crvena zvezda Beograd (Yug)	27	13	UC	4	1
88/89	Brest-Armorique (Fra)	Div 2				
90/91	Crvena zvezda Beograd (Yug)	27	13	#CC	9	2
91/92	Slavia Praha	12	5			

★ Yugoslavia 3 caps, 1 goal

Pavel KUKA
19/07/68   Forward

89/90	Slavia Praha	29	2
90/91	Slavia Praha	27	14
91/92	Slavia Praha	27	19

★ Czechoslovakia 14 caps, 4 goals

Jiří NOVÁK
26/10/69   Forward

87/88	Union Teplice	Div 2	
88/89	Slavia Praha	16	5
89/90	Slavia Praha	24	4
90/91	Slavia Praha	16	-
91/92	Slavia Praha	7	1

Stefan RUSNÁK
07/08/71   Forward

89/90	Dukla Banská Bystrica	2	-
90/91	Dukla Banská Bystrica	27	13
91/92	Slavia Praha	20	2

Frantisek VESELY
27/03/69   Forward

87/88	Slavia Praha	8	3
88/89	RH Cheb	9	-
89/90	RH Cheb	14	1
90/91	Slavia Praha	30	7
91/92	Slavia Praha	6	1

EUROPEAN HONOURS
none

EUROPEAN CUPS RECORD

	Entries	Pd	W	D	L	F	A
Champions' Cup	none						
Cup-winners' Cup	1	2	1	0	1	1	1
UEFA/Fairs' Cup	5	12	5	1	6	17	19
Total - All 3 Cups	6	14	6	1	7	18	20

FC KØBENHAVN

FIVE YEAR RECORD Birthdate/Playing position	LEAGUE Apps	Gls	EURO CUPS Cup	Apps	Gls

Palle PETERSEN
01/06/59   Goalkeeper

87	B 1903	26	-			
88	B 1903	19	-			
89	B 1903	26	-			
90	B 1903	19	-			
91	B 1903	18	-			
91/92	B 1903	32	-	UC	6	-

Thomas RISUM
06/02/65   Goalkeeper

88	Svendborg FB	Div 2				
89	Svendborg FB	Div 2				
90	Svendborg FB	Div 2				
91	B 1903	-	-			
91/92	B 1903	-	-	UC	3	-

Ivan NIELSEN
09/10/56   Defender

87	PSV (Hol)	32	3	#CC	8	-
88	PSV (Hol)	1	-			
89/90	PSV (Hol)	21	1	CC	6	-
90	BK Fremad Anager	Div 2				
91	B 1903	14	-			
91/92	B 1903	25	1	UC	7	1

★ Denmark 51 caps, 0 goals

Torben PIECHNIK
21/05/63   Defender

87	KB	21	2			
88	Ikast FS	24	1	UC	2	-
89	Ikast FS	19	2	CWC	2	-
90	B 1903	25	1			
91	B 1903	15	-			
91/92	B 1903	27	7	UC	8	-

★ Denmark 7 caps, 0 goals

Diego TUR
03/10/71   Defender

89	B 1903	24	-			
90	B 1903	10	-			
91	B 1903	10	-			
91/92	B 1903	26	-	UC	7	-

FIVE YEAR RECORD Birthdate/Playing position	LEAGUE Apps	Gls	EURO CUPS Cup	Apps	Gls

Iørn ULDBJERG
01/02/68   Defender

87	B 1903	5	-			
88	B 1903	24	2			
89	B 1903	21	-			
90	B 1903	26	-			
91	B 1903	18	3			
91/92	B 1903	27	1	UC	8	1

Kenneth WEGNER
03/03/66   Defender

87	Brønshøj BK	24	1			
88	Brønshøj BK	21	-			
89	Brønshøj BK	11	1			
90/91	Neuchâtel Xamax FC (Sui)	-	-			
91	B 1903	17	1			
91/92	B 1903	30	2	UC	8	1

Kenneth BIRKEDAL
19/11/65   Midfield

87	B 1903	20	-			
88	BK Frem	Div 2				
89	BK Frem	19	-			
90	BK Frem	21	2			
91	BK Frem	17	-			
91/92	BK Frem	14	-			
	B 1903	5	-	UC	2	-

Anders BJERRE
27/05/69   Midfield

88	AGF	2	-	CWC	1	-
89	AGF	12	-			
90	KB	25	3			
91	KB	Div 2				
91/92	B 1903	12	2	UC	2	-

Lars Højer NIELSEN
08/12/70   Midfield

89	B 1903	18	2			
90	B 1903	16	1			
91	B 1903	16	3			
91/92	B 1903	32	7	UC	8	1

DENMARK

FIVE YEAR RECORD	LEAGUE		EURO CUPS		
Birthdate/Playing position	Apps	Gls	Cup	Apps	Gls

Jorgen Juul JENSEN
17/11/65   Midfield

87	B 1903	25	8			
88	B 1903	24	6			
89	BK Avarta	Div 2				
90	B 1903	26	13			
91	B 1903	15	2			
91/92	B 1903	19	5	UC	5	1

★ Denmark 1 cap, 0 goals

Brian KAUS
05/07/67   Midfield

87	Brønshøj BK	26	.8			
88	Brønshøj BK	26	6			
89	Brønshøj BK	26	2			
90	B 1903	26	-			
91	B 1903	16	-			
91/92	B 1903	26	1	UC	5	2

Pierre LARSEN
20/01/59   Midfield

87/88	Grasshopper-Club Zürich (Sui)	13	-	UC	2	-
88	B 1903	26	-			
89	B 1903	26	1			
90	B 1903	25	-			
91	B 1903	18	-			
91/92	B 1903	29	2	UC	8	-

★ Denmark 17 caps, 0 goals

Michael GIOLBAS
26/06/70   Midfield

89	B 1903	4	-			
90	B 1903	10	-			
91	B 1903	6	-			
91/92	B 1903	13	-	UC	4	-

Michael JOHANSEN
22/07/72   Forward

90	KB	15	1			
91	KB	Div 2				
91/92	B 1903	26	1	UC	6	1

FIVE YEAR RECORD	LEAGUE		EURO CUPS		
Birthdate/Playing position	Apps	Gls	Cup	Apps	Gls

Martin JOHANSEN
22/07/72   Forward

90	KB	20	4			
91	KB	Div 2				
91/92	B 1903	25	8	UC	5	-

Søren LYNG
08/07/66   Forward

87	BK Frem	Div 2				
88	BK Frem	Div 2				
89	BK Frem	21	4			
90	BK Frem	26	13			
91	BK Frem	18	5			
91/92	BK Frem	17	7			
	1903	5	-	UC	2	-

★ Denmark 2 caps, 0 goals

Michael MANNICHE
17/07/59   Forward

87	B 1903	13	7			
88	B 1903	22	14			
89	B 1903	25	5			
90	B 1903	23	6			
91	B 1903	15	3			
91/92	B 1903	30	12	UC	7	3

★ Denmark 11 caps, 2 goals

EUROPEAN HONOURS
none

EUROPEAN CUPS RECORD (B 1903)

	Entries	Pd	W	D	L	F	A
Champions' Cup	4	11	3	1	7	13	19
Cup-winners' Cup	2	6	3	1	2	10	8
UEFA/Fairs' Cup	8	24	5	4	15	31	51
Total - All 3 Cups	14	41	11	6	24	54	78

EUROPEAN CUPS RECORD (KB)

	Entries	Pd	W	D	L	F	A
Champions' Cup	3	10	3	2	5	13	17
Cup-winners' Cup	1	2	0	1	1	0	3
UEFA/Fairs' Cup	3	8	2	0	6	11	21
Total - All 3 Cups	7	20	5	3	12	24	41

BK FREM

FIVE YEAR RECORD	LEAGUE		EURO CUPS	
Birthdate/Playing position	Apps	Gls	Cup Apps	Gls

Per WIND
15/08/55 Goalkeeper

87	BK Frem	Div 2		
88	BK Frem	Div 2		
89	BK Frem	24	-	
90	BK Frem	1	-	
91	BK Frem	15	-	
91/92	BK Frem	32	-	

★ Denmark 2 caps, 0 goals

Allan JENSEN
01/09/68 Goalkeeper

89	BK Frem	2	-	
90	BK Frem	25	-	
91	BK Frem	3	-	
91/92	BK Frem	-	-	

Tony CARLSEN
26/05/63 Defender

88	Helsingør IF	Div 2		
89	Helsingør IF	Div 2		
90	BK Frem	26	2	
91	BK Frem	16	1	
91/92	BK Frem	28	-	

Lars BROUSTBO
06/01/62 Defender

87	BK Frem	Div 2		
88	BK Frem	Div 2		
89	BK Frem	22	-	
90	BK Frem	23	-	
91	BK Frem	17	-	
91/92	BK Frem	11	-	

Peter FRANK
26/05/70 Defender

89	BK Frem	5	-	
90	BK Frem	-	-	
91	BK Frem	-	-	
91/92	BK Frem	24	1	

Henrik KNUDSEN
05/07/65 Defender

89	BK Frem	13	-	
90	BK Frem	25	2	
91	BK Frem	-	-	
91/92	BK Frem	-	-	

Peter POULSEN
05/04/64 Midfield

87	BK Frem	Div 2		
88	BK Frem	Div 2		
89	BK Frem	24	-	
90	BK Frem	26	2	
91	BK Frem	18	1	
91/92	BK Frem	15	1	

Dan EGGEN (Nor)
13/01/70 Midfield

91	BK Frem	10	2	
91/92	BK Frem	32	6	

Jimmi LÜTHJE
18/01/68 Midfield

88	BK Fremad Amager	Div 2		
89	BK Fremad Amager	Div 2		
90	BK Fremad Amager	Div 2		
91	BK Frem	15	1	
91/92	BK Frem	31	3	

Søren FOLKMANN
09/09/67 Midfield

88	BK Frem	Div 2		
89	BK Frem	-	-	
90	BK Frem	-	-	
91	BK Frem	3	1	
91/92	BK Frem	22	2	

DENMARK

FIVE YEAR RECORD / Birthdate/Playing position — LEAGUE Apps Gls — EURO CUPS Cup Apps Gls

Kim MIKKELSEN
24/11/65 Midfield

Year	Club	Apps	Gls
87	Herfølge BK	13	-
88	Roskilde BK	Div 2	
89	Roskilde BK	Div 2	
90	Roskilde BK	Div 2	
91	BK Frem	10	1
91/92	BK Frem	26	2

Finn JENSEN
29/03/64 Midfield

Year	Club	Apps	Gls
88	Albertsund IF	Div 3	
89	BK Frem	20	1
90	BK Frem	26	-
91	BK Frem	17	2
91/92	BK Frem	31	-

Thomas THØGERSEN
02/04/68 Midfield

Year	Club	Apps	Gls
89	BK Frem	2	-
90	BK Frem	17	-
91	BK Frem	17	2
91/92	BK Frem	20	5

Carsten BIRKEDAL
21/04/70 Midfield

Year	Club	Apps	Gls
89	BK Frem	8	-
90	BK Frem	5	-
91	BK Frem	8	-
91/92	BK Frem	4	-

Peter ERIKSEN
21/08/66 Forward

Year	Club	Apps	Gls
90	BK Frem	11	2
91	BK Frem	1	-
91/92	BK Frem	7	1

Peter LASSEN
04/10/66 Forward

Year	Club	Apps	Gls
89	Brande IF	Div 3	
90	Brande IF	Div 4	
91	BK Frem	13	4
91/92	BK Frem	12	1

Marek CZAKON (Pol)
01/12/63 Forward

Year	Club	Apps	Gls		Cup	Apps	Gls
87/88	Olimpia Poznan (Pol)	7	-				
88/89	Olimpia Poznan (Pol)	-	-				
89	Ilves (Fin)	25	5				
90	Ilves (Fin)	22	16				
91	Ilves (Fin)	33	6		UC	4	3
91/92	BK Frem	10	1				

Mukramin JASAR
29/04/67 Forward

Year	Club	Apps	Gls
88	B 93	Div 2	
89	B 93	Div 2	
90	Helsingør IF	Div 2	
91	Helsingør IF	Div 2	
91/92	BK Frem	14	5

EUROPEAN HONOURS
none

EUROPEAN CUPS RECORD

	Entries	Pd	W	D	L	F	A
Champions' Cup	none						
Cup-winners' Cup	2	4	2	0	2	4	6
UEFA/Fairs' Cup	5	12	2	1	9	13	37
Total - All 3 Cups	7	16	4	1	11	17	43

MANCHESTER UNITED

FIVE YEAR RECORD						FIVE YEAR RECORD					
Birthdate/Playing position	LEAGUE Apps	Gls	EURO CUPS Cup	Apps	Gls	_Birthdate/Playing position_	LEAGUE Apps	Gls	EURO CUPS Cup	Apps	Gls

Peter SCHMEICHEL (Den)
18/11/63   Goalkeeper

87	Brøndby IF (Den)	23	2	UC	4	-
88	Brøndby IF (Den)	26	-	CC	2	-
89	Brøndby IF (Den)	26	-	CC	2	-
90	Brøndby IF (Den)	26	-	UC	10	-
91	Brøndby IF (Den)	18	-			
91/92	Manchester United	40	-	CWC	3	-

★ Denmark 52 caps, 0 goals

Gary WALSH
21/03/68   Goalkeeper

87/88	Manchester United	16	-			
88/89	Manchester United	-	-			
	Airdrieonians (Sco)	Div 2				
89/90	Manchester United	-	-			
90/91	Manchester United	5	-	#CWC	1	-
91/92	Manchester United	2	-	CWC	1	-

Dennis IRWIN (Irl)
31/10/65   Defender

87/88	Oldham Athletic	Div 2				
88/89	Oldham Athletic	Div 2				
89/90	Oldham Athletic	Div 2				
90/91	Manchester United	34	-	#CWC	6	-
91/92	Manchester United	38	4	CWC	2	-

★ Republic of Ireland 13 caps, 1 goal

Clayton BLACKMORE (Wal)
23/09/64   Defender

87/88	Manchester United	22	3			
88/89	Manchester United	28	3			
89/90	Manchester United	28	2			
90/91	Manchester United	35	4	#CWC	9	2
91/92	Manchester United	33	3	CWC	1	-

★ Wales 32 caps, 0 goals

Steve BRUCE
31/12/60   Defender

87/88	Norwich City	19	2			
	Manchester United	21	2			
88/89	Manchester United	38	2			
89/90	Manchester United	34	3			
90/91	Manchester United	31	13	#CWC	8	4
91/92	Manchester United	37	5	CWC	4	-

Paul PARKER
04/04/64   Defender

87/88	Queen's Park Rangers	40	-			
88/89	Queen's Park Rangers	36	-			
89/90	Queen's Park Rangers	32	-			
90/91	Queen's Park Rangers	17	1			
91/92	Manchester United	26	-	CWC	2	-

★ England 17 caps, 0 goals

Gary PALLISTER
30/06/65   Defender

87/88	Middlesbrough	Div 2				
88/89	Middlesbrough	37	1			
89/90	Manchester United	35	3			
90/91	Manchester United	36	-	#CWC	9	1
91/92	Manchester United	39	1	CWC	4	-

★ England 5 caps, 0 goals

Mal DONAGHY (Nir)
13/09/57   Defender

87/88	Luton Town	32	1			
88/89	Manchester United	30	-			
89/90	Manchester United	14	-			
90/91	Manchester United	25	-	#CWC	5	-
91/92	Manchester United	20	-			

★ Northern Ireland 76 caps, 0 goals

Paul INCE
21/10/67   Midfield

87/88	West Ham United	28	3			
88/89	West Ham United	33	3			
89/90	Manchester United	26	-			
90/91	Manchester United	31	3	#CWC	7	-
91/92	Manchester United	33	3	CWC	3	-

ENGLAND

| FIVE YEAR RECORD | LEAGUE | | EURO CUPS | |
| Birthdate/Playing position | Apps | Gls | Cup | Apps Gls |

Bryan ROBSON
11/01/57   Midfield

87/88	Manchester United	36	11		
88/89	Manchester United	34	4		
89/90	Manchester United	20	2		
90/91	Manchester United	17	1	#CWC	4 -
91/92	Manchester United	27	4	CWC	3 -
★ England 90 caps, 26 goals

Andrei KANCHELSKIS (Ukr)
23/01/69   Midfield

88	Dinamo Kiev (Urs)	7	1		
89	Dinamo Kiev (Urs)	15	-	UC	1 -
90	Shakhtyor Donetsk (Urs)	16	2		
90/91	Manchester United	1	-		
91/92	Manchester United	34	5	CWC	1 -
★ USSR/CIS 23 caps, 3 goals

Neil WEBB
30/07/63   Midfield

87/88	Nottingham Forest	40	13		
88/89	Nottingham Forest	36	6		
89/90	Manchester United	11	2		
90/91	Manchester United	32	3	#CWC	6 1
91/92	Manchester United	31	3	CWC	3 -
★ England 26 caps, 4 goals

Mike PHELAN
24/09/62   Midfield

87/88	Norwich City	37	-		
88/89	Norwich City	37	2		
89/90	Manchester United	38	1		
90/91	Manchester United	33	1	#CWC	8 -
91/92	Manchester United	18	-	CWC	4 -
★ England 1 cap, 0 goals

Lee SHARPE
27/05/71   Midfield

87/88	Torquay United	Div 4			
88/89	Manchester United	22	-		
89/90	Manchester United	18	1		
90/91	Manchester United	23	2	#CWC	8 1
91/92	Manchester United	14	1		
★ England 1 cap, 0 goals

Darren FERGUSON (Sco)
09/02/72   Midfield

| 90/91 | Manchester United | 5 | - | | |
| 91/92 | Manchester United | 4 | - | | |

Brian McCLAIR (Sco)
08/12/63   Forward

87/88	Manchester United	40	24		
88/89	Manchester United	38	10		
89/90	Manchester United	37	5		
90/91	Manchester United	36	13	#CWC	9 4
91/92	Manchester United	42	18	CWC	4 1
★ Scotland 26 caps, 1 goal

Mark HUGHES (Wal)
01/11/63   Forward

87/88	FC Bayern München (Ger)	18	6	CC	2 -
88/89	Manchester United	38	14		
89/90	Manchester United	37	13		
90/91	Manchester United	31	10	#CWC	8 3
91/92	Manchester United	39	11	CWC	4 2
★ Wales 42 caps, 9 goals

Ryan GIGGS (Wal)
29/11/73   Forward

| 90/91 | Manchester United | 2 | 1 | | |
| 91/92 | Manchester United | 38 | 4 | CWC | 1 - |
★ Wales 2 caps, 0 goals

EUROPEAN HONOURS
Champions' Cup - (1) 1968.
Cup-winners' Cup - (1) 1991.
Super Cup - (1) 1991.

EUROPEAN CUPS RECORD

	Entries	Pd	W	D	L	F	A
Champions' Cup	5	41	26	7	8	100	45
Cup-winners' Cup	5	31	16	9	6	55	35
UEFA/Fairs' Cup	5	27	12	9	6	47	25
Total - All 3 Cups	15	99	54	25	20	202	105

SHEFFIELD WEDNESDAY

FIVE YEAR RECORD *Birthdate/Playing position*	LEAGUE Apps Gls	EURO CUPS Cup Apps Gls

Chris WOODS
14/11/59   Goalkeeper

87/88	Rangers (Sco)	39	-	CC	6	-
88/89	Rangers (Sco)	24	-	CWC	4	-
89/90	Rangers (Sco)	32	-	CC	1	-
90/91	Rangers (Sco)	36	-	CC	4	-
91/92	Sheffield Wednesday	41	-			

★ England 34 caps, 0 goals

Kevin PRESSMAN
06/11/67   Goalkeeper

87/88	Sheffield Wednesday	11	-
88/89	Sheffield Wednesday	9	-
89/90	Sheffield Wednesday	15	-
90/91	Sheffield Wednesday	Div 2	
91/92	Sheffield Wednesday	1	-

Roland NILSSON (Swe)
27/11/63   Defender

87	IFK Göteborg (Swe)	21	2	UC	2	-
88	IFK Göteborg (Swe)	20	-	CC	6	1
89	IFK Göteborg (Swe)	21	-	UC	2	-
89/90	Sheffield Wednesday	20	-			
90/91	Sheffield Wednesday	Div 2				
91/92	Sheffield Wednesday	39	1			

★ Sweden 47 caps, 1 goal

Phil KING
28/12/67   Defender

87/88	Swindon Town	Div 2	
88/89	Swindon Town	Div 2	
89/90	Swindon Town	Div 2	
	Sheffield Wednesday	25	-
90/91	Sheffield Wednesday	Div 2	
91/92	Sheffield Wednesday	39	1

Nigel PEARSON
21/08/63   Defender

87/88	Sheffield Wednesday	19	2
88/89	Sheffield Wednesday	37	2
89/90	Sheffield Wednesday	33	1
90/91	Sheffield Wednesday	Div 2	
91/92	Sheffield Wednesday	31	2

FIVE YEAR RECORD *Birthdate/Playing position*	LEAGUE Apps Gls	EURO CUPS Cup Apps Gls

Paul WARHURST
26/09/69   Defender

88/89	Oldham Athletic	Div 2	
89/90	Oldham Athletic	Div 2	
90/91	Oldham Athletic	Div 2	
91/92	Sheffield Wednesday	33	-

Viv ANDERSON
29/08/56   Defender

87/88	Manchester United	31	2			
88/89	Manchester United	6	-			
89/90	Manchester United	16	-			
90/91	Manchester United	1	-	#CWC	1	-
	Sheffield Wednesday	Div 2				
91/92	Sheffield Wednesday	22	3			

★ England 30 caps, 2 goals

Peter SHIRTLIFF
06/04/61   Defender

87/88	Charlton Athletic	36	2
88/89	Charlton Athletic	34	2
89/90	Sheffield Wednesday	33	2
90/91	Sheffield Wednesday	Div 2	
91/92	Sheffield Wednesday	12	-

Carlton PALMER
05/12/65   Midfield

87/88	West Bromwich Albion	Div 2	
88/89	West Bromwich Albion	Div 2	
	Sheffield Wednesday	13	1
89/90	Sheffield Wednesday	34	-
90/91	Sheffield Wednesday	Div 2	
91/92	Sheffield Wednesday	42	5

★ England 7 caps, 0 goals

Danny WILSON (Nir)
01/01/60   Midfield

87/88	Luton Town	38	8
88/89	Luton Town	37	9
89/90	Luton Town	35	7
90/91	Sheffield Wednesday	Div 2	
91/92	Sheffield Wednesday	36	3

★ Northern Ireland 24 caps, 1 goal

ENGLAND

FIVE YEAR RECORD *Birthdate/Playing position*	LEAGUE Apps Gls	EURO CUPS Cup Apps Gls

John SHERIDAN (Irl)
01/10/64   Midfield

87/88	Leeds United	Div 2			
88/89	Leeds United	Div 2			
89/90	Nottingham Forest	-	-		
	Sheffield Wednesday	27	2		
90/91	Sheffield Wednesday	Div 2			
91/92	Sheffield Wednesday	24	6		

★ Republic of Ireland 13 caps, 1 goal

Nigel WORTHINGTON (Nir)
04/11/61   Midfield

87/88	Sheffield Wednesday	38	-		
88/89	Sheffield Wednesday	28	-		
89/90	Sheffield Wednesday	32	2		
90/91	Sheffield Wednesday	Div 2			
91/92	Sheffield Wednesday	34	5		

★ Northern Ireland 37 caps, 0 goals

John HARKES (Usa)
08/03/67   Midfield

89/90	USSF (Usa)				
90/91	Sheffield Wednesday	Div 2			
91/92	Sheffield Wednesday	29	3		

★ USA

Chris BART-WILLIAMS
16/06/74   Midfield

90/91	Leyton Orient	Div 3			
91/92	Sheffield Wednesday	15	-		

Chris WADDLE
14/12/60   Midfield

87/88	Tottenham Hotspur	22	2			
88/89	Tottenham Hotspur	38	14			
89/90	Olympique Marseille (Fra)	37	9	CC	8	1
90/91	Olympique Marseille (Fra)	35	6	+CC	9	2
91/92	Olympique Marseille (Fra)	35	7	CC	3	1

★ England 62 caps, 6 goals

FIVE YEAR RECORD *Birthdate/Playing position*	LEAGUE Apps Gls	EURO CUPS Cup Apps Gls

David HIRST
07/12/67   Forward

87/88	Sheffield Wednesday	24	3		
88/89	Sheffield Wednesday	32	7		
89/90	Sheffield Wednesday	38	14		
90/91	Sheffield Wednesday	Div 2			
91/92	Sheffield Wednesday	33	18		

★ England 3 caps, 1 goal

Paul WILLIAMS
16/08/65   Forward

87/88	Charlton Athletic	12	-		
	Brentford	Div 3			
88/89	Charlton Athletic	32	13		
89/90	Charlton Athletic	38	10		
90/91	Sheffield Wednesday	Div 2			
91/92	Sheffield Wednesday	39	9		

Nigel JEMSON
10/08/69   Forward

87/88	Preston North End	Div 3			
88/89	Bolton Wanderers	Div 3			
	Preston North End	Div 3			
89/90	Nottingham Forest	18	4		
90/91	Nottingham Forest	23	8		
91/92	Nottingham Forest	6	1		
	Sheffield Wednesday	22	4		

EUROPEAN HONOURS
none

EUROPEAN CUPS RECORD

	Entries	Pd	W	D	L	F	A
Champions' Cup	none						
Cup-winners' Cup	none						
UEFA/Fairs' Cup	2	10	5	0	5	25	18
Total - All 3 Cups	2	10	5	0	5	25	18

MP

FIVE YEAR RECORD *Birthdate/Playing position*	LEAGUE Apps Gls	EURO CUPS Cup Apps Gls

Esa VIITANEN
23/07/69   Goalkeeper

89	KPV	Div 2				
90	KPV	6	-			
91	MP	33	-	UC	2	-

Pasi KORHONEN
04/01/72   Goalkeeper

91	MP	-	-			

Ilkka MÄKELÄ
25/06/63   Defender

87	Haka	22	3			
88	Haka	18	-			
89	Haka	18	-	CWC	2	-
90	MP	15	-			
91	MP	24	1	UC	2	-

★ Finland 11 caps, 0 goals

Antti RONKAINEN
07/06/58   Defender

87	MP	15	-			
88	MP	-	-			
89	MP	24	-			
90	MP	20	-			
91	MP	32	-	UC	2	-

★ Finland 12 caps, 0 goals

Timo-Pekka VIITIKKO
29/05/67   Defender

87	MP	21	-			
88	MP	15	-			
89	MP	23	-			
90	MP	26	1			
91	MP	27	1	UC	2	-

Niko TERÄSALMI
06/03/69   Defender

90	MP	17	-			
91	MP	13	-	UC	1	-

FIVE YEAR RECORD *Birthdate/Playing position*	LEAGUE Apps Gls	EURO CUPS Cup Apps Gls

Mikko MANNINEN
13/10/65   Defender

87	LauTP	Div 2				
88	MP	27	2			
89	MP	-	-			
90	MP	26	-			
91	MP	29	2	UC	2	-

Jyrki HUHTAMÄKI
27/08/67   Midfield

87	MP	21	8			
88	MP	27	2			
89	MP	27	13			
90	MP	15	4			
91	MP	31	13	UC	2	-

★ Finland 9 caps, 0 goals

Mirka TORNIAINEN
22/09/71   Defender

91	MP	-	-			

John ALLEN (Eng)
14/11/64   Midfield

87	MP	20	6			
88	MP	27	4			
89	Malmö FF (Swe)	5	1			
90	MP	24	3			
91	MP	30	3	UC	2	-

Jokke KANGASKORPI
02/03/72   Midfield

87	MP	1	-			
88	MP	12	1			
89	MP	27	1			
90	MP	22	1			
91	MP	32	1	UC	1	-

FINLAND

FIVE YEAR RECORD *Birthdate/Playing position*	LEAGUE Apps Gls	EURO CUPS Cup Apps Gls	FIVE YEAR RECORD *Birthdate/Playing position*	LEAGUE Apps Gls	EURO CUPS Cup Apps Gls

Tibor GRUBOROVICS (Hun)
09/08/59   Midfield

87/88	Békéscsaba (Hun)	22	-	
88/89	Békéscsaba (Hun)	16	1	CWC 4 2
89	MP	27	1	
90	MP	29	7	
91	MP	32	7	UC 2 -

Harri SAARELMA
25/08/68   Forward

87	MP	14	-
88	TuTo	Div 2	
89	MP	25	3
90	MP	21	3
91	MP	25	2	UC 1 -

Juha KARVINEN
26/09/66   Midfield

87	KuPS	21	3	
88	KuPS	21	4	
89	MP	27	4	
90	MP	29	7	
91	MP	32	16	UC 2 -

★ Finland 3 caps, 1 goal

Antti-Pekka NIKULA
29/08/65   Forward

88	MP	1	-
89	MP	-	-
90	MP	15	-
91	MP	17	-	UC 2 -

Pasi NUIJA
13/04/70   Forward

89	MP	1	-
90	MP	-	-
91	MP	2	-

Jukka RUHANEN
16/04/71   Forward

88	MP	20	2
89	MP	26	4
90	MP	23	-
91	MP	29	13	UC 1 -

★ Finland 1 cap, 0 goals

Jari HUDD
13/04/65   Forward

87	AIK (Swe)	13	-
88	AIK (Swe)	3	-
89	AIK (Swe)	9	-
90	KPV	23	-
91	KPV	Div 2	

EUROPEAN HONOURS
none

EUROPEAN CUPS RECORD

	Entries	Pd	W	D	L	F	A
Champions' Cup	none						
Cup-winners' Cup	2	4	1	1	2	4	12
UEFA/Fairs' Cup	2	4	0	0	4	1	11
Total - All 3 Cups	4	8	1	1	6	5	23

PARIS SAINT-GERMAIN FC

FIVE YEAR RECORD	LEAGUE		EURO CUPS		
Birthdate/Playing position	Apps	Gls	Cup	Apps	Gls

Bernard LAMA
17/04/63   Goalkeeper

87/88	Lille OSC	36	-		
88/89	Lille OSC	36	1		
89/90	FC Metz	38	-		
90/91	Brest-Armorique	38	-		
91/92	RC Lens	36	1		

Richard DUTRUEL
24/12/72   Goalkeeper

91/92	Paris Saint-Germain FC	4	-		

Alain ROCHE
15/10/67   Defender

87/88	Girondins de Bordeaux	34	2	CC	6	-
88/89	Girondins de Bordeaux	33	-	UC	5	1
89/90	Olympique Marseille	25	-	CC	2	-
90/91	AJ Auxerre	38	2			
91/92	AJ Auxerre	38	5	UC	4	-

★ France 2 caps, 0 goals

Antoine KOMBOUARE
16/11/63   Defender

87/88	FC Nantes	31	1		
88/89	FC Nantes	35	1		
89/90	FC Nantes	35	-		
90/91	Paris Saint-Germain FC	20	-		
91/92	Paris Saint-Germain FC	32	2		

RICARDO Gomes (Bra)
13/12/64   Defender

87/88	Fluminense (Bra)					
88/89	SL Benfica (Por)	31	8	UC	4	-
89/90	SL Benfica (Por)	16	2	+CC	8	3
90/91	SL Benfica (Por)	36	9	UC	1	-
91/92	Paris Saint-Germain FC	37	2			

★ Brazil

FIVE YEAR RECORD	LEAGUE		EURO CUPS		
Birthdate/Playing position	Apps	Gls	Cup	Apps	Gls

Patrick COLLETER
06/11/65   Defender

87/88	Brest-Armorique	37	2			
88/89	Brest-Armorique	Div 2				
89/90	Brest-Armorique	35	3			
90/91	Montpellier HSC	31	-	CWC	4	1
91/92	Paris Saint-Germain FC	28	-			

Jean-Luc SASSUS
04/10/62   Defender

87/88	AS Cannes	29	4			
88/89	AS Cannes	20	-			
89/90	AS Cannes	27	2			
90/91	AS Cannes	36	-			
91/92	AS Cannes	37	1	UC	4	-

Laurent FOURNIER
14/09/64   Midfield

87/88	Olympique Lyonnais	Div 2				
88/89	AS Saint-Etienne	34	3			
89/90	AS Saint-Etienne	36	4			
90/91	Olympique Marseille	17	2	+CC	6	1
91/92	Paris Saint-Germain FC	34	3			

Bruno GERMAIN
28/04/60   Midfield

87/88	Matra Racing Paris	36	4			
88/89	SC Toulon	15	2			
	Olympique Marseille	21	1			
89/90	Olympique Marseille	27	2	CC	6	-
90/91	Olympique Marseille	32	6	+CC	8	-
91/92	Paris Saint-Germain FC	34	2			

★ France 1 cap, 0 goals

Paul LE GUEN
01/03/64   Midfield

87/88	Brest-Armorique	38	-		
88/89	Brest-Armorique	Div 2			
89/90	FC Nantes	38	1		
90/91	FC Nantes	38	-		
91/92	Paris Saint-Germain FC	36	2		

FRANCE

FIVE YEAR RECORD	LEAGUE		EURO CUPS		
Birthdate/Playing position	Apps	Gls	Cup	Apps	Gls

Vincent GUERIN
22/11/65   Midfield

87/88	Brest-Armorique	35	8			
88/89	Matra Racing Paris	34	2			
89/90	Montpellier HSC	35	4			
90/91	Montpellier HSC	34	2	CWC	4	1
91/92	Montpellier HSC	29	3			

Pierre REYNAUD
09/01/68   Midfield

87/88	Paris Saint-Germain FC	22	2	
88/89	Paris Saint-Germain FC	-	-	
89/90	Paris Saint-Germain FC	18	-	
90/91	Paris Saint-Germain FC	34	-	
91/92	Paris Saint-Germain FC	21	1	

VALDO Candido(Bra)
12/01/64   Midfield

87/88	Gremio (Bra)					
88/89	SL Benfica (Por)	28	3	UC	3	1
89/90	SL Benfica (Por)	24	3	+CC	9	1
90/91	SL Benfica (Por)	26	5	UC	2	-
91/92	Paris Saint-Germain FC	32	3			
★ Brazil						

David GINOLA
25/01/67   Midfield

87/88	SC Toulon	33	4	
88/89	Matra Racing Paris	29	7	
89/90	Racing Paris 1	32	1	
90/91	Brest-Armorique	33	6	
91/92	Brest-Armorique	Div 2		
	Paris Saint-Germain FC	15	3	
★ France 1 cap, 0 goals				

François CALDERARO
15/06/64   Forward

87/88	Stade de Reims	Div 2	
88/89	Stade de Reims	Div 2	
89/90	Stade de Reims	Div 2	
90/91	FC Metz	32	10
91/92	FC Metz	36	19

George WEAH (Lib)
01/10/66   Forward

88/89	AS Monaco	23	14	CC	5	2
89/90	AS Monaco	17	5	CWC	7	3
90/91	AS Monaco	29	10	UC	5	3
91/92	AS Monaco	34	18	+CWC	9	4
★ Liberia						

Daniel BRAVO
09/02/63   Forward

87/88	OGC Nice	21	3			
88/89	OGC Nice	29	15			
89/90	Paris Saint-Germain FC	30	5	UC	4	1
90/91	Paris Saint-Germain FC	35	8			
91/92	Paris Saint-Germain FC	36	6			
★ France 13 caps, 1 goal						

Amara SIMBA
23/12/61   Forward

87/88	Paris Saint-Germain FC	16	2			
88/89	Paris Saint-Germain FC	8	1			
89/90	Paris Saint-Germain FC	27	6	UC	2	-
90/91	Paris Saint-Germain FC	5	-			
	AS Cannes	28	10			
91/92	Paris Saint-Germain FC	25	6			
★ France 3 caps, 2 goals						

EUROPEAN HONOURS
none

EUROPEAN CUPS RECORD

	Entries	Pd	W	D	L	F	A
Champions' Cup	1	2	0	1	1	2	3
Cup-winners' Cup	2	10	6	2	2	16	9
UEFA/Fairs' Cup	2	8	2	2	4	12	12
Total - All 3 Cups	5	20	8	5	7	30	24

AJ AUXERRE

FIVE YEAR RECORD Birthdate/Playing position	LEAGUE Apps	Gls	EURO CUPS Cup	Apps	Gls

Bruno MARTINI
25/01/62   Goalkeeper

87/88 AJ Auxerre	38	-	UC	2	-
88/89 AJ Auxerre	37	-			
89/90 AJ Auxerre	38	-	UC	10	-
90/91 AJ Auxerre	38	-			
91/92 AJ Auxerre	31	-	UC	4	-

★ France 25 caps, 0 goals

Lionel CHARBONNIER
25/10/66   Goalkeeper

88/89 AJ Auxerre	1	-			
89/90 AJ Auxerre	-	-			
90/91 AJ Auxerre	-	-			
91/92 AJ Auxerre	7	-			

Frank VERLAAT (Hol)
05/03/68   Defender

87/88 Ajax (Hol)	8	2	+CWC	4	-
88/89 Ajax (Hol)	2	-	UC	1	-
89/90 Lausanne-Sports (Sui)	33	4			
90/91 Lausanne-Sports (Sui)	35	5	UC	2	-
91/92 Lausanne-Sports (Sui)	36	6	UC	2	-

William PRUNIER
14/08/67   Defender

87/88 AJ Auxerre	38	1	UC	2	-
88/89 AJ Auxerre	35	3			
89/90 AJ Auxerre	5	-			
90/91 AJ Auxerre	36	2			
91/92 AJ Auxerre	35	4	UC	3	-

Thierry BONALAIR
14/06/66   Defender

87/88 FC Nantes	13	-			
88/89 FC Nantes	35	1			
89/90 FC Nantes	31	-			
90/91 FC Nantes	35	-			
91/92 FC Nantes	31	1			

Stéphane MAHE
23/09/68   Defender

88/89 AJ Auxerre	1	-			
89/90 AJ Auxerre	-	-			
90/91 AJ Auxerre	6	-			
91/92 AJ Auxerre	34	1	UC	4	-

Stéphane MAZZOLINI
28/11/66   Defender

87/88 AJ Auxerre	14	-			
88/89 AJ Auxerre	11	-			
89/90 AJ Auxerre	30	1	UC	9	-
90/91 AJ Auxerre	32	-			
91/92 AJ Auxerre	21	1	UC	1	-

Alain GOMA
05/10/72   Defender

90/91 AJ Auxerre	1	-			
91/92 AJ Auxerre	1	-			

Raphaël GUERREIRO
24/04/68   Midfield

88/89 AJ Auxerre	31	-			
89/90 AJ Auxerre	33	1	UC	9	2
90/91 AJ Auxerre	37	1			
91/92 AJ Auxerre	36	1	UC	4	-

Daniel DUTUEL
10/12/67   Midfield

87/88 AJ Auxerre	35	6	UC	2	1
88/89 AJ Auxerre	14	1			
89/90 AJ Auxerre	13	1	UC	4	1
90/91 AJ Auxerre	35	7			
91/92 AJ Auxerre	38	6	UC	4	-

Jean-Marc FERRERI
26/12/62   Midfield

87/88 Girondins de Bordeaux	34	5	CC	5	4
88/89 Girondins de Bordeaux	32	6	UC	6	1
89/90 Girondins de Bordeaux	35	14			
90/91 Girondins de Bordeaux	34	6	UC	6	3
91/92 AJ Auxerre	26	8	UC	4	3

★ France 37 caps, 3 goals

FRANCE

FIVE YEAR RECORD	LEAGUE		EURO CUPS		
Birthdate/Playing position	Apps	Gls	Cup	Apps	Gls

FIVE YEAR RECORD	LEAGUE		EURO CUPS		
Birthdate/Playing position	Apps	Gls	Cup	Apps	Gls

Didier OTOKORE (Civ)
26/03/69   Midfield

87/88	AJ Auxerre	10	5	UC	1	-
88/89	AJ Auxerre	10	1			
89/90	AJ Auxerre	23	4	UC	7	3
90/91	AJ Auxerre	14	1			
91/92	AJ Auxerre	20	1	UC	3	-

★ Ivory Coast

Corentin MARTINS
11/07/69   Midfield

88/89	Brest-Armorique	Div 2	
89/90	Brest-Armorique	28	1
90/91	Brest-Armorique	36	2
91/92	Brest-Armorique	Div 2	
	AJ Auxerre	15	3

Christophe COCARD
23/11/67   Forward

87/88	AJ Auxerre	5	1			
88/89	AJ Auxerre	34	6			
89/90	AJ Auxerre	32	4	UC	9	2
90/91	AJ Auxerre	38	11			
91/92	AJ Auxerre	37	10	UC	4	1

★ France 5 caps, 0 goals

Pascal VAHIRUA
09/03/66   Forward

87/88	AJ Auxerre	35	9	UC	2	-
88/89	AJ Auxerre	34	6			
89/90	AJ Auxerre	29	4	UC	9	2
90/91	AJ Auxerre	37	6			
91/92	AJ Auxerre	35	3	UC	4	2

★ France 15 caps, 1 goal

Gérald BATICLE
10/09/69   Forward

90/91	Amiens SC	Div 3	
91/92	AJ Auxerre	24	8

Franco VIGNOLA
15/09/66   Forward

88/89	AJ Auxerre	4	-			
89/90	AJ Auxerre	11	2	UC	1	-
90/91	AJ Auxerre	11	-			
91/92	AJ Auxerre	2	-			

Lidian LASLANDES
04/09/71   Forward

91/92	AS Saint-Seurin	Div 2	

EUROPEAN HONOURS
none

EUROPEAN CUPS RECORD

	Entries	Pd	W	D	L	F	A
Champions' Cup	none						
Cup-winners' Cup	none						
UEFA/Fairs' Cup	5	20	10	3	7	36	21
Total - All 3 Cups	5	20	10	3	7	36	21

SM CAEN

Philippe MONTANIER
15/11/64   Goalkeeper

87/88	Evreux AC	Div 3		
88/89	SM Caen	14	-	
89/90	SM Caen	38	-	
90/91	FC Nantes	8	-	
91/92	SM Caen	31	-	

Frédéric PETEREYNS
08/12/69   Goalkeeper

89/90	US Maubeuge	Div 3		
90/91	SM Caen	1	-	
91/92	SM Caen	7	-	

Hippolyte DANGBETO (Ben)
02/11/69   Defender

88/89	Matra Racing Paris	2	-	
89/90	Racing Paris 1	37	-	
90/91	SM Caen	37	1	
91/92	SM Caen	35	1	

Hubert FOURNIER
03/09/67   Defender

88/89	US Maubeuge	Div 3		
89/90	SM Caen	32	-	
90/91	SM Caen	23	2	
91/92	SM Caen	19	-	

Yvan LEBOURGEOIS
26/10/62   Defender

87/88	SM Caen	Div 2		
88/89	SM Caen	36	3	
89/90	SM Caen	27	2	
90/91	SM Caen	28	1	
91/92	SM Caen	38	1	

Christophe POINT
26/05/65   Defender

87/88	SM Caen	Div 2		
88/89	SM Caen	33	2	
89/90	SM Caen	28	-	
90/91	SM Caen	31	1	
91/92	SM Caen	8	-	

Benoît CAUET
02/05/69   Midfield

87/88	Olympique Marseille	11	1	CWC	3	-
88/89	Olympique Marseille	14	-			
89/90	Olympique Marseille	-	-			
90/91	SM Caen	35	1			
91/92	SM Caen	37	3			

Gabriel CALDERON (Arg)
07/02/60   Midfield

87/88	Paris-Saint-Germain FC	32	4			
88/89	Paris-Saint-Germain FC	38	7			
89/90	Paris-Saint-Germain FC	32	9	UC	4	1
90/91	FC Sion (Sui)	22	8			
91/92	FC Sion (Sui)	25	9	CWC	2	-

★ Argentina

Wilhelmus GORTER (Hol)
06/07/63   Midfield

87/88	FC Lugano (Sui)	Div 2	
88/89	FC Lugano (Sui)	18	5
89/90	FC Lugano (Sui)	34	12
90/91	FC Lugano (Sui)	31	11
91/92	SM Caen	36	4

Xavier GRAVELAINE
05/10/68   Midfield

89/90	AS Saint-Seurin	Div 2	
90/91	Stade Lavallois	Div 2	
91/92	SM Caen	34	6

Emmanuel RIVAL
15/02/71   Midfield

91/92	SM Caen	10	-

Stéphane DEDEBANT
17/10/70   Forward

91/92	Racing Paris 92	Div 3	

Christophe DUBOSCQ
15/01/67   Forward

91/92	US Avranches	Div 3	

FRANCE

FIVE YEAR RECORD *Birthdate/Playing position*	LEAGUE Apps Gls	EURO CUPS Cup Apps Gls

Philippe AVENET
16/04/67   Forward

		LEAGUE Apps	Gls
87/88	Matra Racing Paris	11	-
88/89	RC Lens	16	1
89/90	Racing Paris 1	28	3
90/91	SM Caen	21	-
91/92	SM Caen	17	1

Joël GERMAIN
07/12/64   Forward

		LEAGUE Apps	Gls
87/88	CS Cuiseaux-Louhans	Div 2	
88/89	US Orléans	Div 2	
89/90	US Orléans	Div 2	
90/91	SM Caen	34	5
91/92	SM Caen	36	1

Olivier PICKEU
24/02/70   Forward

		LEAGUE Apps	Gls
90/91	FC Tours	Div 3	
91/92	SM Caen	27	4

Stéphane PAILLE
27/06/65   Forward

		LEAGUE Apps	Gls		EURO CUPS Cup Apps	Gls
87/88	FC Sochaux	Div 2				
88/89	FC Sochaux	35	15			
89/90	Montpellier HSC	17	4			
90/91	FC Porto (Por)	17	4	CC	5	4
91/92	SM Caen	38	14			

★ France 8 caps, 1 goal

FIVE YEAR RECORD *Birthdate/Playing position*	LEAGUE Apps Gls	EURO CUPS Cup Apps Gls

Clément GARCIA
26/06/68   Forward

		LEAGUE Apps	Gls		EURO CUPS Cup Apps	Gls
88/89	FC Grenoble	Div 2				
89/90	FC Grenoble	Div 2				
90/91	Montpellier HSC	13	-	CWC	2	-
91/92	Montpellier HSC	3	-			

EUROPEAN HONOURS
none

EUROPEAN CUPS RECORD

	Entries	Pd	W	D	L	F	A
Champions' Cup	none						
Cup-winners' Cup	none						
UEFA/Fairs' Cup	none						
Total - All 3 Cups	none						

BORUSSIA DORTMUND

FIVE YEAR RECORD *Birthdate/Playing position*	LEAGUE Apps	Gls	EURO CUPS Cup	Apps	Gls

Stefan KLOS
16/08/71   Goalkeeper

90/91	Borussia Dortmund	2	-		
91/92	Borussia Dortmund	31	-		

Wolfgang DE BEER
02/01/64   Goalkeeper

87/88	Borussia Dortmund	32	-	UC	6	-
88/89	Borussia Dortmund	34	-			
89/90	Borussia Dortmund	33	-	CWC	4	-
90/91	Borussia Dortmund	32	-	UC	6	-
91/92	Borussia Dortmund	7	-			

Stefan REUTER
16/10/66   Defender

87/88	1.FC Nürnberg	34	2			
88/89	FC Bayern München	32	-	CC	10	1
89/90	FC Bayern München	33	-	CC	8	-
90/91	FC Bayern München	30	4	CC	8	3
91/92	Juventus (Ita)	28	-			
★ Germany 35 caps, 2 goals						

Bodo SCHMIDT
03/09/67   Defender

90/91	SpVgg Unterhaching	Div 3		
91/92	Borussia Dortmund	13	1	

Michael SCHULZ
03/09/61   Defender

87/88	1.FC Kaiserslautern	28	1			
88/89	1.FC Kaiserslautern	21	2			
89/90	Borussia Dortmund	21	1	CWC	4	-
90/91	Borussia Dortmund	26	1	UC	5	1
91/92	Borussia Dortmund	38	1			
★ Germany 2 caps, 0 goals						

Steffen KARL
03/02/70   Defender

87/88	HFC Chemie	6	1	
88/89	HFC Chemie	25	1	
89/90	Borussia Dortmund	2	-	
90/91	Borussia Dortmund	12	-	
91/92	Borussia Dortmund	28	1	

FIVE YEAR RECORD *Birthdate/Playing position*	LEAGUE Apps	Gls	EURO CUPS Cup	Apps	Gls

Ned ZELIC (Aus)
04/07/71   Midfield

91/92	Olympic Sydney (Aus)			
★ Australia				

Günter KUTOWSKI
02/08/65   Defender

87/88	Borussia Dortmund	33	-	UC	6	-
88/89	Borussia Dortmund	33	1			
89/90	Borussia Dortmund	23	-	CWC	3	-
90/91	Borussia Dortmund	25	1	UC	4	-
91/92	Borussia Dortmund	33	-			

Michael RUMMENIGGE
03/02/64   Midfield

87/88	FC Bayern München	31	10	CC	5	-
88/89	FC Bayern München	32	4			
89/90	Borussia Dortmund	29	9	CWC	3	-
90/91	Borussia Dortmund	31	8	UC	6	1
91/92	Borussia Dortmund	36	10			
★ Germany 2 caps, 0 goals						

Gerhard POSCHNER
23/09/69   Midfield

87/88	VfB Stuttgart	15	-			
88/89	VfB Stuttgart	16	-	+UC	3	-
89/90	VfB Stuttgart	14	-	UC	3	-
90/91	Borussia Dortmund	27	4	UC	4	-
91/92	Borussia Dortmund	29	3			

Michael LUSCH
16/06/64   Midfield

87/88	Borussia Dortmund	26	-	UC	3	-
88/89	Borussia Dortmund	21	1			
89/90	Borussia Dortmund	23	2	CWC	4	-
90/91	Borussia Dortmund	22	3	UC	6	-
91/92	Borussia Dortmund	33	2			

GERMANY

FIVE YEAR RECORD *Birthdate/Playing position*	LEAGUE Apps Gls	EURO CUPS Cup Apps Gls

Knut REINHARDT
27/04/68   Midfield

		Apps	Gls	Cup	Apps	Gls
87/88	Bayer 04 Leverkusen	23	1	#UC	8	-
88/89	Bayer 04 Leverkusen	27	1	UC	1	-
89/90	Bayer 04 Leverkusen	31	-			
90/91	Bayer 04 Leverkusen	29	-	UC	5	-
91/92	Borussia Dortmund	36	3			

★ Germany 4 caps, 0 goals

Thomas FRANCK
24/02/71   Midfield

		Apps	Gls	Cup	Apps	Gls
88/89	SV Waldhof Mannheim	1	-			
89/90	SV Waldhof Mannheim	18	2			
90/91	Borussia Dortmund	20	-	UC	3	-
91/92	Borussia Dortmund	27	1			

Michael ZORC
25/08/62   Midfield

		Apps	Gls	Cup	Apps	Gls
87/88	Borussia Dortmund	22	13	UC	2	-
88/89	Borussia Dortmund	27	3			
89/90	Borussia Dortmund	32	10	CWC	4	-
90/91	Borussia Dortmund	30	5	UC	4	2
91/92	Borussia Dortmund	19	6			

Flemming POVLSEN (Den)
03/12/66   Forward

		Apps	Gls	Cup	Apps	Gls
87/88	1.FC Köln	34	14			
88/89	1.FC Köln	34	5	UC	6	1
89/90	PSV (Hol)	29	10	CC	5	1
90/91	Borussia Dortmund	30	5	UC	6	-
91/92	Borussia Dortmund	38	7			

★ Denmark 50 caps, 17 goals

Frank MILL
23/07/58   Forward

		Apps	Gls	Cup	Apps	Gls
87/88	Borussia Dortmund	29	9	UC	6	4
88/89	Borussia Dortmund	26	6			
89/90	Borussia Dortmund	29	2	CWC	4	1
90/91	Borussia Dortmund	13	3	UC	4	3
91/92	Borussia Dortmund	28	4			

★ Germany 17 caps, 0 goals

FIVE YEAR RECORD *Birthdate/Playing position*	LEAGUE Apps Gls	EURO CUPS Cup Apps Gls

Stéphane CHAPUISAT (Sui)
28/06/69   Forward

		Apps	Gls	Cup	Apps	Gls
87/88	Lausanne-Sports (Sui)	33	12			
88/89	Lausanne-Sports (Sui)	21	1			
89/90	Lausanne-Sports (Sui)	30	10			
90/91	Lausanne-Sports (Sui)	20	13	UC	2	1
	Bayer 05 Uerdingen	10	4			
91/92	Borussia Dortmund	37	20			

★ Switzerland 22 caps, 3 goals

Lothar SIPPEL
09/05/65   Forward

		Apps	Gls	Cup	Apps	Gls
88/89	Hessen Kassel	Div 3				
89/90	Eintracht Frankfurt	18	2			
90/91	Eintracht Frankfurt	18	2	UC	2	-
91/92	Eintracht Frankfurt	32	14	UC	3	-

EUROPEAN HONOURS
Cup-winners' Cup - (1) 1966.

EUROPEAN CUPS RECORD

	Entries	Pd	W	D	L	F	A
Champions' Cup	3	18	8	3	7	44	31
Cup-winners' Cup	3	15	9	3	3	32	15
UEFA/Fairs' Cup	4	18	9	1	8	24	26
Total - All 3 Cups	10	51	26	7	18	100	72

EINTRACHT FRANKFURT

FIVE YEAR RECORD _Birthdate/Playing position_	LEAGUE Apps	Gls	EURO CUPS Cup	Apps	Gls
Uli STEIN _23/10/54 Goalkeeper_					
87/88 Eintracht Frankfurt	20	-			
88/89 Eintracht Frankfurt	34	-	CWC	6	-
89/90 Eintracht Frankfurt	34	-			
90/91 Eintracht Frankfurt	34	-	UC	2	-
91/92 Eintracht Frankfurt	38	-	UC	4	-
★ Germany 6 caps, 0 goals					

Thomas ERNST _23/12/67 Goalkeeper_					
91/92 Eintracht Frankfurt	-	-			

Manfred BINZ _22/09/65 Defender_					
87/88 Eintracht Frankfurt	34	2			
88/89 Eintracht Frankfurt	34	2	CWC	6	1
89/90 Eintracht Frankfurt	34	4			
90/91 Eintracht Frankfurt	34	4	UC	2	-
91/92 Eintracht Frankfurt	38	1	UC	4	-
★ Germany 14 caps, 1 goal					

Dietmar ROTH _16/09/63 Defender_					
87/88 Eintracht Frankfurt	27	-			
88/89 Eintracht Frankfurt	33	1	CWC	6	-
89/90 Eintracht Frankfurt	26	1			
90/91 Eintracht Frankfurt	30	-	UC	1	-
91/92 Eintracht Frankfurt	35	2	UC	1	-

Michael KLEIN _22/02/65 Defender_					
88/89 FSV Frankfurt	Div 3				
89/90 Eintracht Frankfurt	12	-			
90/91 Eintracht Frankfurt	14	-	UC	1	-
91/92 Eintracht Frankfurt	16	-	UC	1	-

Uwe BINDEWALD _13/08/68 Defender_					
88/89 Eintracht Frankfurt	3	-			
89/90 Eintracht Frankfurt	19	-			
90/91 Eintracht Frankfurt	13	-	UC	1	-
91/92 Eintracht Frankfurt	36	-	UC	4	-

FIVE YEAR RECORD _Birthdate/Playing position_	LEAGUE Apps	Gls	EURO CUPS Cup	Apps	Gls
André KÖHLER _28/02/65 Defender_					
89/90 Chemie Böhlen	Div 2				
90/91 FC Wismut Aue	Div 2				
91/92 Eintracht Frankfurt	4	-	UC	1	-

Frank MÖLLER _11/07/67 Defender_					
89/90 FSV Mainz 05	Div 2				
90/91 FSV Mainz 05	Div 2				
91/92 Eintracht Frankfurt	13	-			

Ilija NAJDOSKI (Yug) _26/03/64 Defender_					
87/88 Vardar Skoplje (Yug)	25	-			
88/89 Crvena zvezda Beograd (Yug)	23	2	CC	3	-
89/90 Crvena zvezda Beograd (Yug)	29	1	UC	5	-
90/91 Crvena zvezda Beograd (Yug)	32	2	#CC	6	-
91/92 Crvena zvezda Beograd (Yug)	15*	1*	CC	5	-
★ Yugoslavia 11 caps, 1 goal					
* first half of season figures only					

Uwe BEIN _26/09/60 Midfield_					
87/88 Hamburger SV	24	7	CWC	4	-
88/89 Hamburger SV	32	15			
89/90 Eintracht Frankfurt	33	9			
90/91 Eintracht Frankfurt	31	8	UC	1	1
91/92 Eintracht Frankfurt	34	8	UC	4	2
★ Germany 14 caps, 3 goals					

Stefan STUDER _30/01/64 Midfield_					
87/88 FC St. Pauli	Div 2				
88/89 Eintracht Frankfurt	23	2	CWC	4	1
89/90 Eintracht Frankfurt	33	2			
90/91 Eintracht Frankfurt	33	3	UC	2	-
91/92 Eintracht Frankfurt	18	-	UC	3	-

GERMANY

FIVE YEAR RECORD *Birthdate/Playing position*	LEAGUE Apps Gls	EURO CUPS Cup Apps Gls

Ralf WEBER
31/05/69   Midfield

		Apps	Gls		Apps	Gls
88/89	Kickers Offenbach	Div 2				
89/90	Eintracht Frankfurt	18	2			
90/91	Eintracht Frankfurt	13	2	UC	1	-
91/92	Eintracht Frankfurt	34	4	UC	4	-

Heinz GRÜNDEL
13/02/67   Midfield

		Apps	Gls		Apps	Gls
87/88	Hamburger SV	15	-			
88/89	Eintracht Frankfurt	25	1	CWC	3	-
89/90	Eintracht Frankfurt	23	3			
90/91	Eintracht Frankfurt	29	4	UC	1	0
91/92	Eintracht Frankfurt	14	1	UC	2	1

★ Germany 4 caps, 0 goals

Ralf FALKENMAYER
11/02/63   Midfield

		Apps	Gls		Apps	Gls
87/88	Bayer 04 Leverkusen	29	6	#UC	10	-
88/89	Bayer 04 Leverkusen	19	1			
89/90	Eintracht Frankfurt	33	6			
90/91	Eintracht Frankfurt	21	1	UC	2	-
91/92	Eintracht Frankfurt	33	4	UC	3	-

★ Germany 4 caps, 0 goals

Axel KRUSE
28/09/67   Forward

		Apps	Gls		Apps	Gls
87/88	FC Hansa Rostock	26	3			
88/89	FC Hansa Rostock	21	2			
89/90	Hertha BSC	Div 2				
90/91	Hertha BSC	7	2			
	Eintracht Frankfurt	17	3			
91/92	Eintracht Frankfurt	14	5	UC	2	2

Uwe RAHN
21/05/62   Forward

		Apps	Gls		Apps	Gls
87/88	Borussia Mönchengladbach	25	13	UC	1	1
88/89	Borussia Mönchengladbach	10	-			
	1.FC Köln	20	7			
89/90	1.FC Köln	23	6	UC	7	-
90/91	Hertha BSC	21	5			
91/92	Fortuna Düsseldorf	15	5			

★ Germany 14 caps, 5 goals

FIVE YEAR RECORD *Birthdate/Playing position*	LEAGUE Apps Gls	EURO CUPS Cup Apps Gls

Anthony YEBOAH (Gha)
06/06/64   Forward

		Apps	Gls		Apps	Gls
88/89	1.FC Saarbrücken	Div 2				
89/90	1.FC Saarbrücken	Div 2				
90/91	Eintracht Frankfurt	26	8	UC	1	1
91/92	Eintracht Frankfurt	34	15	UC	3	2

★ Ghana

Jorn ANDERSEN (Nor)
03/02/63   Forward

		Apps	Gls		Apps	Gls
87/88	1.FC Nürnberg	27	9			
88/89	Eintracht Frankfurt	26	2	CWC	6	-
89/90	Eintracht Frankfurt	34	18			
90/91	Fortuna Düsseldorf	31	4			
91/92	Fortuna Düsseldorf	9	1			
	Eintracht Frankfurt	26	9			

★ Norway 27 caps, 5 goals

EUROPEAN HONOURS
UEFA Cup - (1) 1980.

EUROPEAN CUPS RECORD

	Entries	Pd	W	D	L	F	A
Champions' Cup	1	7	4	2	1	23	15
Cup-winners' Cup	4	24	14	3	7	41	23
UEFA/Fairs' Cup	10	54	27	9	18	107	67
Total - All 3 Cups	15	85	45	14	26	171	105

1.FC KÖLN

FIVE YEAR RECORD	LEAGUE		EURO CUPS		
Birthdate/Playing position	Apps	Gls	Cup	Apps	Gls

Bodo ILLGNER
07/04/67   Goalkeeper

87/88	1.FC Köln	34	-		
88/89	1.FC Köln	33	-	UC	6	-
89/90	1.FC Köln	34	-	UC	10	-
90/91	1.FC Köln	34	-	UC	6	-
91/92	1.FC Köln	37	-		

★ Germany 39 caps, 0 goals

Alexander BADE
25/08/70   Goalkeeper

89/90	1.FC Köln	-	-
90/91	1.FC Köln	-	-
91/92	1.FC Köln	1	-

Karsten BAUMANN
14/10/69   Defender

89/90	1.FC Köln	-	-		
90/91	1.FC Köln	28	-	UC	2	-
91/92	1.FC Köln	34	2		

Kim CHRISTOFTE (Den)
24/08/60   Defender

87	OB (Den)	24	1		
88	OB (Den)	10	1		
89	Brøndby IF (Den)	17	1	CC	2	-
90	Brøndby IF (Den)	23	2	UC	8	2
91	Brøndby IF (Den)	9	-		
91/92	Brøndby IF (Den)	31	1	CC	4	1

★ Denmark 16 caps, 1 goal

Henrik ANDERSEN (Den)
07/05/65   Defender

87/88	RSC Anderlecht (Bel)	32	2	CC	6	-
88/89	RSC Anderlecht (Bel)	30	1	CWC	3	-
89/90	RSC Anderlecht (Bel)	33	1	+CWC	8	-
90/91	1.FC Köln	27	-	UC	5	-
91/92	1.FC Köln	21	1		

★ Denmark 29 caps, 2 goals

Alfons HIGL
17/12/64   Defender

87/88	SC Freiburg	Div 2			
88/89	SC Freiburg	Div 2			
89/90	1.FC Köln	30	-	UC	9	1
90/91	1.FC Köln	33	3	UC	6	1
91/92	1.FC Köln	31	-		

Olaf JANSSEN
08/10/66   Midfield

87/88	1.FC Köln	13	3		
88/89	1.FC Köln	21	2	UC	5	3
89/90	1.FC Köln	27	3	UC	10	-
90/91	1.FC Köln	12	2	UC	4	1
91/92	1.FC Köln	5	1		

Jan JENSEN (Den)
22/02/69   Midfield

87	B 1909 (Den)	Div 3			
88/89	1.FC Köln	4	-	UC	4	
89/90	1.FC Köln	7	-	UC	3	
90/91	1.FC Köln	5	-	UC	1	
91/92	1.FC Köln	16	-		

André TRULSEN
28/05/65   Midfield

87/88	FC St. Pauli	Div 2	
88/89	FC St. Pauli	33	-
89/90	FC St. Pauli	33	1
90/91	FC St. Pauli	32	-
91/92	1.FC Köln	20	1

Rico STEINMANN
26/12/67   Midfield

87/88	FC Karl-Marx-Stadt	20	1		
88/89	FC Karl-Marx-Stadt	20	8		
89/90	FC Karl-Marx-Stadt	25	7	UC	6	1
90/91	Chemnitzer FC	21	4	UC	1	-
91/92	1.FC Köln	31	2		

★ East Germany 23 caps, 3 goals

GERMANY

FIVE YEAR RECORD *Birthdate/Playing position*	LEAGUE Apps	Gls	EURO CUPS Cup	Apps	Gls

Pierre LITTBARSKI
16/04/60   Midfield

		LEAGUE		EURO CUPS		
87/88	Matra Racing Paris (Fra)	2	-			
	1.FC Köln	31	8			
88/89	1.FC Köln	30	5	UC	6	1
89/90	1.FC Köln	34	8	UC	9	2
90/91	1.FC Köln	15	2			
91/92	1.FC Köln	36	1			

★ Germany 73 caps, 18 goals

Horst HELDT
09/12/69   Midfield

		LEAGUE		EURO CUPS		
89/90	1.FC Köln	-	-			
90/91	1.FC Köln	22	3	UC	4	-
91/92	1.FC Köln	31	3			

Frank GREINER
03/07/66   Midfield

		LEAGUE		EURO CUPS		
87/88	1.FC Nürnberg	5	-			
88/89	1.FC Köln	3	-			
89/90	1.FC Köln	19	1	UC	8	-
90/91	1.FC Köln	32	3	UC	6	-
91/92	1.FC Köln	36	2			

Hans-Dieter FLICK
24/02/65   Midfield

		LEAGUE		EURO CUPS		
87/88	FC Bayern München	28	1	CC	6	-
88/89	FC Bayern München	30	2	UC	8	1
89/90	FC Bayern München	22	1	CC	2	-
90/91	1.FC Köln	19	-	UC	5	-
91/92	1.FC Köln	21	1			

Andrzej RUDY (Pol)
15/10/65   Midfield

		LEAGUE		EURO CUPS		
87/88	Slask Wroclaw (Pol)	21	2			
88/89	GKS Katowice (Pol)	13	1	UC	2	-
89/90	1.FC Köln	18	2	UC	4	-
90/91	1.FC Köln	24	2	UC	4	-
91/92	1.FC Köln	1	-			
	Brøndby IF (Den)	8	1			

★ Poland 11 caps, 3 goals

Ralf STURM
18/10/68   Forward

		LEAGUE		EURO CUPS		
87/88	1.FC Köln	-	-			
88/89	1.FC Köln	15	1	UC	2	-
89/90	1.FC Köln	25	8	UC	9	2
90/91	1.FC Köln	27	9	UC	5	-
91/92	1.FC Köln	22	5			

Frank ORDENEWITZ
25/03/65   Forward

		LEAGUE		EURO CUPS		
87/88	SV Werder Bremen	30	15	UC	10	2
88/89	SV Werder Bremen	26	6	CC	4	-
89/90	1.FC Köln	30	3	UC	8	2
90/91	1.FC Köln	31	7	UC	6	1
91/92	1.FC Köln	35	11			

★ Germany 2 caps, 0 goals

Henri FUCHS
23/06/70   Forward

		LEAGUE		EURO CUPS		
87/88	FC Hansa Rostock	1	-			
88/89	FC Hansa Rostock	10	3			
89/90	FC Hansa Rostock	26	3	UC	2	-
90/91	FC Hansa Rostock	24	12			
91/92	1.FC Köln	35	10			

EUROPEAN HONOURS
none

EUROPEAN CUPS RECORD

	Entries	Pd	W	D	L	F	A
Champions' Cup	3	17	7	8	2	27	19
Cup-winners' Cup	3	14	7	2	5	30	19
UEFA/Fairs' Cup	18	127	69	19	39	251	145
Total - All 3 Cups	24	158	83	29	46	308	183

1.FC KAISERSLAUTERN

FIVE YEAR RECORD *Birthdate/Playing position*	LEAGUE Apps Gls	EURO CUPS Cup Apps Gls

Gerald EHRMANN
18/02/59   Goalkeeper

87/88	1.FC Kaiserslautern	17	-	
88/89	1.FC Kaiserslautern	33	-	
89/90	1.FC Kaiserslautern	21	-	
90/91	1.FC Kaiserslautern	33	-	CWC 2 -
91/92	1.FC Kaiserslautern	38	-	CC 4 -

Michael SERR
14/07/62   Goalkeeper

87/88	1.FC Kaiserslautern	19	-	
88/89	1.FC Kaiserslautern	2	-	
89/90	1.FC Kaiserslautern	14	-	
90/91	1.FC Kaiserslautern	2	-	
91/92	1.FC Kaiserslautern	-	-	

Jan ERIKSSON (Swe)
24/08/67   Defender

87	AIK (Swe)	9	-	UC 2 -
88	AIK (Swe)	21	-	
89	AIK (Swe)	22	-	
90	AIK (Swe)	21	2	
91	IFK Norrköping (Swe)	26	2	CWC 4 2

★ Sweden 23 caps, 3 goals

Thomas DOOLEY (Usa)
12/05/61   Defender

87/88	FC 08 Homburg	24	2	
88/89	1.FC Kaiserslautern	24	2	
89/90	1.FC Kaiserslautern	22	2	
90/91	1.FC Kaiserslautern	23	4	CWC 2 -
91/92	1.FC Kaiserslautern	20	3	CC 3 -

★ United States

Wolfgang FUNKEL
10/08/58   Defender

87/88	Bayer 05 Uerdingen	33	3	
88/89	Bayer 05 Uerdingen	32	4	
89/90	Bayer 05 Uerdingen	32	4	
90/91	Bayer 05 Uerdingen	24	4	
91/92	1.FC Kaiserslautern	35	6	CC 4 2

★ Germany 2 caps, 0 goals

FIVE YEAR RECORD *Birthdate/Playing position*	LEAGUE Apps Gls	EURO CUPS Cup Apps Gls

Thomas RITTER
10/10/67   Defender

87/88	SG Dynamo Dresden (Gdr)	2	-	
88/89	Fortschritt Bischofswerda (Gdr)	Div 2		
89/90	Fortschritt Bischofswerda (Gdr)	6	-	
90/91	Stuttgarter Kickers	Div 2		
91/92	Stuttgarter Kickers	36	1	

Reinhard STUMPF
26/11/61   Defender

87/88	Kickers Offenbach	Div 2		
88/89	Kickers Offenbach	Div 2		
89/90	1.FC Kaiserslautern	28	-	
90/91	1.FC Kaiserslautern	21	1	
91/92	1.FC Kaiserslautern	16	-	CC 2 -

Miroslav KADLEC (Tch)
22/06/64   Defender

87/88	TJ Vitkovice (Tch)	28	2	UC 8 -
88/89	TJ Vitkovice (Tch)	30	8	
89/90	TJ Vitkovice (Tch)	28	8	
90/91	1.FC Kaiserslautern	28	2	CWC 2 -
91/92	1.FC Kaiserslautern	21	1	

★ Czechoslovakia 32 caps, 0 goals

Martin WAGNER
24/02/68   Midfield

88/89	1.FC Nürnberg	30	7	UC 1 -
89/90	1.FC Nürnberg	7	1	
90/91	1.FC Nürnberg	30	2	
91/92	1.FC Nürnberg	33	4	

Guido HOFFMANN
20/12/65   Midfield

87/88	Borussia Mönchengladbach	8	-	
88/89	FC 08 Homburg	Div 2		
89/90	FC 08 Homburg	25	-	
90/91	1.FC Kaiserslautern	29	7	CWC 2 -
91/92	1.FC Kaiserslautern	27	2	CC 2 -

GERMANY

FIVE YEAR RECORD *Birthdate/Playing position*	LEAGUE Apps Gls	EURO CUPS Cup Apps Gls

Oliver SCHÄFER
27/02/69   Midfield

89/90	SC Freiburg	Div 2			
90/91	SC Freiburg	Div 2			
91/92	1.FC Kaiserslautern	24	-	CC	3	-

Marco HABER
21/09/71   Midfield

89/90	1.FC Kaiserslautern	3	-		
90/91	1.FC Kaiserslautern	28	5	CWC	2	-
91/92	1.FC Kaiserslautern	34	-	CC	3	-

Frank LELLE
04/02/65   Midfield

87/88	1.FC Kaiserslautern	21	2		
88/89	1.FC Kaiserslautern	1	-		
89/90	1.FC Kaiserslautern	22	2		
90/91	1.FC Kaiserslautern	13	3	CWC	2	-
91/92	1.FC Kaiserslautern	15	1	CC	1	-

Bjarne GOLDBAEK (Den)
06/10/68   Midfield

87	Naestved IF (Den)	17	4		
87/88	FC Schalke 04	22	3		
88/89	FC Schalke 04	Div 2			
89/90	FC Schalke 04	Div 2			
	1.FC Kaiserslautern	3	-		
90/91	1.FC Kaiserslautern	22	4	CWC	1	-
91/92	1.FC Kaiserslautern	24	2	CC	3	1

★ Denmark 4 caps, 0 goals

Stefan KUNTZ
30/10/62   Forward

87/88	Bayer 05 Uerdingen	32	13		
88/89	Bayer 05 Uerdingen	33	13		
89/90	1.FC Kaiserslautern	32	15		
90/91	1.FC Kaiserslautern	27	11	CWC	2	1
91/92	1.FC Kaiserslautern	31	11	CC	2	-

FIVE YEAR RECORD *Birthdate/Playing position*	LEAGUE Apps Gls	EURO CUPS Cup Apps Gls

Demir HOTIC (Yug)
09/07/62   Forward

87/88	Stuttgarter Kickers	Div 2			
88/89	Stuttgarter Kickers	23	7		
89/90	VfB Stuttgart	13	3	UC	5	-
	1.FC Kaiserslautern	12	3		
90/91	1.FC Kaiserslautern	29	9	CWC	2	-
91/92	1.FC Kaiserslautern	38	10	CC	4	2

Marcel WITECZEK
18/10/68   Forward

87/88	Bayer 05 Uerdingen	29	3		
88/89	Bayer 05 Uerdingen	29	4		
89/90	Bayer 05 Uerdingen	32	7		
90/91	Bayer 05 Uerdingen	31	5		
91/92	1.FC Kaiserslautern	36	5	CC	4	-

Marcus MARIN
13/12/66   Forward

88/89	Hamburger SV	5	-		
89/90	Hamburger SV	10	-	UC	2	-
90/91	Stuttgarter Kickers	Div 2			
91/92	Stuttgarter Kickers	32	13		

EUROPEAN HONOURS
none

EUROPEAN CUPS RECORD

	Entries	pd	W	D	L	F	A
Champions' Cup	1	4	2	1	1	6	4
Cup-winners' Cup	1	2	1	0	1	1	2
UEFA/Fairs' Cup	7	44	24	3	17	91	69
Total - All 3 Cups	9	50	27	4	19	98	75

PANATHINAIKOS

FIVE YEAR RECORD *Birthdate/Playing position*	LEAGUE Apps Gls	EURO CUPS Cup Apps Gls

Jozef WANDZIK (Pol)
13/08/63   Goalkeeper

87/88	Górnik Zabrze (Pol)	30	-	CC	4	-
88/89	Górnik Zabrze (Pol)	27	-	CC	4	-
89/90	Górnik Zabrze (Pol)	28	-	UC	2	-
90/91	Panathinaikos	34	-	CC	2	-
91/92	Panathinaikos	32	-	CC	10	-

★ Poland 46 caps, 0 goals

Yorgos ABADIOTAKIS
21/03/67   Goalkeeper

87/88	Korinthos	Div 2				
88/89	Panathinaikos	3	-	CWC	2	-
89/90	Panathinaikos	14	-	CWC	2	-
90/91	Panathinaikos	-	-			
91/92	Panathinaikos	2	-			

Stratos APOSTOLAKIS
11/05/64   Defender

87/88	Olympiakos	26	-			
88/89	Olympiakos	21	2			
89/90	Olympiakos	32	2	UC	5	-
90/91	Panathinaikos	31	3	CC	1	-
91/92	Panathinaikos	28	1	CC	10	-

★ Greece 46 caps, 1 goal

Yannis KALITZAKIS
10/12/61   Defender

87/88	Panathinaikos	18	-	UC	6	-
88/89	Panathinaikos	22	-	CWC	1	-
89/90	Panathinaikos	31	3	CWC	4	-
90/91	Panathinaikos	31	3	CWC	4	-
90/91	Panathinaikos	28	-	CC	1	-
91/92	Panathinaikos	26	2	CC	8	-

★ Greece 25 caps, 0 goals

Kostas MAVRIDIS
07/07/62   Defender

87/88	Panathinaikos	27	1	UC	8	1
88/89	Panathinaikos	30	2	CWC	4	1
89/90	Panathinaikos	16	-	CWC	4	-
90/91	Panathinaikos	18	2			
91/92	Panathinaikos	33	3	CC	10	-

★ Greece 30 caps, 1 goal

Nikos KARAYEORYIOU
08/12/62   Defender

87/88	PAOK	25	1			
88/89	PAOK	26	1	UC	2	-
89/90	PAOK	25	1			
90/91	PAOK	30	5	UC	2	-
91/92	Panathinaikos	31	-	CC	10	-

★ Greece 16 caps, 0 goals

Nikos KOURBANAS
22/03/62   Defender

87/88	Panahaiki	25	3			
88/89	Panathinaikos	21	-	CWC	3	-
89/90	Panathinaikos	26	-	CWC	1	-
90/91	Panathinaikos	29	2	CC	2	-
91/92	Panathinaikos	15	1	CC	2	-

★ Greece 7 caps, 0 goals

Hristos KALATZIS
27/07/67   Midfield

87/88	Olympic Sydney (Aus)					
	Panathinaikos	15	1	UC	1	-
88/89	Panathinaikos	23	2	CWC	4	-
89/90	Panathinaikos	26	3	CWC	4	-
90/91	Panathinaikos	24	2	CC	2	-
91/92	Panathinaikos	30	2	CC	9	-

Marinos OUZOUNIDIS
10/10/68   Midfield

88/89	Xanthi	Div 2	
89/90	Xanthi	33	2
90/91	Xanthi	31	5
91/92	Xanthi	33	8

★ Greece 1 cap, 0 goals

Asterios YOTSAS
20/01/66   Midfield

90/91	Pierikos	Div 2	
91/92	Pierikos	32	2

★ Greece 3 caps, 0 goals

GREECE

FIVE YEAR RECORD	LEAGUE		EURO CUPS		
Birthdate/Playing position	Apps	Gls	Cup	Apps	Gls

Leonidas HRISTODOULOU
07/08/67   Midfield

87/88	Adelaide City (Aus)					
	Panathinaikos	4	1			
88/89	Panathinaikos	14	3	CWC	4	-
89/90	Panathinaikos	15	1	CWC	1	-
90/91	Panathinaikos	25	2			
91/92	Panathinaikos	30	2	CC	10	2

Spiros MARAGOS
03/07/67   Midfield

87/88	Panionios	25	-			
88/89	Panionios	24	-			
89/90	Panionios	11	1			
	Panathinaikos	20	1			
90/91	Panathinaikos	30	-	CC	1	-
91/92	Panathinaikos	31	4	CC	9	2

★ Greece 12 caps, 0 goals

Kostas ANTONIOU
19/04/62   Midfield

87/88	Panathinaikos	25	3	UC	8	2
88/89	Panathinaikos	15	2			
89/90	Panathinaikos	34	13	CWC	4	-
90/91	Panathinaikos	29	8	CC	2	-
91/92	Panathinaikos	17	4	CC	9	-

★ Greece 30 caps, 2 goals

Dimitris SARAVAKOS
26/07/61   Forward

87/88	Panathinaikos	26	5	UC	8	6
88/89	Panathinaikos	25	5	CWC	2	-
89/90	Panathinaikos	24	11	CWC	3	3
90/91	Panathinaikos	30	23	CC	2	1
91/92	Panathinaikos	33	24	CC	10	3

★ Greece 70 caps, 20 goals

Yorgos DONIS
08/05/70   Forward

90/91	Panaryiakos	Div 2				
	Yannina	22	3			
91/92	Panathinaikos	30	4	CC	10	-

★ Greece 3 caps, 1 goal

FIVE YEAR RECORD	LEAGUE		EURO CUPS		
Birthdate/Playing position	Apps	Gls	Cup	Apps	Gls

Dimitris MARKOU
1971   Forward

91/92	Naoussa	Div 2				

★ Greece 2 caps, 0 goals

Kostas FRANTZESKOS
04/01/69   Forward

90/91	Panathinaikos	22	5			
91/92	Panathinaikos	26	5	CC	4	-

Krzysztof WARZYCHA (Pol)
17/11/64   Forward

87/88	Ruch Chorzów (Pol)	Div 2				
88/89	Ruch Chorzów (Pol)	30	24			
89/90	Ruch Chorzów (Pol)	15	12	CC	2	1
	Panathinaikos	21	14			
90/91	Panathinaikos	31	18	CC	2	-
91/92	Panathinaikos	21	12	CC	4	-

★ Poland 36 caps, 6 goals

EUROPEAN HONOURS
none

EUROPEAN CUPS RECORD

	Entries	Pd	W	D	L	F	A
Champions' Cup	13	53	13	19	21	60	71
Cup-winners' Cup	5	14	4	2	8	13	28
UEFA/Fairs' Cup	**8**	**24**	**7**	**3**	**14**	**30**	**40**
Total - All 3 Cups	26	91	24	24	43	103	139

PAOK

FIVE YEAR RECORD	LEAGUE		EURO CUPS		
Birthdate/Playing position	Apps	Gls	Cup	Apps	Gls

Tonci GABRIC (Cro)
11/03/61   Goalkeeper

87/88	Hajduk Split (Yug)	2	-		
88/89	NK Rijeka (Yug)	25	-		
89/90	NK Rijeka (Yug)	32	-		
90/91	NK Rijeka (Yug)	35	-		
91/92	PAOK	31	-	UC	4	-

Yannis GITSIOUDIS
17/03/62   Goalkeeper

87/88	PAOK	28	-			
88/89	PAOK	29	-	UC	2	-
89/90	PAOK	34	-			
90/91	PAOK	27	-	UC	2	-
91/92	PAOK	4	-			

★ Greece 4 caps, 0 goals

Kostas MALIOUFAS
01/09/63   Defender

87/88	PAOK	20	1			
88/89	PAOK	23	-	UC	2	-
89/90	PAOK	31	1			
90/91	PAOK	19	-	UC	1	-
91/92	PAOK	24	1	UC	3	-

Kostas ILIADIS
02/04/62   Defender

87/88	Iraklis	28	4			
88/89	Iraklis	27	1			
89/90	Iraklis	31	-	UC	2	-
90/91	Iraklis	27	4	UC	2	-
91/92	Iraklis	33	4			

Alexandros ALEXIOU
08/09/62   Defender

87/88	Olympiakos	27	4	CC	2	1
88/89	Olympiakos	23	2			
89/90	Olympiakos	22	1	UC	4	1
90/91	PAOK	12	1			
91/92	PAOK	30	6	UC	4	-

★ Greece 3 caps, 0 goals

FIVE YEAR RECORD	LEAGUE		EURO CUPS		
Birthdate/Playing position	Apps	Gls	Cup	Apps	Gls

Yorgos TOURSOUNIDIS
21/08/70   Midfield

88/89	PAOK	2	-			
89/90	PAOK	23	3			
90/91	PAOK	32	2	UC	2	-
91/92	PAOK	30	5	UC	4	-

★ Greece 12 caps, 0 goals

Kostas LAGONIDIS
01/07/65   Midfield

87/88	PAOK	16	4			
88/89	PAOK	23	1	UC	2	-
89/90	PAOK	33	3			
90/91	PAOK	29	2	UC	2	-
91/92	PAOK	28	6	UC	3	-

★ Greece 4 caps, 0 goals

Ioakim HAVOS
05/09/69   Midfield

87/88	Olympiakos	3	-	
	Apollon Kalamarias	3	-	
88/89	Panserraikos	Div 2		
89/90	Panserraikos	20	1	
90/91	Panserraikos	30	3	
91/92	Panserraikos	32	4	

Dimitris KAPEPANOPOULOS
1969   Midfield

91/92	Panaryiakos	Div 2	

MAGDI TOLBA (Egy)
25/02/64   Midfield

88/89	Egypt					
89/90	PAOK	32	4			
90/91	PAOK	23	5	UC	2	-
91/92	PAOK	11	2	UC	2	-

★ Egypt

GREECE

FIVE YEAR RECORD	LEAGUE		EURO CUPS			FIVE YEAR RECORD	LEAGUE		EURO CUPS		
Birthdate/Playing position	Apps	Gls	Cup	Apps	Gls	*Birthdate/Playing position*	Apps	Gls	Cup	Apps	Gls

Mihalis LEONTIADIS
25/01/66   Midfield

87/88	PAOK	16	3		
88/89	PAOK	20	1	UC	1	-
89/90	PAOK	18	2		
90/91	PAOK	15	1	UC	2	-
91/92	PAOK	23	2	UC	4	-

★ Greece 1 cap, 0 goals

Hristos HIONAS
11/10/66   Midfield

88/89	Alexandropoulos	Div 4	
89/90	Doxa	30	8
90/91	Doxa	32	6
91/92	Doxa	10	6
	PAOK	19	1

★ Greece 1 cap, 0 goals

Yannis ALEXOULIS
22/04/64   Midfield

87/88	Larissa	28	4			
88/89	Larissa	26	2	CC	2	-
89/90	PAOK	24	3			
90/91	PAOK	28	-	UC	2	-
91/92	PAOK	4	-	UC	3	-

Nikos PLITSIS
29/02/68   Forward

89/90	PAOK	10	1			
90/91	PAOK	18	1			
91/92	PAOK	23	-	UC	2	-

Stefanos BORBOKIS
01/09/66   Forward

87/88	PAOK	26	9			
88/89	PAOK	25	3	UC	2	-
89/90	PAOK	32	2			
90/91	PAOK	29	6	UC	1	-
91/92	PAOK	30	3	UC	4	1

★ Greece 28 caps, 6 goals

Thanassis DIMOPOULOS
21/04/63   Forward

87/88	Panathinaikos	4	-	UC	1	-
	Iraklis	13	7			
88/89	Iraklis	29	13			
89/90	Iraklis	29	11	UC	2	-
90/91	Iraklis	33	7	UC	2	-
91/92	Iraklis	30	12			

★ Greece 3 caps, 0 goals

Milan DJURDJEVIC (Yug)
04/11/67   Forward

87/88	OFK Beograd (Yug)	Div 2				
88/89	OFK Beograd (Yug)	Div 2				
89/90	Partizan Beograd (Yug)	23	9	CWC	5	2
90/91	Partizan Beograd (Yug)	21	9	UC	4	1
91/92	PAOK	23	6			

Kostas IKONOMIDIS
18/07/66   Forward

87/88	Aris	23	-			
88/89	Aris	21	2			
89/90	Aris	26	1			
90/91	Aris	28	-			
91/92	PAOK	29	1	UC	2	-

★ Greece 2 caps, 0 goals

EUROPEAN HONOURS
none

EUROPEAN CUPS RECORD

	Entries	Pd	W	D	L	F	A
Champions' Cup	2	6	1	1	4	5	12
Cup-winners' Cup	6	18	8	5	5	24	23
UEFA/Fairs' Cup	9	24	9	6	9	20	37
Total - All 3 Cups	17	48	18	12	18	49	72

AJAX

FIVE YEAR RECORD *Birthdate/Playing position*	LEAGUE Apps	Gls	EURO CUPS Cup	Apps	Gls
Stanley MENZO					
15/10/63 Goalkeeper					
87/88 Ajax	34	-	+CWC 9	-	
88/89 Ajax	32	-	UC 2	-	
89/90 Ajax	29	-	UC 2	-	
90/91 Ajax	26	-			
91/92 Ajax	34	-	#UC 12	-	
★ Holland 3 caps, 0 goals					
Edwin VAN DER SAR					
29/10/70 Goalkeeper					
90/91 Ajax	9	-			
91/92 Ajax	-	-			
Danny BLIND					
01/08/61 Defender					
87/88 Ajax	31	-	+CWC 8	1	
88/89 Ajax	30	2			
89/90 Ajax	34	-			
90/91 Ajax	34	2			
91/92 Ajax	30	2	#UC 12	1	
★ Holland 20 caps, 1 goal					
Sonny SILOOY					
31/08/63 Defender					
87/88 Ajax	6	1			
Matra Racing Paris (Fra)	21	-			
88/89 Matra Racing Paris (Fra)	34	-			
89/90 Ajax	2	-			
90/91 Ajax	16	-			
91/92 Ajax	21	-	#UC 7	-	
★ Holland 22 caps, 0 goals					
Frank DE BOER					
15/05/70 Defender					
88/89 Ajax	28	-			
89/90 Ajax	25	-	UC 1	-	
90/91 Ajax	34	1			
91/92 Ajax	30	1	#UC 12	-	
★ Holland 9 caps, 1 goal					

FIVE YEAR RECORD *Birthdate/Playing position*	LEAGUE Apps	Gls	EURO CUPS Cup	Apps	Gls
Marciano VINK					
17/10/70 Defender					
88/89 Ajax	2	1	UC 1	-	
89/90 Ajax	23	2	UC 2	-	
90/91 Ajax	27	1			
91/92 Ajax	26	1	#UC 9	-	
★ Holland 2 caps, 0 goals					
John HANSEN (Den)					
11/07/66 Defender					
87 OB (Den)	24	2			
88 OB (Den)	16	1			
89 OB (Den)	24	-			
90 OB (Den)	20	2			
91 OB (Den)	17	4			
91/92 Ajax	1	-			
★ Denmark 12 caps, 0 goals					
Michel KREEK					
16/01/71 Midfield					
89/90 Ajax	2	-			
90/91 Ajax	13	2			
91/92 Ajax	25	2	#UC 9	1	
Ron WILLEMS					
20/09/66 Midfield					
87/88 FC Twente	32	11			
88/89 Ajax	1	-			
89/90 Ajax	19	7	UC 1	-	
90/91 Ajax	22	6			
91/92 Ajax	3	-			
Bryan ROY					
12/02/70 Midfield					
87/88 Ajax	12	2	+CWC 2	-	
88/89 Ajax	29	5			
89/90 Ajax	29	3	UC 2	-	
90/91 Ajax	29	4			
91/92 Ajax	22	3	#UC 10	1	
★ Holland 12 caps, 2 goals					

HOLLAND

Wim JONK
12/10/66   Midfield

		Apps	Gls	Cup	Apps	Gls
87/88	FC Volendam	23	5			
88/89	Ajax	17	6	UC	2	-
89/90	Ajax	13	3			
90/91	Ajax	17	1			
91/92	Ajax	26	5	#UC	10	3

★ Holland 4 caps, 0 goals

Dan PETERSEN (Den)
06/05/72   Midfield

		Apps	Gls	Cup	Apps	Gls
91	OB (Den)	14	2	CC	1	-
91/92	Ajax	16	1	#UC	1	-

Alphons GROENENDIJK
17/05/64   Midfield

		Apps	Gls	Cup	Apps	Gls
87/88	Roda JC	32	8			
88/89	Roda JC	21	6	UC	3	-
89/90	Roda JC	31	5			
90/91	Roda JC	23	1	UC	1	-
91/92	Ajax	20	1	#UC	3	-

Rob ALFLEN
07/05/68   Midfield

		Apps	Gls	Cup	Apps	Gls
87/88	FC Utrecht	28	2	UC	3	-
88/89	FC Utrecht	31	4			
89/90	FC Utrecht	25	-			
90/91	FC Utrecht	33	6			
91/92	Ajax	9	2	#UC	5	-

Dennis BERGKAMP
10/05/69   Forward

		Apps	Gls	Cup	Apps	Gls
87/88	Ajax	25	5	+CWC	6	1
88/89	Ajax	30	13	UC	1	-
89/90	Ajax	25	8	UC	1	-
90/91	Ajax	33	25			
91/92	Ajax	30	24	#UC	11	6

★ Holland 17 caps, 9 goals

Marc OVERMARS
29/03/73   Forward

90/91	Go Ahead Eagles	Div 2		
91/92	Willem II	31	1	

Stefan PETTERSSON (Swe)
22/03/63   Forward

		Apps	Gls	Cup	Apps	Gls
87	IFK Göteborg (Swe)	18	10	UC	2	-
88	IFK Göteborg (Swe)	8	7			
88/89	Ajax	25	13	UC	2	2
89/90	Ajax	18	6			
90/91	Ajax	19	13			
91/92	Ajax	30	15	#UC	12	4

★ Sweden 26 caps, 2 goals

John VAN LOEN
04/02/65   Forward

		Apps	Gls	Cup	Apps	Gls
87/88	FC Utrecht	31	13	UC	4	1
88/89	Roda JC	31	8	UC	6	1
89/90	Roda JC	25	17			
90/91	RSC Anderlecht (Bel)	26	3	UC	5	-
91/92	Ajax	30	10	#UC	7	1

★ Holland 7 caps, 1 goal

EUROPEAN HONOURS
Champions' Cup - (3) 1971, 1972, 1973.
Cup-winners' Cup - (1) 1987.
UEFA Cup - (1) 1992.
Super Cup - (2) 1972, 1973.

EUROPEAN CUPS RECORD

	Entries	Pd	W	D	L	F	A
Champions' Cup	15	75	42	15	18	141	74
Cup-winners' Cup	4	22	15	1	6	41	18
UEFA/Fairs' Cup	9	50	27	7	16	100	47
Total - All 3 Cups	28	147	84	23	40	282	139

VITESSE

FIVE YEAR RECORD *Birthdate/Playing position*	LEAGUE Apps Gls	EURO CUPS Cup Apps Gls

Raymond VAN DER GOUW
24/03/63   Goalkeeper

87/88	Go Ahead Eagles	Div 2		
88/89	Vitesse	Div 2		
89/90	Vitesse	34	-	
90/91	Vitesse	31	-	UC 6 -
91/92	Vitesse	34	-	

Abe KNOOP
28/08/63   Goalkeeper

89/90	Wageningen	Div 2	
90/91	Ajax	-	-
91/92	Vitesse	-	-

Edward STURING
13/06/63   Defender

87/88	Vitesse	Div 2		
88/89	Vitesse	Div 2		
89/90	Vitesse	34	-	
90/91	Vitesse	14	-	UC 3 -
91/92	Vitesse	33	-	

★ Holland 3 caps, 0 goals

Theo BOS
05/10/65   Defender

87/88	Vitesse	Div 2		
88/89	Vitesse	Div 2		
89/90	Vitesse	33	1	
90/91	Vitesse	32	1	UC 6 -
91/92	Vitesse	28	-	

Arjan VERMEULEN
19/03/69   Defender

88/89	Vitesse	Div 2		
89/90	Vitesse	32	1	
90/91	Vitesse	30	1	UC 5 -
91/92	Vitesse	30	3	

FIVE YEAR RECORD *Birthdate/Playing position*	LEAGUE Apps Gls	EURO CUPS Cup Apps Gls

Roberto STRAAL
19/12/66   Defender

87/88	Vitesse	Div 2		
88/89	Vitesse	Div 2		
89/90	Vitesse	19	-	
90/91	Vitesse	26	-	UC 6 -
91/92	Vitesse	21	1	

Ton VAN BREMEN
02/03/68   Defender

87/88	Excelsior	Div 2		
88/89	Excelsior	Div 2		
89/90	Excelsior	Div 2		
90/91	Vitesse	18	-	UC 4 -
91/92	Vitesse	3	-	

John VAN DEN BROM
04/10/66   Midfield

87/88	Vitesse	Div 2		
88/89	Vitesse	Div 2		
89/90	Vitesse	33	14	
90/91	Vitesse	33	8	UC 6 1
91/92	Vitesse	32	10	

★ Holland 1 cap, 0 goals

Martin LAAMERS
02/08/67   Midfield

87/88	Vitesse	Div 2		
88/89	Vitesse	Div 2		
89/90	Vitesse	31	2	
90/91	Vitesse	3	1	UC 5 -
91/92	Vitesse	34	2	

★ Holland 2 caps, 0 goals

René EIJER
01/01/63   Midfield

87/88	VVV	32	4	
88/89	VVV	29	4	
89/90	Vitesse	32	3	
90/91	Vitesse	33	6	UC 6 2
91/92	Vitesse	32	1	

HOLLAND

FIVE YEAR RECORD	LEAGUE		EURO CUPS		
Birthdate/Playing position	Apps	Gls	Cup	Apps	Gls

Bart LATUHERU
08/11/65   Midfield

87/88	Excelsior	Div 2				
88/89	Excelsior	Div 2				
89/90	Vitesse	23	2			
90/91	Vitesse	34	6	UC	6	2
91/92	Vitesse	33	4			

★ Holland 1 cap, 0 goals

Marlon KEIZER
24/03/69   Midfield

88/89	Vitesse	Div 2	
89/90	Vitesse	-	-
90/91	Vitesse	1	-
	NEC	5	-
91/92	Vitesse	-	-

Huub LOEFFEN
11/01/72   Forward

90/91	Vitesse	16	4	UC	5	1
91/92	Vitesse	34	9			

Hans VAN ARUM
23/12/66   Forward

88/89	SDVB	Div 3				
89/90	Vitesse	31	10			
90/91	Vitesse	30	5	UC	6	1
91/92	Vitesse	28	8			

Philip COCU
29/10/70   Forward

88/89	AZ	Div 2	
89/90	AZ	Div 2	
90/91	Vitesse	8	-
91/92	Vitesse	33	3

FIVE YEAR RECORD	LEAGUE		EURO CUPS		
Birthdate/Playing position	Apps	Gls	Cup	Apps	Gls

Rick HILGERS
31/08/62   Forward

87/88	Vitesse	Div 2				
88/89	Vitesse	Div 2				
89/90	Vitesse	30	13			
90/91	Vitesse	22	1	UC	4	-
91/92	Vitesse	26	5			

Dennis KRIJGSMAN
21/07/72   Forward

91/92	Vitesse	8	-

Richard ROELOFSEN
13/07/69   Forward

88/89	PEC Zwolle	17	1
89/90	PEC Zwolle	Div 2	
90/91	Vitesse	12	1
91/92	Vitesse	10	-

EUROPEAN HONOURS							
none							

EUROPEAN CUPS RECORD							
	Entries	Pd	W	D	L	F	A
Champions' Cup	none						
Cup-winners' Cup	none						
UEFA/Fairs' Cup	1	6	3	1	2	7	4
Total - All 3 Cups	1	6	3	1	2	7	4

FC GRONINGEN

FIVE YEAR RECORD	LEAGUE		EURO CUPS		
Birthdate/Playing position	Apps	Gls	Cup	Apps	Gls

Patrick LODEWIJKS
21/02/67   Goalkeeper

		Apps	Gls	Cup	Apps	Gls
87/88	PSV	1	-			
88/89	PSV	10	-	CC	2	-
89/90	FC Groningen	31	-	CWC	4	-
90/91	FC Groningen	32	-			
91/92	FC Groningen	34	-	UC	2	-

Theo MIGCHELSEN
13/12/69   Goalkeeper

		Apps	Gls			
90/91	FC Groningen	2	-			
91/92	FC Groningen	-	-			

Jan VEENHOF
28/01/69   Defender

		Apps	Gls	Cup	Apps	Gls
88/89	FC Groningen	5	-			
89/90	FC Groningen	27	-			
90/91	FC Groningen	25	1			
91/92	FC Groningen	13	-	UC	1	-

Claus BOEKWEG
03/03/66   Defender

		Apps	Gls	Cup	Apps	Gls
87/88	FC Groningen	32	2			
88/89	FC Groningen	28	-	UC	5	-
89/90	FC Groningen	27	-	CWC	4	-
90/91	FC Groningen	29	-			
91/92	FC Groningen	33	1	UC	2	-

Ulrich WILSON
05/05/64

		Apps	Gls	Cup	Apps	Gls
87/88	FC Twente	-	-			
88/89	Ipswich Town (Eng)	Div 2				
88/89	Go Ahead Eagles	Div 2				
89/90	FC Groningen	33	-	CWC	4	-
90/91	FC Groningen	26	2			
91/92	FC Groningen	32	2	UC	2	-

Jan VAN DIJK
10/12/56   Defender

		Apps	Gls	Cup	Apps	Gls
87/88	FC Groningen	22	-			
88/89	FC Groningen	27	-	UC	5	-
89/90	FC Groningen	31	2	CWC	4	-
90/91	FC Groningen	28	1			
91/92	FC Groningen	18	-	UC	1	-

Andrei ZYGMANTOVICH (Cis)
07/12/62   Defender

		Apps	Gls	Cup	Apps	Gls
87	Dinamo Minsk (Urs)	30	2	CWC	6	1
88	Dinamo Minsk (Urs)	23	2	UC	4	1
89	Dinamo Minsk (Urs)	29	2			
90	Dinamo Minsk (Urs)	22	1			
91	Dinamo Minsk (Urs)	2	-			
91/92	FC Groningen	29	2	UC	2	-

★ USSR 36 caps, 3 goals

Edwin OLDE RIEKERINK
28/09/61   Midfield

		Apps	Gls	Cup	Apps	Gls
87/88	FC Groningen	23	3			
88/89	FC Groningen	31	4	UC	6	-
89/90	FC Groningen	20	2	CWC	1	-
90/91	FC Groningen	29	2			
91/92	FC Groningen	34	2	UC	2	-

Jos ROOSSIEN
16/11/60   Midfield

		Apps	Gls	Cup	Apps	Gls
87/88	FC Groningen	26	4			
88/89	FC Groningen	34	3	UC	6	-
89/90	FC Groningen	34	7	CWC	4	1
90/91	FC Groningen	33	10			
91/92	FC Groningen	31	5	UC	2	-

Grafton HOLBAND
25/02/65   Midfield

		Apps	Gls	Cup	Apps	Gls
89/90	FC Groningen	19	2			
90/91	FC Groningen	26	2			
91/92	FC Groningen	30	1	UC	1	-

HOLLAND

FIVE YEAR RECORD *Birthdate/Playing position*	LEAGUE Apps Gls	EURO CUPS Cup Apps Gls

Erik VAN KESSEL
28/02/66   Midfield

87/88	PSV	-	-
88/89	KSK Beveren (Bel)	31	2
89/90	KSK Beveren (Bel)	26	2
90/91	KSK Beveren (Bel)	Div 2	
91/92	De Graafschap	34	1

Martin VAN DUREN
27/10/64   Midfield

87/88	FC Den Bosch	31	4			
88/89	BVV Den Bosch	34	15			
89/90	BVV Den Bosch	31	5			
90/91	FC Groningen	26	2			
91/92	FC Groningen	29	6	UC	2	-

Harris HUIZINGH
10/02/63   Midfield

87/88	Veendam	Div 2				
88/89	Veendam	24	4			
89/90	Veendam	Div 2				
90/91	FC Groningen	30	8			
91/92	FC Groningen	18	2	UC	1	-

Hennie MEIJER
17/02/62   Forward

87/88	Ajax	26	11	#CWC	6	3
88/89	FC Groningen	34	15	UC	6	3
89/90	FC Groningen	29	8	CWC	4	2
90/91	FC Groningen	34	12			
91/92	FC Groningen	30	10	UC	2	-

★ Holland 1 cap, 0 goals

Milko DJUROVSKI (Yug)
26/02/63   Forward

87/88	Partizan Beograd (Yug)	16	9	UC	1	-
88/89	Partizan Beograd (Yug)	-	-			
89/90	Partizan Beograd (Yug)	23	11	CWC	6	4
90/91	FC Groningen	28	14			
91/92	FC Groningen	24	8	UC	2	-

★ Yugoslavia 6 caps, 2 goals

FIVE YEAR RECORD *Birthdate/Playing position*	LEAGUE Apps Gls	EURO CUPS Cup Apps Gls

Martin DRENT
31/03/70   Forward

91/92	FC Groningen	10	2	UC	2	-

Marcel VAN BUUREN
14/03/64   Forward

87/88	Veendam	Div 2				
88/89	Veendam	24	8			
89/90	Veendam	Div 2				
90/91	FC Groningen	9	2			
91/92	FC Groningen	12	-	UC	1	-

Arnold BOS
19/12/69   Forward

90/91	FC Groningen	9	-
91/92	FC Groningen	15	1

EUROPEAN HONOURS
none

EUROPEAN CUPS RECORD

	Entries	Pd	W	D	L	F	A
Champions' Cup	none						
Cup-winners' Cup	1	4	3	0	1	8	7
UEFA/Fairs' Cup	4	18	7	3	8	23	23
Total - All 3 Cups	5	22	10	3	9	31	30

VÁC FC SAMSUNG

FIVE YEAR RECORD *Birthdate/Playing position*	LEAGUE Apps Gls	EURO CUPS Cup Apps Gls

János KOSZTA
18/03/59   Goalkeeper

87/88	Videoton SC	10	-		
88/89	Videoton SC	8	-		
89/90	Videoton-Waltham SC	-	-		
	Váci Izzó MTE	15	-		
90/91	Váci Izzó MTE	29	-		
91/92	Vác FC Samsung	30	-	UC	2	-

★ Hungary 1 cap, 0 goals

Attila HAJDU
13/04/71   Goalkeeper

89/90	Ferencváros	-	-		
	Váci Izzó MTE				
90/91	Váci Izzó MTE	-	-		
91/92	Vác FC Samsung	1	-		

Péter BERECZKY
11/08/67   Defender

88/89	FC Bihor Oradea (Rom)	2	-		
89/90	FC Bihor Oradea (Rom)	14	-		
90/91	FC Bihor Oradea (Rom)	25	-		
91/92	Vác FC Samsung	13	-	UC	1	-

Árpád HAHN
12/03/65   Defender

87/88	Szekszárdi DSE	Div 2			
88/89	MTK-VM	14	-		
89/90	MTK-VM	24	1	UC	2	-
90/91	MTK-VM	24	2	UC	2	-
91/92	Vác FC Samsung	30	2	UC	2	1

Attila SZALAI
09/07/65   Defender

87/88	MTK-VM	27	-	CC	1	-
88/89	MTK-VM	21	-		
89/90	MTK-VM	5	-		
90/91	Váci Izzó MTE	26	1		
91/92	Vác FC Samsung	22	7		

FIVE YEAR RECORD *Birthdate/Playing position*	LEAGUE Apps Gls	EURO CUPS Cup Apps Gls

Tibor NAGY
24/09/62   Defender

87/88	Váci Izzó MTE	28	3		
88/89	Váci Izzó MTE	30	2		
89/90	Váci Izzó MTE	29	2		
90/91	Váci Izzó MTE	30	2		
91/92	Vác FC Samsung	26	1	UC	1	-

★ Hungary 7 caps, 0 goals

Gábor KRISKA
10/09/67   Defender

90/91	Dunakészi VSE	Div 3			
91/92	Vác FC Samsung	29	2	UC	2	-

LUIS CARLOS (Bra)
12/04/66   Defender

90/91	Internacional Porto Alegre (Bra)				
91/92	Vác FC Samsung	21	-	UC	1	-

Gábor PUGLITS
26/12/67   Defender

89/90	Budapesti Honvéd SE	1	-		
90/91	Budapesti Honvéd SE	-	-		
91/92	Vác FC Samsung	18	-	UC	2	-

Imre ARÁNYOS
13/06/66   Defender

91/92	Eger SE	Div 2			

András ZOMBORI
06/12/65   Midfield

87/88	Dunaújvárosi KSE	Div 2			
88/89	Dunaújvárosi KSE	15	-		
89/90	Váci Izzó MTE	17	-		
90/91	Váci Izzó MTE	23	2		
91/92	Vác FC Samsung	28	3	UC	2	-

★ Hungary 2 caps, 0 goals

HUNGARY

FIVE YEAR RECORD
Birthdate/Playing position

| | LEAGUE Apps Gls | EURO CUPS Cup Apps Gls |

László HORVÁTH
01/12/66   Midfield

	League Apps	Gls	Euro Cup	Apps	Gls
87/88 Békéscsaba	2	-			
88/89 Békéscsaba	20	2	CWC	3	-
89/90 Békéscsaba	19	-			
90/91 Békéscsaba	24	4			
91/92 Vác FC Samsung	25	6	UC	2	-

Antal SIMON
27/09/65   Midfield

	League Apps	Gls	Euro Cup	Apps	Gls
89/90 Eger SE	Div 2				
90/91 Volán FC	16	3			
91/92 Vác FC Samsung	20	3	UC	1	-

Sándor CSERESZYNIK
02/08/67   Midfield

	League Apps	Gls	Euro Cup	Apps	Gls
90/91 Váci Izzó MTE	1	-			
91/92 Vác FC Samsung	-	-			

Elek NYILAS
03/05/69   Forward

	League Apps	Gls
91/92 Vác FC Samsung	18	2

János ROMANEK
28/03/66   Forward

	League Apps	Gls	Euro Cup	Apps	Gls
87/88 Budapesti Honvéd SE	21	1	UC	4	-
88/89 Budapesti Honvéd SE	8	-			
Dunaújvárosi KSE	6	-			
89/90 Váci Izzó MTE	11	1			
90/91 Váci Izzó MTE	27	1			
91/92 Vác FC Samsung	23	1	UC	2	1

FIVE YEAR RECORD
Birthdate/Playing position

| | LEAGUE Apps Gls | EURO CUPS Cup Apps Gls |

László RÉPÁSI
23/03/66   Forward

	League Apps	Gls	Euro Cup	Apps	Gls
87/88 Ferencváros	1	-			
88/89 Ferencváros	-	-			
89/90 Váci Izzó MTE	28	10			
90/91 Váci Izzó MTE	28	8			
91/92 Vác FC Samsung	16	2	UC	1	-

Antal FÜLE
26/11/66   Forward

	League Apps	Gls	Euro Cup	Apps	Gls
88/89 Budapesti Honvéd SE	14	3	CC	1	-
89/90 Budapesti Honvéd SE	12	1	CC	3	-
Váci Izzó MTE	2	-			
90/91 Váci Izzó MTE	29	8			
91/92 Vác FC Samsung	18	6	UC	2	-

EUROPEAN HONOURS
none

EUROPEAN CUPS RECORD

	Entries	Pd	W	D	L	F	A
Champions' Cup	none						
Cup-winners' Cup	none						
UEFA/Fairs' Cup	1	2	1	0	1	2	4
Total - All 3 Cups	1	2	1	0	1	2	4

FRAM

FIVE YEAR RECORD Birthdate/Playing position	LEAGUE Apps Gls	EURO CUPS Cup Apps Gls

Birkir KRISTINSSON
15/08/64   Goalkeeper

87	ÍA	18	-	CWC	2	-
88	Fram	18	-	CWC	2	-
89	Fram	18	-	CC	2	-
90	Fram	18	-	CWC	4	-
91	Fram	18	-	CC	2	-

★ Iceland 10 caps, 0 goals

Fridrik THORSTEINSSON
05/12/73   Goalkeeper

91	Fram	-	-

Jón SVEINSSON
05/08/65   Defender

87	Fram	11	-	CC	2	-
88	Fram	17	-	CWC	2	-
89	Fram	13	-	CC	1	-
90	Fram	18	-	CWC	4	-
91	Fram	17	-	CC	2	-

Kristján JÓNSSON
29/10/63   Defender

87	Fram	17	3	CC	2	-
88	Fram	15	-	CWC	2	-
89	Fram	18	-	CC	2	-
90	Fram	18	-	CWC	4	-
91	Fram	16	-	CC	2	-

★ Iceland 18 caps, 0 goals

Pétur ÓSKARSSON
10/02/68   Defender

88	Fylkir	Div 2	
89	Fylkir	18	-
90	Fylkir	Div 2	
91	Fylkir	Div 2	

Saevar GUDJÓNSSON
01/02/72   Defender

91	Fram	-	-

Gudmundur GÍSLASON
05/05/73   Midfield

91	Fram	-	-

Ómar SIGTRYGGSSON
28/01/73   Midfield

91	Fram	-	-

Pétur ORMSLEV
28/07/58   Midfield

87	Fram	18	12	CC	1	-
88	Fram	18	8	CWC	2	-
89	Fram	17	4	CC	2	-
90	Fram	18	3	CWC	3	1
91	Fram	18	4	CC	2	-

★ Iceland 41 caps, 5 goals

Asgeir ASGEIRSSON
30/03/72   Midfield

91	Fram	15	-	CC	1	-

Pétur ARNTHÓRSSON
08/05/65   Midfield

87	Fram	18	3	CC	2	-
88	Fram	18	4	CWC	2	-
89	Fram	17	1	CC	2	-
90	Fram	14	4	CWC	4	1
91	Fram	13	-	CC	2	1

★ Iceland 28 caps, 0 goals

Steinar GUDGEIRSSON
19/08/71   Midfield

89	Fram	8	-	CC	2	-
90	Fram	12	1	CWC	4	-
91	Fram	18	2	CC	2	-

★ Iceland 1 cap, 0 goals

ICELAND

FIVE YEAR RECORD *Birthdate/Playing position*	LEAGUE Apps Gls	EURO CUPS Cup Apps Gls

Kristinn R. JÓNSSON
23/06/64   Midfield

87	Fram	17	1	CC	2	-
88	Fram	18	-	CWC	2	-
89	Fram	18	-	CC	2	-
90	Fram	16	2	CWC	4	-
91	Fram	18	2	CC	2	-

★ Iceland 8 caps, 0 goals

Anton Björn MARKÚSSON
06/01/71   Midfield

89	Fram	1	-			
90	Fram	10	1	CWC	4	-
91	Fram	8	-	CC	2	-

Ingólfur INGÓLFSSON
28/10/70   Midfield

89	Stjarnan	Div 2		
90	Stjarnan	18	4	
91	Stjarnan	18	7	

Jon Erling RAGNARSSON
18/05/64   Forward

87	FH	10	2			
88	FH	Div 2				
89	FH	4	-			
90	Fram	14	8	CWC	4	2
91	Fram	18	11	CC	2	1

Rikhardur DADASON
26/04/72   Forward

89	Fram	13	1			
90	Fram	17	5	CWC	4	1
91	Fram	18	4	CC	1	-

★ Iceland 2 caps, 0 goals

FIVE YEAR RECORD *Birthdate/Playing position*	LEAGUE Apps Gls	EURO CUPS Cup Apps Gls

Valdimir KRISTÓFERSSON
22/03/70   Forward

89	Stjarnan	Div 2		
90	Stjarnan	18	3	
91	Stjarnan	15	6	

EUROPEAN HONOURS
none

EUROPEAN CUPS RECORD

	Entries	Pd	W	D	L	F	A
Champions' Cup	4	8	0	2	6	4	28
Cup-winners' Cup	8	20	5	1	14	14	42
UEFA/Fairs' Cup	3	6	0	0	6	0	23
Total - All 3 Cups	15	34	5	3	26	18	93

JUVENTUS

FIVE YEAR RECORD	LEAGUE		EURO CUPS		
Birthdate/Playing position	Apps	Gls	Cup	Apps	Gls

Angelo PERUZZI
16/02/70 Goalkeeper

87/88 Roma	1	-			
88/89 Roma	12	-	UC	1	-
89/90 Verona	29	-			
90/91 Roma	3	-	UC	2	-
91/92 Juventus	6	-			

Michelangelo RAMPULLA
10/08/62 Goalkeeper

87/88 Cremonese	Div 2	
88/89 Cremonese	Div 2	
89/90 Cremonese	27	-
90/91 Cremonese	Div 2	
91/92 Cremonese	34	1

Massimo CARRERA
22/04/64 Defender

87/88 Bari	Div 2	
88/89 Bari	Div 2	
89/90 Bari	30	2
90/91 Bari	30	-
91/92 Juventus	31	1

★ Italy 1 cap, 0 goals

Dino BAGGIO
24/07/71 Defender

89/90 Torino	Div 2				
90/91 Torino	25	2			
91/92 Interniazionale	27	1	UC	2	-

★ Italy 1 cap, 0 goals

Jürgen KOHLER (Ger)
06/10/65 Defender

87/88 1.FC Köln (Ger)	30	3			
88/89 1.FC Köln (Ger)	27	-	UC	6	-
89/90 FC Bayern München (Ger)	26	2	CC	6	-
90/91 FC Bayern München (Ger)	29	4	CC	7	-
91/92 Juventus	27	3			

★ Germany 47 caps, 0 goals

FIVE YEAR RECORD	LEAGUE		EURO CUPS		
Birthdate/Playing position	Apps	Gls	Cup	Apps	Gls

JULIO CÉSAR Silva (Bra)
08/03/63 Defender

87/88 Montpellier PSC (Fra)	37	5			
88/89 Montpellier PSC (Fra)	26	1	UC	2	-
89/90 Montpellier HSC (Fra)	30	3			
90/91 Juventus	29	1	CWC	8	2
91/92 Juventus	33	1			

★ Brazil

Andreas MÖLLER (Ger)
02/09/67 Midfield

87/88 Eintracht Frankfurt (Ger)	12	4			
Borussia Dortmund (Ger)	14	3			
88/89 Borussia Dortmund (Ger)	29	11			
89/90 Borussia Dortmund (Ger)	32	10	CWC	4	-
90/91 Eintracht Frankfurt (Ger)	32	16	UC	2	1
91/92 Eintracht Frankfurt (Ger)	37	12	UC	4	2

* Germany 24 caps, 4 goals

David PLATT (Eng)
10/06/66 Midfield

87/88 Aston Villa (Eng)	Div 2				
88/89 Aston Villa (Eng)	38	7			
89/90 Aston Villa (Eng)	37	19			
90/91 Aston Villa (Eng)	35	19	UC	4	2
91/92 Bari	29	11			

★ England 32 caps, 11 goals

Giancarlo MAROCCHI
04/07/65 Midfield

87/88 Bologna	Div 2				
88/89 Juventus	34	1	UC	7	-
89/90 Juventus	32	5	#UC	11	2
90/91 Juventus	31	3	CWC	7	-
91/92 Juventus	31	1			

★ Italy 11 caps, 0 goals

Frederico GIAMPAOLO
03/03/70 Midfield

90/91 Spezia	Div 3	
91/92 Bari	20	1

ITALY

FIVE YEAR RECORD *Birthdate/Playing position*	LEAGUE Apps Gls	EURO CUPS Cup Apps Gls

Roberto BAGGIO
18/02/67   Midfield

		Apps	Gls	Cup	Apps	Gls
87/88	Fiorentina	27	7			
88/89	Fiorentina	30	16			
89/90	Fiorentina	32	17	+UC	12	1
90/91	Juventus	33	14	CWC	8	9
91/92	Juventus	32	18			

★ Italy 22 caps, 12 goals

Roberto GALIA
16/02/63   Midfield

		Apps	Gls	Cup	Apps	Gls
87/88	Verona	28	2	UC	8	-
88/89	Juventus	32	3	UC	7	2
89/90	Juventus	31	1	#UC	11	3
90/91	Juventus	23	-	CWC	6	-
91/92	Juventus	32	1			

Italy 3 caps, 0 goals

Marco Antonio DE MARCHI
08/09/66   Midfield

		Apps	Gls	Cup	Apps	Gls
87/88	Bologna	Div 2				
88/89	Bologna	32	2			
89/90	Bologna	26	2			
90/91	Juventus	17	-			
91/92	Juventus	10	-	CWC	4	-

Antonio CONTE
31/07/69   Midfield

		Apps	Gls	Cup	Apps	Gls
87/88	Lecce	Div 2				
88/89	Lecce	18	-			
89/90	Lecce	28	1			
90/91	Lecce	28	-			
91/92	Lecce	Div 2				
	Juventus	14	-			

Paolo DI CANIO
09/07/68   Forward

		Apps	Gls	Cup	Apps	Gls
87/88	Lazio	Div 2				
88/89	Lazio	30	1			
89/90	Lazio	24	3			
90/91	Juventus	23	3	CWC	5	-
91/92	Juventus	24	1			

FIVE YEAR RECORD *Birthdate/Playing position*	LEAGUE Apps Gls	EURO CUPS Cup Apps Gls

Gianluca VIALLI
09/07/64   Forward

		Apps	Gls	Cup	Apps	Gls
87/88	Sampdoria	30	10			
88/89	Sampdoria	30	14	+CWC	7	5
89/90	Sampdoria	22	10	#CWC	8	7
90/91	Sampdoria	26	19	CWC	3	1
91/92	Sampdoria	31	11	+CC	11	6

★ Italy 56 caps, 14 goals

Pierluigi CASIRAGHI
04/03/69   Forward

		Apps	Gls	Cup	Apps	Gls
87/88	Monza	Div 3				
88/89	Monza	Div 2				
89/90	Juventus	23	4	#UC	11	3
90/91	Juventus	24	8	CWC	6	4
91/92	Juventus	33	7			

★ Italy 7 caps, 1 goal

Fabrizio RAVANELLI
11/12/68   Forward

		Apps	Gls	Cup	Apps	Gls
88/89	Casertana	Div 3				
89/90	Reggiana	Div 2				
90/91	Reggiana	Div 2				
91/92	Reggiana	Div 2				

EUROPEAN HONOURS
Champions' Cup - (1) 1985.
Cup-winners' Cup - (1) 1984.
UEFA Cup - (2) 1977, 1990.
Super Cup - (1) 1984.

EUROPEAN CUPS RECORD

	Entries	Pd	W	D	L	F	A
Champions' Cup	14	77	41	15	21	124	71
Cup-winners' Cup	4	27	17	5	5	53	19
UEFA/Fairs' Cup	**13**	**104**	**64**	**16**	**24**	**191**	**87**
Total - All 3 Cups	31	208	122	36	50	368	177

TORINO

FIVE YEAR RECORD Birthdate/Playing position	LEAGUE Apps	Gls	EURO CUPS Cup	Apps	Gls

Luca MARCHEGIANI
22/02/66   Goalkeeper

87/88	Brescia	Div 2				
88/89	Torino	17	-			
89/90	Torino	Div 2				
90/91	Torino	29	-			
91/92	Torino	33	-	+UC	12	-

★ Italy 1 cap, 0 goals

Raffaele DI FUSCO
06/10/61   Goalkeeper

87/88	Napoli	1	-			
88/89	Napoli	3	-			
89/90	Napoli	2	-			
90/91	Torino	-	-			
91/92	Torino	3	-			

Pasquale BRUNO
19/06/62   Defender

87/88	Juventus	25	-	UC	2	-
88/89	Juventus	21	-	UC	5	1
89/90	Juventus	19	-	#UC	8	-
90/91	Torino	28	-			
91/92	Torino	22	1	+UC	9	-

Raffaele SERGIO
27/08/66   Defender

87/88	Mantova	Div 4				
88/89	Mantova	Div 3				
89/90	Lazio	31	-			
90/91	Lazio	34	-			
91/92	Lazio	25	1			

Enrico ANNONI
01/07/66   Defender

87/88	Como	28	1			
88/89	Como	33	1			
89/90	Como	Div 2				
90/91	Torino	22	1			
91/92	Torino	29	1	+UC	11	2

Roberto MUSSI
25/08/63   Defender

87/88	Milan	11	-	UC	3	-
88/89	Milan	18	-	#CC	3	-
89/90	Torino	Div 2				
90/91	Torino	18	-			
91/92	Torino	25	1	+UC	10	1

Antonio ALOISI
28/08/68   Defender

87/88	Ascoli	2	-			
88/89	Ascoli	28	1			
89/90	Ascoli	30	1			
90/91	Ascoli	Div 2				
91/92	Ascoli	29	1			

Marco SINIGAGLIA
29/02/68   Midfield

90/91	Como	Div 3				
91/92	Torino	2	-			

Gianluca SORDO
02/12/68   Midfield

87/88	Torino	-	-			
88/89	Trento	Div 3				
89/90	Torino	Div 2				
90/91	Torino	24	-			
91/92	Torino	20	1	+UC	8	-

Luca FUSI
07/06/63   Midfield

87/88	Sampdoria	30	-			
88/89	Napoli	31	-	#UC	11	-
89/90	Napoli	29	2	UC	5	-
90/91	Torino	31	-			
91/92	Torino	31	1	+UC	10	1

★ Italy 8 caps, 0 goals

ITALY

FIVE YEAR RECORD *Birthdate/Playing position*	LEAGUE Apps Gls	EURO CUPS Cup Apps Gls

Giorgio VENTURIN
09/07/68   Midfield

87/88	Torino		· ·	
88/89	Cosenza	Div 2		
89/90	Torino	Div 2		
90/91	Napoli	31	-	CC 3 -
91/92	Torino	32	1	+UC 12 -

★ Italy 1 cap, 0 goals

Enzo SCIFO (Bel)
19/02/66   Midfield

87/88	Internazionale	28	4	UC 6 1
88/89	Girondins de Bordeaux (Fra)	24	7	UC 6 1
89/90	AJ Auxerre (Fra)	33	11	UC 9 5
90/91	AJ Auxerre (Fra)	34	14	
91/92	Torino	30	9	+UC 11 2

★ Belgium 54 caps, 11 goals

Rafael MARTIN VAZQUEZ (Esp)
25/09/65   Midfield

87/88	Real Madrid (Esp)	35	5	CC 7 -
88/89	Real Madrid (Esp)	36	7	CC 8 1
89/90	Real Madrid (Esp))	34	14	CC 3 -
90/91	Torino	24	1	
91/92	Torino	28	1	+UC 12 1

★ Spain 33 caps, 1 goal

Giuseppe CARILLO
24/05/65   Midfield

87/88	Ascoli	25	3	
88/89	Ascoli	28	-	
89/90	Ascoli	25	2	
90/91	Torino	18	-	
91/92	Torino	4	-	+UC 2 1

Andrea SILENZI
10/02/66   Forward

87/88	Arezzo	Div 2		
88/89	Reggiana	Div 3		
90/91	Reggiana	Div 2		
90/91	Napoli	19	2	CC 3 -
91/92	Napoli	20	4	

FIVE YEAR RECORD *Birthdate/Playing position*	LEAGUE Apps Gls	EURO CUPS Cup Apps Gls

Carlos AGUILERA (Uru)
21/09/64   Forward

88/89	Peñarol (Uru)			
89/90	Genoa	31	8	
90/91	Genoa	31	15	
91/92	Genoa	34	10	UC 9 8

★ Uruguay

Walter CASAGRANDE (Bra)
15/04/63   Forward

87/88	Ascoli	27	6	
88/89	Ascoli	8	4	
89/90	Ascoli	24	6	
90/91	Ascoli	Div 2		
91/92	Torino	23	6	+UC 10 6

★ Brazil

Christian VIERI
12/07/73   Forward

91/92	Torino	6	1

EUROPEAN HONOURS
none

EUROPEAN CUPS RECORD

	Entries	Pd	W	D	L	F	A
Champions' Cup	1	4	1	2	1	4	4
Cup-winners' Cup	3	19	9	4	6	28	17
UEFA/Fairs' Cup	11	48	20	13	15	70	53
Total - All 3 Cups	15	71	30	19	22	102	74

NAPOLI

FIVE YEAR RECORD Birthdate/Playing position	LEAGUE Apps	Gls	EURO CUPS Cup	Apps	Gls

Giovanni GALLI
29/04/58   Goalkeeper

87/88	Milan	30	-	UC	4	-
88/89	Milan	32	-	#CC	9	-
89/90	Milan	11	-	#CC	8	-
90/91	Napoli	33	-	CC	4	-
91/92	Napoli	33	-			

★ Italy 19 caps, 0 goals

Marco SANSONETTI
28/01/65   Goalkeeper

87/88	Internazionale	-	-
88/89	Sambenedettese	Div 2	
89/90	Giarre	Div 3	
90/91	Giarre	Div 3	
91/92	Napoli	1	-

Ciro FERRARA
11/02/67   Defender

87/88	Napoli	23	1	CC	2	-
88/89	Napoli	27	-	#UC	12	1
89/90	Napoli	33	-	UC	6	-
90/91	Napoli	29	2	CC	3	-
91/92	Napoli	32	1			

★ Italy 25 caps, 0 goals

Giovanni FRANCINI
03/08/63   Defender

87/88	Napoli	30	2	CC	1	1
88/89	Napoli	26	1	#UC	11	2
89/90	Napoli	26	3	UC	4	-
90/91	Napoli	25	1	CC	4	-
91/92	Napoli	31	2			

★ Italy 8 caps, 0 goals

Giancarlo CORRADINI
24/02/61   Defender

87/88	Torino	29	-			
88/89	Napoli	32	-	#UC	12	-
89/90	Napoli	28	2	UC	4	-
90/91	Napoli	30	-	CC	2	-
91/92	Napoli	30	-			

Laurent BLANC (Fra)
19/11/65   Defender

87/88	Montpellier PSC (Fra)	24	6			
88/89	Montpellier PSC (Fra)	35	15	UC	2	-
89/90	Montpellier HSC (Fra)	36	12			
90/91	Montpellier HSC (Fra)	38	14	CWC	6	1
91/92	Napoli	31	6			

★ France 25 caps, 4 goals

Carlo CORNACCHIA
04/05/65   Defender

87/88	Reggiana	Div 3	
88/89	Reggiana	Div 3	
89/90	Cagliari	Div 2	
90/91	Cagliari	25	4
91/92	Atalanta	20	3

Massimo TARANTINO
20/05/71   Defender

87/88	Catania	Div 3	
88/89	Catania	Div 3	
89/90	Napoli	1	-
	Monza	Div 2	
90/91	Barletta	Div 2	
91/92	Napoli	14	-

Angelo CARBONE
23/03/68   Midfield

88/89	Bari	Div 2	
89/90	Bari	26	1
90/91	Milan	21	-
91/92	Bari	26	1

Massimo CRIPPA
17/05/65   Midfield

87/88	Torino	29	3			
88/89	Napoli	31	2	#UC	10	-
89/90	Napoli	32	4	UC	5	-
90/91	Napoli	30	-	CC	4	-
91/92	Napoli	28	2			

★ Italy 10 caps, 0 goals

ITALY

FIVE YEAR RECORD	LEAGUE		EURO CUPS		
Birthdate/Playing position	Apps	Gls	Cup	Apps	Gls

Fausto PARI
15/09/62   Midfield

87/88	Sampdoria	30	1			
88/89	Sampdoria	30	1	+CWC	9	-
89/90	Sampdoria	33	-	#CWC	9	-
90/91	Sampdoria	33	-	CWC	6	-
91/92	Sampdoria	32	2	+CC	11	-

Gianfranco ZOLA
05/07/66   Midfield

87/88	Torres	Div 3				
88/89	Torres	Div 3				
89/90	Napoli	18	2	UC	2	-
90/91	Napoli	20	6	CC	2	-
91/92	Napoli	34	12			

★ Italy 3 caps, 0 goals

Jonas THERN (Swe)
20/03/67   Midfield

87	Malmö FF (Swe)	19	3	CC	2	-
88	Malmö FF (Swe)	18	4	UC	4	-
89	Malmö FF (Swe)	13	1			
89/90	SL Benfica (Por)	21	2	+CC	9	1
90/91	SL Benfica (Por)	24	4	UC	1	-
91/92	SL Benfica (Por)	27	2	CC	8	-

★ Sweden 35 caps, 6 goals

Ricardo ALEMÃO (Bra)
22/11/61   Midfield

87/88	Atlético Madrid (Esp)	31	5			
88/89	Napoli	16	3	#UC	8	-
89/90	Napoli	27	2	UC	5	1
90/91	Napoli	21	1	CC	4	1
91/92	Napoli	29	2			

★ Brazil

Roberto POLICANO
19/02/64   Midfield

87/88	Roma	17	2			
88/89	Roma	18	3	UC	5	1
89/90	Torino	Div 2				
90/91	Torino	28	6			
91/92	Torino	23	5	+UC	8	2

FIVE YEAR RECORD	LEAGUE		EURO CUPS		
Birthdate/Playing position	Apps	Gls	Cup	Apps	Gls

Daniel FONSECA (Uru)
13/09/69   Forward

89/90	Nacional (Uru)					
90/91	Cagliari	27	10			
91/92	Cagliari	23	9			

★ Uruguay

Antonio CARECA (Bra)
05/10/60   Forward

87/88	Napoli	26	13	CC	1	-
88/89	Napoli	29	19	#UC	12	6
89/90	Napoli	22	10	UC	6	1
90/91	Napoli	29	9	CC	2	-
91/92	Napoli	33	15			

★ Brazil

Marco FERRANTE
04/02/71   Forward

90/91	Reggiana	Div 2	
91/92	Pisa	Div 2	

ROMA

FIVE YEAR RECORD *Birthdate/Playing position*	LEAGUE Apps Gls	EURO CUPS Cup Apps Gls

Giuseppe ZINETTI
22/06/58 Goalkeeper

87/88	Pescara	16	-	
88/89	Pescara	14	-	
89/90	Pescara	Div 2		
90/91	Roma	10	-	+UC 4 -
91/92	Roma	14	-	CWC 2 -

Giovanni CERVONE
16/11/62 Goalkeeper

87/88	Parma	Div 2		
88/89	Verona	34	-	
89/90	Roma	27	-	
90/91	Roma	21	-	+UC 6 -
91/92	Roma	21	-	CWC 4 -

Amedeo CARBONI
06/04/65 Defender

87/88	Parma	Div 2		
88/89	Sampdoria	31	1	+CWC 4 1
89/90	Sampdoria	29	1	#CWC 7 -
90/91	Roma	30	1	+UC 4 -
91/92	Roma	33	-	CWC 6 -

★ Italy 2 caps, 0 goals

ALDAIR dos Santos (Bra)
30/11/65 Defender

88/89	Flamengo (Bra)			
89/90	SL Benfica (Por)	24	5	+CC 8 1
90/91	Roma	29	2	+UC 11 -
91/92	Roma	33	3	CWC 6 -

★ Brazil

Sebastiano NELA
13/03/61 Defender

87/88	Roma	6	-	
88/89	Roma	32	2	UC 6 -
89/90	Roma	30	1	
90/91	Roma	28	1	+UC 11 -
91/92	Roma	27	-	CWC 6 -

★ Italy 5 caps, 0 goals

Silvano BENEDETTI
05/10/65 Defender

87/88	Torino	15	-	
88/89	Torino	22	1	
89/90	Torino	Div 2		
90/91	Torino	27	1	
91/92	Torino	25	1	+UC 9 -

Luigi GARZYA
07/07/69 Defender

87/88	Lecce	Div 2		
	Reggina	Div 3		
88/89	Lecce	21	1	
89/90	Lecce	33	-	
90/91	Lecce	23	-	
91/92	Roma	23	-	CWC 4 -

Antonio COMI
26/07/64 Defender

87/88	Torino	29	3	
88/89	Torino	28	-	
89/90	Roma	31	1	
90/91	Roma	18	-	+UC 11 -
91/92	Roma	10	-	CWC 1 -

Fabio PETRUZZI
24/10/70 Defender

91/92	Casertana	Div 2	

Thomas HÄSSLER (Ger)
30/05/66 Midfield

87/88	1.FC Köln (Ger)	34	5	
88/89	1.FC Köln (Ger)	33	5	UC 6 -
89/90	1.FC Köln (Ger)	34	6	UC 10 -
90/91	Juventus	32	1	CWC 8 1
91/92	Roma	32	3	CWC 6 -

★ Germany 34 caps, 5 goals

ITALY

FIVE YEAR RECORD *Birthdate/Playing position*	LEAGUE Apps Gls	EURO CUPS Cup Apps Gls

Walter BONACINA
30/07/64   Midfield

87/88	Atalanta	Div 2		CWC	4	-
88/89	Atalanta	27	3			
89/90	Atalanta	31	2	UC	2	-
90/91	Atalanta	30	2	UC	6	2
91/92	Roma	28	1	CWC	4	-

Giuseppe GIANNINI
20/08/64   Midfield

87/88	Roma	28	11			
88/89	Roma	32	6	UC	5	1
89/90	Roma	31	3			
90/91	Roma	24	3	+UC	10	2
91/92	Roma	24	4	CWC	4	1

★ Italy 47 caps, 6 goals

Giovanni PIACENTINI
09/04/68   Midfield

87/88	Padova	Div 2				
88/89	Padova	Div 2				
89/90	Padova	Div 2				
	Roma	16	-			
90/91	Roma	20	-	+UC	7	-
91/92	Roma	25	-	CWC	3	-

Fausto SALSANO
18/12/62   Midfield

87/88	Sampdoria	28	3			
88/89	Sampdoria	29	2	+CWC	6	2
89/90	Sampdoria	32	2	#CWC	7	-
90/91	Roma	29	4	+UC	5	-
91/92	Roma	20	1	CWC	3	-

Sinisa MIHAJLOVIC (Yug)
20/02/69   Midfield

88/89	Vojvodina Novi Sad (Yug)	31	4			
89/90	Vojvodina Novi Sad (Yug)	28	11	CC	2	1
90/91	Vojvodina Novi Sad (Yug)	14	4			
	Crvena zvezda Beograd (Yug)	14	1	#CC	5	1
91/92	Crvena zvezda Beograd (Yug)	13*	4*	CC	10	4

★ Yugoslavia 4 caps, 0 goals
* first half of season figures only.

FIVE YEAR RECORD *Birthdate/Playing position*	LEAGUE Apps Gls	EURO CUPS Cup Apps Gls

Ruggiero RIZZITELLI
02/09/67   Forward

87/88	Cesena	30	5			
88/89	Roma	20	2	UC	2	-
89/90	Roma	34	5			
90/91	Roma	24	5	+UC	8	4
91/92	Roma	26	6	CWC	5	2

★ Italy 9 caps, 2 goals

Claudio CANIGGIA (Arg)
09/10/67   Forward

87/88	River Plate (Arg)					
88/89	Verona	21	3			
89/90	Atalanta	31	8	UC	2	-
90/91	Atalanta	23	10	UC	5	-
91/92	Atalanta	31	8			

★ Argentina

Roberto MUZZI
29/01/71   Forward

89/90	Roma	1	-			
90/91	Roma	15	3	+UC	5	-
91/92	Roma	10	1	CWC	1	-

EUROPEAN HONOURS
Fairs' Cup - (1) 1961.

EUROPEAN CUPS RECORD

	Entries	Pd	W	D	L	F	A
Champions' Cup	1	9	5	1	3	14	7
Cup-winners' Cup	6	29	12	9	8	34	24
UEFA/Fairs' Cup	11	70	35	12	23	113	77
Total - All 3 Cups	18	108	52	22	34	161	108

SPORA LUXEMBOURG

FIVE YEAR RECORD *Birthdate/Playing position*	LEAGUE Apps	Gls	EURO CUPS Cup	Apps	Gls

Fernand FELTEN
20/01/62 Goalkeeper

87/88 Spora Luxembourg	28	-			
88/89 Spora Luxembourg	28	-			
89/90 Spora Luxembourg	28	-	CC	2	-
90/91 Spora Luxembourg	28	-			
91/92 Spora Luxembourg	28	-	UC	2	-

Patrick PENNING
1971 Goalkeeper

91/92 Spora Luxembourg	-	-			

Marc JANES
11/11/61 Defender

87/88 Spora Luxembourg	16	-			
88/89 Spora Luxembourg	25	1			
89/90 Spora Luxembourg	21	-	CC	2	-
90/91 Spora Luxembourg	26	-			
91/92 Spora Luxembourg	23	-	UC	2	-

John KREMER
06/01/60 Defender

87/88 Spora Luxembourg	27	1			
88/89 Spora Luxembourg	28	-			
89/90 Spora Luxembourg	23	-	CC	2	-
90/91 Spora Luxembourg	22	-			
91/92 Spora Luxembourg	17	-	UC	2	-

Ralph STANGE
09/02/59 Defender

90/91 Spora Luxembourg	18	2			
91/92 Spora Luxembourg	15	-	UC	1	-

Gérard URBING
21/02/59 Defender

87/88 Spora Luxembourg	24	1			
88/89 Spora Luxembourg	28	2			
89/90 Spora Luxembourg	27	2	CC	1	-
90/91 Spora Luxembourg	28	-			
91/92 Spora Luxembourg	22	1	UC	2	-

FIVE YEAR RECORD *Birthdate/Playing position*	LEAGUE Apps	Gls	EURO CUPS Cup	Apps	Gls

Patrick BEI
16/03/73 Midfield

89/90 Spora Luxembourg	1	-			
90/91 Spora Luxembourg	7	-			
91/92 Spora Luxembourg	16	-			

Rico CARDONI
15/08/66 Midfield

87/88 US Dudelange	Div 2				
88/89 US Dudelange	Div 2				
89/90 Spora Luxembourg	21	1	CC	1	-
90/91 Spora Luxembourg	28	7			
91/92 Spora Luxembourg	25	1	UC	2	-

Eduardo DINIS
27/02/70 Midfield

90/91 Spora Luxembourg	3	-			
91/92 Spora Luxembourg	18	-			

Heinz EIMER
06/04/57 Midfield

87/88 FSV Salmrohr (Ger)	Div 3				
88/89 CS Grevenmacher	28	6			
89/90 CS Grevenmacher	14	4			
90/91 CS Grevenmacher	26	1			
91/92 Spora Luxembourg	22	6	UC	2	-

Léon LAERA
12/04/64 Midfield

87/88 Etzella Ettelbrück	Div 2				
88/89 Etzella Ettelbrück	Div 2				
89/90 Spora Luxembourg	27	2	CC	2	-
90/91 Spora Luxembourg	27	1			
91/92 Spora Luxembourg	26	3	UC	2	-

Jorge LOPES
19/03/72 Midfield

88/89 CS Grevenmacher	1	-			
89/90 CS Grevenmacher	18	3			
90/91 CS Grevenmacher	17	1			
91/92 Spora Luxembourg	28	-	UC	2	-

LUXEMBOURG

FIVE YEAR RECORD	LEAGUE		EURO CUPS		
Birthdate/Playing position	Apps	Gls	Cup	Apps	Gls

Jean-Marc RIGAUD
04/09/62   Midfield

88/89	Spora Luxembourg	28	5			
89/90	Spora Luxembourg	25	4	CC	2	-
90/91	Spora Luxembourg	25	9			
91/92	Spora Luxembourg	26	8	UC	2	1

João CRUZ
16/04/69   Midfield

90/91	Spora Luxembourg	21	7
91/92	Spora Luxembourg	17	10

Sidney FERREIRA DE LIMA
14/11/62   Forward

91/92	Spora Luxembourg	17	4	UC	1	-

Marc CHAUSSY
07/04/72   Forward

89/90	Union Luxembourg	3	-	CWC	1	-
90/91	Union Luxembourg	13	-	CC	1	-
91/92	Union Luxembourg	18	1	CC	1	-

FIVE YEAR RECORD	LEAGUE		EURO CUPS		
Birthdate/Playing position	Apps	Gls	Cup	Apps	Gls

Pascal WAMPACH
24/01/70   Forward

90/91	Spora Luxembourg	10	6			
91/92	Spora Luxembourg	17	2	UC	2	-

Marciano GOMES
03/07/66   Forward

91/92	Spora Luxembourg	22	6

EUROPEAN HONOURS
none

EUROPEAN CUPS RECORD

	Entries	Pd	W	D	L	F	A
Champions' Cup	3	7	1	0	6	7	36
Cup-winners' Cup	3	6	0	0	6	2	23
UEFA/Fairs' Cup	4	8	1	0	7	4	39
Total - All 3 Cups	10	21	2	0	19	13	98

FLORIANA

FIVE YEAR RECORD *Birthdate/Playing position*	LEAGUE Apps Gls	EURO CUPS Cup Apps Gls

David CLUETT
02/08/65   Goalkeeper

87/88 Floriana	14	-	
88/89 Floriana	15	-	CWC 2 -
89/90 Floriana	15	-	
90/91 Floriana	16	-	
91/92 Floriana	18	-	UC 2 -

★ Malta 34 caps, 0 goals

David BRINCAT
12/11/71   Goalkeeper

90/91 Floriana	- -	
91/92 Floriana	- -	

Joseph John AQUILINA
16/02/57   Defender

87/88 Floriana	10	-	
88/89 Floriana	13	3	CWC 2 -
89/90 Floriana	8	2	
90/91 Floriana	14	2	
91/92 Floriana	9	-	UC 2 -

★ Malta 13 caps, 0 goals

Pierre BRINCAT
17/02/61   Defender

87/88 Zurrieq	11	-	
88/89 Floriana	15	-	CWC 2 -
89/90 Floriana	15	-	
90/91 Floriana	16	3	
91/92 Floriana	17	1	UC 2 -

Richard BUHAGIAR
17/03/72   Defender

89/90 Mosta	Div 2	
90/91 Floriana	6	-	
91/92 Floriana	9	2	UC 2 -

★ Malta 5 caps, 0 goals

FIVE YEAR RECORD *Birthdate/Playing position*	LEAGUE Apps Gls	EURO CUPS Cup Apps Gls

John BUTTIGIEG
05/10/63   Defender

87/88 Sliema Wanderers	13	1	CWC 2 -
88/89 Sliema Wanderers	1	1	
Brentford (Eng)	Div 3	
89/90 Brentford (Eng)	Div 3	
90/91 Brentford (Eng)	Div 3	
91/92 Floriana	17	1	UC 2 -

★ Malta 45 caps, 0 goals

Jesmond DELIA
20/03/70   Defender

87/88 St. George's	Div 3	
88/89 Floriana	8	-	CWC 1 -
89/90 Floriana	16	1	
90/91 Floriana	14	-	
91/92 Floriana	16	-	UC 2 -

★ Malta 5 caps, 0 goals

David GALEA
29/03/73   Defender

89/90 Floriana	7	-	
90/91 Floriana	12	-	
91/92 Floriana	17	-	UC 2 -

James BRISCOE
13/05/65   Midfield

87/88 Floriana	9	-	
88/89 Floriana	4	-	CWC 1 -
89/90 Floriana	- -	
90/91 Floriana	- -	
91/92 Floriana	11	-	UC 1 -

Dennis CAUCHI
15/01/65   Midfield

87/88 Floriana	11	-	
88/89 Floriana	16	-	CWC 2 -
89/90 Floriana	15	1	
90/91 Floriana	15	1	
91/92 Floriana	16	1	UC 2 -

★ Malta 3 caps, 0 goals

MALTA

Mark MILLER (Eng)
22/09/62   Midfield

		Apps	Gls	Cup	Apps	Gls
87/88	Floriana	13	-			
88/89	Floriana	15	1	CWC	2	-
89/90	Floriana	10	2			
90/91	Floriana	16	-			
91/92	Floriana	15	2	UC	2	-

Charlie SCIBERRAS
26/06/71   Midfield

		Apps	Gls	Cup	Apps	Gls
88/89	Gzira United	Div 3				
89/90	Floriana	15	3			
90/91	Rabat Ajax	16	-			
91/92	Floriana	12	4			

Robert AGIUS
27/06/72   Midfield

		Apps	Gls	Cup	Apps	Gls
90/91	Melita	Div 4				
91/92	Floriana	3	-			

Ian BUHAGIAR
06/09/64   Forward

		Apps	Gls	Cup	Apps	Gls
89/90	Naxxar Lions	6	-			
90/91	Floriana	-	-			
91/92	Floriana	4	-	UC	1	-

Albert BUSUTTIL
08/10/70   Forward

		Apps	Gls	Cup	Apps	Gls
90/91	Kirkop United	Div 3				
91/92	Floriana	15	2			

Oscar MAGRI
21/06/67   Forward

		Apps	Gls	Cup	Apps	Gls
88/89	Fgura United	Div 3				
89/90	Floriana	15	8			
90/91	Floriana	14	3			
91/92	Floriana	17	8	UC	2	-

★ Malta 1 cap, 0 goals

Jesmond CARDONA
09/10/68   Forward

		Apps	Gls	Cup	Apps	Gls
87/88	Birkirkara	9	-			
88/89	Birkirkara	-	-			
89/90	Birkirkara	Div 2				
90/91	Birkirkara	12	1			
91/92	Floriana	10	-			

Mark MARLOW
18/11/71   Forward

		Apps	Gls	Cup	Apps	Gls
87/88	Hamrun Spartans	2	-			
88/89	Hamrun Spartans	-	-			
89/90	Floriana	8	1			
90/91	Floriana	11	-			
91/92	Floriana	11	2			

EUROPEAN HONOURS
none

EUROPEAN CUPS RECORD

	Entries	Pd	W	D	L	F	A
Champions' Cup	6	12	0	2	10	3	49
Cup-winners' Cup	8	16	1	2	13	10	69
UEFA/Fairs' Cup	2	4	1	1	2	1	8
Total - All 3 Cups	16	32	2	5	25	14	126

PORTADOWN

| FIVE YEAR RECORD | LEAGUE | | EURO CUPS | | |
Birthdate/Playing position	Apps	Gls	Cup	Apps	Gls

Michael KEENAN
1958   Goalkeeper

87/88 Portadown	26	-			
88/89 Portadown	26	-			
89/90 Portadown	26	-			
90/91 Portadown	29	-	CC	2	-
91/92 Portadown	29	-	CC	2	-

Jim ARNOTT
10/02/67   Goalkeeper

90/91 Portadown	1	-			
91/92 Portadown	1	-			

Ian CURLISS
1966   Defender

87/88 Portadown	23	1			
88/89 Portadown	24	-			
89/90 Portadown	26	-			
90/91 Portadown	26	2	CC	2	-
91/92 Portadown	7	-	CC	1	-

Philip MAJOR
1970   Defender

88/89 Portadown	22	-			
89/90 Portadown	24	-			
90/91 Portadown	25	-	CC	2	-
91/92 Portadown	24	2	CC	2	-

Alfie STEWART
1962   Defender

87/88 Glentoran	25	2	CWC	2	-
88/89 Portadown	16	-			
89/90 Portadown	23	-			
90/91 Portadown	30	-	CC	2	-
91/92 Portadown	27	-	CC	2	-

Brian STRAIN
1969   Defender

87/88 Portadown	23	2			
88/89 Portadown	23	1			
89/90 Portadown	15	2			
90/91 Portadown	27	3	CC	2	-
91/92 Portadown	28	5	CC	2	-

John TREANOR
24/12/63   Defender

91/92 Portadown	15	-			

Robert CASEY
20/11/72   Midfield

91/92 Portadown	13	2			

Gregg DAVIDSON
1966   Midfield

87/88 Portadown	20	3			
88/89 Portadown	23	4			
89/90 Portadown	15	1			
90/91 Portadown	28	4	CC	2	-
91/92 Portadown	19	5	CC	2	-

Peter MURRAY
11/11/63   Midfield

87/88 Cliftonville	18	2			
88/89 Cliftonville	21	5			
89/90 Cliftonville	17	3			
90/91 Cliftonville	28	6			
91/92 Portadown	19	2			

Kevin McKEEVER
1968   Midfield

87/88 Portadown	11	1			
88/89 Portadown	25	1			
89/90 Portadown	19	5			
90/91 Portadown	17	1	CC	2	-
91/92 Portadown	19	-	CC	1	-

Martin RUSSELL (Irl)
27/04/67   Midfield

87/88 Leicester City (Eng)	Div 2				
88/89 Leicester City (Eng)	Div 2				
Scarborough (Eng)	Div 4				
89/90 Scarborough (Eng)	Div 4				
90/91 Middlesbrough (Eng)	Div 2				
91/92 Portadown	30	6	CC	2	-

NORTHERN IRELAND

FIVE YEAR RECORD	LEAGUE		EURO CUPS		
Birthdate/Playing position	Apps	Gls	Cup	Apps	Gls

David MILLS
1963   Midfield

		Apps	Gls			
87/88	Portadown	18	1			
88/89	Portadown	20	-			
89/90	Portadown	23	1			
90/91	Portadown	19	1			
91/92	Portadown	9	1			

John CAMPBELL
27/03/72   Forward

		Apps	Gls	Cup	Apps	Gls
90/91	Glenavon	8	-	UC	1	-
91/92	Portadown	12	-			

Stevie COWAN (Sco)
17/02/63   Forward

		Apps	Gls	Cup	Apps	Gls
87/88	Motherwell (Sco)	32	9			
88/89	Motherwell (Sco)	18	2			
89/90	Motherwell (Sco)	-	-			
	Portadown	8	7			
90/91	Portadown	30	18	CC	2	-
91/92	Portadown	22	14	CC	2	-

Sandy FRASER (Sco)
31/08/67   Forward

		Apps	Gls	Cup	Apps	Gls
87/88	Hamilton Academical (Sco)	Div 2				
88/89	Hamilton Academical (Sco)	8	-			
89/90	Portadown	25	7			
90/91	Portadown	25	11	CC	2	1
91/92	Portadown	22	12	CC	2	-

FIVE YEAR RECORD	LEAGUE		EURO CUPS		
Birthdate/Playing position	Apps	Gls	Cup	Apps	Gls

Michael SURGEON
14/11/65   Forward

		Apps	Gls			
87/88	Distillery	12	1			
88/89	Distillery	25	6			
89/90	Distillery	26	2			
90/91	Distillery	23	5			
91/92	Portadown	15	1			

Barry MEEHAN
16/05/73   Forward

		Apps	Gls			
91/92	Portadown	10	4			

EUROPEAN HONOURS
none

EUROPEAN CUPS RECORD

	Entries	Pd	W	D	L	F	A
Champions' Cup	2	4	0	0	4	1	21
Cup-winners' Cup	1	2	1	0	1	4	7
UEFA/Fairs' Cup	**1**	**4**	**1**	**2**	**1**	**3**	**7**
Total - All 3 Cups	4	10	2	2	6	8	35

ROSENBORG BK

FIVE YEAR RECORD — Birthdate/Playing position — LEAGUE Apps Gls — EURO CUPS Cup Apps Gls

Ola BY RISE
14/11/60   Goalkeeper

		Apps	Gls	Cup	Apps	Gls
87	Rosenborg BK	22	-			
88	Rosenborg BK	22	-			
89	Rosenborg BK	22	-	CC	2	-
90	Rosenborg BK	21	-	UC	2	-
91	Rosenborg BK	21	-	CC	2	-

★ Norway 23 caps, 0 goals

Ivar SELNAES
10/09/62   Goalkeeper

		Apps	Gls
91	Rosenborg BK	1	-

Øivind HUSBY
03/08/60   Defender

		Apps	Gls	Cup	Apps	Gls
87	Vålerengens IF	20	4			
88	Vålerengens IF	20	3			
89	Rosenborg BK	22	-	CC	2	-
90	Rosenborg BK	17	-	UC	2	-
91	Rosenborg BK	16	1	CC	1	-

★ Norway 2 caps, 0 goals

Rune TANGEN
16/12/64   Defender

		Apps	Gls	Cup	Apps	Gls
87	Moss FK	21	1			
88	Moss FK	16	2	CC	1	-
89	Moss FK	20	2			
90	Moss FK	21	3			
91	Rosenborg BK	20	3	CC	2	-

★ Norway 3 caps, 1 goal

Trond HENRIKSEN
28/04/64   Defender

		Apps	Gls	Cup	Apps	Gls
87	Rosenborg BK	22	1			
88	Rosenborg BK	22	1			
89	Rosenborg BK	21	1	CC	2	-
90	Rosenborg BK	22	2	UC	2	-
91	Rosenborg BK	22	-	CC	2	-

Bjørn Otto BRAGSTAD
05/01/71   Defender

		Apps	Gls	Cup	Apps	Gls
89	Rosenborg BK	1	-			
90	Rosenborg BK	9	-			
91	Rosenborg BK	6	1	CC	2	-

Hugo HANSEN
01/08/67   Defender

		Apps	Gls	Cup	Apps	Gls
87	Bryne IL	20	3			
88	Bryne IL	22	1	CWC	2	-
89	Bryne IL	Div 2				
90	Bryne IL	Div 2				
91	Rosenborg BK	19	-	CC	2	-

Stig Inge BJØRNEBYE
11/12/69   Midfield

		Apps	Gls
87	Strømmen IF	Div 2	
88	Strømmen IF	19	-
89	Kongsvinger IL	21	2
90	Kongsvinger IL	20	-
91	Kongsvinger IL	21	1

★ Norway 17 caps, 0 goals

Kåre INGEBRIGTSEN
11/11/65   Midfield

		Apps	Gls	Cup	Apps	Gls
87	Frigg FK	Div 3				
88	Rosenborg BK	22	3			
89	Rosenborg BK	22	3	CC	2	-
90	Rosenborg BK	21	4	UC	2	-
91	Rosenborg BK	21	1	CC	2	-

★ Norway 10 caps, 1 goal

Bent SKAMMELSRUD
18/05/66   Midfield

		Apps	Gls	Cup	Apps	Gls
88	Frigg FK	Div 3				
89	Frigg FK	Div 2				
90	Malmö FF (Swe)	20	2	CC	3	1
91	Rosenborg BK	18	2	CC	2	-

★ Norway 10 caps, 2 goals

NORWAY

FIVE YEAR RECORD	LEAGUE		EURO CUPS		
Birthdate/Playing position	Apps	Gls	Cup	Apps	Gls

Bjørn Tore KVARME
17/06/72   Midfield

91	Rosenborg BK	9	1			

Øyvind LEONHARDSEN
17/08/70   Midfield

88	Clausenengen FK	Div 3				
89	Molde FK	22	5			
90	Molde FK	21	2			
91	Molde FK	21	2			

★ Norway 13 caps, 1 goals

Karl Petter LØKEN
14/06/66   Midfield

87	Rosenborg BK	17	4			
88	Rosenborg BK	20	5			
89	Rosenborg BK	22	13	CC	2	-
90	Rosenborg BK	17	7	UC	1	-
91	Rosenborg BK	20	12	CC	2	-

★ Norway 30 caps, 1 goal

Goran SØRLOTH
16/07/62   Forward

87	Rosenborg BK	22	7			
88	Rosenborg BK	21	10			
88/89	Borussia M'gladbach (Ger)	5	-			
89	Rosenborg BK	13	8	CC	2	-
90	Rosenborg BK	21	8	UC	2	1
91	Rosenborg BK	22	9	CC	2	-

★ Norway 43 caps, 11 goals

Roar STRAND
02/02/70   Forward

89	Rosenborg BK	12	-	CC	1	-
90	Rosenborg BK	19	6	UC	2	-
91	Rosenborg BK	21	3	CC	2	1

FIVE YEAR RECORD	LEAGUE		EURO CUPS		
Birthdate/Playing position	Apps	Gls	Cup	Apps	Gls

Harald BRATBAKK
01/02/71   Forward

90	Rosenborg BK	3	1			
91	Rosenborg BK	11	1	CC	2	-

Arild NORDFJAERN
25/11/65   Forward

91	Strindheim IL	Div 2				

Tore Andre DAHLUM
21/06/68   Forward

87	IK Start	1				
88	IK Start	Div 2				
89	IK Start	22	5			
90	IK Start	19	20			
91	IK Start	22	8			

★ Norway 11 caps, 5 goals

EUROPEAN HONOURS
none

EUROPEAN CUPS RECORD

	Entries	Pd	W	D	L	F	A
Champions' Cup	6	14	1	3	10	10	38
Cup-winners' Cup	1	4	2	0	2	7	8
UEFA/Fairs' Cup	4	10	5	0	5	15	22
Total - All 3 Cups	11	28	8	3	17	32	68

GKS KATOWICE

FIVE YEAR RECORD *Birthdate/Playing position*	LEAGUE Apps Gls	EURO CUPS Cup Apps Gls

Janusz JOJKO
20/04/60 Goalkeeper

87/88	Ruch Chorzów	Div 2			
	GKS Katowice	15	-		
88/89	GKS Katowice	29	-	UC	2	-
89/90	GKS Katowice	29	-	UC	2	-
90/91	GKS Katowice	12	-	UC	1	-
91/92	GKS Katowice	34	-	CWC	4	-

★ Poland 1 cap, 0 goals

Marek BARAN
12/02/63 Goalkeeper

90/91	GKS Katowice	1	-
91/92	GKS Katowice	-	-

Adam LEDWON
15/01/74 Defender

91/92	Ddra Opole	Div 4	
	GKS Katowice	19	-

Roman SZEWCZYK
18/03/65 Defender

87/88	Szombierki Bytom	30	3			
88/89	Szombierki Bytom	9	2			
	Slask Wroclaw	14	1			
89/90	Slask Wroclaw	12	1			
	GKS Katowice	12	-			
90/91	GKS Katowice	27	3	UC	4	1
91/92	GKS Katowice	26	2	CWC	2	1

★ Poland 21 caps, 2 goals

Krzysztof MACIEJEWSKI
22/08/64 Defender

90/91	GKS Katowice	12	-			
91/92	GKS Katowice	30	2	CWC	4	-

★ Poland 2 caps, 0 goals

Piotr PIEKARCZYK
01/10/58 Defender

87/88	GKS Katowice	30	4	UC	2	-
88/89	GKS Katowice	30	5	UC	2	-
89/90	GKS Katowice	26	3	UC	2	-
90	GAIS (Swe)	14	-	UC	2	-
91	GAIS (Swe)	18	-			
91/92	Naprzód Rydultowy	Div 2				

Robert RAZAKOWSKI
22/11/68 Defender

87/88	GKS Katowice	8	-	UC	1	-
88/89	GKS Katowice	1	-			
89/90	GKS Katowice	18	1			
90/91	Slask Wroclaw	15	-			
91/92	GKS Katowice	6	-			

Marek SZYMINSKI
27/09/68 Defender

90/91	MKG Katowice	Div 4				
91/92	GKS Katowice	10	-	CWC	2	-

Dariusz GRZESIK
10/01/66 Midfield

87/88	GKS Katowice	27	-	UC	1	-
88/89	GKS Katowice	26	1			
89/90	GKS Katowice	22	-	UC	2	-
90/91	GKS Katowice	24	1	UC	3	-
91/92	GKS Katowice	33	1	CWC	4	-

★ Poland 2 caps, 0 goals

Zdzislaw STROJEK
06/12/64 Midfield

87/88	Wisla Kraków	Div 2				
88/89	Wisla Kraków	12	3			
89/90	GKS Katowice	21	2			
90/91	GKS Katowice	24	2	UC	4	1
91/92	GKS Katowice	33	1	CWC	4	-

POLAND

FIVE YEAR RECORD	LEAGUE		EURO CUPS		
Birthdate/Playing position	Apps	Gls	Cup	Apps	Gls

Marek SWIERCZEWSKI
02/03/67   Midfield

87/88	Wisla Kraków	Div 2			
88/89	Wisla Kraków	26	5		
89/90	GKS Katowice	29	5	UC	2	-
90/91	GKS Katowice	29	6	UC	4	-
91/92	GKS Katowice	21	3		

Piotr SWIERCZEWSKI
08/04/72   Midfield

88/89	GKS Katowice	1	-		
89/90	GKS Katowice	15	1		
90/91	GKS Katowice	28	-	UC	3	1
91/92	GKS Katowice	30	2	CWC	3	-

Dariusz RZEZNICZEK
22/01/68   Midfield

87/88	GKS Katowice	11	1		
88/89	GKS Katowice	20	2	UC	2	-
89/90	Slask Wroclaw	7	-		
90/91	GKS Katowice	19	-	UC	2	-
91/92	GKS Katowice	31	-	CWC	4	1

Grzegorz BORAWSKY
1967   Midfield

91/92	Naprzód Rydultowy	Div 2

Arkadiusz WOLOWICZ
04/05/67   Midfield

87/88	Wisla Kraków	Div 2			
88/89	Wisla Kraków	11	2		
	GKS Katowice	9	-		
89/90	GKS Katowice	3	-		
90/91	GKS Katowice	19	1		
91/92	GKS Katowice	15	1	CWC	2	-

FIVE YEAR RECORD	LEAGUE		EURO CUPS		
Birthdate/Playing position	Apps	Gls	Cup	Apps	Gls

Adam KUCZ
26/06/71   Forward

91/92	Zaglebie Sosnowiec	33	4

Krzysztof WALCZAK
04/02/63   Forward

87/88	Polonia Bytom	Div 2			
88/89	GKS Katowice	28	8	UC	2	-
89/90	GKS Katowice	27	5	UC	2	-
90/91	GKS Katowice	27	7	UC	4	-
91/92	GKS Katowice	27	7	UC	4	-
91/92	GKS Katowice	26	13	CWC	4	-

Dariusz WOLNY
30/04/69   Forward

90/91	Odra Wodzislaw	Div 2			
91/92	GKS Katowice	34	7	CWC	4	1

EUROPEAN HONOURS
none

EUROPEAN CUPS RECORD

	Entries	Pd	W	D	L	F	A
Champions' Cup	none						
Cup-winners' Cup	2	8	3	1	4	9	12
UEFA/Fairs' Cup	5	12	2	1	9	11	20
Total - All 3 Cups	7	20	5	2	13	20	32

WIDZEW LÓDZ

FIVE YEAR RECORD *Birthdate/Playing position*	LEAGUE Apps Gls	EURO CUPS Cup Apps Gls

Piotr WOJDYGA
11/09/62 Goalkeeper

87/88	Stal Mielec	Div 2	
88/89	Stal Mielec	27	-
89/90	Stal Mielec	30	-
90/91	Stal Mielec	30	-
91/92	Widzew Lódz	34	-

Andrzej KRETEK
27/05/63 Goalkeeper

87/88	Piast Nowa Ruda	Div 2	
88/89	GKS Jastrzebie	19	-
89/90	Widzew Lódz	14	-
90/91	Widzew Lódz	Div 2	
91/92	Widzew Lódz	-	-

Miroslaw MYSLINSKI
06/12/63 Defender

87/88	Widzew Lódz	30	7
88/89	Widzew Lódz	30	1
89/90	Widzew Lódz	19	2
90/91	Widzew Lódz	Div 2	
91/92	Widzew Lódz	29	2

Zdzislaw OSMIALOWSKI
11/10/69 Defender

90/91	Widzew Lódz	Div 2	
91/92	Widzew Lódz	14	-

Tomasz LAPINSKI
01/08/69 Defender

87/88	Widzew Lódz	16	-
88/89	Widzew Lódz	22	-
89/90	Widzew Lódz	19	-
90/91	Widzew Lódz	Div 2	
91/92	Widzew Lódz	25	1

Marek BAJOR
10/01/70 Defender

89/90	Igloopol Debica	Div 2	
90/91	Pegrotour Debica	27	1
91/92	Widzew Lódz	33	-

FIVE YEAR RECORD *Birthdate/Playing position*	LEAGUE Apps Gls	EURO CUPS Cup Apps Gls

Wieslaw CISEK
02/01/63 Defender

87/88	Widzew Lódz	27	2
88/89	Widzew Lódz	28	-
89/90	Widzew Lódz	22	-
90/91	Widzew Lódz	Div 2	
91/92	Widzew Lódz	33	4

★ Poland 12 caps, 2 goals

Anatoly DEMYANENKO (Ukr)
19/02/59 Defender

87	Dinamo Kiev (Urs)	29	1	CC	1	-
88	Dinamo Kiev (Urs)	30	1			
89	Dinamo Kiev (Urs)	5	2			
90	Dinamo Kiev (Urs)	15	-	CWC	1	-
90/91	1.FC Magdeburg (Gdr)	3	-			
91/92	Widzew Lódz	13	-			

★ USSR 80 caps, 6 goals

Andrzej SZULC
17/10/67 Defender

87/88	Widzew Lódz	29	-
88/89	Widzew Lódz	26	1
89/90	Widzew Lódz	25	3
90/91	Widzew Lódz	Div 2	
91/92	Widzew Lódz	18	-

Bogdan JOZWIAK
17/07/70 Midfield

90/91	Wisla Ploch	Div 4	
91/92	Widzew Lódz	32	3

Leszek IWANICKI
12/08/59 Midfield

87/88	Widzew Lódz	29	4
88/89	Widzew Lódz	20	5
89/90	Widzew Lódz	11	1
90/91	Widzew Lódz	Div 2	
91/92	Widzew Lódz	33	8

★ Poland 2 caps, 0 goals

POLAND

FIVE YEAR RECORD	LEAGUE		EURO CUPS		
Birthdate/Playing position	Apps	Gls	Cup	Apps	Gls

Marek GODLEWSKI
28/04/65   Midfield

87/88	Zaglebie Lubin	27	-			
88/89	Zaglebie Lubin	Div 2				
89/90	Zaglebie Lubin	28	8			
90/91	Zaglebie Lubin	21	2	UC	2	-
91/92	Widzew Lódz	14	1			

★ Poland 3 caps, 0 goals

Pawel MIASZKIEWICZ
26/11/70   Midfield

89/90	Gwardia Warszawa	Div 2	
90/91	Gwardia Warszawa	Div 2	
91/92	Widzew Lódz	28	6

Piotr KUPKA
03/06/71   Midfield

89/90	Widzew Lódz	15	1
90/91	Widzew Lódz	Div 2	
91/92	Widzew Lódz	7	-

Marek KONIAREK
29/05/62   Forward

87/88	GKS Katowice	28	5	UC	2	1
88/89	GKS Katowice	1	-			
	FC Rot-Weiss Essen (Gdr)	Div 2				
89/90	FC Rot-Weiss Essen (Gdr)	Div 2				
91/92	Zaglebie Sosnowiec	13	4			
	Widzew Lódz	17	5			

★ Poland 2 caps, 1 goal

FIVE YEAR RECORD	LEAGUE		EURO CUPS		
Birthdate/Playing position	Apps	Gls	Cup	Apps	Gls

Ryszard CZERWIEC
28/02/68   Forward

88/89	Victoria Jaworzno	Div 3	
89/90	Zaglebie Sosnowiec	26	3
90/91	Zaglebie Sosnowiec	29	6
91/92	Zaglebie Sosnowiec	33	9

Radoslawa GILEWICZ
1969   Forward

91/92	GKS Tychy	Div 3

Andrzej MICHALCZUK
1967   Forward

91/92	Chemik Bydgoszcz	Div 2

EUROPEAN HONOURS
none

EUROPEAN CUPS RECORD

	Entries	Pd	W	D	L	F	A
Champions' Cup	2	10	4	1	5	21	20
Cup-winners' Cup	1	2	1	0	1	2	2
UEFA/Fairs' Cup	**6**	**26**	**8**	**8**	**10**	**24**	**36**
Total - All 3 Cups	9	38	13	9	16	47	58

SL BENFICA

NENO
27/01/62   Goalkeeper

FIVE YEAR RECORD	League Apps	Gls	Cup	Apps	Gls
87/88 Vitória Setúbal	5	-			
88/89 Vitória Guimarães	37	-	CWC	2	-
89/90 Vitória Guimarães	21	-			
90/91 SL Benfica	21	-			
91/92 SL Benfica	34	-	CC	9	-

★ Portugal 3 caps, 0 goals

SILVINO
05/03/59   Goalkeeper

FIVE YEAR RECORD	League Apps	Gls	Cup	Apps	Gls
87/88 SL Benfica	38	-	+CC	8	-
88/89 SL Benfica	38	-	UC	4	-
89/90 SL Benfica	33	-	+CC	9	-
90/91 SL Benfica	17	-	UC	2	-
91/92 SL Benfica	1	-	CC	1	-

★ Portugal 19 caps, 0 goals

JOSÉ CARLOS
02/08/66   Defender

FIVE YEAR RECORD	League Apps	Gls	Cup	Apps	Gls
87/88 Portimonense SC	36	2			
88/89 Portimonense SC	37	-			
89/90 SL Benfica	25	-	+CC	6	-
90/91 SL Benfica	26	1			
91/92 SL Benfica	29	1	CC	6	-

★ Portugal 1 cap, 0 goals

Carlos MOZER (Bra)
19/09/60   Defender

FIVE YEAR RECORD	League Apps	Gls	Cup	Apps	Gls
87/88 SL Benfica	32	6	+CC	8	1
88/89 SL Benfica	29	2	UC	3	1
89/90 Olympique Marseille (Fra)	27	4	CC	8	-
90/91 Olympique Marseille (Fra)	31	-	+CC	8	-
91/92 Olympique Marseille (Fra)	31	-	CC	3	-

★ Brazil

PAULO MADEIRA
06/09/70   Defender

FIVE YEAR RECORD	League Apps	Gls	Cup	Apps	Gls
89/90 SL Benfica	7	-			
90/91 SL Benfica	8	-	UC	2	-
91/92 SL Benfica	32	1	CC	9	1

★ Portugal 4 caps, 0 goals

VELOSO
31/01/57   Defender

FIVE YEAR RECORD	League Apps	Gls	Cup	Apps	Gls
87/88 SL Benfica	22	-	+CC	8	-
88/89 SL Benfica	37	2	UC	4	-
89/90 SL Benfica	30	-	+CC	8	-
90/91 SL Benfica	36	-	UC	2	-
91/92 SL Benfica	32	-	CC	9	-

★ Portugal 35 caps, 0 goals

Vasily KULKOV (Rus)
11/06/66   Defender

FIVE YEAR RECORD	League Apps	Gls	Cup	Apps	Gls
88 Spartak Ordzhonikidze (Urs) Div 2					
89 Spartak Moskva (Urs)	30	1	UC	4	-
90 Spartak Moskva (Urs)	23	2	CC	8	-
91 Spartak Moskva (Urs)	22	1			
91/92 SL Benfica	19	3	CC	6	1

★ USSR/CIS 21 caps, 0 goals

RUI COSTA
29/03/72   Midfield

FIVE YEAR RECORD	League Apps	Gls	Cup	Apps	Gls
90/91 AD Fafe	Div 3				
91/92 SL Benfica	21	4	CC	7	-

VÍTOR PANEIRA
16/02/66   Midfield

FIVE YEAR RECORD	League Apps	Gls	Cup	Apps	Gls
87/88 FC Vizela	Div 2				
88/89 SL Benfica	32	1		UC	4
89/90 SL Benfica	26	3	+CC	8	-
90/91 SL Benfica	36	9	UC	2	-
91/92 SL Benfica	29	-	CC	8	1

★ Portugal 28 caps, 4 goals

Stefan SCHWARZ (Swe)
18/04/69   Midfield

FIVE YEAR RECORD	League Apps	Gls	Cup	Apps	Gls
88 Malmö FF (Swe)	7	-	UC	4	-
89 Malmö FF (Swe)	15	-	CC	4	-
90 Malmö FF (Swe)	7	-			
90/91 SL Benfica	9	3	UC	1	-
91/92 SL Benfica	16	-	CC	9	-

★ Sweden 16 caps, 4 goals

PORTUGAL

FIVE YEAR RECORD	LEAGUE		EURO CUPS		
Birthdate/Playing position	Apps	Gls	Cup	Apps	Gls

PAULO SOUSA
30/08/70   Midfield

89/90	SL Benfica	2	-			
90/91	SL Benfica	36	-	UC	2	-
91/92	SL Benfica	23	1	CC	3	-

★ Portugal 5 caps, 0 goals

RUI ÁGUAS
28/04/60   Forward

87/88	SL Benfica	26	12	+CC	8	4
88/89	FC Porto	33	13	CC	3	2
89/90	FC Porto	31	18	CWC	5	3
90/91	SL Benfica	37	25	UC	2	-
91/92	SL Benfica	14	5	CC	3	1

★ Portugal 23 caps, 8 goals

JOÃO PINTO
19/08/71   Forward

88/89	Boavista FC	6	-			
89/90	Boavista FC	11	3	UC	2	2
90/91	Atlético Madrileño (Esp)	Div 2				
91/92	Boavista FC	34	8	UC	4	-

★ Portugal 8 caps, 1 goal

Aleksandr MOSTOVOY (Rus)
22/08/68   Forward

87	Spartak Moskva (Urs)	18	6	UC	4	3
88	Spartak Moskva (Urs)	27	3	CC	4	-
89	Spartak Moskva (Urs)	11	3	UC	2	-
90	Spartak Moskva (Urs)	23	9	CC	7	1
91	Spartak Moskva (Urs)	27	13	UC	4	2

★ USSR/CIS 15 caps, 3 goals

PACHECO
01/02/66   Forward

87/88	SL Benfica	25	4	+CC	6	-
88/89	SL Benfica	26	5	UC	2	-
89/90	SL Benfica	30	4	+CC	7	1
90/91	SL Benfica	28	7	UC	1	-
91/92	SL Benfica	27	7	CC	8	2

★ Portugal 6 caps, 0 goals

FIVE YEAR RECORD	LEAGUE		EURO CUPS		
Birthdate/Playing position	Apps	Gls	Cup	Apps	Gls

ISAÍAS (Bra)
18/10/63   Forward

87/88	Rio Ave FC	33	5			
88/89	Boavista FC	35	10			
89/90	Boavista FC	33	12	UC	2	-
90/91	SL Benfica	24	5	UC	2	-
91/92	SL Benfica	26	12	CC	8	5

Sergei YURAN (Ukr)
11/06/69   Forward

90	Dinamo Kiev (Urs)	13	9	CWC	5	5
91	Dinamo Kiev (Urs)	18	6			
91/92	SL Benfica	21	7	CC	9	7

★ USSR/CIS 16 caps, 4 goals

CÉSAR BRITO
21/10/64   Forward

87/88	Portimonense SC	36	5			
88/89	Portimonense SC	17	7			
89/90	SL Benfica	24	5	+4	2	
90/91	SL Benfica	19	7			
91/92	SL Benfica	23	7	CC	7	4

★ Portugal 13 caps, 2 goals

EUROPEAN HONOURS
Champions' Cup - (2) 1961, 1962.

EUROPEAN CUPS RECORD

	Entries	Pd	W	D	L	F	A
Champions' Cup	22	133	67	29	37	266	139
Cup-winners' Cup	5	28	13	8	7	42	19
UEFA/Fairs' Cup	**6**	**28**	**12**	**9**	**7**	**38**	**26**
Total - All 3 Cups	33	189	92	46	51	346	184

SPORTING CP

FIVE YEAR RECORD *Birthdate/Playing position*	LEAGUE Apps Gls	EURO CUPS Cup Apps Gls

Tomislav IVKOVIC (Cro)
11/08/60   Goalkeeper

87/88	FC Swarovski Tirol (Aut)	30	1	CWC	2	-
88/89	Wiener Sport-Club (Aut)	15	-			
	RKC Genk (Bel)	14	-			
89/90	Sporting CP	30	-	UC	2	-
90/91	Sporting CP	37	-	UC	10	-
91/92	Sporting CP	34	-	UC	2	-

★ Yugoslavia 38 caps, 0 goals

SÉRGIO
03/01/66   Goalkeeper

87/88	Portimonense SC	6	-
88/89	Portimonense SC	24	-
89/90	Sporting CP	-	-
90/91	Sporting CP	1	-
91/92	Sporting CP	-	-

LEAL
23/03/65   Defender

87/88	Académico Viseu	Div 2				
88/89	Académico Viseu	35	3			
89/90	Sporting CP	17	-	UC	2	-
90/91	Sporting CP	37	5	UC	10	-
91/92	Sporting CP	34	5	UC	2	-

★ Portugal 15 caps, 1 goal

MARINHO
24/11/70   Defender

89/90	Sporting CP	14	-			
90/91	Sporting CP	2	-			
91/92	Sporting CP	21	-	UC	2	-

Stan VALCKX (Hol)
20/10/63   Defender

87/88	VVV (Hol)	32	4			
88/89	PSV (Hol)	32	-	CC	4	-
89/90	PSV (Hol)	24	1	CC	2	-
90/91	PSV (Hol)	31	-	CWC	2	-
91/92	PSV (Hol)	28	4	CC	3	-

★ Holland 3 caps, 0 goals

FIVE YEAR RECORD *Birthdate/Playing position*	LEAGUE Apps Gls	EURO CUPS Cup Apps Gls

BARNY
20/06/66   Defender

87/88	Boavista FC	16	-			
88/89	CF Estrela Amadora	34	-			
89/90	CF Estrela Amadora	30	-			
90/91	Boavista FC	35	3			
91/92	Boavista FC	34	1	UC	4	1

PAULO TORRES
25/11/71   Defender

89/90	Sporting CP	11	-
90/91	Sporting CP	2	-
91/92	Sporting CP	6	-

★ Portugal 2 caps, 0 goals

NÉLSON
05/11/71   Defender

89/90	SC Salgueiros	Div 2	
90/91	SC Salgueiros	24	-
91/92	Sporting CP	2	-

CARLOS JORGE
08/11/66   Defender

87/88	CS Marítimo	-	-
88/89	CS Marítimo	21	-
89/90	CS Marítimo	29	1
90/91	CS Marítimo	38	5
91/92	CS Marítimo	32	3

CAPUCHO
21/02/72   Midfield

89/90	Gil Vicente FC	Div 2	
90/91	Gil Vicente FC	20	-
91/92	Gil Vicente FC	30	3

FIGO
04/11/72   Midfield

89/90	Sporting CP	3	-			
90/91	Sporting CP	-	-			
91/92	Sporting CP	34	1	UC	2	-

★ Portugal 7 caps, 0 goals

PORTUGAL

FIVE YEAR RECORD	LEAGUE		EURO CUPS		
Birthdate/Playing position	Apps	Gls	Cup	Apps	Gls

FILIPE
21/04/70   Midfield

88/89	SCU Torriense	Div 2				
89/90	Sporting CP	6	-			
90/91	Sporting CP	34	1	UC	9	-
91/92	Sporting CP	31	-	UC	1	-

★ Portugal 2 caps, 0 goals

Krasimir BALAKOV (Bul)
28/04/66   Midfield

87/88	Etar Veliko Tarnovo (Bul)	18	2			
88/89	Etar Veliko Tarnovo (Bul)	29	9			
89/90	Etar Veliko Tarnovo (Bul)	30	9			
90/91	Etar Veliko Tarnovo (Bul)	11	3			
	Sporting CP	18	5	UC	2	-
91/92	Sporting CP	32	7	UC	2	-

★ Bulgaria 21 caps, 1 goal

PEIXE
16/01/73   Midfield

90/91	Sporting CP	1	-			
91/92	Sporting CP	27	-	UC	2	-

★ Portugal 7 caps, 0 goals

CADETE
27/08/68   Forward

87/88	Sporting CP	6	-	CWC	1	-
88/89	Vitória Setúbal	29	8			
89/90	Sporting CP	29	7			
90/91	Sporting CP	30	3	UC	10	6
91/92	Sporting CP	34	25	UC	2	-

★ Portugal 14 caps, 1 goal

Ivailo YORDANOV (Bul)
12/01/66   Forward

89/90	Lokomotiv Gorna Oriahovitsa (Bul)	23	2			
90/91	Lokomotiv Gorna Oriahovitsa (Bul)	29	21			
91/92	Sporting CP	29	9	UC	1	1

★ Bulgaria 4 caps, 0 goals

FIVE YEAR RECORD	LEAGUE		EURO CUPS		
Birthdate/Playing position	Apps	Gls	Cup	Apps	Gls

Andrzej JUSKOWIAK (Pol)
03/11/70   Forward

87/88	Lech Poznan (Pol)	3	-			
88/89	Lech Poznan (Pol)	12	2	CWC	2	-
89/90	Lech Poznan (Pol)	27	18			
90/91	Lech Poznan (Pol)	29	12	CC	4	1
91/92	Lech Poznan (Pol)	24	11			

★ Poland 1 cap, 0 goals

Boncho GENCHEV (Bul)
07/07/64   Forward

87/88	Etar Veliko Tarnovo (Bul)	29	5			
88/89	Etar Veliko Tarnovo (Bul)	30	6			
89/90	Etar Veliko Tarnovo (Bul)	29	11			
90/91	Etar Veliko Tarnovo (Bul)	27	15			
91/92	Sporting CP	2	-			

★ Bulgaria 1 cap, 0 goals

EUROPEAN HONOURS
Cup-winners' Cup - (1) 1964.

EUROPEAN CUPS RECORD

	Entries	Pd	W	D	L	F	A
Champions' Cup	8	28	9	5	14	41	48
Cup-winners' Cup	7	36	16	8	12	76	45
UEFA/Fairs' Cup	**16**	**73**	**33**	**19**	**21**	**127**	**69**
Total - All 3 Cups	31	137	58	32	47	244	162

VITÓRIA GUIMARÃES

FIVE YEAR RECORD	LEAGUE		EURO CUPS		
Birthdate/Playing position	Apps	Gls	Cup	Apps	Gls

MADUREIRA
08/02/65   Goalkeeper

87/88	CD Nacional	Div 2			
88/89	CD Nacional	2	-		
89/90	Vitória Guimarães	3	-		
90/91	Vitória Guimarães	-	-		
91/92	Vitória Guimarães	13	-		

JESUS
11/02/55   Goalkeeper

87/88	Vitória Guimarães	34	-	UC	6	-
88/89	Leixões SC	36	-			
89/90	GD Chaves	27	-			
90/91	Vitória Guimarães	38	-	UC	2	-
91/92	Vitória Guimarães	19	-			

★ Portugal 7 caps, 0 goals

MATIAS
18/03/64   Defender

87/88	SC Salgueiros	11	-
88/89	SC Salgueiros	Div 2	
89/90	Rio Ave FC	Div 2	
90/91	CF União	37	2
91/92	Vitória Guimarães	20	2

NANDO
02/02/63   Defender

87/88	SC Farense	38	-			
88/89	Vitória Guimarães	38	2	CWC	2	-
89/90	Vitória Guimarães	25	-			
90/91	Vitória Guimarães	28	-	UC	1	-
91/92	SC Braga	30	1			

DIMAS
16/02/64   Defender

87/88	Académica Coimbra	35	1			
88/89	Académica Coimbra	Div 2				
89/90	Académica Coimbra	Div 2				
90/91	CF Estrela Amadora	32	2	CWC	3	-
91/92	CF Estrela Amadora	Div 2				

FIVE YEAR RECORD	LEAGUE		EURO CUPS		
Birthdate/Playing position	Apps	Gls	Cup	Apps	Gls

GERMANO
27/11/65   Defender

87/88	SC Covilhã	32	2			
88/89	Vitória Guimarães	28	2	CWC	2	-
89/90	Vitória Guimarães	30	1			
90/91	Vitória Guimarães	23	-	UC	2	-
91/92	Vitória Guimarães	6	-			

TAOUFIK (Tun)
08/01/65   Defender

90/91	Espérance (Tun)		
91/92	Vitória Guimarães	16	1

TANTÃ (Bra)
12/02/66   Defender

89/90	Brazil		
90/91	FC Famalicão	38	4
91/92	FC Famalicão	29	1

BASÍLIO
09/05/66   Defender

87/88	Vitória Guimarães	15	-	UC	1	-
88/89	Vitória Guimarães	23	-	CWC	2	-
89/90	Vitória Guimarães	6	-			
90/91	Vitória Guimarães	36	-	UC	2	-
91/92	Vitória Guimarães	25	-			

PAULO BENTO
20/06/69   Midfield

89/90	CF Estrela Amadora	12	-			
90/91	CF Estrela Amadora	25	-	CWC	4	-
91/92	Vitória Guimarães	32	3			

BASAULA Lemba (Zai)
03/03/65   Midfield

87/88	O Elvas	30	4			
88/89	CF Estrela Amadora	36	3			
89/90	Estrela Amadora	25	-			
90/91	Vitória Guimarães	32	1	UC	2	1
91/92	Vitória Guimarães	21	2			

★ Zaire

PORTUGAL

FIVE YEAR RECORD — *Birthdate/Playing position* | LEAGUE Apps Gls | EURO CUPS Cup Apps Gls

Dane KUPRESANIN (Yug)
12/06/66 Midfield

		Apps	Gls			
87/88	FK Sarajevo (Yug)	14	3			
88/89	FK Sarajevo (Yug)	27	2			
89/90	FK Sarajevo (Yug)	32	10			
90/91	FK Sarajevo (Yug)	31	8			
91/92	FC Famalicão	31	8			

PEDRO BARBOSA
06/08/70 Midfield

89/90	SC Freamunde	Div 2				
90/91	SC Freamunde	Div 2				
91/92	Vitória Guimarães	17	2			

N'DINGA Mbote (Zai)
11/09/66 Midfield

		Apps	Gls	Cup	Apps	Gls
87/88	Vitória Guimarães	18	-	UC	4	-
88/89	Vitória Guimarães	31	2	CWC	1	-
89/90	Vitória Guimarães	31	5			
90/91	Vitória Guimarães	38	2	UC	2	-
91/92	Vitória Guimarães	26	-			

★ Zaire

PAULO JORGE
22/02/63 Midfield

87/88	CF Estrela Amadora	Div 2				
88/89	CF Estrela Amadora	33	4			
89/90	CF Estrela Amadora	26	2			
90/91	CF Estrela Amadora	28	-	CWC	4	-
91/92	Vitória Guimarães	19	2			

ZIAD Tlemcani (Tun)
26/04/63 Forward

		Apps	Gls	Cup	Apps	Gls
90/91	Vitória Guimarães	34	8	UC	2	-
91/92	Vitória Guimarães	32	15			

★ Tunisia

LIMA
16/10/66 Forward

		Apps	Gls	Cup	Apps	Gls
87/88	Sporting CP	8	2			
88/89	Sporting CP	17	3	UC	1	-
89/90	Sporting CP	12	-	UC	1	-
90/91	Sporting CP	4	-			
91/92	Sporting CP	12	1			

MOREIRA DE SÁ
03/02/66 Forward

87/88	Leixões SC	Div 2				
88/89	Leixões SC	32	5			
89/90	CS Marítimo	6	-			
90/91	FC Penafiel	36	9			
91/92	Vitória Guimarães	13	1			

EUROPEAN HONOURS
none

EUROPEAN CUPS RECORD

	Entries	pd	W	D	L	F	A
Champions' Cup	none						
Cup-winners' Cup	1	2	1	0	1	1	2
UEFA/Fairs' Cup	6	26	10	5	11	30	39
Total - All 3 Cups	7	28	11	5	12	31	41

DERRY CITY

FIVE YEAR RECORD *Birthdate/Playing position*	LEAGUE Apps Gls	EURO CUPS Cup Apps Gls

Dermot O'NEILL
Goalkeeper

		Apps	Gls		Apps	Gls
87/88	Bohemians	33	-	UC	2	-
88/89	Bohemians	33	-			
89/90	Bohemians	32	-			
90/91	Bohemians	31	-			
91/92	Derry City	33	-			

Paul CURRAN
05/10/66   Defender

		Apps	Gls		Apps	Gls
87/88	Derry City	26	-			
88/89	Derry City	31	2	CWC	2	-
89/90	Derry City	33	4	CC	2	-
90/91	Derry City	33	3	UC	2	-
91/92	Derry City	32	3			

Stuart GAULD
06/09/66   Defender

		Apps	Gls		Apps	Gls
87/88	Derry City	11	1			
88/89	Derry City	20	5	CWC	1	-
89/90	Derry City	4	-	CC	2	-
90/91	Derry City	31	8	UC	2	-
91/92	Derry City	31	7			

Peter HUTTON
Defender

		Apps	Gls			
89/90	Coleraine	3	-			
90/91	Derry City	2	-			
91/92	Derry City	31	1			

Sean CAMPBELL
Midfield

		Apps	Gls			
90/91	Derry City	7	-			
91/92	Derry City	7	-			

Paul CARLYLE
19/07/66   Midfield

		Apps	Gls		Apps	Gls
87/88	Derry City	8	1			
88/89	Derry City	32	6	CWC	2	-
89/90	Derry City	28	-	CC	2	1
90/91	Derry City	33	5	UC	2	-
91/92	Derry City	27	3			

Marty McCANN
Midfield

		Apps	Gls			
90/91	Derry City	5	-			
91/92	Derry City	17	1			

Damian DUNLEAVY
21/01/71   Midfield

		Apps	Gls			
90/91	Raith Rovers (Sco)	Div 2				
91/92	Raith Rovers (Sco)	Div 2				
	Sligo Rovers	3	-			

Declan ROCHE
09/10/70   Midfield

		Apps	Gls			
90/91	Partick Thistle (Sco)	Div 2				
91/92	Shelbourne	13	1			

Paul MOONEY
Midfield

		Apps	Gls		Apps	Gls
87/88	Linfield (Nir)	24	-			
88/89	Linfield (Nir)	20	3	UC	2	-
89/90	Linfield (Nir)	20	2	CC	2	1
90/91	Linfield (Nir)	11	-			
91/92	Derry City	27	2			

Martin McGINLEY
Midfield

		Apps	Gls			
91/92	Bradford City (Eng)	Div 3				

Mark ENNIS
12/02/64   Forward

		Apps	Gls		Apps	Gls
87/88	St. Patrick's Athletic	31	10			
88/89	St. Patrick's Athletic	33	12			
89/90	St. Patrick's Athletic	30	19			
90/91	St. Patrick's Athletic	30	12	CC	1	-
91/92	St. Patrick's Athletic	32	14			

Liam CURRAN
Forward

		Apps	Gls			
91	Derry City	-	-			

REPUBLIC OF IRELAND

FIVE YEAR RECORD *Birthdate/Playing position*	LEAGUE Apps Gls	EURO CUPS Cup Apps Gls

Gary HEANEY
Forward

90/91 Derry City	2	-
91/92 Derry City	2	-

Paul HEGARTY
30/06/67 Forward

87/88 Derry City	10	1	
88/89 Derry City	9	1	
89/90 Derry City	13	3	
90/91 Derry City	27	1	UC 1 -
91/92 Derry City	13	-	

Gregory KEARNEY
Forward

91/92 Derry City	26	4

Donal O'BRIEN
Forward

90/91 Derry City	9	5
91/92 Derry City	25	6

FIVE YEAR RECORD *Birthdate/Playing position*	LEAGUE Apps Gls	EURO CUPS Cup Apps Gls

Michael DEENEY
27/03/62 Forward

88/89 Morton (Sco)	Div 2
89/90 Morton (Sco)	Div 2
90/91 Morton (Sco)	Div 2
91/92 Morton (Sco)	Div 2

EUROPEAN HONOURS
none

EUROPEAN CUPS RECORD

	Entries	Pd	W	D	L	F	A
Champions' Cup	2	5	1	0	4	9	21
Cup-winners' Cup	2	4	0	1	3	0	9
UEFA/Fairs' Cup	1	2	0	1	1	0	1
Total - All 3 Cups	5	11	1	2	8	9	31

ELECTROPUTERE CRAIOVA

FIVE YEAR RECORD	LEAGUE		EURO CUPS	
Birthdate/Playing position	Apps	Gls	Cup	Apps Gls

Silviu LUNG
09/11/56   Goalkeeper

87/88	Universitatea Craiova	27	-	UC	1 -
88/89	Steaua Bucuresti	29	-	+CC	9 -
89/90	Steaua Bucuresti	20	-	CC	4 -
90/91	CD Logroñés	9	-		
91/92	Electroputere Craiova	22	-		

★ Romania 76 caps, 0 goals

Liviu PERDUT
08/11/63   Goalkeeper

90/91	Electroputere Craiova	Div 2	
91/92	Electroputere Craiova	14	-

Gheorghe BITA
08/09/63   Defender

87/88	Universitatea Craiova	17	7
88/89	Universitatea Craiova	9	2
89/90	Universitatea Craiova	-	-
90/91	Electroputere Craiova	Div 2	
91/92	Electroputere Craiova	32	2

Mihai MATEI
14/08/68   Defender

88/89	ASA Tirgu Mures	17	-
89/90	ASA Tirgu Mures	Div 2	
90/91	Electroputere Craiova	Div 2	
91/92	Electroputere Craiova	32	1

Stefan NANU
08/09/68   Defender

90/91	Electroputere Craiova	Div 2	
91/92	Electroputere Craiova	28	-

Ion BARBUCEANU
07/01/63   Defender

90/91	Electroputere Craiova	Div 2	
91/92	Electroputere Craiova	10	-

FIVE YEAR RECORD	LEAGUE		EURO CUPS	
Birthdate/Playing position	Apps	Gls	Cup	Apps Gls

Mircea ION
10/01/70   Midfield

89/90	Universitatea Craiova	2	-
90/91	Electroputere Craiova	Div 2	
91/92	Electroputere Craiova	21	2

Ionel LUTA
14/03/65   Midfield

88/89	Universitatea Craiova	10	-
89/90	Universitatea Craiova	-	-
90/91	Electroputere Craiova	Div 2	
91/92	Electroputere Craiova	31	9

Dumitru MITRITA
23/06/71   Midfield

90/91	Universitatea Craiova	2	-
91/92	Electroputere Craiova	31	4

Vintila POPESCU
07/10/66   Midfield

90/91	Electroputere Craiova	Div 2	
91/92	Electroputere Craiova	18	1

Viorel PRUNA
24/02/68   Midfield

87/88	Universitatea Craiova	2	-
88/89	Universitatea Craiova	-	-
89/90	Universitatea Craiova	-	-
90/91	Universitatea Craiova	9	1
91/92	Electroputere Craiova	8	-

Dumitru SOROHAN
13/05/63   Midfield

90/91	Electroputere Craiova	Div 2	
91/92	Electroputere Craiova	15	-

Grigore TUDOR
10/10/73   Midfield

90/91	Electroputere Craiova	Div 2	
91/92	Electroputere Craiova	14	-

ROMANIA

FIVE YEAR RECORD	LEAGUE		EURO CUPS		
Birthdate/Playing position	Apps	Gls	Cup	Apps	Gls

Claudiu Constantin STOICA
25/06/70   Forward

88/89	Universitatea Craiova	2	-			
89/90	Universitatea Craiova	4	-			
90/91	Universitatea Craiova	4	-			
91/92	Universitatea Craiova	3	-			
	Electroputere Craiova	12	1			

Cristian ALBEANU
05/10/71   Forward

90/91	Electroputere Craiova	Div 2	
91/92	Electroputere Craiova	15	4

Marian CALAFETEANU
08/11/65   Forward

88/89	Universitatea Craiova	4	-
89/90	Universitatea Craiova	-	-
90/91	Electroputere Craiova	Div 2	
91/92	Electroputere Craiova	26	6

Ion DUDAN
11/09/66   Forward

87/88	FC Olt Scornicesti	10	-			
88/89	FC Olt Scornicesti	21	2			
89/90	FC Olt Scornicesti	16	1			
	Universitatea Craiova	9	-			
90/91	Petrolul Ploiesti	9	-	UC	2	-
	Universitatea Craiova	4	-			
91/92	Electroputere Craiova	25	2			

FIVE YEAR RECORD	LEAGUE		EURO CUPS		
Birthdate/Playing position	Apps	Gls	Cup	Apps	Gls

Tersinio Ionel GANE
12/10/71   Forward

88/89	Universitatea Craiova	1	-
89/90	Universitatea Craiova	-	-
90/91	Electroputere Craiova	Div 2	
91/92	Electroputere Craiova	30	9

★ Romania 1 cap, 0 goals

EUROPEAN HONOURS
none

EUROPEAN CUPS RECORD

	Entries	Pd	W	D	L	F	A
Champions' Cup	none						
Cup-winners' Cup	none						
UEFA/Fairs' Cup	**none**						
Total - All 3 Cups	none						

UNIVERSITATEA CRAIOVA

FIVE YEAR RECORD *Birthdate/Playing position*	LEAGUE Apps Gls	EURO CUPS Cup Apps Gls

Florin DUMITRU
13/02/68   Goalkeeper

		Apps	Gls		
88/89	Universitatea Craiova	1	-		
89/90	Jiul Petrosani	9	-		
90/91	Jiul Petrosani	28	-		
91/92	Universitatea Craiova	5	-		

Gabriel BOLDICI
28/03/57   Goalkeeper

		Apps	Gls		
87/88	Chimia Rimnicu Vilcea	Div 2			
88/89	Universitatea Craiova	17	-		
89/90	Universitatea Craiova	17	-		
90/91	Universitatea Craiova	2	-		
91/92	Universitatea Craiova	13	-		

Emil SANDOI
01/03/65   Defender

		Apps	Gls	Cup	Apps Gls
87/88	Universitatea Craiova	30	1	UC	2 -
88/89	Universitatea Craiova	31	6		
89/90	Universitatea Craiova	23	2		
90/91	Universitatea Craiova	33	13	UC	4 -
91/92	Universitatea Craiova	25	2	CC	2 -

★ Romania 24 caps, 0 goals

Adrian POPESCU
26/07/60   Defender

		Apps	Gls	Cup	Apps Gls
87/88	Universitatea Craiova	28	1	UC	1 -
88/89	Universitatea Craiova	30	1		
89/90	Universitatea Craiova	28	3		
90/91	Universitatea Craiova	29	1	UC	4 -
91/92	Universitatea Craiova	31	1	CC	2 1

★ Romania 7 caps, 1 goal

Catalin GIRLISTEANU
19/12/70   Defender

		Apps	Gls		
89/90	Universitatea Craiova	4	-		
90/91	Universitatea Craiova	4	-		
91/92	Universitatea Craiova	10	-		

FIVE YEAR RECORD *Birthdate/Playing position*	LEAGUE Apps Gls	EURO CUPS Cup Apps Gls

Gheorghe BARBU
20/07/68   Defender

		Apps	Gls		
88/89	Universitatea Craiova	5	-		
89/90	Universitatea Craiova	-	-		
90/91	Universitatea Craiova	-	-		
91/92	Universitatea Craiova	18	-		

Nicolae ZAMFIR
26/04/67   Defender

		Apps	Gls	Cup	Apps Gls
87/88	Universitatea Craiova	10	1		
88/89	Universitatea Craiova	20	-		
89/90	Universitatea Craiova	22	-		
90/91	Universitatea Craiova	27	3	UC	3 1
91/92	Universitatea Craiova	23	-	CC	2 -

★ Romania 4 caps, 0 goals

Daniel Emil MOGOSANU
01/12/67   Defender

		Apps	Gls	Cup	Apps Gls
89/90	Universitatea Craiova	4	-		
90/91	Universitatea Craiova	27	2	UC	2 -
91/92	Universitatea Craiova	24	-		

Victor COJOCARU
01/05/59   Defender

		Apps	Gls	Cup	Apps Gls
87/88	Victoria Bucuresti	33	3		
88/89	Victoria Bucuresti	28	1	UC	8 -
89/90	Victoria Bucuresti	8	1	UC	2 -
89/90	Universitatea Craiova	14	-		
90/91	Universitatea Craiova	16	-		
91/92	Electroputere Craiova	23	-		
	Universitatea Craiova	8	-		

Gheorghe CIUREA
12/10/62   Midfield

		Apps	Gls	Cup	Apps Gls
87/88	Universitatea Craiova	34	15	UC	2 1
88/89	Universitatea Craiova	22	2		
89/90	Universitatea Craiova	29	5		
90/91	Universitatea Craiova	31	13	UC	4 1
91/92	Universitatea Craiova	25	9	CC	1 -

ROMANIA

FIVE YEAR RECORD	LEAGUE		EURO CUPS		
Birthdate/Playing position	Apps	Gls	Cup	Apps	Gls

Ion OLARU
24/08/61   Midfield

		Apps	Gls	Cup	Apps	Gls
88/89	Universitatea Craiova	16	2			
89/90	Universitatea Craiova	13	2			
90/91	Universitatea Craiova	31	2	UC	4	-
91/92	Universitatea Craiova	33	1	CC	1	-

Pavel BADEA
10/06/67   Midfield

		Apps	Gls	Cup	Apps	Gls
87/88	Universitatea Craiova	34	9	UC	2	-
88/89	Universitatea Craiova	29	4			
89/90	Universitatea Craiova	31	8			
90/91	Universitatea Craiova	31	10	UC	4	-
91/92	Universitatea Craiova	30	7	CC	2	-

★ Romania 8 caps, 2 goals

Silvian CRISTESCU
29/10/70   Midfield

		Apps	Gls	Cup	Apps	Gls
88/89	Universitatea Craiova	8	-			
89/90	Universitatea Craiova	8	-			
90/91	Universitatea Craiova	10	3	UC	1	-
91/92	Universitatea Craiova	25	3	CC	2	-

Danut BICA
23/08/64   Midfield

		Apps	Gls	Cup	Apps	Gls
87/88	Universitatea Craiova	12	-			
88/89	Universitatea Craiova	24	1			
89/90	Universitatea Craiova	26	1			
90/91	Universitatea Craiova	26	-	UC	4	-
91/92	Universitatea Craiova	17	-	CC	1	-

Ovidiu STINGA
05/12/72   Midfield

		Apps	Gls
90/91	Universitatea Craiova	1	-
91/92	Universitatea Craiova	17	2

FIVE YEAR RECORD	LEAGUE		EURO CUPS		
Birthdate/Playing position	Apps	Gls	Cup	Apps	Gls

Adrian PIGULEA
12/05/68   Forward

		Apps	Gls	Cup	Apps	Gls
88/89	Universitatea Craiova	3	-			
89/90	Universitatea Craiova	19	3			
90/91	Universitatea Craiova	31	12	UC	4	-
91/92	Universitatea Craiova	28	1	CC	2	-

★ Romania 1 cap, 0 goals

Eugen NEAGOE
22/08/67   Forward

		Apps	Gls	Cup	Apps	Gls
87/88	Universitatea Craiova	3	-			
88/89	Universitatea Craiova	21	7			
89/90	Universitatea Craiova	26	7			
90/91	Universitatea Craiova	20	5	UC	2	-
91/92	Universitatea Craiova	22	5	CC	2	-

Gheorghe CRAIOVEANU
14/02/68   Forward

		Apps	Gls	Cup	Apps	Gls
90/91	Universitatea Craiova	13	3			
91/92	Universitatea Craiova	24	4	CC	1	-

EUROPEAN HONOURS
none

EUROPEAN CUPS RECORD

	Entries	Pd	W	D	L	F	A
Champions' Cup	4	12	4	2	6	14	17
Cup-winners' Cup	3	10	4	2	4	19	15
UEFA/Fairs' Cup	10	42	21	6	15	44	40
Total - All 3 Cups	17	64	29	10	25	77	72

POLITEHNICA TIMISOARA

FIVE YEAR RECORD	LEAGUE		EURO CUPS		
Birthdate/Playing position	Apps	Gls	Cup	Apps	Gls

Ion ALMASAN
22/06/62   Goalkeeper

87/88	Politehnica Timisoara	18	-			
88/89	Politehnica Timisoara	30	-			
90/91	Politehnica Timisoara	8	-			
91/92	Politehnica Timisoara	30	-			

Dorin ARCANU
29/03/70   Goalkeeper

91/92	Politehnica Timisoara	3	-	

Constantin VARGA
18/09/64   Defender

87/88	Politehnica Timisoara	33	6			
88/89	Politehnica Timisoara	Div 2				
89/90	Politehnica Timisoara	31	9			
90/91	Politehnica Timisoara	27	10	UC	3	1
91/92	Politehnica Timisoara	31	5			

Adrian Gheorghe CRACIUN
09/09/63   Defender

87/88	Politehnica Timisoara	31	-			
88/89	Politehnica Timisoara	Div 2				
89/90	Politehnica Timisoara	28	8			
90/91	Politehnica Timisoara	33	2	UC	4	-
91/92	Politehnica Timisoara	16	-			

Petru ANDREAS
13/05/62   Defender

87/88	Politehnica Timisoara	5	-			
88/89	Politehnica Timisoara	Div 2				
89/90	Politehnica Timisoara	25	-			
90/91	Politehnica Timisoara	25	-	UC	4	-
91/92	Politehnica Timisoara	30	1			

Adrian STOICOV
12/11/67   Defender

87/88	Politehnica Timisoara	12	-			
88/89	Politehnica Timisoara	Div 2				
89/90	Politehnica Timisoara	29	-			
90/91	Politehnica Timisoara	31	2	UC	4	-
91/92	Politehnica Timisoara	28	-			

FIVE YEAR RECORD	LEAGUE		EURO CUPS		
Birthdate/Playing position	Apps	Gls	Cup	Apps	Gls

Florin BATRINU
19/03/71   Defender

90/91	Politehnica Timisoara	11	1	UC	1	-
91/92	Politehnica Timisoara	27	1			

Tiberiu CSIK
12/12/71   Defender

91/92	Politehnica Timisoara	23	-	

Emilian Mario DIACONESCU
16/04/70   Midfield

91/92	Politehnica Timisoara	29	3	

Octavian POPESCU
07/01/64   Midfield

87/88	Otelul Galati	29	4			
88/89	Otelul Galati	32	8	UC	2	-
89/90	Otelul Galati	Div 2				
90/91	Politehnica Timisoara	24	1	UC	4	1
91/92	Politehnica Timisoara	28	2			

Sorin VLAICU
03/06/65   Midfield

87/88	Politehnica Timisoara	7	-			
88/89	Politehnica Timisoara	Div 2				
89/90	Politehnica Timisoara	25	5			
90/91	Politehnica Timisoara	31	3	UC	4	1
91/92	Politehnica Timisoara	30	2			

★ Romania 4 caps, 0 goals

Ionel Aurel BARBOSU
12/08/67   Midfield

88/89	Politehnica Timisoara	Div 2				
89/90	Politehnica Timisoara	26	-			
90/91	Politehnica Timisoara	30	3	UC	2	-
91/92	Politehnica Timisoara	26	1			

Eugen VOICA
02/12/69   Midfield

90/91	Gloria Bistrita	16	-	
91/92	Politehnica Timisoara	18	3	

ROMANIA

FIVE YEAR RECORD	LEAGUE		EURO CUPS		
Birthdate/Playing position	Apps	Gls	Cup	Apps	Gls

Ion ROSU
23/01/67   Midfield

91/92	Politehnica Timisoara	1	-			

Marcel BABAN
16/10/68   Forward

91/92	Politehnica Timisoara	32	10			

Calin ROSENBLUM
26/05/64   Forward

89/90	Politehnica Timisoara	13	4			
90/91	Politehnica Timisoara	33	8	UC	4	-
91/92	Politehnica Timisoara	28	5			

Liviu Corneliu VUIA
17/06/68   Forward

91/92	Politehnica Timisoara	16	1			

FIVE YEAR RECORD	LEAGUE		EURO CUPS		
Birthdate/Playing position	Apps	Gls	Cup	Apps	Gls

Ovidiu Lucian CUC
14/01/73   Forward

89/90	Politehnica Timisoara	2	1			
90/91	Politehnica Timisoara	8	-			
91/92	Politehnica Timisoara	8	1			

EUROPEAN HONOURS
none

EUROPEAN CUPS RECORD

	Entries	Pd	W	D	L	F	A
Champions' Cup	none						
Cup-winners' Cup	2	6	3	0	3	5	11
UEFA/Fairs' Cup	2	8	4	0	4	9	14
Total - All 3 Cups	4	14	7	0	7	14	25

TORPEDO MOSKVA

FIVE YEAR RECORD Birthdate/Playing position	LEAGUE Apps Gls	EURO CUPS Cup Apps Gls

Aleksandr PODSHIVALOV
06/09/63   Goalkeeper

87	Ararat Erevan	21	-	
88	Ararat Erevan	30	-	
89	Ararat Erevan	24	-	
90	Ararat Erevan	23	-	
91	Torpedo Moskva	14	-	UC 3 -

Vladimir POHEINIKOV
30/03/70   Goalkeeper

88	Spartak Moskva	3	-
89	Torpedo Moskva	-	-
90	Torpedo Moskva	-	-
91	Torpedo Moskva	-	-

Andrey AFANASYEV
15/05/64   Defender

87	CSKA Moskva	15	1	
88	CSKA Moskva	Div 2		
89	Torpedo Moskva	7	-	CWC 2 1
90	Torpedo Moskva	8	1	UC 4 -
91	Torpedo Moskva	27	1	UC 4 -

Andrey KALAYCHEV
26/10/63   Defender

88	Lokomotiv Moskva	29	4	
89	Lokomotiv Moskva	30	-	
90	Torpedo Moskva	22	1	UC 4 -
91	Torpedo Moskva	23	2	UC 2 -

★ USSR 1 cap, 0 goals

Maxim CHELTSOV
04/09/70   Defender

88	Torpedo Moskva	3	-	
89	Torpedo Moskva	-	-	
90	Torpedo Moskva	-	-	
91	Torpedo Moskva	5	-	UC 2 -

Boris VOSTROSABLIN
07/10/68   Defender

91	Fakel Voronezh	Div 2

FIVE YEAR RECORD Birthdate/Playing position	LEAGUE Apps Gls	EURO CUPS Cup Apps Gls

Mikhail SOLOVYEV
23/12/68   Defender

87	CSKA Moskva	1	-	
88	CSKA Moskva (II)	Div 3		
89	Torpedo Moskva	24	-	CWC 3 -
90	Torpedo Moskva	8	-	UC 3 -
91	Torpedo Moskva	17	-	UC 3 -

Dmitry ULYANOV
28/11/70   Defender

91	Torpedo Moskva	16	1	UC 4 -

Nikolai SAVICHEV
19/02/65   Midfield

87	Torpedo Moskva	18	3	
88	Torpedo Moskva	25	6	UC 2 -
89	Torpedo Moskva	29	2	CWC 4 -
90	Torpedo Moskva	22	1	UC 5 2
91	Torpedo Moskva	21	3	

★ USSR 3 caps, 0 goals

Dmitry IVANOV
17/09/70   Midfield

91	Krylya Sovetov Samara	Div 2

Sergei SHUSTIKOV
30/09/70   Midfield

88	Torpedo Moskva	1	-	
89	Torpedo Moskva	-	-	
90	Torpedo Moskva	14	-	UC 6 -
91	Torpedo Moskva	28	1	UC 3 -

★ CIS 2 caps, 0 goals

Igor CHUGAYNOV
06/04/70   Midfield

87	Torpedo Moskva	1	-	
88	Torpedo Moskva	-	-	
89	Torpedo Moskva	1	-	
90	Lokomotiv Moskva	Div 2		
91	Torpedo Moskva	28	2	UC 4 1

★ CIS 4 caps, 0 goals

RUSSIA

FIVE YEAR RECORD	LEAGUE		EURO CUPS		
Birthdate/Playing position	Apps	Gls	Cup	Apps	Gls

Sergei CHUMACHENKO
14/02/73   Midfield

91	Torpedo Moskva	-	-		

Yury TISHKOV
22/03/71   Forward

88	Torpedo Moskva	1	-		
89	Torpedo Moskva	-	-		
90	Torpedo Moskva	14	4	UC	5	6
91	Torpedo Moskva	24	8	UC	4	1

Gennady GRISHIN
25/11/64   Forward

87	Torpedo Moskva	24	3		
88	Torpedo Moskva	27	1	UC	2	-
89	Torpedo Moskva	28	2	CWC	4	-
90	Torpedo Moskva	11	2	UC	5	1
91	Torpedo Moskva	29	7	UC	4	1

Sergei SKACHENKO
18/11/72   Forward

90	Traktor Pavograd	Div 3	
91	Metallist Kharkov	9	2

FIVE YEAR RECORD	LEAGUE		EURO CUPS		
Birthdate/Playing position	Apps	Gls	Cup	Apps	Gls

Sergei BORISOV
10/10/72   Forward

91	Torpedo Moskva	7	-	UC	2	-

Andrey TALALAYEV
05/10/72   Forward

91	Torpedo Moskva	5	-	UC	3	-

EUROPEAN HONOURS
none

EUROPEAN CUPS RECORD

	Entries	Pd	W	D	L	F	A
Champions' Cup	2	4	0	3	1	0	1
Cup-winners' Cup	6	23	10	8	5	32	20
UEFA/Fairs' Cup	5	24	13	4	7	44	29
Total - All 3 Cups	13	51	23	15	13	76	50

DINAMO MOSKVA

FIVE YEAR RECORD *Birthdate/Playing position*	LEAGUE Apps Gls	EURO CUPS Cup Apps Gls

Andrey SMETANIN
21/06/69   Goalkeeper

		Apps	Gls	Cup	Apps	Gls
89	Dinamo Moskva	-	-			
90	Dinamo Moskva	3	-			
91	Dinamo Moskva	10	-	UC	6	-

Valery KLEYMENOV
10/09/65   Goalkeeper

		Apps	Gls	Cup	Apps	Gls
87	Rotor Volgograd	Div 2				
88	Rotor Volgograd	Div 2				
89	Rotor Volgograd	27	-			
90	Rotor Volgograd	19	-			
91	Rotor Volgograd	Div 2				

★ CIS 2 caps, 0 goals

Yevgeny DOLGOV
20/06/69   Defender

		Apps	Gls	Cup	Apps	Gls
89	Iskra Smolensk	Div 3				
90	Dinamo Moskva	16	-			
91	Dinamo Moskva	14	-	UC	3	-

★ USSR 1 cap, 0 goals

Viktor LOSEV
25/06/59   Defender

		Apps	Gls	Cup	Apps	Gls
87	Dinamo Moskva	28	-	UC	3	-
88	Dinamo Moskva	30	-			
89	Dinamo Moskva	28	-			
90	Dinamo Moskva	20	-			
91	Dinamo Moskva	29	-	UC	2	-

★ USSR 3 caps, 0 goals

Sarkis OGANESYAN
17/08/68   Defender

		Apps	Gls	Cup	Apps	Gls
87	Ararat Erevan	1	-			
88	Ararat Erevan	12	-			
89	Ararat Erevan	28	2			
90	Ararat Erevan	19	3			
91	Ararat Erevan	29	4			

FIVE YEAR RECORD *Birthdate/Playing position*	LEAGUE Apps Gls	EURO CUPS Cup Apps Gls

Igor SKLYAROV
31/08/66   Defender

		Apps	Gls	Cup	Apps	Gls
87	Dinamo Moskva	21	-	UC	4	-
88	Dinamo Moskva	24	-			
89	Dinamo Moskva	20	-			
90	Dinamo Moskva	21	1			
91	Dinamo Moskva	14	-	UC	4	-

Yevgeny SMERTIN
17/01/69   Defender

		Apps	Gls	Cup	Apps	Gls
87	Dinamo Barnaul	Div 3				
88	Dinamo Moskva	17	-			
89	Dinamo Moskva	15	-			
90	Dinamo Moskva	18	-			
91	Dinamo Moskva	26	-	UC	6	-

Vyacheslav TSAREV
04/05/71   Defender

		Apps	Gls	Cup	Apps	Gls
90	Dinamo Moskva	10	-			
91	Dinamo Moskva	21	-	UC	6	-

Yury DROZDOV
16/01/72   Midfield

		Apps	Gls	Cup	Apps	Gls
91	Dinamo Moskva	6	-			

Vitaly BUT
16/11/72   Midfield

		Apps	Gls	Cup	Apps	Gls
91	Dinamo Moskva	5	1			

Sergei DERKACH
14/11/66   Midfield

		Apps	Gls	Cup	Apps	Gls
87	Dinamo Minsk	18	3	CWC	5	1
88	Dinamo Minsk	18	4	UC	4	-
89	Dinamo Moskva	24	2			
90	Dinamo Moskva	19	4			
91	Dinamo Moskva	14	-	UC	2	-

RUSSIA

FIVE YEAR RECORD *Birthdate/Playing position*	LEAGUE Apps Gls	EURO CUPS Cup Apps Gls

Yury KALITVINTSEV
05/05/68   Midfield

87	SKA Rostov	Div 2	
88	SKA Rostov	Div 2	
	Rotor Volgograd	Div 2	
89	Rotor Volgograd	28	1
90	Rotor Volgograd	22	1
91	Rotor Volgograd	Div 2	

Andrey KOBELEV
22/10/68   Midfield

87	Dinamo Moskva	10	-			
88	Dinamo Moskva	12	-			
89	Dinamo Moskva	26	2			
90	Dinamo Moskva	21	4			
91	Dinamo Moskva	23	9	UC	5	2

Badri SPANDERASHVILI
10/11/69   Midfield

87	SKA Rostov	Div 2	
88	SKA Rostov	Div 2	
89	Spartak Vladikavkaz	Div 2	
90	Spartak Vladikavkaz	Div 2	
91	Spartak Vladikavkaz	5	-
	Dila Gori (Geo)		

Omari TETRADZE
13/10/69   Midfield

88	Dinamo Tbilisi	9	-			
89	Dinamo Tbilisi	15	-			
90	Mertskhali Ozurgeti (Geo)					
91	Dinamo Moskva	21	-	UC	5	-

★ CIS 3 caps, 0 goals

Igor GAVRILIN
10/02/72   Forward

91	FC Moskovski	Div 4	

Velli KASUMOV
04/10/68   Forward

87	Neftchi Baku	23	-
88	Neftchi Baku	25	2
89	Neftchi Baku	Div 2	
90	Neftchi Baku	Div 2	
91	Neftchi Baku	Div 2	

Igor SIMUTENKOV
04/03/73   Forward

90	Dinamo Moskva	1	-			
91	Dinamo Moskva	18	3	UC	5	-

EUROPEAN HONOURS
none

EUROPEAN CUPS RECORD

	Entries	Pd	W	D	L	F	A
Champions' Cup	none						
Cup-winners' Cup	4	29	15	8	6	46	25
UEFA/Fairs' Cups	6	20	7	5	8	21	20
Total - All 3 Cups	10	49	22	13	14	67	45

HIBERNIAN

FIVE YEAR RECORD Birthdate/Playing position	LEAGUE Apps	 Gls	EURO CUPS Cup	 Apps	 Gls

John BURRIDGE (Eng)
08/12/51   Goalkeeper

87/88	Southampton (Eng)	31	-		
88/89	Southampton (Eng)	31	-		
90/91	Newcastle United (Eng)	Div 2			
90/91	Newcastle United (Eng)	Div 2			
91/92	Hibernian	35	-		

Chris REID
04/11/71   Goalkeeper

89/90	Hibernian	2	-
90/91	Hibernian	1	-
91/92	Hibernian	9	-

Willie MILLER
01/11/69   Defender

89/90	Hibernian	11	-
90/91	Hibernian	27	1
91/92	Hibernian	30	-

Graham MITCHELL
02/11/62   Defender

87/88	Hibernian	41	1		
88/89	Hibernian	20	-		
89/90	Hibernian	31	-	UC 4	1
90/91	Hibernian	28	-		
91/92	Hibernian	27	-		

Neil ORR
13/05/59   Defender

87/88	Hibernian	38	1		
88/89	Hibernian	33	-		
89/90	Hibernian	24	1	UC 4	-
90/91	Hibernian	18	1		
91/92	Hibernian	30	-		

Tommy McINTYRE
26/12/63   Defender

87/88	Hibernian	26	-
88/89	Hibernian	17	2
89/90	Hibernian	-	-
90/91	Hibernian	11	-
91/92	Hibernian	37	6

Gordon HUNTER
03/05/67   Defender

87/88	Hibernian	36	-		
88/89	Hibernian	33	1		
89/90	Hibernian	34	-	UC 4	-
90/91	Hibernian	20	1		
91/92	Hibernian	37	2		

Joe TORTOLANO
06/04/66   Defender

87/88	Hibernian	21	4
88/89	Hibernian	25	-
89/90	Hibernian	6	-
90/91	Hibernian	20	1
91/92	Hibernian	25	1

Dave BEAUMONT
10/12/63   Defender

87/88	Dundee United	9	1	UC 2	-
88/89	Dundee United	18	1	CWC 2	1
	Luton Town (Eng)	15	-		
89/90	Luton Town (Eng)	19	-		
90/91	Luton Town (Eng)	33	-		
91/92	Luton Town (Eng)	9	-		
	Hibernian	26	-		

Murdo MacLEOD
24/09/58   Midfield

87/88	Borussia Dortmund (Ger)	32	1	UC 6	-
88/89	Borussia Dortmund (Ger)	31	-		
89/90	Borussia Dortmund (Ger)	31	2	CWC 4	-
90/91	Borussia Dortmund (Ger)	7	1	UC 2	-
	Hibernian	25	2		
91/92	Hibernian	22	-		

★ Scotland 20 caps, 1 goal

Brian HAMILTON
05/08/67   Midfield

87/88	St. Mirren	28	-	CWC 2	-
88/89	St. Mirren	23	1		
89/90	Hibernian	26	-	UC 4	-
90/91	Hibernian	26	2		
91/92	Hibernian	40	3		

SCOTLAND

FIVE YEAR RECORD *Birthdate/Playing position*	LEAGUE Apps Gls	EURO CUPS Cup Apps Gls

Pat McGINLAY
30/05/67   Midfield

		Apps	Gls		Cup	Apps	Gls
88/89	Hibernian	2	-				
89/90	Hibernian	22	3	UC	2	-	
90/91	Hibernian	32	1				
91/92	Hibernian	43	9				

Billy FINDLAY
29/08/70   Midfield

		Apps	Gls		Cup	Apps	Gls
88/89	Hibernian	3	1				
89/90	Hibernian	9	-				
90/91	Hibernian	23	2				
91/92	Hibernian	12	-				

Darren JACKSON
25/07/66   Forward

		Apps	Gls		Cup	Apps	Gls
87/88	Newcastle United (Eng)	31	2				
88/89	Newcastle United (Eng)	15	2				
	Dundee United	1	-				
89/90	Dundee United	25	7	UC	1	-	
90/91	Dundee United	32	12	UC	3	1	
91/92	Dundee United	28	11				

Michael WEIR
16/01/66   Forward

		Apps	Gls		Cup	Apps	Gls
87/88	Luton Town (Eng)	8	-				
	Hibernian	18	4				
88/89	Hibernian	7	-				
89/90	Hibernian	15	3	UC	2	-	
90/91	Hibernian	20	1				
91/92	Hibernian	31	11				

Mark McGRAW
05/01/71   Forward

		Apps	Gls		Cup	Apps	Gls
89/90	Morton	Div 2					
90/91	Hibernian	17	-				
91/92	Hibernian	24	1				

FIVE YEAR RECORD *Birthdate/Playing position*	LEAGUE Apps Gls	EURO CUPS Cup Apps Gls

Keith WRIGHT
17/05/65   Forward

		Apps	Gls		Cup	Apps	Gls
87/88	Dundee	42	15				
88/89	Dundee	35	8				
89/90	Dundee	34	11				
90/91	Dundee	Div 2					
91/92	Hibernian	40	9				

★ Scotland 1 cap, 0 goals

Gareth EVANS (Eng)
14/01/67   Forward

		Apps	Gls		Cup	Apps	Gls
87/88	Rotherham United (Eng)	Div 3					
	Hibernian	12	2				
88/89	Hibernian	35	5				
89/90	Hibernian	26	3	UC	4	1	
90/91	Hibernian	14	2				
91/92	Hibernian	41	6				

EUROPEAN HONOURS
none

EUROPEAN CUPS RECORD

	Entries	Pd	W	D	L	F	A
Champions' Cup	1	6	3	1	2	9	5
Cup-winners' Cup	1	6	3	1	2	19	10
UEFA/Fairs' Cup	13	58	28	11	19	97	84
Total - All 3 Cups	15	70	34	13	23	125	99

HEART OF MIDLOTHIAN

FIVE YEAR RECORD *Birthdate/Playing position*	LEAGUE Apps Gls		EURO CUPS Cup Apps Gls		

Henry SMITH
10/03/56   Goalkeeper

		Apps	Gls		Cup	Apps	Gls
87/88	Heart of Midlothian	44	-				
88/89	Heart of Midlothian	36	-		UC	8	-
89/90	Heart of Midlothian	36	-				
90/91	Heart of Midlothian	23	-		UC	4	-
91/92	Heart of Midlothian	44	-				

★ Scotland 3 caps, 0 goals

Nicky WALKER
29/09/62   Goalkeeper

		Apps	Gls
87/88	Rangers	5	-
88/89	Rangers	12	-
89/90	Heart of Midlothian	-	-
90/91	Heart of Midlothian	13	-
91/92	Heart of Midlothian	-	-

Alan McLAREN
04/01/71   Defender

		Apps	Gls		Cup	Apps	Gls
87/88	Heart of Midlothian	1	-				
88/89	Heart of Midlothian	12	1		UC	2	-
89/90	Heart of Midlothian	27	1				
90/91	Heart of Midlothian	23	1		UC	4	-
91/92	Heart of Midlothian	38	1				

★ Scotland 3 caps, 0 goals

Tosh McKINLAY
03/12/64   Defender

		Apps	Gls		Cup	Apps	Gls
87/88	Dundee	19	-				
88/89	Dundee	18	-				
	Heart of Midlothian	17	1		UC	2	-
89/90	Heart of Midlothian	29	1				
90/91	Heart of Midlothian	33	2		UC	4	-
91/92	Heart of Midlothian	39	2				

Craig LEVEIN
22/10/64   Defender

		Apps	Gls		Cup	Apps	Gls
87/88	Heart of Midlothian	21	-				
88/89	Heart of Midlothian	9	-		UC	2	-
89/90	Heart of Midlothian	35	-				
90/91	Heart of Midlothian	33	3		UC	4	-
91/92	Heart of Midlothian	36	2				

★ Scotland 8 caps, 0 goals

Graeme HOGG
17/06/64   Defender

		Apps	Gls
87/88	Manchester United (Eng)	10	-
	West Bromwich A. (Eng)	Div 2	
88/89	Portsmouth (Eng)	Div 2	
89/90	Portsmouth (Eng)	Div 2	
90/91	Portsmouth (Eng)	Div 2	
91/92	Heart of Midlothian	18	1

Gary MACKAY
23/01/64   Midfield

		Apps	Gls		Cup	Apps	Gls
87/88	Heart of Midlothian	41	5				
88/89	Heart of Midlothian	29	2		UC	8	-
89/90	Heart of Midlothian	33	1				
90/91	Heart of Midlothian	30	3		UC	2	-
91/92	Heart of Midlothian	43	1				

★ Scotland 4 caps, 1 goal

Derek FERGUSON
31/07/67   Midfield

		Apps	Gls		Cup	Apps	Gls
87/88	Rangers	32	4		CC	5	-
88/89	Rangers	16	3		CWC	3	-
89/90	Rangers	5	-		CC	1	-
	Dundee	Div 2					
90/91	Heart of Midlothian	28	2		UC	2	-
91/92	Heart of Midlothian	38	1				

★ Scotland 2 caps, 0 goals

Ally MAUCHLEN
29/06/60   Midfield

		Apps	Gls
87/88	Leicester City (Eng)	Div 2	
88/89	Leicester City (Eng)	Div 2	
89/90	Leicester City (Eng)	Div 2	
90/91	Leicester City (Eng)	Div 2	
91/92	Leicester City (Eng)	Div 2	

Peter VAN DE VEN (Hol)
08/01/61   Midfield

		Apps	Gls		Cup	Apps	Gls
87/88	RSC Charleroi (Bel)	26	2				
88/89	RSC Charleroi (Bel)	26	-				
89/90	Willem II (Hol)	30	4				
90/91	Aberdeen (Sco)	32	-		CWC	4	-
91/92	Aberdeen	25	2		UC	1	-

SCOTLAND

FIVE YEAR RECORD *Birthdate/Playing position*	LEAGUE Apps Gls	EURO CUPS Cup Apps Gls

Ian BAIRD (Eng)
01/04/64   Midfield

		Apps	Gls	Cup	Apps	Gls
87/88	Portsmouth (Eng)	20	1			
	Leeds United (Eng)	Div 2				
88/89	Leeds United (Eng)	Div 2				
89/90	Leeds United (Eng)	Div 2				
	Middlesbrough (Eng)	Div 2				
90/91	Middlesbrough (Eng)	Div 2				
91/92	Heart of Midlothian	30	6			

John MILLAR
08/12/66   Midfield

		Apps	Gls	Cup	Apps	Gls
87/88	Blackburn Rovers (Eng)	Div 2				
88/89	Blackburn Rovers (Eng)	Div 2				
89/90	Blackburn Rovers (Eng)	Div 2				
90/91	Blackburn Rovers (Eng)	Div 2				
91/92	Heart of Midlothian	41	7			

Eamonn BANNON
18/04/58   Midfield

		Apps	Gls	Cup	Apps	Gls
87/88	Dundee United	26	1	UC	3	-
88/89	Heart of Midlothian	30	2	UC	8	1
89/90	Heart of Midlothian	33	2			
90/91	Heart of Midlothian	19	2	UC	3	-
91/92	Heart of Midlothian	13	3			

★ Scotland 11 caps, 1 goal

George WRIGHT
22/12/69   Midfield

		Apps	Gls	Cup	Apps	Gls
89/90	Heart of Midlothian	1	-			
90/91	Heart of Midlothian	17	2	UC	2	-
91/92	Heart of Midlothian	25	1			

Scott CRABBE
12/08/68   Forward

		Apps	Gls	Cup	Apps	Gls
87/88	Heart of Midlothian	5	-			
88/89	Heart of Midlothian	1	-			
89/90	Heart of Midlothian	35	12			
90/91	Heart of Midlothian	21	3	UC	1	-
91/92	Heart of Midlothian	41	15			

FIVE YEAR RECORD *Birthdate/Playing position*	LEAGUE Apps Gls	EURO CUPS Cup Apps Gls

John ROBERTSON
02/10/64   Forward

		Apps	Gls	Cup	Apps	Gls
87/88	Heart of Midlothian	39	26			
88/89	Newcastle United (Eng)	12	-			
	Heart of Midlothian	15	4	UC	1	-
89/90	Heart of Midlothian	32	17			
90/91	Heart of Midlothian	31	12	UC	3	3
91/92	Heart of Midlothian	42	14			

★ Scotland 6 caps, 2 goals

Iain FERGUSON
04/08/62   Forward

		Apps	Gls	Cup	Apps	Gls
87/88	Dundee United	39	11	UC	3	1
88/89	Heart of Midlothian	29	5	UC	6	1
89/90	Heart of Midlothian	11	1			
	Charlton Athletic	1	-			
	Bristol City	Div 3				
90/91	Heart of Midlothian	12	2	UC	3	1
	Motherwell	15	7			
91/92	Heart of Midlothian	30	4			

Wayne FOSTER (Eng)
11/09/63   Forward

		Apps	Gls	Cup	Apps	Gls
87/88	Heart of Midlothian	39	4			
88/89	Heart of Midlothian	9	1	UC	5	1
89/90	Heart of Midlothian	17	1			
90/91	Heart of Midlothian	28	1	UC	2	2
91/92	Heart of Midlothian	6	-			

EUROPEAN HONOURS
none

EUROPEAN CUPS RECORD

	Entries	Pd	W	D	L	F	A
Champions' Cup	2	4	1	0	3	4	11
Cup-winners' Cup	1	4	1	0	3	8	11
UEFA/Fairs' Cup	**7**	**28**	**12**	**7**	**9**	**43**	**41**
Total - All 3 Cups	10	36	14	7	15	55	63

CELTIC

FIVE YEAR RECORD Birthdate/Playing position	LEAGUE Apps	Gls	EURO CUPS Cup	Apps	Gls

Gordon MARSHALL
19/04/64   Goalkeeper

87/88 Falkirk	44	-			
88/89 Falkirk	Div 2				
89/90 Falkirk	Div 2				
90/91 Falkirk	Div 2				
91/92 Celtic	25	-			

★ Scotland 1 cap, 0 goals

Pat BONNER (Irl)
25/05/60   Goalkeeper

87/88 Celtic	32	-			
88/89 Celtic	26	-	CC	2	-
89/90 Celtic	36	-	CWC	2	-
90/91 Celtic	36	-			
91/92 Celtic	19	-	UC	4	-

★ Republic of Ireland 57 caps, 0 goals

Chris MORRIS (Irl)
24/12/63   Defender

87/88 Celtic	44	3	UC	2	-
88/89 Celtic	33	3	CC	4	-
89/90 Celtic	32	1	CWC	1	-
90/91 Celtic	18	-			
91/92 Celtic	31	1	UC	2	-

★ Republic of Ireland 34 caps, 0 goals

Tom BOYD
24/11/65   Defender

87/88 Motherwell	42	2			
88/89 Motherwell	36	1			
89/90 Motherwell	33	1			
90/91 Motherwell	30	2			
91/92 Chelsea (Eng)	23	-			
Celtic	13	1			

★ Scotland 10 caps, 0 goals

Steve FULTON
10/8/70   Midfield

88/89 Celtic	3	-			
89/90 Celtic	14	-			
90/91 Celtic	20	-			
91/92 Celtic	30	2	UC	3	-

Derek WHYTE
31/08/68   Defender

87/88 Celtic	41	3	UC	2	1
88/89 Celtic	22	-	CC	4	-
89/90 Celtic	35	1	CWC	2	-
90/91 Celtic	24	2			
91/92 Celtic	40	1	UC	4	-

★ Scotland 4 caps, 0 goals

Gary GILLESPIE
05/07/60   Defender

87/88 Liverpool (Eng)	35	4			
88/89 Liverpool (Eng)	15	1			
89/90 Liverpool (Eng)	13	4			
90/91 Liverpool (Eng)	30	1			
91/92 Celtic	24	2	UC	2	-

★ Scotland 13 caps, 0 goals

Tony MOWBRAY (Eng)
22/11/63   Defender

87/88 Middlesbrough (Eng)	Div 2				
88/89 Middlesbrough (Eng)	37	3			
89/90 Middlesbrough (Eng)	Div 2				
90/91 Middlesbrough (Eng)	Div 2				
91/92 Middlesbrough (Eng)	Div 2				
Celtic	15	2			

Dariusz WDOWCZYK (Pol)
25/09/62   Defender

87/88 Legia Warszawa (Pol)	18	3			
88/89 Legia Warszawa (Pol)	26	3	UC	2	-
89/90 Legia Warszawa (pol)	13	4	CWC	2	-
Celtic	23	1			
90/91 Celtic	24	-			
91/92 Celtic	19	-	UC	4	-

★ Poland 53 caps, 2 goals

Brian O'NEIL
06/09/72   Midfield

91/92 Celtic	28	1	UC	3	1

SCOTLAND

FIVE YEAR RECORD Birthdate/Playing position	LEAGUE Apps	Gls	EURO CUPS Cup	Apps	Gls

John COLLINS
31/01/68   Midfield

87/88	Hibernian	44	6		
88/89	Hibernian	35	2		
89/90	Hibernian	35	6	UC	4	1
90/91	Celtic	35	1		
91/92	Celtic	38	11	UC	3	-

★ Scotland 8 caps, 2 goals

Mike GALLOWAY
30/05/65   Midfield

87/88	Halifax Town (Eng)	Div 4			
	Heart of Midlothian	25	6		
88/89	Heart of Midlothian	31	2	UC	8	5
89/90	Celtic	32	2	CWC	2	1
90/91	Celtic	7	1		
91/92	Celtic	34	2	UC	2	1

★ Scotland 1 cap, 0 goals

Peter GRANT
30/08/65   Midfield

87/88	Celtic	37	2	UC	2	-
88/89	Celtic	21	-	CC	1	-
89/90	Celtic	26	-	CWC	2	-
90/91	Celtic	28	-		
91/92	Celtic	22	-	UC	3	-

★ Scotland 2 caps, 0 goals

Paul McSTAY
22/10/64   Midfield

87/88	Celtic	44	5	UC	2	-
88/89	Celtic	33	5	CC	4	-
89/90	Celtic	35	3	CWC	2	-
90/91	Celtic	30	2		
91/92	Celtic	32	7	UC	2	-

★ Scotland 60 caps, 9 goals

Charlie NICHOLAS
30/12/61   Forward

87/88	Arsenal (Eng)	3	-		
	Aberdeen	16	3		
88/89	Aberdeen	29	16	UC	1	-
89/90	Aberdeen	33	11	UC	2	-

FIVE YEAR RECORD Birthdate/Playing position	LEAGUE Apps	Gls	EURO CUPS Cup	Apps	Gls
90/91	Celtic	14	6		
91/92	Celtic	37	21	UC	4	2

★ Scotland 20 caps, 5 goals

Joe MILLER
08/12/67   Forward

87/88	Aberdeen	14	4	UC	4	1
	Celtic	27	3		
88/89	Celtic	23	8	CC	3	-
89/90	Celtic	23	5	CWC	1	-
90/91	Celtic	30	8		
91/92	Celtic	26	2	UC	3	1

Tommy COYNE (Irl)
14/11/62   Forward

87/88	Dundee	43	33		
88/89	Dundee	26	9		
	Celtic	7	-		
89/90	Celtic	19	7	CWC	1	-
90/91	Celtic	26	18		
91/92	Celtic	39	15	UC	3	-

★ Republic of Ireland 5 caps, 2 goals

Gerry CREANEY
13/04/70   Forward

89/90	Celtic	6	1		
90/91	Celtic	30	7		
91/92	Celtic	32	14	UC	1	-

EUROPEAN HONOURS
Champions' Cup - (1) 1967.

EUROPEAN CUPS RECORD

	Entries	Pd	W	D	L	F	A
Champions' Cup	15	78	42	15	21	143	73
Cup-winners' Cup	7	34	19	4	11	68	31
UEFA/Fairs' Cup	6	20	7	6	7	29	28
Total - All 3 Cups	28	132	68	25	39	240	132

REAL MADRID

FIVE YEAR RECORD *Birthdate/Playing position*	LEAGUE Apps Gls	EURO CUPS Cup Apps Gls

Francisco BUYO
13/01/58   Goalkeeper

		Apps	Gls		Cup Apps	Gls
87/88	Real Madrid	35	-	CC	8	-
88/89	Real Madrid	31	-	CC	7	-
89/90	Real Madrid	35	-	CC	4	-
90/91	Real Madrid	31	-	CC	2	-
91/92	Real Madrid	35	-	UC	10	-

★ Spain 7 caps, 0 goals

Pedro Luis JARO
22/02/63   Goalkeeper

		Apps	Gls		Cup Apps	Gls
87/88	Cádiz CF	30	-			
88/89	CD Málaga	34	-			
89/90	CD Málaga	37	-			
90/91	Real Madrid	8	-	CC	4	-
91/92	Real Madrid	3	-			

Miguel CHENDO
12/10/61   Defender

		Apps	Gls		Cup Apps	Gls
87/88	Real Madrid	31	1	CC	8	-
88/89	Real Madrid	26	-	CC	5	-
89/90	Real Madrid	37	1	CC	3	-
90/91	Real Madrid	36	-	CC	5	-
91/92	Real Madrid	37	-	UC	10	-

★ Spain 26 caps, 0 goals

Manuel SANCHIS
23/05/65   Defender

		Apps	Gls		Cup Apps	Gls
87/88	Real Madrid	33	9	CC	8	1
88/89	Real Madrid	33	3	CC	7	-
89/90	Real Madrid	34	3	CC	4	-
90/91	Real Madrid	31	2	CC	1	-
91/92	Real Madrid	37	1	UC	9	1

★ Spain 48 caps, 1 goal

RICARDO ROCHA (Bra)
11/09/62   Defender

		Apps	Gls		Cup Apps	Gls
90/91	FC São Paulo (Bra)					
91/92	Real Madrid	36	-	UC	9	-

★ Brazil

FIVE YEAR RECORD *Birthdate/Playing position*	LEAGUE Apps Gls	EURO CUPS Cup Apps Gls

Rafael GORDILLO
24/02/57   Defender

		Apps	Gls		Cup Apps	Gls
87/88	Real Madrid	35	6	CC	8	-
88/89	Real Madrid	34	6	CC	8	-
89/90	Real Madrid	33	-	CC	3	-
90/91	Real Madrid	12	2	CC	2	-
91/92	Real Madrid	10	-	UC	7	-

★ Spain 75 caps, 3 goals

Juan José MAQUEDA
23/01/69   Defender

		Apps	Gls		Cup Apps	Gls
87/88	Real Madrid	10	1			
88/89	Real Madrid	5	-			
89/90	CD Logroñés	29	1			
90/91	Real Madrid	24	1	CC	3	1
91/92	Real Madrid	13	2	UC	2	-

Francisco José Pérez VILLARROYA
06/08/66   Midfield

		Apps	Gls		Cup Apps	Gls
87/88	Real Zaragoza	23	1			
88/89	Real Zaragoza	37	1			
89/90	Real Zaragoza	37	4	UC	4	-
90/91	Real Madrid	36	-	CC	6	1
91/92	Real Madrid	34	1	UC	7	1

★ Spain 14 caps, 0 goals

Fernando Muñoz "NANDO"
30/10/67   Defender

		Apps	Gls		Cup Apps	Gls
87/88	Sevilla FC	10	-			
88/89	Sevilla FC	17	-			
89/90	Sevilla FC	37	-			
90/91	FC Barcelona	34	-	+CWC	6	-
91/92	FC Barcelona	30	-	#CC	8	-

★ Spain 8 caps, 0 goals

Fernando HIERRO
23/03/68   Midfield

		Apps	Gls		Cup Apps	Gls
87/88	Real Valladolid	29	1			
88/89	Real Valladolid	29	2			
89/90	Real Madrid	37	7	CC	4	-
90/91	Real Madrid	35	7	CC	5	1
91/92	Real Madrid	37	21	UC	9	2

★ Spain 11 caps, 4 goals

SPAIN

FIVE YEAR RECORD *Birthdate/Playing position*	LEAGUE Apps Gls	EURO CUPS Cup Apps Gls

Miguel González "MICHEL"
23/03/63 Midfield

		Apps	Gls	Cup	Apps	Gls
87/88	Real Madrid	35	14	CC	8	-
88/89	Real Madrid	36	12	CC	5	-
89/90	Real Madrid	37	8	CC	3	2
90/91	Real Madrid	36	8	CC	6	1
91/92	Real Madrid	38	11	UC	10	2

★ Spain 63 caps, 21 goals

Luis MILLA
12/03/69 Midfield

		Apps	Gls	Cup	Apps	Gls
88/89	FC Barcelona	28	-	#CWC	8	-
89/90	FC Barcelona	25	1	CWC	3	-
90/91	Real Madrid	6	-			
91/92	Real Madrid	36	-	UC	8	-

★ Spain 5 caps, 0 goals

Robert PROSINECKI (Cro)
12/01/69 Midfield

		Apps	Gls	Cup	Apps	Gls
87/88	Crvena zvezda Beograd (Yug)	23	4	UC	3	-
88/89	Crvena zvezda Beograd (Yug)	33	4	CC	3	-
89/90	Crvena zvezda Beograd (Yug)	32	5	UC	6	1
90/91	Crvena zvezda Beograd (Yug)	29	11	#CC	9	4
91/92	Real Madrid	3	1	UC	2	1

★ Yugoslavia 15 caps, 4 goals

Emilio BUTRAGUEÑO
22/07/63 Forward

		Apps	Gls	Cup	Apps	Gls
87/88	Real Madrid	33	12	CC	8	2
88/89	Real Madrid	33	16	CC	8	4
89/90	Real Madrid	32	10	CC	2	2
90/91	Real Madrid	35	19	CC	4	4
91/92	Real Madrid	35	14	UC	9	1

★ Spain 68 caps, 26 goals

ALFONSO Pérez
26/09/72 Forward

		Apps	Gls	Cup	Apps	Gls
90/91	Real Madrid	9	-			
91/92	Real Madrid	19	3	UC	3	1

FIVE YEAR RECORD *Birthdate/Playing position*	LEAGUE Apps Gls	EURO CUPS Cup Apps Gls

Iván ZAMORANO (Chi)
18/01/67 Forward

		Apps	Gls	Cup	Apps	Gls
87/88	Cobreloa (Chi)					
88/89	FC St. Gallen (Sui)	17	10			
89/90	FC St. Gallen (Sui)	33	23			
90/91	FC St. Gallen (Sui)	6	1			
	Sevilla FC	29	9			
91/92	Sevilla FC	30	12			

★ Chile

Francisco LLORENTE
21/05/65 Forward

		Apps	Gls	Cup	Apps	Gls
87/88	Real Madrid	21	2	CC	5	-
88/89	Real Madrid	24	1	CC	7	-
89/90	Real Madrid	22	1	CC	4	-
90/91	Real Madrid	6	-	CC	2	-
91/92	Real Madrid	18	2	UC	5	-

★ Spain 1 cap, 1 goal

LUIS ENRIQUE Martínez
08/05/70 Forward

		Apps	Gls	Cup	Apps	Gls
89/90	Sporting Gijón	1	-			
90/91	Sporting Gijón	35	15			
91/92	Real Madrid	29	4	UC	6	-

★ Spain 1 cap, 0 goals

EUROPEAN HONOURS
Champions' Cup - (6) 1956, 1957, 1958, 1959, 1960, 1966.
UEFA Cup - (2) 1985, 1986.

EUROPEAN CUPS RECORD

	Entries	Pd	W	D	L	F	A
Champions' Cup	26	170	101	25	44	401	186
Cup-winners' Cup	3	25	13	7	5	46	20
UEFA/Fairs' Cup	7	50	25	8	17	82	56
Total - All 3 Cups	36	245	139	40	66	529	262

VALENCIA CF

FIVE YEAR RECORD — LEAGUE — EURO CUPS
Birthdate/Playing position — Apps Gls — Cup Apps Gls

José Manuel SEMPERE
15/02/58 Goalkeeper

		Apps	Gls	Cup	Apps	Gls
87/88	Valencia CF	18	-			
88/89	Valencia CF	1	-			
89/90	Valencia CF	1	-			
90/91	Valencia CF	8	-			
91/92	Valencia CF	38	-			

José Luis GONZALEZ
27/08/62 Goalkeeper

		Apps	Gls	Cup	Apps	Gls
87/88	Real Sociedad	-	-			
88/89	Real Sociedad	7	-			
89/90	Real Sociedad	37	-			
90/91	Real Sociedad	37	-	UC	4	-
91/92	Real Sociedad	36	-			

Francisco José CAMARASA
27/09/67 Defender

		Apps	Gls	Cup	Apps	Gls
87/88	Valencia CF	1	-			
88/89	Valencia CF	16	-			
89/90	Valencia CF	22	-	UC	4	-
90/91	Valencia CF	32	2	UC	1	-
91/92	Valencia CF	38	1			

Fernando GINER
31/12/64 Defender

		Apps	Gls	Cup	Apps	Gls
87/88	Valencia CF	28	4			
88/89	Valencia CF	35	1			
89/90	Valencia CF	21	1	UC	2	-
90/91	Valencia CF	34	1	UC	4	-
91/92	Valencia CF	37	3			

★ Spain 5 caps, 0 goals

Salvador González "VORO"
09/10/63 Defender

		Apps	Gls	Cup	Apps	Gls
87/88	Valencia CF	36	2			
88/89	Valencia CF	26	1			
89/90	Valencia CF	37	2	UC	4	-
90/91	Valencia CF	24	-	UC	4	-
91/92	Valencia CF	32	2			

LEONARDO Nascimento (Bra)
05/09/69 Defender

		Apps	Gls	Cup	Apps	Gls
90/91	FC São Paulo (Bra)					
91/92	Valencia CF	36	4			
★ Brazil						

Miodrag BELODEDICI (Rom)
20/05/64 Defender

		Apps	Gls	Cup	Apps	Gls
87/88	Steaua Bucuresti (Rom)	31	3	CC	8	-
88/89	Steaua Bucuresti (Rom)	17	5	CC	4	-
89/90	Crvena zvezda Beograd (Yug)	14	1			
90/91	Crvena zvezda Beograd (Yug)	34	1	#CC	9	-
91/92	Crvena zvezda Beograd (Yug)	15*	-*	CC	8	-

★ Romania 21 caps, 4 goals
* first half of season figures only.

Enrique Sánchez "QUIQUE"
02/02/65 Defender

		Apps	Gls	Cup	Apps	Gls
87/88	Valencia CF	21	1			
88/89	Valencia CF	28	-			
89/90	Valencia CF	19	3	UC	2	1
90/91	Valencia CF	30	2	UC	3	-
91/92	Valencia CF	26	3			

★ Spain 15 caps, 0 goals

Fernando Martínez "NANDO"
03/05/67 Midfield

		Apps	Gls	Cup	Apps	Gls
87/88	Valencia CF	30	1			
88/89	Valencia CF	34	1			
89/90	Valencia CF	29	4	UC	4	-
90/91	Valencia CF	25	1	UC	1	-
91/92	Valencia CF	22	-			

★ Spain 1 cap, 0 goals

TOMAS González
03/03/63 Midfield

		Apps	Gls	Cup	Apps	Gls
87/88	Real Oviedo	Div 2				
88/89	Real Oviedo	36	6			
89/90	Valencia CF	27	2	UC	2	-
90/91	Valencia CF	30	1	UC	1	-
91/92	Valencia CF	28	2			

SPAIN

FIVE YEAR RECORD	LEAGUE		EURO CUPS		
Birthdate/Playing position	Apps	Gls	Cup	Apps	Gls

Carlos ARROYO
16/02/66   Midfield

87/88	Valencia CF	32	3			
88/89	Valencia CF	28	4			
89/90	Valencia CF	35	4	UC	3	1
90/91	Valencia CF	18	1	UC	3	-
91/92	Valencia CF	20	5			

ROBERTO Fernández
05/07/62   Midfield

87/88	FC Barcelona	34	5	UC	7	-
88/89	FC Barcelona	37	11	#CWC	9	5
89/90	FC Barcelona	33	9	CWC	4	-
90/91	Valencia CF	29	4	UC	3	1
91/92	Valencia CF	31	7			

★ Spain 29 caps, 2 goals

FERNANDO Gómez
11/09/65   Midfield

87/88	Valencia CF	33	10			
88/89	Valencia CF	35	14			
89/90	Valencia CF	37	13	UC	4	-
90/91	Valencia CF	24	10	UC	4	2
91/92	Valencia CF	36	9			

★ Spain 7 caps, 2 goals

Liuboslav PENEV (Bul)
31/08/66   Forward

87/88	CFKA Sredets Sofia (Bul)	26	21	CC	2	-
88/89	CFKA Sredets Sofia (Bul)	22	21	CWC	6	6
89/90	CSKA Sofia (Bul)	6	12	CC	2	2
	Valencia CF	27	13			
90/91	Valencia CF	30	7	UC	3	-
91/92	Valencia CF	35	13			

★ Bulgaria 29 caps, 6 goals

ALVARO Cervera
22/09/64   Forward

87/88	RCD Mallorca	29	2			
88/89	RCD Mallorca	Div 2				
89/90	RCD Mallorca	33	1			
90/91	RCD Mallorca	13	-			
91/92	RCD Mallorca	28	1			

ROMMEL Fernández (Pan)
15/01/66   Forward

87/88	CD Tenerife	Div 2			·	
88/89	CD Tenerife	Div 2				
89/90	CD Tenerife	33	10			
90/91	CD Tenerife	31	13			
91/92	Valencia CF	21	2			

★ Panama

ELOY Olaya
10/07/64   Forward

87/88	Sporting Gijón	37	3	UC	2	-
88/89	Valencia CF	35	8			
89/90	Valencia CF	29	8	UC	3	-
90/91	Valencia CF	36	6	UC	4	-
91/92	Valencia CF	37	10			

★ Spain 15 caps, 1 goal

Antonio José Gomes "TONI" (Bra)
25/10/65   Forward

88/89	São José (Bra)					
89/90	Valencia CF	36	6	UC	4	2
90/91	Valencia CF	26	1	UC	3	-
91/92	Valencia CF	12	-			

EUROPEAN HONOURS
Cup-winners' Cup - (1) 1980.
Fairs' Cup - (2) 1962, 1963.
Super Cup - (1) 1980.

EUROPEAN CUPS RECORD

	Entries	Pd	W	D	L	F	A
Champions' Cup	1	6	2	2	2	6	5
Cup-winners' Cup	3	19	10	5	4	39	20
UEFA/Fairs' Cup	15	86	42	19	25	160	110
Total - All 3 Cups	19	111	54	26	31	205	135

REAL SOCIEDAD

FIVE YEAR RECORD	LEAGUE		EURO CUPS		
Birthdate/Playing position	Apps	Gls	Cup	Apps	Gls

Francisco Hernández "PAXTI"
03/11/67   Goalkeeper

89/90	Real Sociedad	-	-			
90/91	Real Sociedad	-	-			
91/92	Real Socedad	1	-			

Javier YUBERO
21/01/72   Goalkeeper

91/92	Real Sociedad	1	-	

IMANOL Aguazil
1970   Defender

90/91	Real Sociedad	1	-	
91/92	Real Sociedad	22	-	

José URIA
12/02/65   Defender

87/88	Real Sociedad	20	-	CWC	3	-
88/89	Real Sociedad	15	-	UC	3	-
89/90	Real Sociedad	14	-			
90/91	Real Sociedad	19	3	UC	1	-
91/92	Real Sociedad	30	2			

Juan Antonio LARRAÑAGA
03/07/58   Defender

87/88	Real Sociedad	38	-	CWC	3	-
88/89	Real Sociedad	38	1	UC	8	-
89/90	Real Sociedad	38	4			
90/91	Real Sociedad	38	-	UC	4	1
91/92	Real Sociedad	38	1			

★ Spain 1 cap, 0 goals

Alberto GORRIZ
16/02/58   Defender

87/88	Real Sociedad	37	6	CWC	4	-
88/89	Real Sociedad	36	1	UC	8	-
89/90	Real Sociedad	38	2			
90/91	Real Sociedad	37	-	UC	4	-
91/92	Real Sociedad	36	1			

★ Spain 12 caps, 1 goal

Augustin GAJATE
22/03/58   Defender

87/88	Real Sociedad	38	2	CWC	4	1
88/89	Real Sociedad	36	1	UC	7	-
89/90	Real Sociedad	34	1			
90/91	Real Sociedad	36	-	UC	4	1
91/92	Real Sociedad	17	-			

Iñaki ALABA
14/11/66   Defender

87/88	Real Sociedad	1	-	
88/89	Real Sociedad	5	-	
89/90	Real Sociedad	-	-	
91/92	Real Sociedad	23	-	

OCEANO Andrade (Por)
29/07/62   Midfield

87/88	Sporting CP (Por)	34	2	CWC	6	-
88/89	Sporting CP (Por)	34	4	UC	4	1
89/90	Sporting CP (Por)	27	1	UC	1	-
90/91	Sporting CP (Por)	35	5	UC	10	-
91/92	Real Sociedad	34	7			

★ Portugal 16 caps, 2 goals

Miguel Angel FUENTES
06/08/64   Midfield

87/88	Real Sociedad	24	-	CWC	1	-
88/89	Real Sociedad	24	2	UC	5	1
89/90	Real Sociedad	32	1			
90/91	Real Sociedad	33	-	UC	4	-
91/92	Real Sociedad	37	1			

Bittor ALKIZA
26/10/70   Midfield

91/92	Real Sociedad	26	3	

LUIS PEREZ
09/02/71   Midfield

90/91	Real Sociedad	13	-	
91/92	Real Sociedad	24	2	

SPAIN

FIVE YEAR RECORD
Birthdate/Playing position LEAGUE EURO CUPS
Apps Gls Cup Apps Gls

FIVE YEAR RECORD
Birthdate/Playing position LEAGUE EURO CUPS
Apps Gls Cup Apps Gls

José María LUMBRERAS
06/01/61   Midfield

		Apps	Gls	Cup	Apps	Gls
87/88	Real Zaragoza	29	2			
88/89	Real Zaragoza	33	-			
89/90	Real Sociedad	10	-			
90/91	Real Sociedad	18	-	UC	4	1
91/92	Real Sociedad	28	1			

José Luis AGUIRRE
14/09/65   Midfield

		Apps	Gls
87/88	Sestao Sport	Div 2	
88/89	Real Sociedad	12	-
89/90	Real Sociedad	10	-
90/91	Real Sociedad	19	-
91/92	Real Sociedad	17	-

CARLOS XAVIER (Por)
26/01/62   Midfield

		Apps	Gls	Cup	Apps	Gls
87/88	Sporting CP (Por)	19	-	CWC	3	-
88/89	Sporting CP (Por)	18	1	UC	2	-
89/90	Sporting CP (Por)	24	1	UC	1	-
90/91	Sporting CP (Por)	35	-	UC	9	1
91/92	Real Sociedad	31	7			

★ Portugal 8 caps, 0 goals

Meho KODRO (Yug)
12/01/67   Forward

		Apps	Gls	Cup	Apps	Gls
87/88	Velez Mostar (Yug)	22	3	UC	2	1
88/89	Velez Mostar (Yug)	15	2	UC	5	-
89/90	Velez Mostar (Yug)	31	18			
90/91	Velez Mostar (Yug)	34	13			
91/92	Velez Mostar (Yug)	6	5			
	Real Sociedad	24	13			

★ Yugoslavia 2 caps, 0 goals

Mikel LOINAZ
28/03/67   Forward

		Apps	Gls	Cup	Apps	Gls
88/89	Real Sociedad	20	8	UC	5	4
89/90	Real Sociedad	7	1			
90/91	Real Sociedad	7	1	UC	2	-
91/92	Real Sociedad	9	1			

José Javier BELLOSO
14/04/67   Forward

		Apps	Gls
91/92	Real Sociedad	4	-

EUROPEAN HONOURS
none

EUROPEAN CUPS RECORD

	Entries	Pd	W	D	L	F	A
Champions' Cup	2	10	4	2	4	11	9
Cup-winners' Cup	1	4	1	3	0	3	1
UEFA/Fairs' Cup	6	26	9	7	10	28	39
Total - All 3 Cups	9	40	14	12	14	42	49

REAL ZARAGOZA

Andoni CEDRUN
05/06/60   Goalkeeper

Five Year Record	League Apps	Gls	Cup	Apps	Gls
87/88 Real Zaragoza	36	-			
88/89 Real Zaragoza	-	-			
89/90 Real Zaragoza	4	-			
90/91 Real Zaragoza	30	-			
91/92 Real Zaragoza	38	-			

MARIO García
29/03/68   Goalkeeper

Five Year Record	League Apps	Gls	Cup	Apps	Gls
90/91 Real Zaragoza	-	-			
91/92 Real Zaragoza	2	-			

Jesús Angel SOLANA
25/12/64   Defender

Five Year Record	League Apps	Gls	Cup	Apps	Gls
87/88 Real Madrid	22	-	CC	4	-
88/89 Real Madrid	21	1	CC	4	-
89/90 Real Madrid	21	-	CC	1	-
90/91 Real Madrid	26	-	CC	5	-
91/92 Real Zaragoza	26	1			

★ Spain 1 cap, 0 goals

Andreas BREHME (Ger)
09/11/60   Defender

Five Year Record	League Apps	Gls	Cup	Apps	Gls
87/88 FC Bayern München (Ger)	28	3	CC	6	1
88/89 Internazionale (Ita)	31	3	UC	6	-
89/90 Internazionale (Ita)	32	6	CC	2	-
90/91 Internazionale (Ita)	23	1	#UC	9	-
91/92 Internazionale (Ita)	30	1	UC	2	-

★ Germany 74 caps, 8 goals

Narciso JULIA
24/05/63   Defender

Five Year Record	League Apps	Gls	Cup	Apps	Gls
87/88 Real Zaragoza	15	-			
88/89 Real Zaragoza	29	-			
89/90 Real Zaragoza	34	-	UC	4	-
90/91 Real Zaragoza	35	1			
91/92 Real Zaragoza	26	-			

ESTEBAN Gutiérrez
20/10/60   Defender

Five Year Record	League Apps	Gls	Cup	Apps	Gls
87/88 Sporting Gijón	30	-			
88/89 Real Madrid	29	-	CC	5	-
89/90 Real Madrid	7	-			
90/91 Real Zaragoza	33	-			
91/92 Real Zaragoza	34	-			

Alberto BELSUE
02/03/68   Defender

Five Year Record	League Apps	Gls	Cup	Apps	Gls
88/89 Real Zaragoza	16	1			
89/90 Real Zaragoza	30	-	UC	2	-
90/91 Real Zaragoza	24	1			
91/92 Real Zaragoza	15	-			

Javier AGUADO
05/06/68   Defender

Five Year Record	League Apps	Gls	Cup	Apps	Gls
88/89 CE Sabadell FC	Div 2				
89/90 CE Sabadell FC	Div 2				
90/91 Real Zaragoza	30	-			
91/92 Real Zaragoza	33	1			

Dario FRANCO (Arg)
17/01/69   Midfield

Five Year Record	League Apps	Gls	Cup	Apps	Gls
90/91 Newell's Old Boys (Arg)					
91/92 Real Zaragoza	36	3			

★ Argentina

José GAY
10/12/65   Midfield

Five Year Record	League Apps	Gls	Cup	Apps	Gls
87/88 Castilla CF	Div 2				
88/89 RCD Español	17	2			
89/90 RCD Español	Div 2				
90/91 RCD Español	36	6			
91/92 Real Zaragoza	34	8			

SPAIN

FIVE YEAR RECORD	LEAGUE		EURO CUPS		
Birthdate/Playing position	Apps	Gls	Cup	Apps	Gls

Dorin MATEUT (Rom)
05/08/65 Midfield

		Apps	Gls		Apps	Gls
87/88	Dinamo Bucuresti (Rom)	31	17	CWC	2	-
88/89	Dinamo Bucuresti (Rom)	34	43	CWC	6	2
89/90	Dinamo Bucuresti (Rom)	22	9	CWC	8	4
90/91	Dinamo Bucuresti (Rom)	8	5	CC	2	2
	Real Zaragoza	29	7			
91/92	Real Zaragoza	29	3			

★ Romania 56 caps, 10 goals

Ignacio LIZARRALDE
06/08/66 Midfield

		Apps	Gls		Apps	Gls
87/88	Athletic Bilbao	27	-			
88/89	Athletic Bilbao	21	-	UC	4	-
89/90	Athletic Bilbao	16	-			
90/91	Real Zaragoza	31	-			
91/92	Real Zaragoza	17	-			

GARCIA SANJUAN
22/08/71 Midfield

		Apps	Gls
90/91	Real Zaragoza	7	-
91/92	Real Zaragoza	30	1

Gustavo POYET (Uru)
15/11/67 Midfield

		Apps	Gls
89/90	Bellavista (Uru)		
90/91	Real Zaragoza	31	7
91/92	Real Zaragoza	33	3

MOISES García
10/07/71 Forward

		Apps	Gls
91/92	Real Zaragoza	11	2

Francisco HIGUERA
03/01/65 Forward

		Apps	Gls		Apps	Gls
87/88	RCD Mallorca	37	8			
88/89	Real Zaragoza	15	6			
89/90	Real Zaragoza	36	10	UC	4	-
90/91	Real Zaragoza	37	5			
91/92	Real Zaragoza	37	8			

★ Spain 1 cap, 0 goals

FIVE YEAR RECORD	LEAGUE		EURO CUPS		
Birthdate/Playing position	Apps	Gls	Cup	Apps	Gls

Manuel PEÑA
18/10/65 Forward

		Apps	Gls		Apps	Gls
87/88	Real Valladolid	29	8			
88/89	Real Valladolid	34	5			
89/90	Real Valladolid	24	2	CWC	2	-
90/91	Real Zaragoza	15	-			
91/92	Real Zaragoza	13	3			

Miguel PARDEZA
08/02/65 Forward

		Apps	Gls		Apps	Gls
87/88	Real Zaragoza	28	11			
88/89	Real Zaragoza	20	4			
89/90	Real Zaragoza	37	15	UC	4	2
90/91	Real Zaragoza	37	13			
91/92	Real Zaragoza	22	6			

★ Spain 5 caps, 0 goals

EUROPEAN HONOURS
Fairs' Cup - (1) 1964.

EUROPEAN CUPS RECORD

	Entries	Pd	W	D	L	F	A
Champions' Cup	none						
Cup-winners' Cup	3	22	10	5	7	36	26
UEFA/Fairs' Cup	8	48	26	6	16	94	71
Total - All 3 Cups	11	70	36	11	23	130	97

IFK NORRKÖPING

FIVE YEAR RECORD	LEAGUE		EURO CUPS		
Birthdate/Playing position	Apps	Gls	Cup	Apps	Gls

Lars ERIKSSON
21/09/65   Goalkeeper

87	Hammarby IF	22	-			
88	Hammarby IF	19	-			
89	IFK Norrköping	22	-			
90	IFK Norrköping	26	-	UC	2	-
91	IFK Norrköping	28	-	CWC	4	-

★ Sweden 8 caps, 0 goals

Anders JONANDER
26/01/73   Goalkeeper

Sulo VAATTOVAARA
18/07/62   Defender

87	Hammarby IF	22	2			
88	IFK Norrköping	22	3	CWC	2	-
89	IFK Norrköping	22	1			
90	IFK Norrköping	26	1	UC	2	-
91	IFK Norrköping	28	2	CWC	4	1

★ Sweden 6 caps, 0 goals

Jan KALÉN
19/09/62   Defender

87	IFK Norrköping	20	1			
88	IFK Norrköping	21	1	CWC	2	-
89	IFK Norrköping	15	-			
90	IFK Norrköping	25	-	UC	2	-
91	IFK Norrköping	21	-	CWC	4	-

Jonas LIND
06/06/62   Defender

87	IFK Norrköping	21	3			
88	IFK Norrköping	21	1	CWC	2	-
89	IFK Norrköping	22	3			
90	IFK Norrköping	24	2	UC	2	-
91	IFK Norrköping	27	1	CWC	4	-

FIVE YEAR RECORD	LEAGUE		EURO CUPS		
Birthdate/Playing position	Apps	Gls	Cup	Apps	Gls

Slobodan MAROVIC (Yug)
13/08/64   Defender

87/88	Crvena zvezda Beograd (Yug)	30	1	UC	3	-
88/89	Crvena zvezda Beograd (Yug)	23	-	CC	1	-
89/90	Crvena zvezda Beograd (Yug)	27	2	UC	6	-
90/91	Crvena zvezda Beograd (Yug)	26	1	#CC	9	-

★ Yugoslavia 4 caps, 0 goals

Peter LÖNN
13/07/62   Defender

87	IFK Norrköping	21	2			
88	IFK Norrköping	22	7		.	
89	IFK Norrköping	11	1			
89/90	Neuchâtel Xamax FC (Sui)	35	5			
90/91	Neuchâtel Xamax FC (Sui)	19	2	CWC	1	-
91/92	Neuchâtel Xamax FC (Sui)	-	-			

★ Sweden 7 caps, 0 goals

Per BLOHM
10/02/67   Midfield

87	BK Forward	Div 2				
88	BK Forward	Div 2				
89	Örebro SK	18	2			
90	Örebro SK	24	3			
91	Örebro SK	27	1	UC	2	-

★ Sweden 1 cap, 0 goals

Göran BERGORT
14/02/68   Midfield

87	Falu BS	Div 3				
88	IK Brage	9	2	UC	2	-
89	IK Brage	22	4			
90	IK Brage	22	4			
91	IFK Norrköping	15	1	CWC	2	-

Yevgeny KUZNETSOV (Rus)
30/08/61   Midfield

87	Spartak Moskva (Urs)	17	-	UC	4	-
88	Spartak Moskva (Urs)	22	1	CC	3	-
89	Spartak Moskva (Urs)	26	2	UC	4	-
90	IFK Norrköping	26	2	UC	2	-
91	IFK Norrköping	13	2	CWC	3	-

SWEDEN

FIVE YEAR RECORD *Birthdate/Playing position*	LEAGUE Apps Gls	EURO CUPS Cup Apps Gls

Jonny RÖDLUND
22/12/71   Midfield

89	IFK Norrköping	16	3			
90	IFK Norrköping	23	-	UC	2	-
91	IFK Norrköping	25	4	CWC	4	-

★ Sweden 2 caps, 0 goals

Mikael HANSSON
15/03/68   Midfield

90	IFK Norrköping	1	-			
91	IFK Norrköping	19	4	CWC	4	-

Magnus SAMUELSSON
15/04/72   Midfield

90	IFK Norrköping	3	-			
91	IFK Norrköping	9	-	CWC	2	-

Tor-Arne FREDHEIM
05/11/62   Midfield

87	IFK Norrköping	17	3			
88	IFK Norrköping	22	2	CWC	2	-
89	IFK Norrköping	13	-			
90	IFK Norrköping	24	7	UC	2	-
91	IFK Norrköping	18	1			

Niklas KINDVALL
19/02/67   Forward

87	AIK	13	2	UC	2	1
88	AIK	21	-			
89	AIK	22	6			
90	AIK	20	5			
91	IFK Norrköping	20	5	CWC	4	1

★ Sweden 1 cap, 0 goals

Jens NILSSON
30/07/72   Forward

90	Kalmar FF	Div 2				
91	IFK Norrköping	7	1			

FIVE YEAR RECORD *Birthdate/Playing position*	LEAGUE Apps Gls	EURO CUPS Cup Apps Gls

Jan HELLSTRÖM
21/02/60   Forward

87	IFK Norrköping	21	7			
88	IFK Norrköping	19	13	CWC	2	1
89	IFK Norrköping	22	16			
90	IFK Norrköping	18	9	UC	2	1
91	IFK Norrköping	26	8	CWC	3	2

★ Sweden 6 caps, 0 goals

Patrik ANDERSSON
30/11/67   Forward

87	IFK Norrköping	9	3			
88	IFK Norrköping	17	3	CWC	2	1
89	IFK Norrköping	19	10			
90	IFK Norrköping	22	8	UC	2	-
91	IFK Norrköping	21	5	CWC	4	-

★ Sweden 1 cap, 0 goals

EUROPEAN HONOURS
none

EUROPEAN CUPS RECORD

	Entries	Pd	W	D	L	F	A
Champions' Cup	4	12	2	5	5	14	20
Cup-winners' Cup	4	14	6	2	6	23	17
UEFA/Fairs' Cup	4	12	3	5	4	12	14
Total - All 3 Cups	12	38	11	12	15	49	51

ÖREBRO SK

FIVE YEAR RECORD *Birthdate/Playing position*	LEAGUE Apps Gls	EURO CUPS Cup Apps Gls

Anders KARLSSON
27/04/63   Goalkeeper

87	Örebro SK	Div 2				
88	Örebro SK	Div 2				
89	Örebro SK	22	-			
90	Örebro SK	14	-			
91	Örebro SK	25	-	UC	1	-

Jonas LARSSON
23/07/69   Goalkeeper

Patrick MILLESKOG
14/01/66   Defender

91	Karlslunds IF	Div 3	

Lars ZETTERLUND
11/02/64   Defender

87	IFK Göteborg	18	1	UC	2	-
88	IFK Göteborg	22	5	CC	6	2
89	IFK Göteborg	13	1	UC	1	-
90	Örebro SK	24	2			
91	Örebro SK	10	-	UC	1	-

Magnus SKÖLDMARK
22/09/68   Defender

89	Örebro SK	21	1			
90	Örebro SK	23	3			
91	Örebro SK	28	1	UC	2	-

Tommy STÅHL
12/11/65   Defender

87	Örebro SK	Div 2				
88	Örebro SK	Div 2				
89	Örebro SK	-	-			
90	Örebro SK	14	-			
91	Örebro SK	24	1	UC	1	-

FIVE YEAR RECORD *Birthdate/Playing position*	LEAGUE Apps Gls	EURO CUPS Cup Apps Gls

Hlynur STÉFANSSON (Isl)
08/10/64   Midfield

87	ÍBV (Isl)	Div 2				
88	Víkingur (Isl)	18	-			
89	ÍBV (Isl)	Div 2				
90	ÍBV (Isl)	18	9			
91	ÍBV (Isl)	18	2			

★ Iceland 7 caps, 0 goals

Lennart SJÖGREN
21/11/65   Midfield

87	Västerås SK	Div 2				
88	Örebro SK	Div 2				
89	Örebro SK	19	3			
90	Örebro SK	19	3			
91	Örebro SK	24	2	UC	2	-

Magnus ERLINGMARK
08/07/68   Midfield

87	BK Forward	Div 2				
88	BK Forward	Div 2				
89	Örebro SK	22	2			
90	Örebro SK	24	2			
91	Örebro SK	27	4	UC	2	-

★ Sweden 17 caps, 1 goal

Mikael LINDGREN
26/09/69   Midfield

90	Gefle IF	Div 2	
91	Örebro SK	1	-

Mikael LINDKVIST
01/09/67   Midfield

89	Hammarby IF	Div 2	
90	Hammarby IF	20	2
91	Hammarby IF	Div 2	

SWEDEN

FIVE YEAR RECORD	LEAGUE		EURO CUPS		
Birthdate/Playing position	Apps	Gls	Cup	Apps	Gls

Hans HOLMQVIST
27/04/60   Midfield

		Apps	Gls	Cup	Apps	Gls
87	Hammarby IF	9	1			
87/88	BSC Young Boys (Sui)	28	10	CWC	6	-
88/89	Cesena (Ita)	19	1			
89/90	Cesena (Ita)	1	-			
91	Örebro SK	24	5	UC	2	-

★ Sweden 27 caps, 4 goals

Christer FURSTH
06/07/70   Midfield

		Apps	Gls	Cup	Apps	Gls
88	Örebro SK	Div 2				
89	Örebro SK	17	1			
90	Örebro SK	14	-			
91	Örebro SK	26	4	UC	2	-

★ Sweden 3 caps, 0 goals

Richard LARSSON
09/04/72   Midfield

		Apps	Gls	Cup	Apps	Gls
91	Örebro SK	20	-			

Pär MILLQVIST
24/05/67   Midfield

		Apps	Gls	Cup	Apps	Gls
87	IFK Göteborg	2	-			
88	IFK Göteborg	5	2	CC	3	-
89	Örebro SK	22	2			
90	Örebro SK	21	2			
91	Örebro SK	10	-	UC	1	-

Miroslaw KUBISZTAL (Pol)
12/02/62   Forward

		Apps	Gls	Cup	Apps	Gls
87/88	GKS Katowice (Pol)	29	5	UC	2	-
88/89	GKS Katowice (Pol)	29	11	UC	2	1
89/90	GKS Katowice (Pol)	28	5	UC	2	1
90/91	GKS Katowice (Pol)	15	4	UC	4	-
91	Örebro SK	27	8	UC	2	-

★ Poland 1 cap, 0 goals

FIVE YEAR RECORD	LEAGUE		EURO CUPS		
Birthdate/Playing position	Apps	Gls	Cup	Apps	Gls

Mikael ANDERSSON
21/03/71   Forward

		Apps	Gls	Cup	Apps	Gls
89	Örebro SK	1	-			
90	Örebro SK	-	-			
91	Örebro SK	10	1	UC	1	-

Jörgen DUNBERG
11/02/65   Forward

		Apps	Gls	Cup	Apps	Gls
89	Örebro SK	1	-			
90	Örebro SK	14	2			
91	BK Forward	Div 2				

EUROPEAN HONOURS
none

EUROPEAN CUPS RECORD

	Entries	Pd	W	D	L	F	A
Champions' Cup	none						
Cup-winners' Cup	none						
UEFA/Fairs' Cup	1	2	0	0	2	0	4
Total - All 3 Cups	1	2	0	0	2	0	4

NEUCHATEL XAMAX FC

FIVE YEAR RECORD	LEAGUE		EURO CUPS		
Birthdate/Playing position	Apps	Gls	Cup	Apps	Gls

Joël CORMINBOEUF
16/03/64   Goalkeeper

87/88	Neuchâtel Xamax FC	30	-	CC	3	-
88/89	Neuchâtel Xamax FC	20	-	CC	3	-
89/90	Neuchâtel Xamax FC	-	-			
90/91	Neuchâtel Xamax FC	3	-			
	FC Zürich	Div 2				
91/92	Neuchâtel Xamax FC	25	-	UC	1	-

★ Switzerland 6 caps, 0 goals

Florent DELAY
23/08/71   Goalkeeper

91/92	Neuchâtel Xamax FC	12	-	UC	5	-

Franҫis FROIDEVAUX
26/04/71   Defender

90/91	Neuchâtel Xamax FC	11	-	CWC	1	-
91/92	Neuchâtel Xamax FC	10	-	UC	3	-

Daniel FASEL
03/05/67   Defender

87/88	Neuchâtel Xamax FC	32	3	UC	3	-
88/89	Neuchâtel Xamax FC	23	1	CC	3	-
89/90	Neuchâtel Xamax FC	24	-			
90/91	FC Wettingen	16	1			
91/92	Neuchâtel Xamax FC	14	-	UC	3	-

Walter FERNANDEZ (Esp)
20/08/65   Defender

87/88	Lausanne-Sports	35	-			
88/89	Lausanne-Sports	19	1			
89/90	Lausanne-Sports	26	-			
90/91	Neuchâtel Xamax FC	36	2	CWC	2	-
91/92	Neuchâtel Xamax FC	19	2	UC	5	-

Hany RAMZY (Egy)
10/03/69   Defender

89/90	Al Ahly (Egy)					
90/91	Neuchâtel Xamax FC	11	1			
91/92	Neuchâtel Xamax FC	28	3	UC	6	-

★ Egypt

Ronald ROTHENBÜHLER
15/08/71   Defender

89/90	Neuchâtel Xamax FC	2	-			
90/91	Neuchâtel Xamax FC	-	-			
91/92	Neuchâtel Xamax FC	9	-	UC	1	-

Robert LÜTHI
12/07/58   Defender

87/88	Neuchâtel Xamax FC	31	15	CC	2	1
88/89	Neuchâtel Xamax FC	29	14	CC	4	3
89/90	Neuchâtel Xamax FC	31	2			
90/91	Neuchâtel Xamax FC	17	-	CWC	1	-
91/92	Neuchâtel Xamax FC	11	1	UC	5	-

★ Switzerland 3 caps, 0 goals

Philippe CRAVERO
02/09/70   Midfield

90/91	Neuchâtel Xamax FC	1	-			
91/92	Neuchâtel Xamax FC	14	1			

Guerino GOTTARDI
18/12/70   Midfield

89/90	BSC Young Boys	4	-			
90/91	BSC Young Boys	34	1			
91/92	Neuchâtel Xamax FC	29	2	UC	1	-

Régis ROTHENBÜHLER
11/10/70   Midfield

88/89	Neuchâtel Xamax FC	1	-			
89/90	Neuchâtel Xamax FC	11	-			
90/91	Neuchâtel Xamax FC	28	1	CWC	2	-
91/92	Neuchâtel Xamax FC	26	1	UC	5	-

★ Switzerland 2 caps, 0 goals

Philippe PERRET
17/10/61   Midfield

87/88	Neuchâtel Xamax FC	35	1	CC	4	-
88/89	Neuchâtel Xamax FC	27	-	CC	4	-
89/90	Neuchâtel Xamax FC	33	-			
90/91	Neuchâtel Xamax FC	32	1	CWC	2	-
91/92	Neuchâtel Xamax FC	33	1	UC	5	-

★ Switzerland 13 caps, 0 goals

SWITZERLAND

FIVE YEAR RECORD / Birthdate/Playing position — LEAGUE Apps Gls — EURO CUPS Cup Apps Gls

José ZÉ MARIA (Bra)
14/08/68   Midfield

		Apps	Gls	Cup	Apps	Gls
89/90	Neuchâtel Xamax FC	10	2			
90/91	Neuchâtel Xamax FC	28	1			
91/92	Neuchâtel Xamax FC	20	5	UC	2	-

Admir SMAJIC (Yug)
07/09/63   Midfield

		Apps	Gls	Cup	Apps	Gls
87/88	Partizan Beograd (Yug)	27	-	UC	2	-
88/89	Neuchâtel Xamax FC	31	2	CC	4	-
88/89	Neuchâtel Xamax FC	31	8			
89/90	Neuchâtel Xamax FC	14	3			
91/92	Neuchâtel Xamax FC	6	2			

★ Yugoslavia 5 caps, 0 goals

Beat SUTTER
12/12/62   Midfield

		Apps	Gls	Cup	Apps	Gls
87/88	Neuchâtel Xamax FC	34	13	CC	4	3
88/89	Neuchâtel Xamax FC	27	10	CC	2	-
89/90	Neuchâtel Xamax FC	17	5			
90/91	Neuchâtel Xamax FC	33	9	CWC	2	2
91/92	Neuchâtel Xamax FC	35	9	UC	6	-

★ Switzerland 56 caps, 12 goals

Christophe BONVIN
14/04/65   Forward

		Apps	Gls	Cup	Apps	Gls
87/88	FC Sion	21	4	UC	2	-
88/89	Servette FC Genève	24	4	UC	4	-
89/90	Servette FC Genève	22	6			
90/91	Neuchâtel Xamax FC	36	8	CWC	2	-
91/92	Neuchâtel Xamax FC	35	11	UC	6	1

★ Switzerland 27 caps, 7 goals

Frédéric CHASSOT
31/03/69   Forward

		Apps	Gls	Cup	Apps	Gls
87/88	Neuchâtel Xamax FC	23	6	CC	1	-
88/89	Neuchâtel Xamax FC	22	4	CC	2	-
89/90	Neuchâtel Xamax FC	34	11			
90/91	Neuchâtel Xamax FC	33	6	CWC	2	-
91/92	Neuchâtel Xamax FC	27	8	UC	4	-

★ Switzerland 8 caps, 2 goals

Giuseppe MANFREDA (Ita)
04/01/69   Forward

		Apps	Gls	Cup	Apps	Gls
87/88	FC Lugano	Div 2				
88/89	FC Lugano	16	2			
89/90	FC Lugano	27	11			
90/91	FC Lugano	34	7			
91/92	FC Sion	33	10	CWC	4	-

EUROPEAN HONOURS
none

EUROPEAN CUPS RECORD

	Entries	Pd	W	D	L	F	A
Champions' Cup	2	8	4	0	4	14	13
Cup-winners' Cup	1	2	0	2	0	2	2
UEFA/Fairs' Cup	5	28	12	9	7	41	28
Total - All 3 Cups	8	38	16	11	11	57	43

GRASSHOPPER-CLUB ZÜRICH

FIVE YEAR RECORD	LEAGUE		EURO CUPS		
Birthdate/Playing position	Apps	Gls	Cup	Apps	Gls

Martin BRUNNER
23/04/63 Goalkeeper

87/88	Grasshopper-Club Zürich	36	-			
88/89	Grasshopper-Club Zürich	36	-	CWC	2	-
89/90	Grasshopper-Club Zürich	36	-	CWC	6	-
90/91	Grasshopper-Club Zürich	36	-	CC	2	-
91/92	Grasshopper-Club Zürich	27	-	CC	2	-

★ Switzerland 33 caps, 0 goals

Pascal ZUBERBÜHLER
08/01/71 Goalkeeper

91/92	Grasshopper-Club Zürich	9	-

Urs MEIER
07/07/61 Defender

87/88	AC Bellinzona	14	1			
88/89	AC Bellinzona	29	1			
89/90	Grasshopper-Club Zürich	34	1	CWC	6	-
90/91	Grasshopper-Club Zürich	33	-	CC	2	-
91/92	Grasshopper-Club Zürich	33	-	CC	2	-

Mats GREN (Swe)
20/12/63 Defender

87/88	Grasshopper-Club Zürich	30	7	UC	1	-
88/89	Grasshopper-Club Zürich	33	6	CWC	2	-
89/90	Grasshopper-Club Zürich	29	3	CWC	6	3
90/91	Grasshopper-Club Zürich	34	4	CC	2	-
91/92	Grasshopper-Club Zürich	31	-	CC	2	-

★ Sweden 22 caps, 0 goals

Marcel KOLLER
11/11/60 Defender

87/88	Grasshopper-Club Zürich	31	-	UC	2	-
88/89	Grasshopper-Club Zürich	23	2			
89/90	Grasshopper-Club Zürich	33	1	CWC	6	-
90/91	Grasshopper-Club Zürich	27	1	CC	2	-
91/92	Grasshopper-Club Zürich	1	-			

★ Switzerland 46 caps, 2 goals

FIVE YEAR RECORD	LEAGUE		EURO CUPS		
Birthdate/Playing position	Apps	Gls	Cup	Apps	Gls

Harald GÄMPERLE
11/05/68 Defender

87/88	FC St. Gallen	29	1			
88/89	FC St. Gallen	4	-			
89/90	FC St. Gallen	33	2			
90/91	FC St. Gallen	29	-	CC	2	-
91/92	Grasshopper-Club Zürich	20	2			

★ Switzerland 3 caps, 0 goals

Georgios NEMTSOUDIS (Gre)
01/01/73 Defender

89/90	Grasshopper-Club Zürich	17	-	CWC	4	-
90/91	Grasshopper-Club Zürich	21	-			
91/92	Grasshopper-Club Zürich	26	2	CC	2	1

Alain SUTTER
22/01/68 Midfield

87/88	BSC Young Boys	28	5	CWC	6	-
88/89	Grasshopper-Club Zürich	33	5	CWC	2	-
89/90	Grasshopper-Club Zürich	29	2	CWC	6	-
90/91	Grasshopper-Club Zürich	34	7	CC	2	-
91/92	Grasshopper-Club Zürich	34	10	CC	2	-

★ Switzerland 29 caps, 3 goals

Thomas BICKEL
06/10/63 Midfield

87/88	FC Zürich	20	2			
88/89	Grasshopper-Club Zürich	24	2			
89/90	Grasshopper-Club Zürich	30	2	CWC	6	-
90/91	Grasshopper-Club Zürich	33	1	CC	2	-
91/92	Grasshopper-Club Zürich	35	7	CC	2	-

★ Switzerland 32 caps, 2 goals

Ciriaco SFORZA
02/03/70 Midfield

87/88	Grasshopper-Club Zürich	29	3			
88/89	Grasshopper-Club Zürich	16	1	CWC	2	-
89/90	FC Aarau	22	3			
90/91	Grasshopper-Club Zürich	28	1	CC	1	-
91/92	Grasshopper-Club Zürich	26	4	CC	2	-

★ Switzerland 6 caps, 0 goals

SWITZERLAND

FIVE YEAR RECORD *Birthdate/Playing position*	LEAGUE Apps	Gls	EURO CUPS Cup	Apps	Gls
Heinz HERMANN					
28/03/58 Midfielder					
87/88 Neuchâtel Xamax FC	35	12	CC	4	1
88/89 Neuchâtel Xamax FC	31	4	CC	4	1
89/90 Neuchâtel Xamax FC	13	3			
Servette FC Genève	8	1			
90/91 Servette FC Genève	34	2			
91/92 Servette FC Genève	35	5			

★ Switzerland 117 caps, 14 goals

Sigurdur GRÉTARSSON (Isl)					
02/05/62 Midfield					
87/88 FC Luzern	24	8			
88/89 FC Luzern	29	8			
89/90 FC Luzern	31	9	CC	2	-
90/91 Grasshopper-Club Zürich	22	2	CC	2	-
91/92 Grasshopper-Club Zürich	27	3			

★ Iceland 43 caps, 8 goals

Adrian DE VICENTE (Arg)					
25/07/64 Forward					
88/89 Platense (Arg)					
89/90 Grasshopper-Club Zürich	30	12	CWC	3	-
90/91 Grasshopper-Club Zürich	30	15	CC	2	-
91/92 Grasshopper-Club Zürich	11	1			

Peter KÖZLE (Ger)					
18/11/67 Forward					
87/88 BSC Young Boys	7	-			
88/89 BSC Young Boys	32	17			
89/90 BSC Young Boys	30	10			
90/91 Grasshopper-Club Zürich	28	7	CC	2	2
91/92 Grasshopper-Club Zürich	18	12	CC	2	-

FIVE YEAR RECORD *Birthdate/Playing position*	LEAGUE Apps	Gls	EURO CUPS Cup	Apps	Gls
Mario CANTALUPPi					
11/04/74 Forward					
90/91 Grasshopper-Club Zürich	8	1			
91/92 Grasshopper-Club Zürich	25	1	CC	2	-

Ramon VEGA					
14/06/71 Forward					
90/91 Grasshopper-Club Zürich	3	-	CC	1	-
91/92 Grasshopper-Club Zürich	34	2	CC	2	-

André WIEDERKEHR					
20/04/70 Forward					
88/89 Grasshopper-Club Zürich	1	-			
89/90 Grasshopper-Club Zürich	12	2	CWC	4	1
90/91 Grasshopper-Club Zürich	11	2	CC	1	-
91/92 Grasshopper-Club Zürich	21	2	CC	2	-

ELBER de Souza Giovane (Bra)					
23/07/72 Forward					
90/91 Londrina (Bra)					
91/92 Grasshopper-Club Zürich	21	9			

EUROPEAN HONOURS
none

EUROPEAN CUPS RECORD

	Entries	Pd	W	D	L	F	A
Champions' Cup	8	26	6	6	14	43	48
Cup-winners' Cup	2	8	2	2	4	9	9
UEFA/Fairs' Cup	**12**	**50**	**22**	**6**	**22**	**84**	**75**
Total - All 3 Cups	22	84	30	14	40	136	132

FENERBAHÇE

FIVE YEAR RECORD	LEAGUE		EURO CUPS		
Birthdate/Playing position	Apps	Gls	Cup	Apps	Gls

ENGIN Ipekoglu
07/06/61   Goalkeeper

87/88	Sakaryaspor	18	-		
88/89	Sakaryaspor	29	-	CWC	4	-
89/90	Besiktas	34	-	CWC	2	-
90/91	Besiktas	28	-	CC	2	-
91/92	Fenerbahçe	28	-		

★ Turkey 16 caps, 0 goals

NESET Muharremoglu
20/04/55   Goalkeeper

87/88	Sakaryaspor	18	-
88/89	Sakaryaspor	6	-
89/90	Fenerbahçe	2	-
90/91	Fenerbahçe	1	-
91/92	Fenerbahçe	3	-

Miroslav TANJGA (Yug)
22/07/64   Defender

88/89	Vojvodina Novi Sad (Yug)	14	1			
89/90	Vojvodina Novi Sad (Yug)	33	4	CC	2	1
90/91	Vojvodina Novi Sad	32	4			
91/92	Crvena zvezda Beograd (Yug)	6*	-*	CC	7	1

* first half of season figures only.

AHMET SUPHI Evke
26/06/65   Defender

87/88	Bursaspor	12	-			
88/89	Bursaspor	32	1			
89/90	Bursaspor	31	1			
90/91	Fenerbahçe	10	-	UC	2	-
91/92	Fenerbahçe	15	-			

SEMIH Yuvakuran
01/09/63   Defender

87/88	Galatasaray	37	1	CC	2	-
88/89	Galatasaray	32	1	CC	8	-
89/90	Galatasaray	26	2	UC	1	-
90/91	Fenerbahçe	20	-	UC	4	-
91/92	Fenerbahçe	26	-			

★ Turkey 20 caps, 0 goals

ISMAIL Kartal
15/06/61   Defender

87/88	Fenerbahçe	35	8			
88/89	Fenerbahçe	24	1			
89/90	Fenerbahçe	25	-	CC	2	-
90/91	Fenerbahçe	19	2	UC	2	1
91/92	Fenerbahçe	15	-			

Dzoni NOVAK (Slo)
04/09/69   Defender

88/89	Olimpija Ljubljana (Yug)	Div 2				
89/90	Olimpija Ljubljana (Yug)	30	2			
90/91	Partizan Beograd (Yug)	6	-			
91/92	Partizan Beograd (Yug)	14*	3*	UC	2	-

★ Yugoslavia 4 caps, 0 goals
* first half of season figures only.

MÜJDAT Yetkiner
16/11/61   Midfield

87/88	Fenerbahçe	19	2			
88/89	Fenerbahçe	30	-			
89/90	Fenerbahçe	29	1	CC	2	-
90/91	Fenerbahçe	25	-	UC	3	1
91/92	Fenerbahçe	28	-			

TURAN Sofuoglu
19/08/65   Midfield

87/88	Sakaryaspor	35	3			
88/89	Fenerbahçe	26	9			
89/90	Fenerbahçe	13	1			
90/91	Fenerbahçe	21	5	UC	2	1
91/92	Fenerbahçe	27	4			

★ Turkey 7 caps, 0 goals

HAKAN Tecimer
06/01/67   Midfield

87/88	Rizespor	28	5			
88/89	Fenerbahçe	29	5			
89/90	Fenerbahçe	28	5	CC	2	1
90/91	Fenerbahçe	15	3	UC	2	-
91/92	Fenerbahçe	13	1			

★ Turkey 3 caps, 0 goals

TURKEY

FIVE YEAR RECORD	LEAGUE		EURO CUPS		
Birthdate/Playing position	Apps	Gls	Cup	Apps	Gls

OGUZ Çetin
15/02/63   Midfield

		Apps	Gls		Apps	Gls
87/88	Fenerbahçe	35	6			
88/89	Fenerbahçe	32	10			
89/90	Fenerbahçe	34	14	CC	2	1
90/91	Fenerbahçe	26	6	UC	4	-
91/92	Fenerbahçe	29	3			

★ Turkey 26 caps, 2 goals

ÜMIT Birol
26/03/63   Midfield

		Apps	Gls			
89/90	Altay	19	6			
90/91	Altay	Div 2				
91/92	Fenerbahçe	28	2			

★ Turkey 2 caps, 0 goals

SENOL Çorlu
03/02/61   Midfield

		Apps	Gls		Apps	Gls
87/88	Fenerbahçe	34	4			
88/89	Fenerbahçe	18	-			
89/90	Fenerbahçe	32	16	CC	2	-
90/91	Fenerbahçe	25	1	UC	3	1
91/92	Fenerbahçe	8	-			

SERCAN Gorgülü
15/02/60   Midfield

		Apps	Gls			
87/88	Sariyer	33	9			
88/89	Sariyer	31	10			
89/90	Sariyer	31	8			
90/91	Fenerbahçe	17	5			
91/92	Fenerbahçe	5	-			

TANJU Çolak
10/11/63   Forward

		Apps	Gls		Apps	Gls
87/88	Galatasaray	38	39	CC	2	1
88/89	Galatasaray	34	27	CC	6	5
89/90	Galatasaray	24	19			
90/91	Galatasaray	28	31			
91/92	Fenerbahçe	30	23			

★ Turkey 31 caps, 10 goals

FIVE YEAR RECORD	LEAGUE		EURO CUPS		
Birthdate/Playing position	Apps	Gls	Cup	Apps	Gls

Stanimir STOILOV (Bul)
13/02/67   Forward

		Apps	Gls		Apps	Gls
89/90	Khaskovo (Bul)	Div 2				
90/91	Levski Sofia (Bul)	30	11			
91/92	Levski Sofia (Bul)	25	7	CWC	1	-

AYKUT Kocaman
05/04/65   Forward

		Apps	Gls		Apps	Gls
87/88	Sakaryaspor	28	16			
88/89	Fenerbahçe	34	29			
89/90	Fenerbahçe	31	10	CC	2	-
90/91	Fenerbahçe	20	13	UC	4	1
91/92	Fenerbahçe	25	26			

★ Turkey 3 caps, 0 goals

RIDVAN Dilmen
15/08/62   Forward

		Apps	Gls		Apps	Gls
87/88	Fenerbahçe	32	6			
88/89	Fenerbahçe	34	19			
89/90	Fenerbahçe	8	1	CC	1	-
90/91	Fenerbahçe	13	2	UC	2	-
91/92	Fenerbahçe	7	3			

★ Turkey 24 caps, 5 goals

EUROPEAN HONOURS
none

EUROPEAN CUPS RECORD

	Entries	Pd	W	D	L	F	A
Champions' Cup	12	33	9	4	20	30	70
Cup-winners' Cup	2	9	3	1	5	11	11
UEFA/Fairs' Cup	**8**	**20**	**6**	**2**	**12**	**21**	**37**
Total - All 3 Cups	22	62	18	7	37	62	118

GALATASARY

FIVE YEAR RECORD	LEAGUE		EURO CUPS		
Birthdate/Playing position	Apps	Gls	Cup	Apps	Gls

HAYRETTIN Demirbas
26/06/63   Goalkeeper

87/88	Galatasaray	5	-		
88/89	Galatasaray	6	-		
89/90	Galatasaray	5	-		
90/91	Galatasaray	29	-		
91/92	Galatasaray	27	-	CWC	6	-

★ Turkey 9 caps, 0 goals

NEZIHI Bologlu
04/08/64   Goalkeeper

88/89	Gençlerbirligi	Div 2			
89/90	Gençlerbirligi	25	-		
90/91	Galatasaray	1	-		
91/92	Galatasaray	4	-		

BÜLENT Korkmaz
24/11/68   Defender

88/89	Galatasaray	11	-	CC	7	-
89/90	Galatasaray	19	-	UC	2	-
90/91	Galatasaray	30	2		
91/92	Galatasaray	27	3	CWC	5	-

★ Turkey 13 caps, 0 goals

YUSUF Altintas
07/08/61   Defender

87/88	Galatasaray	27	2	CC	2	-
88/89	Galatasaray	20	3	CC	4	-
89/90	Galatasaray	15	-	UC	1	-
90/91	Galatasaray	23	-		
91/92	Galatasaray	19	3	CWC	5	1

★ Turkey 29 caps, 2 goals

TUGAY Kerimoglu
24/08/68   Defender

87/88	Galatasaray	4	-		
88/89	Galatasaray	16	-	CC	1	-
89/90	Galatasaray	23	-	UC	2	-
90/91	Galatasaray	12	-		
91/92	Galatasaray	26	3	CWC	5	-

★ Turkey 13 caps, 0 goals

FIVE YEAR RECORD	LEAGUE		EURO CUPS		
Birthdate/Playing position	Apps	Gls	Cup	Apps	Gls

ISMAIL Demiriz
01/04/62   Defender

87/88	Galatasaray	33	1	CC	1	-
88/89	Galatasaray	26	2	CC	8	-
89/90	Galatasaray	26	-	UC	1	-
90/91	Galatasaray	22	1		
91/92	Galatasaray	30	1	CWC	5	-

★ Turkey 25 caps, 0 goals

HAMZA Hamzaoglu
01/01/70   Defender

90/91	Izmirspor	Div 2			
91/92	Galatasaray	25	3	CWC	3	-

ERHAN Önal
16/12/57   Defender

87/88	Galatasaray	34	3	CC	2	-
88/89	Galatasaray	28	1	CC	6	-
89/90	Galatasaray	27	1	UC	1	-
90/91	Galatasaray	9	-		
91/92	Galatasaray	16	2	CWC	3	-

★ Turkey 4 caps, 0 goals

Falko GÖTZ (Ger)
26/03/62   Defender

87/88	Bayer 04 Leverkusen (Ger)	29	8	#UC	12	2
88/89	1.FC Köln (Ger)	31	5	UC	5	1
89/90	1.FC Köln (Ger)	33	11	UC	10	6
90/91	1.FC Köln (Ger)	30	3	UC	6	1
91/92	1.FC Köln (Ger)	33	1		

UGUR Tütüneker
02/08/63   Midfield

87/88	Galatasaray	33	5	CC	2	-
88/89	Galatasaray	31	8	CC	7	2
89/90	Galatasaray	29	4		
90/91	Galatasaray	20	4		
91/92	Galatasaray	19	5	CWC	1	-

★ Turkey 17 caps, 1 goal

TURKEY

FIVE YEAR RECORD *Birthdate/Playing position*	LEAGUE Apps	Gls	EURO CUPS Cup	Apps	Gls

MUHAMMET Altintas
30/03/64   Midfield

87/88	Galatasaray	31	1	CC	2	-
88/89	Galatasaray	12	-	CC	3	-
89/90	Galatasaray	29	1	UC	2	-
90/91	Galatasaray	28	3			
91/92	Galatasaray	27	-	CWC	6	-

★ Turkey 8 caps, 0 goals

MUSTAFA Yücedag
24/04/66   Midfield

87/88	PEC Zwolle (Hol)	34	7			
88/89	Sariyer	27	9			
89/90	Sariyer	28	7			
90/91	Galatasaray	16	3			
91/92	Galatasaray	25	1	CWC	4	1

★ Turkey 9 caps, 0 goals

TAYFUN Hut
19/07/67   Midfield

89/90	Muglaspor	Div 2				
90/91	Galatasaray	18	-			
91/92	Galatasaray	19	-	CWC	5	-

★ Turkey 1 cap, 0 goals

Fahrudin DURAK (Yug)
18/07/66   Midfield

87/88	Pristina (Yug)	20	-			
88/89	Pristina (Yug)	Div 2				
89/90	Rad Beograd (Yug)	15	2			
90/91	Rad Beograd (Yug)	30	5			
91/92	Rad Beograd (Yug)	14*	2*			

* first half of season figures only.

Elvir BOLIC (Yug)
1970   Midfield

91/92	Crvena zvezda Beograd (Yug)	-*	-*	CC	4	-

* first half of season figures only.

FIVE YEAR RECORD *Birthdate/Playing position*	LEAGUE Apps	Gls	EURO CUPS Cup	Apps	Gls

ERDAL Keser
20/06/61   Forward

87/88	Sariyer	31	17			
88/89	Sariyer	28	12			
89/90	Galatasaray	28	7	UC	1	-
90/91	Galatasaray	22	3			
91/92	Galatasaray	11	5	CWC	2	1

★ Turkey 24 caps, 2 goals

ARIF Erdem
08/10/70   Forward

90/91	Zeytinburnu	2	-			
91/92	Galatasaray	27	4	CWC	6	1

TANER Alpak
27/11/67   Forward

89/90	Fatih Karagümrük	Div 2				
90/91	Galatasaray	4	-			
91/92	Galatasaray	10	2	CWC	1	-

EUROPEAN HONOURS
none

EUROPEAN CUPS RECORD

	Entries	Pd	W	D	L	F	A
Champions' Cup	9	35	12	8	15	42	53
Cup-winners' Cup	7	28	9	7	12	33	49
UEFA/Fairs' Cup	5	12	2	2	8	11	24
Total - All 3 Cups	21	75	23	17	35	86	126

LATE UEFA ADMISSIONS TO THE EUROPEAN CUPS

NORMA TALLINN - ESTONIA

FIVE YEAR RECORD Birthdate/Playing position	LEAGUE Apps	Gls	EURO CUPS Cup	Apps	Gls

Tonu VANAKESA
14/10/62   Goalkeeper

92	Norma Tallinn	9	-			

Gennadi ASTAFYEV
26/06/59   Goalkeeper

92	Norma Tallinn	2	-			

Vladimir URYUPIN
22/05/64   Defender

92	Norma Tallinn	8	-			

Eduard VINOGRADOV
31/07/69   Defender

92	Norma Tallinn	7	-			

Aivar TIIDUS
20/04/63   Defender

92	Norma Tallinn	7	-			

Yuri BORISENKO
24/12/58   Defender

92	Norma Tallinn	4	-			

Yuri GARIFULIN
16/03/57   Defender

92	Norma Tallinn	8	-			

Leonid KURILOV
12/04/55   Defender

92	Norma Tallinn	9	-			

Janno GRÜNMANN
28/07/71   Defender

92	Norma Tallinn	1	-			

Sergei BRAGIN
19/03/67   Midfield

92	Norma Tallinn	9	18			

Andrei BORISOV
01/08/69   Midfield

92	Norma Tallinn	9	3			

Valeri CHMIL
08/03/66   Midfield

92	Norma Tallinn	8	4			

Andrei BELOKHVOSTOV
05/09/64   Midfield

92	Norma Tallinn	8	-			

Yuri VOLKOV
19/12/70   Midfield

92	Norma Tallinn	9	-			

Alexander ZHURKIN
24/02/63   Forward

92	Norma Tallinn	9	7			

Albert DUBNITSKI
10/10/73   Forward

92	Norma Tallinn	1	-			

Mikhail MARCHENKO
16/08/58   Forward

92	Norma Tallinn	1	1			

Mikhail BORISOV
27/01/74   Forward

92	Norma Tallinn	3	1			

EUROPEAN HONOURS
none

EUROPEAN CUPS RECORD

KI - FAEROE ISLES

FIVE YEAR RECORD	LEAGUE		EURO CUPS		
Birthdate/Playing position	Apps	Gls	Cup	Apps	Gls

Jakup MIKKELSEN
14/08/70   Goalkeeper

| 91 | KÍ | 18 | - | | | |

★ Faeroe Isles 4 caps, 0 goals

William JOENSEN
Goalkeeper

| 91 | KÍ | - | - | | | |

Kurt MØRKØRE
20/02/69   Defender

| 91 | KÍ | 16 | 3 | | | |

★ Faeroe Isles 26 caps, 6 goals

Eydfinn POULSEN
Defender

| 91 | KÍ | 8 | - | | | |

John HANSEN
Defender

| 91 | KÍ | - | - | | | |

Petur Ove ELLINGSGAARD
Defender

| 91 | KÍ | - | - | | | |

Fridin LISKASON
Defender

| 91 | KÍ | 7 | - | | | |

Jan JOENSEN
Midfield

| 91 | KÍ | 14 | 1 | | | |

Jogvan JACOBSEN
Midfield

| 91 | KÍ | 17 | - | | | |

Harley BERTOLSEN
Midfield

| 91 | KÍ | 3 | 2 | | | |

Todi JONSSON
02/02/72   Midfield

| 91 | KÍ | 17 | 7 | | | |

★ Faeroe Isles 9 caps, 1 goal

Allan MØRKØRE
22/11/71   Midfield

| 91 | KÍ | 18 | 3 | | | |

★ Faeroe Isles 12 caps, 1 goal

Allan JOENSEN
Midfield

| 91 | KÍ | 12 | 1 | | | |

Olgar DANIELSEN
Forward

| 91 | KÍ | 17 | 2 | | | |

Aksel JOHANNESEN
Forward

| 91 | KÍ | 12 | 1 | | | |

Arnold JOENSEN
Forward

| 91 | KÍ | 3 | 2 | | | |

Stig ELTTOR
Forward

| 91 | KÍ | 14 | 3 | | | |

EUROPEAN HONOURS
none

EUROPEAN CUPS RECORD

MACCABI TEL-AVIV - ISRAEL

FIVE YEAR RECORD	LEAGUE		EURO CUPS		
Birthdate/Playing position	Apps	Gls	Cup	Apps	Gls

Aleksandr UVAROV (Rus)
13/01/60   Goalkeeper

87	Dinamo Moskva (Urs)	9	-	UC	1	-
88	Dinamo Moskva (Urs)	11	-			
89	Dinamo Moskva (Urs)	10	-			
90	Dinamo Moskva (Urs)	20	-			
91	Dinamo Moskva (Urs)	21	-			
91/92	Maccabi Tel-Aviv					

★ USSR 11 caps, 0 goals

Yaron MELIKA
04/04/72   Goalkeeper

91/92	Maccabi Tel-Aviv

Bromer GADI
11/11/73   Defender

91/92	Maccabi Tel-Aviv

Avi COHEN
12/06/62   Defender

91/92	Maccabi Tel-Aviv

Amit LEVY
14/04/71   Defender

91/92	Maccabi Tel-Aviv

Nini ASOR
28/07/69   Defender

91/92	Maccabi Tel-Aviv

Aleksandr POLUKAROV (Ukr)
27/11/59   Defender

87	Torpedo Moskva (Urs)	30	1			
88	Torpedo Moskva (Urs)	29	-	UC	2	-
89	Torpedo Moskva	8	-	CWC	4	-
90	Torpedo Moskva (Urs)	24	-	UC	7	-
91	Torpedo Moskva (Urs)	19	1			
91/92	Maccabi Tel-Aviv					

Amir SHELACH
11/07/70   Defender

91/92	Maccabi Tel-Aviv

FIVE YEAR RECORD	LEAGUE		EURO CUPS		
Birthdate/Playing position	Apps	Gls	Cup	Apps	Gls

Yitzhak ZOHAR
30/10/70   Midfield

91/92	Maccabi Tel-Aviv

Avi NIMNI
26/04/72   Midfield

91/92	Maccabi Tel-Aviv

Nir KLINGER
22/05/66   Midfield

91/92	Maccabi Tel-Aviv

Noam SHOAM
04/04/70   Midfield

91/92	Maccabi Tel-Aviv

Yaron DRORI
02/07/67   Midfield

91/92	K Beerschot Vav (Bel)	Div 2

Eli DRICKX
13/10/64   Forward

91/92	Maccabi Tel-Aviv

Meir MELIKA
01/08/69   Forward

91/92	Maccabi Tel-Aviv

Nir SEVILIA
26/05/75   Forward

91/92	Maccabi Tel-Aviv

Netzach MASOBI
09/06/67   Forward

91/92	Hapoel Jerusalem

Nir LEVIN
14/03/62   Forward

91/92	Hapoel Petacch-Tikva

EUROPEAN HONOURS none
EUROPEAN CUPS RECORD none

SKONTO RIGA - LATVIA

FIVE YEAR RECORD	LEAGUE		EURO CUPS		
Birthdate/Playing position	Apps	Gls	Cup	Apps	Gls

J. TROFIMOVS
1967   Goalkeeper

Aleksandrs KULAKOVS
1956   Goalkeeper
★ Latvia

O. GRISINS
1967   Defender

O. BLAGONADEZDINS
1973   Defender

Mihails ZEMLINSKIS
1968   Defender
★ Latvia

Einars GNEDOJS
1965   Defender
★ Latvia

A. LAPSA
1968   Defender

A. ROZKOVS
1972   Defender

V. LOBANOVS
1971   Midfield

V. ASTAFJEVS
1971   Midfield

Arturs SKETOVS
1968   Midfield
★ Latvia

FIVE YEAR RECORD	LEAGUE		EURO CUPS		
Birthdate/Playing position	Apps	Gls	Cup	Apps	Gls

Alexandrs DIBRIVNIJS
1969   Midfield
★ Latvia

Igors STEPANOVS
1966   Midfield
★ Latvia

Aivars DRUPASS
1963   Forward
★ Latvia

A. SEMJONOVS
1973   Forward

S. TARASOVS
1971   Forward

Aleksandrs JELISEJEVS
1971   Forward
★ Latvia

A. ALOHINS
1971   Forward

EUROPEAN HONOURS
none

EUROPEAN CUPS RECORD

ZHALGIRIS VILNIUS - LITHUANIA

| FIVE YEAR RECORD | LEAGUE | | EURO CUPS | |
Birthdate/Playing position	Apps	Gls	Cup	Apps	Gls

Darius SPETYLA
1969 Goalkeeper

91/92 Zhalgiris Vilnius	23	-			

Dainius BARZDAITIS
1973 Goalkeeper

91/92 Zhalgiris Vilnius	5	-			

Rytis NARUSEVICIUS
1968 Defender

91 Zhalgiris Vilnius	5	-			
91/92 Zhalgiris Vilnius	7	-			

Vaidas PETRAUSKAS
1969 Defender

91 Zhalgiris Vilnius	14	-			
91/92 Zhalgiris Vilnius	7	-			

Arunas ZEKAS
1966 Defender

89 Zhalgiris Vilnius	11	-	UC	2	-
91 Zhalgiris Vilnius	17	1			
91/92 Zhalgiris Vilnius	6	-			

Tomas ZIUKAS
1970 Defender

91 Zhalgiris Vilnius	15	1			
91/92 Zhalgiris Vilnius	17	-			

★ Lithuania 2 caps, 0 goals

Virginius BALTUSHNIKAS
1968 Midfield

87 Zhalgiris Vilnius	4	-			
88 Zhalgiris Vilnius	8	1	UC	1	1
89 Zhalgiris Vilnius	21	2	UC	2	-
91 Zhalgiris Vilnius	6	2			
91/92 Zhalgiris Vilnius	10	-			

Aidas PREIKSHAITIS
1970 Midfield

91 Zhalgiris Vilnius	2	-			
91/92 Zhalgiris Vilnius	22	1			

Andreius TERESHKINAS
1970 Midfield

91 Zhalgiris Vilnius	15	2			
91/92 Zhalgiris Vilnius	20	-			

Dainius SHULIAUSKAS
1973 Midfield

91/92 Zhalgiris Vilnius	16	3			

Gintaras RIMKUS
1968 Midfield

91 Zhalgiris Vilnius	12	7			
91/92 Zhalgiris Vilnius	7	-			

Vytautas KARVELIS
1972 Midfield

91 Zhalgiris Vilnius	7	-			
91/92 Zhalgiris Vilnius	16	1			

Edgaras JANKAUSKAS
1975 Midfield

91 Panerys Vilnius	3	-			
91/92 Zhalgiris Vilnius	14	2			

Darius MACIULEVICIUS
1973 Midfield

91/92 Zhalgiris Vilnius	16	3			

Ramunas STONKUS
1970 Midfield

91 Banga Kaunas	16	8			
91/92 Zhalgiris Vilnius	24	5			

Richardas ZDANCIUS
1967 Forward

91 Zhalgiris Vilnius	17	5			
91/92 Zhalgiris Vilnius	13	5			

★ Lithuania 3 caps, 0 goals

Aurelius SKARBALIUS
1973 Forward

91 Zhalgiris Vilnius	7	1			
91/92 Zhalgiris Vilnius	20	3			

Eimantas PODERIS
73 Forward

91 Zhalgiris Vilnius	3	1			
91/92 Zhalgiris Vilnius	19	13			

★ Lithuania 1 cap, 0 goals

EUROPEAN HONOURS none

EUROPEAN CUPS RECORD

	Entries	Pd	W	D	L	F	A
Champions' Cup	none						
Cup-winners' Cup	none						
UEFA/Fairs' Cup	2	6	2	0	4	7	11
Total - All 3 Cups	2	6	2	0	4	7	11

SCT OLIMPIJA LJUBLJANA - SLOVENIA

FIVE YEAR RECORD	LEAGUE		EURO CUPS	
Birthdate/Playing position	Apps	Gls	Cup	Apps Gls

Marko SIMEUNOVIC
06/12/67   Goalkeeper

91/92	SCT Olimpija Ljubljana	26	-

★ Slovenia 2 caps, 0 goals

Nihad PEJKOVIC
23/10/68   Goalkeeper

91/92	SCT Olimpija Ljubljana	3	-

Robert ENGLARO
26/08/69   Defender

88/89	Olimpija Ljubljana (Yug)	Div 2	
89/90	Olimpija Ljubljana (Yug)	20	-
90/91	Olimpija Ljubljana (Yug)	23	2
91/92	SCT Olimpija Ljubljana	31	1

★ Slovenia 2 caps, 0 goals

Damir VRABAC (Bos)
10/05/62   Defender

88/89	Olimpija Ljubljana (Yug)	Div 2	
89/90	Olimpija Ljubljana (Yug)	20	4
90/91	Olimpija Ljubljana (Yug)	30	3
91/92	SCT Olimpija Ljubljana	33	6

Agron SHALA
20/08/72   Defender

91/92	SCT Olimpija Ljubljana	27	-

Milos HUDARIN
18/06/72   Defender

91/92	SCT Olimpija Ljubljana	30	1

Nenad PODGAJSKI
31/03/63   Defender

88/89	Olimpija Ljubljana (Yug)	Div 2	
89/90	Olimpija Ljubljana (Yug)	12	-
90/91	Olimpija Ljubljana (Yug)	6	-
91/92	SCT Olimpija Ljubljana	37	3

Samir ZULIC
08/01/66   Defender

91/92	SCT Olimpija Ljubljana	30	8

★ Slovenia 3 caps, 0 goals

Zeljko MILINOVIC
12/10/69   Defender

91/92	SCT Olimpija Ljubljana	11	2

Edin HADJIALAGIC
02/02/62   Defender

91/92	Maribor Branik	35	2

Nenad PROTEGA
11/10/69   Midfield

91/92	SCT Olimpija Ljubljana	16	2

Dejan DJURANOVIC
05/05/68   Midfield

91/92	SCT Olimpija Ljubljana	34	8

★ Slovenia 1 cap, 0 goals

Andrej ZELKO
20/03/68   Midfield

91/92	Belvedur Izola	33	11

★ Slovenia 1 cap, 0 goals

Igor BENEDEJCIC
28/07/69   Midfield

91/92	Koper	31	5

★ Slovenia 2 caps, 1 goal

Nedeljko TOPIC (Bos)
24/10/60   Forward

90/91	Olimpija Ljubljana (Yug)	25	3
91/92	SCT Olimpija Ljubljana	32	22

Zoran UBAVIC
28/10/65   Forward

88/89	Olimpija Ljubljana (Yug)	Div 2	
89/90	Olimpija Ljubljana (Yug)	10	-
91/92	SCT Olimpija Ljubljana	34	29

★ Slovenia 1 cap, 0 goals

Sandi VALENTINCIC
25/08/67   Forward

91/92	SCT Olimpija Ljubljana	16	3

Damir SABOTIC
27/08/72   Forward

91/92	SCT Olimpija Ljubljana	24	1

EUROPEAN HONOURS none

EUROPEAN CUPS RECORD

	Entries	Pd	W	D	L	F	A
Champions' Cup	none						
Cup-winners' Cup	1	2	0	1	1	2	9
UEFA/Fairs' Cup	2	4	0	1	3	4	11
Total - All 3 Cups	3	6	0	2	4	6	20

TAVRIA SIMFEROPOL - UKRAINE

FIVE YEAR RECORD	LEAGUE		EURO CUPS	
Birthdate/Playing position	Apps	Gls	Cup	Apps Gls

Dmitri GULENKOV
22/05/68   Goalkeeper

Oleg KOLESOV
05/02/69   Goalkeeper

Sefer ALIBAYEV
25/05/67   Defender

Igor VOLKOV
13/03/65   Defender

Alexandr GOLOVKO
06/01/71   Defender

Mikola TURCHINENKO
23/04/61   Defender

Sergei SHELEST
17/03/65   Defender

Vidmantas VISHNIAUSKAS
13/09/69   Midfield

Yuri GETIKOV
19/06/71   Midfield

Igor IGNATOV
13/09/70   Midfield

Vladislav NOVIKOV
06/09/71   Midfield

Andrei OLARIN
28/05/63   Midfield

FIVE YEAR RECORD	LEAGUE		EURO CUPS	
Birthdate/Playing position	Apps	Gls	Cup	Apps Gls

Dmitri SMIRNOV
14/08/69   Midfield

Sergei ANDREYEV
14/09/70   Forward

Sergei GLADYSHEV
09/12/60   Forward

Yuri GUDIMENKO
10/03/66   Forward

Murat MULASHEV
07/01/68   Forward

Tolyat SHEJHAMETOV
24/04/66   Forward

EUROPEAN HONOURS
none

EUROPEAN CUPS RECORD

B36 - FAEROE ISLES

FIVE YEAR RECORD *Birthdate/Playing position*	LEAGUE Apps Gls	EURO CUPS Cup Apps Gls

Wiscek ZAKREWSKI
Goalkeeper

91	B 71	18	-		

Egin HOGNESEN
Goalkeeper

91	B 36	18	-		

Rogvi THORSTEINSSON
Defender

91	B 36	-	-		

Danjal Petur JOHANSEN
Defender

91	B 36	8	-		

Tummas Eli HANSEN
11/02/66 Defender

91	B 36	16	1		

★ Faeroe Isles 14 caps, 0 goals

Joannes GUTTESEN
Defender

91	B 36	-	-		

Bogi JACOBSEN
Defender

91	B 36	18	-		

Petur Amon DALBO
Midfield

91	B 36	16	-		

Frodi MADSEN
Midfield

91	B 36	-	-		

Karl LEONSON
Midfield

FIVE YEAR RECORD *Birthdate/Playing position*	LEAGUE Apps Gls	EURO CUPS Cup Apps Gls

Jakup Simun SIMONSEN
17/02/66 Midfield

91	B 36	15	5		

★ Faeroe Isles 7 caps, 0 goals

Jens Christian HANSEN
Midfield

91	B 36	18	4		

Bogi MIDJORD
Midfield

91	Sumba	16	-		

Pall Magnar KJAERBAEK
Midfield

91	Sumba	17	2		

Regin ARGE
Forward

91	B 36	18	4		

Karl REYNHEIM
15/02/64 Forward

91	B 36	18	11		

★ Faeroe Isles 34 caps, 4 goals

Jan POULSEN
Forward

91	Sumba	18	4		

Jakup MORK
Forward

91	B 36	-	-		

EUROPEAN HONOURS
none

EUROPEAN CUPS RECORD

HAPOEL PETACH-TIKVA - ISRAEL

FIVE YEAR RECORD Birthdate/Playing position	LEAGUE Apps Gls	EURO CUPS Cup Apps Gls

Rafi COHEN
28/11/70   Goalkeeper

| 91/92   Hapoel Petach-Tikva | | |

Shachar YELIN
15/12/66   Goalkeeper

| 91/92   Hapoel Petach-Tikva | | |

Carlos OLERAN (Arg)
17/11/61   Defender

| 91/92   Hapoel Petach-Tikva | | |

Gay GAT
24/09/70   Defender

| 91/92   Hapoel Petach-Tikva | | |

Benny KOZOSHVILY
16/09/67   Defender

| 91/92   Hapoel Petach-Tikva | | |

Geva MARCOS
10/03/65   Defender

| 91/92   Hapoel Petach-Tikva | | |

Alex BREMCHER
06/04/67   Defender

| 91/92   Hapoel Petach-Tikva | | |

Oz ILIA
06/04/67   Defender

| 91/92   Hapoel Petach-Tikva | | |

Noam KEISY
30/01/65   Midfield

| 91/92   Hapoel Petach-Tikva | | |

Ely MACHPOD
25/03/61   Midfield

| 91/92   Hapoel Petach-Tikva | | |

FIVE YEAR RECORD Birthdate/Playing position	LEAGUE Apps Gls	EURO CUPS Cup Apps Gls

Alon HAZAN
04/10/67   Midfield

| 91/92   Hapoel Petach-Tikva | | |

Gay LEVY
08/05/66   Midfield

| 91/92   Maccabi Petach-Tikva | | |

Yossi LEVY
01/02/66   Midfield

| 91/92   Hapoel Petach-Tikva | | |

Haim SIROTKIN
21/01/72   Midfield

| 91/92   Hapoel Petach-Tikva | | |

Rudolf PAVLÍK (Tch)
04/05/62   Midfield

			LEAGUE Apps	Gls	EURO CUPS Cup	Apps	Gls
87/88	DAC Dunajská Streda (Tch)		30	2	CWC	4	1
88/89	DAC Dunajská Streda (Tch)		30	4	UC	4	1
89/90	DAC Dunajská Streda (Tch)		27	5			
90/91	DAC Dunajská Streda (Tch)		30	5			
91/92	DAC Dunajská Streda (Tch)		28	8			

Danny NIRON
14/01/71   Forward

| 91/92   Hapoel Petach-Tikva | | |

Meny BASON
22/08/68   Forward

| 91/92   Hapoel Petach-Tikva | | |

Rafi COHEN
02/03/65   Forward

| 91/92   Hapoel Petach-Tikva | | |

EUROPEAN HONOURS none
EUROPEAN CUPS RECORD none

FC VADUZ - LIECHTENSTEIN

FIVE YEAR RECORD	LEAGUE		EURO CUPS		
Birthdate/Playing position	Apps	Gls	Cup	Apps	Gls

Oliver GASSNER
1973   Goalkeeper

Peter HARTMANN (Sui)
1964   Goalkeeper

Hans Joachim ABEL (Ger)
1952   Defender

Patrik HEFTI
1968   Defender

Daniel HEMMERLE
1972   Defender

Beat LOHNER
1969   Defender

Roland MOSER
1962   Defender

Heinrich NIGG (Sui)
1963   Defender

Daniel HASLER
1974   Midfield

Franco ROTUNNO
1970   Midfield

Wolfgang OSPELT
1965   Midfield

FIVE YEAR RECORD	LEAGUE		EURO CUPS		
Birthdate/Playing position	Apps	Gls	Cup	Apps	Gls

Alexander QUADERER
1971   Midfield

Patrik SIDLER (Sui)
1965   Midfield

Thomas VERLING
1974   Midfield

Giuseppe ZARRA (Ita)
1967   Midfield

Franz SCHÄDLER
1968   Forward

Christian STÖBER (Sui)
1969   Forward

Harry SCHÄDLER
1967   Forward

EUROPEAN HONOURS
none

EUROPEAN CUPS RECORD

MARIBOR BRANIK - SLOVENIA

FIVE YEAR RECORD *Birthdate/Playing position*	LEAGUE Apps Gls	EURO CUPS Cup Apps Gls

Mladen DABANOVIC
13/09/71   Goalkeeper

91/92 Maribor Branik	39	-		

Darko DUBRAVICA
06/08/72   Goalkeeper

91/92 Maribor Branik	1	-		

Emil STERBAL
15/06/70   Defender

91/92 Maribor Branik	32	-		

Saso LUKIC
24/04/73   Defender

91/92 Maribor Branik	28	2		

Zarko TARANA (Bos)
04/02/67   Defender

91/92 Maribor Branik	36	-		

Ales KRIZAN
25/07/71   Defender

91/92 Maribor Branik	37	-		

Bostjan RATKOVIC
03/01/71   Defender

91/92 Maribor Branik	32	-		

Bostjan DAMIS
16/12/72   Defender

91/92 Maribor Branik	11	1		

Enver CIRIC
08/10/72   Defender

91/92 SCT Olimpija Ljubljana	7	-		

Peter BINKOVSKI
28/06/72   Midfield

91/92 Maribor Branik	29	5		

Renato KOTNIK
01/03/70   Midfield

91/92 Maribor Branik	31	3		

Zoran VOLK
10/05/73   Midfield

91/92 Maribor Branik	10	-		

Marijan BAKULA (Bos)
17/04/66   Midfield

91/92 Maribor Branik	35	9		

Dejan BAUMAN
08/09/70   Midfield

91/92 Maribor Branik	14	2		

Ermin SUSIC (Bos)
18/01/70   Midfield

91/92 Maribor Branik	18	3		

Ante SIMUNDZA
28/09/71   Forward

91/92 Maribor Branik	34	17		

Igor POZNIC
13/08/67   Forward

91/92 Maribor Branik	30	27		
★ Slovenia 1 cap, 0 goals

Mirsad BICAKCIC (Bos)
14/04/65   Forward

91/92 Belvedur Izola	30	6		

EUROPEAN HONOURS none
EUROPEAN CUPS RECORD none

CHERNOMORETS ODESSA

FIVE YEAR RECORD *Birthdate/Playing position*	LEAGUE Apps Gls		EURO CUPS Cup Apps Gls		

Oleg SUSLOV
02/01/69   Goalkeeper

91	Chernomorets Odessa	1	-			

Igor KRAPIVKIN
1966   Goalkeeper

Yury SAK
03/01/67   Defender

91	Chernomorets Odessa	26	7			

Andrey TELESNENKO
12/04/66   Defender

88	Chernomorets Odessa	8	-			
89	Chernomorets Odessa	3	-			
90	Chernomorets Odessa	6	-	UC	2	-
91	Chernomorets Odessa	29	2			

Aleksandr SPITSYN
22/01/63   Defender

87	CSKA Moskva	7	-			
88	Chernomorets Odessa	15	-			
89	Chernomorets Odessa	17	1			
90	Chernomorets Odessa	21	1	UC	3	-
91	Chernomorets Odessa	27	2			

Dmitry DEMYANENKO
11/06/69   Defender

91	Chernomorets Odessa	14	-			

Dmitro PARFONOV
11/09/74   Defender

Sergei TRETYAK
07/09/63   Defender

87	Chernomorets Odessa	Div 2				
88	Chernomorets Odessa	24	1			
89	Chernomorets Odessa	22	2			
90	Chernomorets Odessa	9	-	UC	4	-
91	Chernomorets Odessa	27	1			

FIVE YEAR RECORD *Birthdate/Playing position*	LEAGUE Apps Gls		EURO CUPS Cup Apps Gls		

Ilya TSYMBALAR
17/06/69   Midfield

89	Chernomorets Odessa	15	1			
90	Chernomorets Odessa	24	3	UC	4	1
91	Chernomorets Odessa	30	4			

Yury NIKIFOROV
16/09/70   Midfield

88	Chernomorets Odessa	1	-			
89	Chernomorets Odessa	-	-			
90	Chernomorets Odessa	17	-	UC	2	-
91	Chernomorets Odessa	30	2			

★ CIS 4 caps, 0 goals

Oleg KOSHELYUK
07/09/69   Midfield

91	Chernomorets Odessa	29	6			

Vitaly KOLISNICHENKO
10/06/73   Midfield

Sergei GUSEV
01/07/67   Forward

87	Chernomorets Odessa	Div 2				
88	Chernomorets Odessa	23	1			
89	Chernomorets Odessa	2	-			
90	Chernomorets Odessa	11	2	UC	3	-
91	Chernomorets Odessa	3	-			

Ivan GETSKO
06/04/68   Forward

89	Chernomorets Odessa	13	4			
90	Chernomorets Odessa	21	5	UC	4	1
91	Chernomorets Odessa	26	5			

★ USSR 5 caps, 0 goals

Ruslan ROMANCHUK
09/11/74   Forward

UKRAINE

FIVE YEAR RECORD	LEAGUE		EURO CUPS		
Birthdate/Playing position	Apps	Gls	Cup	Apps	Gls

Aleksandr SCHERBAKOV
1960   Forward

87	Chernomorets Odessa	Div 2		
88	Chernomorets Odessa	22	5
89	Chernomorets Odessa	22	7
90	Chernomorets Odessa	9	-
91	Chernomorets Odessa	26	3

Viktor YABLONSKY
1969   Forward

91	Metallist Kharkov	17	3

FIVE YEAR RECORD	LEAGUE		EURO CUPS		
Birthdate/Playing position	Apps	Gls	Cup	Apps	Gls

Oleg MOCHULYAK
27/09/74   Forward

91	Chernomorets Odessa	3	-

EUROPEAN HONOURS
none

EUROPEAN CUPS RECORD

	Entries	Pd	W	D	L	F	A
Champions' Cup	none						
Cup-winners' Cup	none						
UEFA/Fairs' Cup	3	10	3	2	5	10	13
Total - All 3 Cups	3	10	3	2	5	10	13

DINAMO KIEV

FIVE YEAR RECORD	LEAGUE		EURO CUPS		
Birthdate/Playing position	Apps	Gls	Cup	Apps	Gls

Igor KUTEPOV
17/12/65   Goalkeeper

87	Metallist Kharkov	3	-			
88	Metallist Kharkov	17	-	CWC	1	-
89	Metallist Kharkov	29	-			
90	Metallist Kharkov	9	-			
91	Dinamo Kiev	27	-	CC	8	-

Valdemaras MARTINKENAS (Lit)
1965   Goalkeeper

89	Zhalgiris Vilnius	25	-	UC	4	-
90	Zhalgiris Vilnius (Lit)					
91	Dinamo Kiev	2	-	CC	2	-
★ Lithuania

Oleg LUZHNY
05/08/68   Defender

89	Dinamo Kiev	27	-	UC	4	-
90	Dinamo Kiev	12	-	CWC	2	-
91	Dinamo Kiev	28	-	CC	9	-
★ USSR 8 caps, 0 goals

Sergei ZAETS
18/08/69   Defender

89	Dinamo Kiev	22	4	UC	5	1
90	Dinamo Kiev	17	1	CWC	4	1
91	Dinamo Kiev	25	3	CC	9	-

Akhrik TSVEIBA
10/09/66   Defender

87	Dinamo Tbilisi	23	-	UC	6	-
88	Dinamo Tbilisi	24	-			
89	Dinamo Tbilisi	28	-			
90	Dinamo Kiev	20	-	CWC	4	-
91	Dinamo Kiev	24	1	CC	8	-
★ USSR/CIS 25 caps, 2 goals

Andrey ANNENKOV
21/01/69   Defender

90	Dinamo Kiev	8	-	CWC	4	-
91	Dinamo Kiev	12	-	CC	5	-

FIVE YEAR RECORD	LEAGUE		EURO CUPS		
Birthdate/Playing position	Apps	Gls	Cup	Apps	Gls

Sergei SHMATOVALENKO
29/01/67   Defender

87	CSKA Moskva	15	-			
	Dinamo Kiev	13	-			
88	Dinamo Kiev	21	-			
89	Dinamo Kiev	26	-	UC	6	-
90	Dinamo Kiev	22	1	CWC	6	-
91	Dinamo Kiev	24	2	CC	8	-
★ USSR 2 caps, 0 goals

Yervand SUKIASYAN
20/01/67   Defender

88	Ararat Erevan	21	1			
89	Ararat Erevan	13	-			
90	Ararat Erevan	19	2			
91	Ararat Erevan	30	3			

Sergei KOVALETS
05/09/68   Midfield

90	Dinamo Kiev	11	2	CWC	5	-
91	Dinamo Kiev	23	5	CC	7	1

Pavel YAKOVENKO
19/12/64   Midfield

87	Dinamo Kiev	23	-	CC	2	-
88	Dinamo Kiev	6	1			
89	Dinamo Kiev	10	-	UC	1	1
90	Dinamo Kiev	6	-			
91	Dinamo Kiev	3	-	CC	6	1
★ USSR 19 caps, 1 goal

Oleg MATVEEV
18/03/70   Midfield

91	Dinamo Kiev	13	-	CC	1	-

Stepan BETSA
29/04/70   Midfield

91	Dinamo Kiev	29	1	CC	5	-

Viktor MOROZ
10/01/68   Midfield

91	Dinamo Kiev	22	-	CC	4	-

UKRAINE

FIVE YEAR RECORD Birthdate/Playing position	LEAGUE Apps	Gls	EURO CUPS Cup	Apps	Gls

Yury MOROZ
27/09/70   Midfield

90	Dinamo Kiev	2	-	CWC	2	-
91	Dinamo Kiev	27	1	CC	7	1

Gintaras KVITKAUSKAS (Lit)
03/01/67   Midfield

88	Zhalgiris Vilnius	3	-			
89	Zhalgiris Vilnius	27	7	UC	4	-
90	Zhalgiris (Lit)					
91	Pakhtakor Tashkent	15	3			
	Dinamo Kiev			CC	2	-

★ Lithuania

Yury GRITSYNA
16/04/71   Forward

91	Dinamo Kiev	10	1	CC	7	1

Vladimir SHARAN
1971   Forward

91	Dinamo Kiev	11	2	CC	10	1

FIVE YEAR RECORD Birthdate/Playing position	LEAGUE Apps	Gls	EURO CUPS Cup	Apps	Gls

Oleg SALENKO
25/10/69   Forward

87	Zenit Leningrad	10	-			
88	Zenit Leningrad	26	7			
89	Dinamo Kiev	26	3	UC	6	1
90	Dinamo Kiev	21	4	CWC	6	3
91	Dinamo Kiev	28	14	CC	10	3

EUROPEAN HONOURS
Cup-winners' Cup - (2) 1975, 1986.
Super Cup - (1) 1975.

EUROPEAN CUPS RECORD

Entries	Pd		W	D	L	F	A
Champions' Cup	11	62	33	12	17	81	55
Cup-winners' Cup	4	30	20	6	4	72	27
UEFA/Fairs' Cup	6	24	11	8	5	29	15
Total - All 3 Cups	21	116	64	26	26	182	97

BELVEDUR IZOLA - SLOVENIA

FIVE YEAR RECORD *Birthdate/Playing position*	LEAGUE Apps Gls	EURO CUPS Cup Apps Gls

Dragan TALAJIC (Bos)
25/08/65 Goalkeeper

91/92 Belvedur Izola	35	-

Iztok KAPUN
21/05/64 Goalkeeper

91/92 Belvedur Izola	5	-

Davor PERKAT
24/10/66 Defender

91/92 Belvedur Izola	38	3

★ Slovenia 2 caps, 0 goals

Amir RUZNIC
30/10/72 Defender

91/92 Belvedur Izola	37	1

★ Slovenia 1 cap, 0 goals

Peter TOSIC
07/01/69 Defender

91/92 Belvedur Izola	38	3

★ Slovenia 1 cap, 0 goals

Slaven CUCEK (Cro)
06/01/69 Defender

91/92 Belvedur Izola	18	3

Andrej BIZJAK
26/06/70 Defender

91/92 Koper	31	2

Damir BAN
07/09/66 Defender

91/92 Koper	31	2

Aljosa COTAR
16/10/71 Defender

91/92 Koper	27	-

Andrej TRIPAR
12/10/65 Midfield

91/92 Koper	17	2

Marjan CENDAK
05/12/72 Midfield

91/92 Belvedur Izola	29	8

Danijel RADESIC
28/12/72 Midfield

91/92 Belvedur Izola	17	1

Igor ZOBEC
17/09/71 Midfield

91/92 Koper	31	4

Samo ZUPANC
23/12/68 Midfield

91/92 Steklar	38	2

Miroslav STAMPFER
05/10/72 Midfield

91/92 Belvedur Izola	29	1

Danijel GREGORIC
21/12/69 Forward

91/92 Belvedur Izola	28	4

Vergilio VELKOVSKI
11/07/71 Forward

91/92 Belvedur Izola	2	-

Mladen RUDONJA
26/07/71 Forward

91/92 Koper	34	8

EUROPEAN HONOURS
none

EUROPEAN CUPS RECORD

CHAMPIONS' CUP FINALS

1956	Paris	Real Madrid (Esp)	4	Stade de Reims (Fra)	3
1957	Madrid	Real Madrid (Esp)	2	Fiorentina (Ita)	0
1958	Brussels	Real Madrid (Esp)	3	Milan (Ita)	2
1959	Stuttgart	Real Madrid (Esp)	2	Stade de Reims (Fra)	0
1960	Glasgow	Real Madrid (Esp)	7	Eintracht Frankfurt (Frg)	3
1961	Berne	SL Benfica (Por)	3	FC Barcelona (Esp)	2
1962	Amsterdam	SL Benfica (Por)	5	Real Madrid (Esp)	3
1963	Wembley	Milan (Ita)	2	SL Benfica (Por)	1
1964	Vienna	Internazionale (Ita)	3	Real Madrid (Esp)	1
1965	Milan	Internazionale (Ita)	1	SL Benfica (Por)	0
1966	Brussels	Real Madrid (Esp)	2	Partizan Beograd (Yug)	1
1967	Lisbon	Celtic (Sco)	2	Internazionale (Ita)	1
1968	Wembley	Manchester United (Eng)	4	SL Benfica (Por)	1
1969	Madrid	Milan (Ita)	4	Ajax (Hol)	1
1970	Milan	Feyenoord (Hol)	2	Celtic (Sco)	1
1971	Wembley	Ajax (Hol)	2	Panathinaikos (Gre)	0
1972	Rotterdam	Ajax (Hol)	2	Internazionale (Ita)	0
1973	Belgrade	Ajax (Hol)	1	Juventus (Ita)	0
1974	Brussels	FC Bayern München (Frg)	1	Atlético Madrid (Esp)	1
rep.	Brussels	FC Bayern München (Frg)	4	Atlético Madrid (Esp)	0
1975	Paris	FC Bayern München (Frg)	2	Leeds United (Eng)	0
1976	Glasgow	FC Bayern München (Frg)	1	AS Saint-Etienne (Fra)	0
1977	Rome	Liverpool (Eng)	3	Borussia Mönchengladbach (Frg)	1
1978	Wembley	Liverpool (Eng)	1	Club Brugge KV (Bel)	0
1979	Munich	Nottingham Forest (Eng)	1	Malmö FF (Swe)	0
1980	Madrid	Nottingham Forest (Eng)	1	Hamburger SV (Frg)	0
1981	Paris	Liverpool (Eng)	1	Real Madrid (Esp)	0
1982	Rotterdam	Aston Villa (Eng)	1	FC Bayern München (Frg)	0
1983	Athens	Hamburger SV (Ger)	1	Juventus (Ita)	0
1984	Rome	Liverpool (Eng)	*1	Roma (Ita)	1
1985	Brussels	Juventus (Ita)	1	Liverpool (Eng)	0
1986	Seville	Steaua Bucuresti (Rom)	*0	FC Barcelona (Esp)	0
1987	Vienna	FC Porto (Por)	2	FC Bayern München (Frg)	1
1988	Stuttgart	PSV (Hol)	*0	SL Benfica (Por)	0
1989	Barcelona	Milan (Ita)	4	Steaua Bucuresti (Rom)	0
1990	Vienna	Milan (Ita)	1	SL Benfica (Por)	0
1991	Bari	Crvena zvezda Beograd (Yug)	*0	Olympique Marseille (Fra)	0
1992	Wembley	FC Barcelona (Esp)	1	Sampdoria (Ita)	0

N.B. * indicates winners of penalty shoot-out

CUP-WINNERS' CUP FINALS

1961	†	Fiorentina (Ita)	4 (2,2)	Rangers (Sco)	1 (0,1)
1962	Glasgow	Atlético Madrid (Esp)	1	Fiorentina (Ita)	1
rep.	Stuttgart	Atlético Madrid (Esp)	3	Fiorentina (Ita)	1
1963	Rotterdam	Tottenham Hotspur (Eng)	5	Atlético Madrid (Esp)	1
1964	Brussels	Sporting CP (Por)	3	MTK-VM (Hun)	3
rep.	Antwerp	Sporting CP (Por)	1	MTK-VM (Hun)	0
1965	Wembley	West Ham United (Eng)	2	TSV München 1860 (Frg)	0
1966	Glasgow	Borussia Dortmund (Frg)	2	Liverpool (Eng)	1
1967	Nuremberg	FC Bayern München (Frg)	1	Rangers (Sco)	0
1968	Rotterdam	Milan (Ita)	2	Hamburger SV (Frg)	0
1969	Basle	Slovan Bratislava (Tch)	3	FC Barcelona (Esp)	2
1970	Vienna	Manchester City (Eng)	2	Górnik Zabrze (Pol)	1
1971	Athens	Chelsea (Eng)	1	Real Madrid (Esp)	1
rep.	Athens	Chelsea (Eng)	2	Real Madrid (Esp)	1
1972	Barcelona	Rangers (Sco)	3	Dinamo Moskva (Urs)	2
1973	Salonika	Milan (Ita)	1	Leeds United (Eng)	0
1974	Rotterdam	1.FC Magdeburg (Gdr)	2	Milan (Ita)	0
1975	Basle	Dinamo Kiev (Urs)	3	Ferencváros (Hun)	0
1976	Brussels	RSC Anderlecht (Bel)	4	West Ham United (Eng)	2
1977	Amsterdam	Hamburger SV (Frg)	2	RSC Anderlecht (Bel)	0
1978	Paris	RSC Anderlecht (Bel)	4	FK Austria (Aut)	0
1979	Basle	FC Barcelona (Esp)	4	Fortuna Düsseldorf (Frg)	3
1980	Brussels	Valencia CF (Esp)	*0	Arsenal (Eng)	0
1981	Düsseldorf	Dinamo Tbilisi (Urs)	2	FC Carl Zeiss Jena (Gdr)	1
1982	Barcelona	FC Barcelona (Esp)	2	R Standard Liège (Bel)	1
1983	Gothenburg	Aberdeen (Sco)	2	Real Madrid (Esp)	1
1984	Basle	Juventus (Ita)	2	FC Porto (Por)	1
1985	Rotterdam	Everton (Eng)	3	SK Rapid Wien (Aut)	1
1986	Lyon	Dinamo Kiev (Urs)	3	Atlético Madrid (Esp)	0
1987	Athens	Ajax (Hol)	1	1.FC Lokomotive Leipzig (Gdr)	0
1988	Strasbourg	KV Mechelen (Bel)	1	Ajax (Hol)	0
1989	Berne	FC Barcelona (Esp)	2	Sampdoria (Ita)	0
1990	Gothenburg	Sampdoria (Ita)	2	RSC Anderlecht (Bel)	0
1991	Rotterdam	Manchester United (Eng)	2	FC Barcelona (Esp)	1
1992	Lisbon	SV Werder Bremen (Ger)	2	AS Monaco (Fra)	0

N.B. * indicates winners of penalty shoot-out   † indicates played over two legs

FAIRS/UEFA CUP FINALS

FAIRS CUP

			1st Leg	2nd Leg	Aggregate
1958	FC Barcelona (Esp)	London XI (Eng)	6-0	2-2	(8-2)
1960	FC Barcelona (Esp)	Birmingham City (Eng)	4-1	0-0	(4-1)
1961	Roma (Ita)	Birmingham City (Eng)	2-0	2-2	(4-2)
1962	Valencia CF (Esp)	FC Barcelona (Esp)	6-2	1-1	(7-3)
1963	Valencia CF (Esp)	Dinamo Zagreb (Yug)	2-1	2-0	(4-1)
1964	Real Zaragoza (Esp)	Valencia CF (Esp)	2-1	in Barcelona	
1965	Ferencváros (Hun)	Juventus (Ita)	1-0	in Turin	
1966	FC Barcelona (Esp)	Real Zaragoza (Esp)	4-2	0-1	(4-3)
1967	Dinamo Zagreb (Yug)	Leeds United (Eng)	2-0	0-0	(2-0)
1968	Leeds United (Eng)	Ferencváros (Hun)	1-0	0-0	(1-0)
1969	Newcastle United (Eng)	Újpesti Dózsa SC (Hun)	3-0	3-2	(6-2)
1970	Arsenal (Eng)	RSC Anderlecht (Bel)	3-0	1-3	(4-3)
1971	Leeds United (Eng)#	Juventus (Ita)	1-1	2-2	(3-3)

UEFA CUP

			1st Leg	2nd Leg	Aggregate
1972	Tottenham Hotspur (Eng)	Wolverhampton Wanderers (Eng)	1-1	2-1	(3-2)
1973	Liverpool (Eng)	Borussia M'chengladbach (Frg)	3-0	0-2	(3-2)
1974	Feyenoord (Hol)	Tottenham Hotspur (Eng)	2-0	2-2	(4-2)
1975	Borussia M'gladbach (Frg)	FC Twente (Hol)	0-0	5-1	(5-1)
1976	Liverpool (Eng)	Club Brugge KV (Bel)	3-2	1-1	(4-3)
1977	Juventus (Ita)#	Athletic Bilbao (Esp)	1-0	1-2	(2-2)
1978	PSV (Hol)	SEC Bastia (Fra)	3-0	0-0	(3-0)
1979	Borussia M'gladbach (Frg)	Crvena zvezda Beograd (Yug)	1-0	1-1	(2-1)
1980	Eintracht Frankfurt (Frg)#	Borussia M'chengladbach (Frg)	1-0	2-3	(3-3)
1981	Ipswich Town (Eng)	AZ '67 (Hol)	3-0	2-4	(5-4)
1982	IFK Göteborg (Swe)	Hamburger SV (Frg)	1-0	3-0	(4-0)
1983	RSC Anderlecht (Bel)	SL Benfica (Por)	1-0	1-1	(2-1)
1984	Tottenham Hotspur (Eng)*	RSC Anderlecht (Bel)	1-1	1-1	(2-2)
1985	Real Madrid (Esp)	Videoton SC (Hun)	0-1	3-0	(3-1)
1986	Real Madrid (Esp)	1.FC Köln (Frg)	5-1	0-2	(5-3)
1987	IFK Göteborg (Swe)	Dundee United (Sco)	1-0	1-1	(2-1)
1988	Bayer 04 Leverkusen (Frg)*	RCD Español (Esp)	3-0	0-3	(3-3)
1989	Napoli (Ita)	VfB Stuttgart (Frg)	2-1	3-3	(5-2)
1990	Juventus (Ita)	Fiorentina (Ita)	3-1	0-0	(4-1)
1991	Internazionale (Ita)	Roma (Ita)	2-0	0-1	(2-1)
1992	Ajax (Hol)#	Torino (Ita)	0-0	2-2	(2-2)

N.B.   # indicates winners on away goals

          * indicates winners of penalty shoot-out

NOTES

NOTES

NOTES

NOTES

NOTES